Author's Message:

NOBUYUKI ANZAI
安西信行
PRESENTS

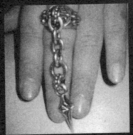

An original ring I got
from designer Takacho of
Loud Style Design.

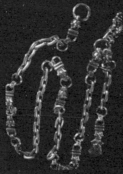

A custom chain *Wazawai
nasu mono* (creator of
calamity) created for me
by Loud Style Design.

MÄR
Vol. 13
Story and Art by Nobuyuki Anzai

English Adaptation/Gerard Jones
Translation/Kaori Inoue
Touch-up Art & Lettering/James Gaubatz
Design/Izumi Evers
Editor/Andy Nakatani

Editor in Chief, Books/Alvin Lu
Editor in Chief, Magazines/Marc Weidenbaum
VP of Publishing Licensing/Rika Inouye
VP of Sales/Gonzalo Ferreyra
Sr. VP of Marketing/Liza Coppola
Publisher/Hyoe Narita

Printed in the U.S.A.

Published by VIZ Media, LLC
P.O. Box 77010
San Francisco, CA 94107

10 9 8 7 6 5 4 3 2
First printing, May 2007
Second printing, June 2007

www.viz.com
store.viz.com

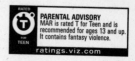

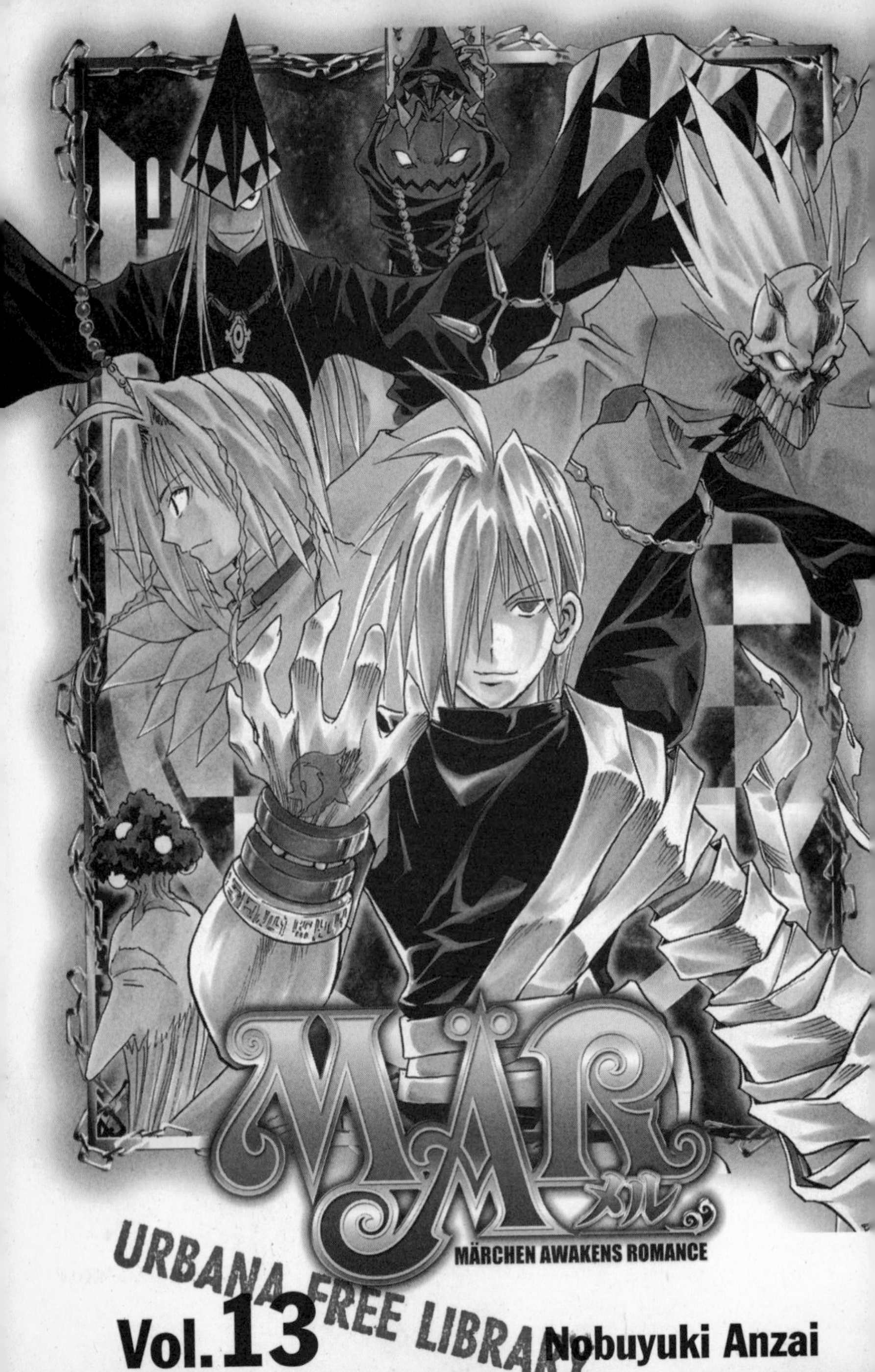
MÄR
メル

MÄRCHEN AWAKENS ROMANCE

Vol. 13

Nobuyuki Anzai

Characters

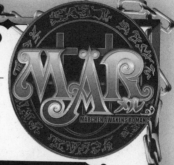

Alan

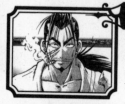

A warrior who played a major role in the war six years ago. For a while a curse trapped him in the form of Edward.

Edward

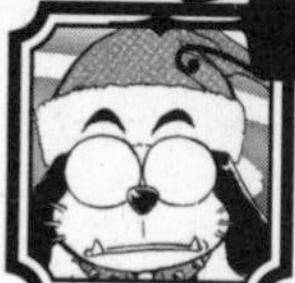

The dog who devotedly serves Princess Snow.

Snow

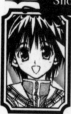

Princess of the Kingdom of Lestava. She was kidnapped by Diana in the middle of the sixth battle.

Nanashi

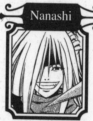

Leader of the Thieves Guild, Luberia. Detests the Chess Pieces who killed his comrades.

Alviss

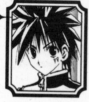

He is the one who brought Ginta to Mär Heaven using the Dimensional ÄRM called the "GateKeeper Clown."

Ginta Toramizu

A second-year middle school student who dreamed about the world of fairy tales. Now, in order to save that world, he must fight the Chess Pieces.

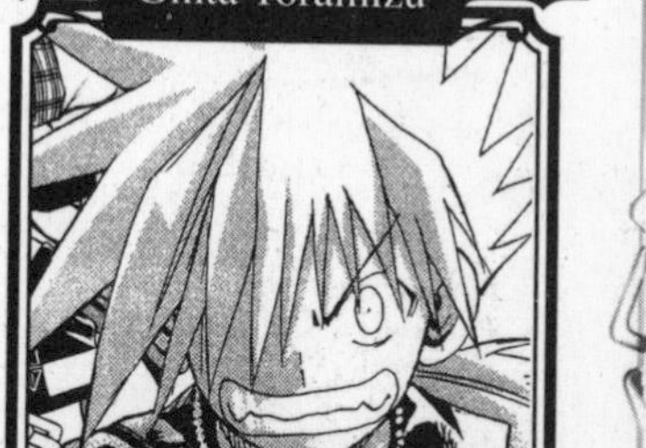

Babbo

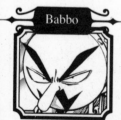

A rare talking ÄRM, who by synchronizing with Ginta is able to change shape—now up to version five.

Jack

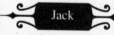

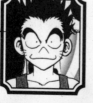

A farmboy who has left his mother and his farm to join Ginta in battle.

Previous Volume

Ginta jumps through a "door" that suddenly appears in his classroom, and finds himself in the magical world of his dreams. Now, at the "request" of the Chess Pieces, the War Games have begun—and Ginta and his eight friends, calling themselves Team Mär, must battle the Chess warriors. Team Mär remains undefeated through the first six battles, but Phantom has proclaimed that the seventh battle will be the last. It's going to be a six-on-six bout with Jack up first, against the man who fought his father in the previous war games!

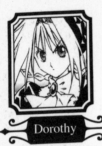

Dorothy

A witch from Caldia, Kingdom of Magic. She has accepted the painful duty of killing the Queen of the Chess—her own sister.

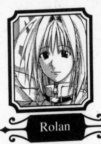

Rolan

A Knight of the Chess who received the Zombie Tattoo from Phantom. Beat Alviss in the third battle.

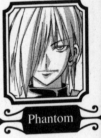

Phantom

A Chess Knight. The most powerful in the group, and the leader of its combat force.

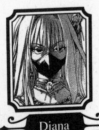

Diana

Queen of the Chess, Dorothy's older sister and Snow's stepmother.

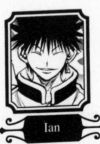

Ian

A chess Knight. His lover Gido was subjected to a terrible transformation.

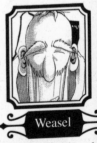

Weasel

A chess knight. Weasel i an 84-year-old plant wielder. Weasel fatally wounded Jack's father ir the previous war games.

CONTENTS

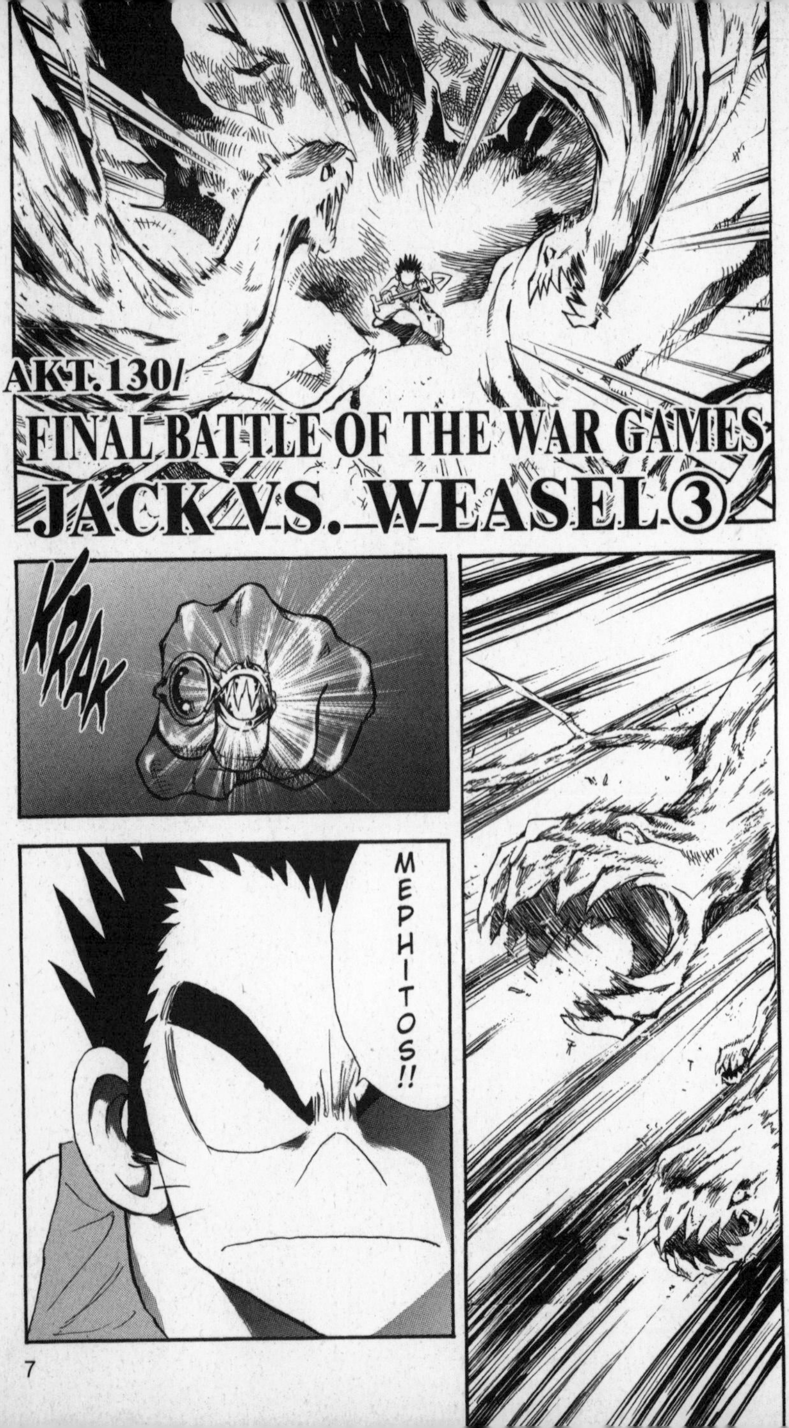
AKT.130/
FINAL BATTLE OF THE WAR GAMES
JACK VS. WEASEL③
KRAK
MEPHITOS!!

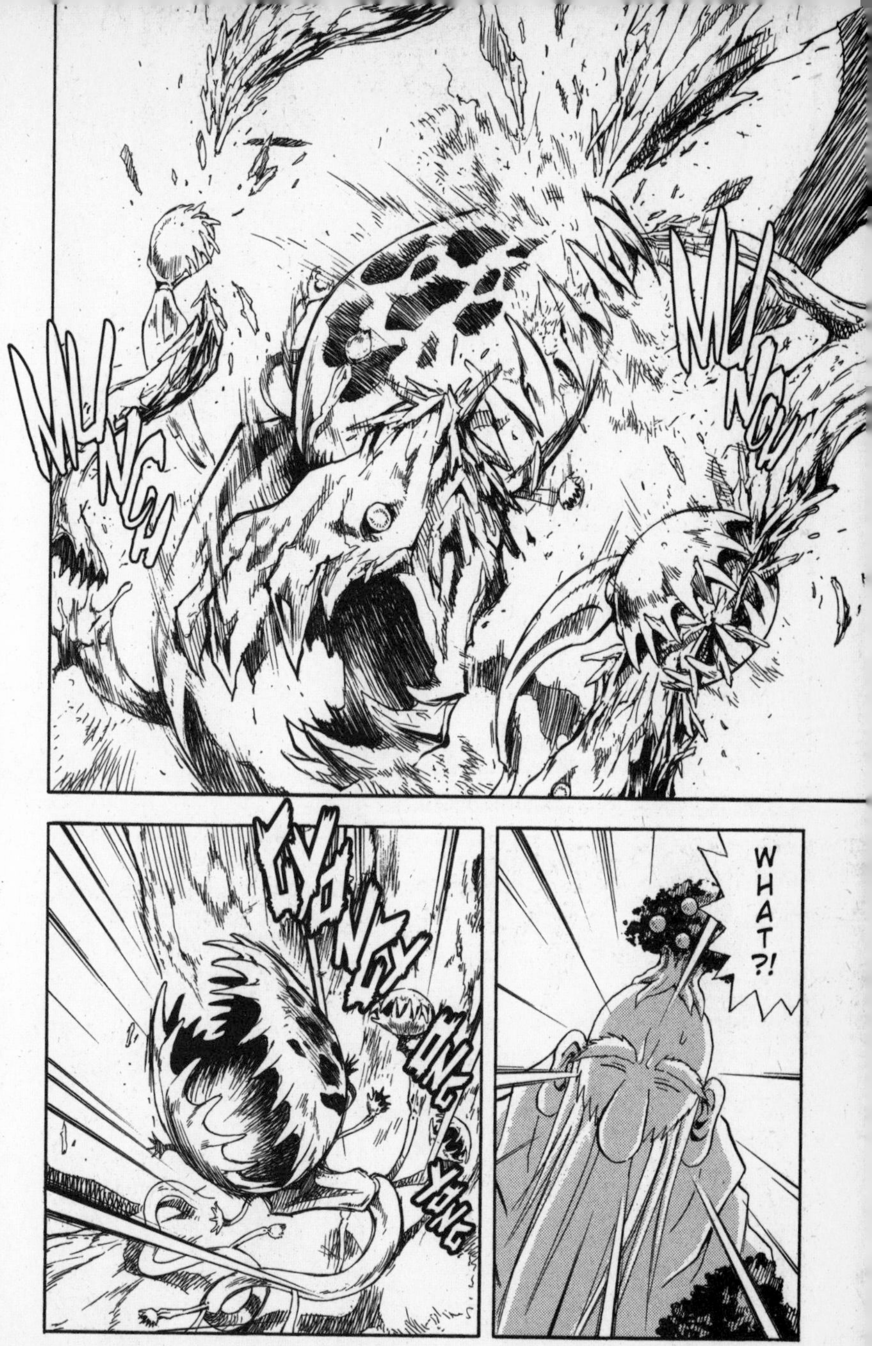
MUNCH
MUNCH
WHAT?!
GYONNYONG
YONG

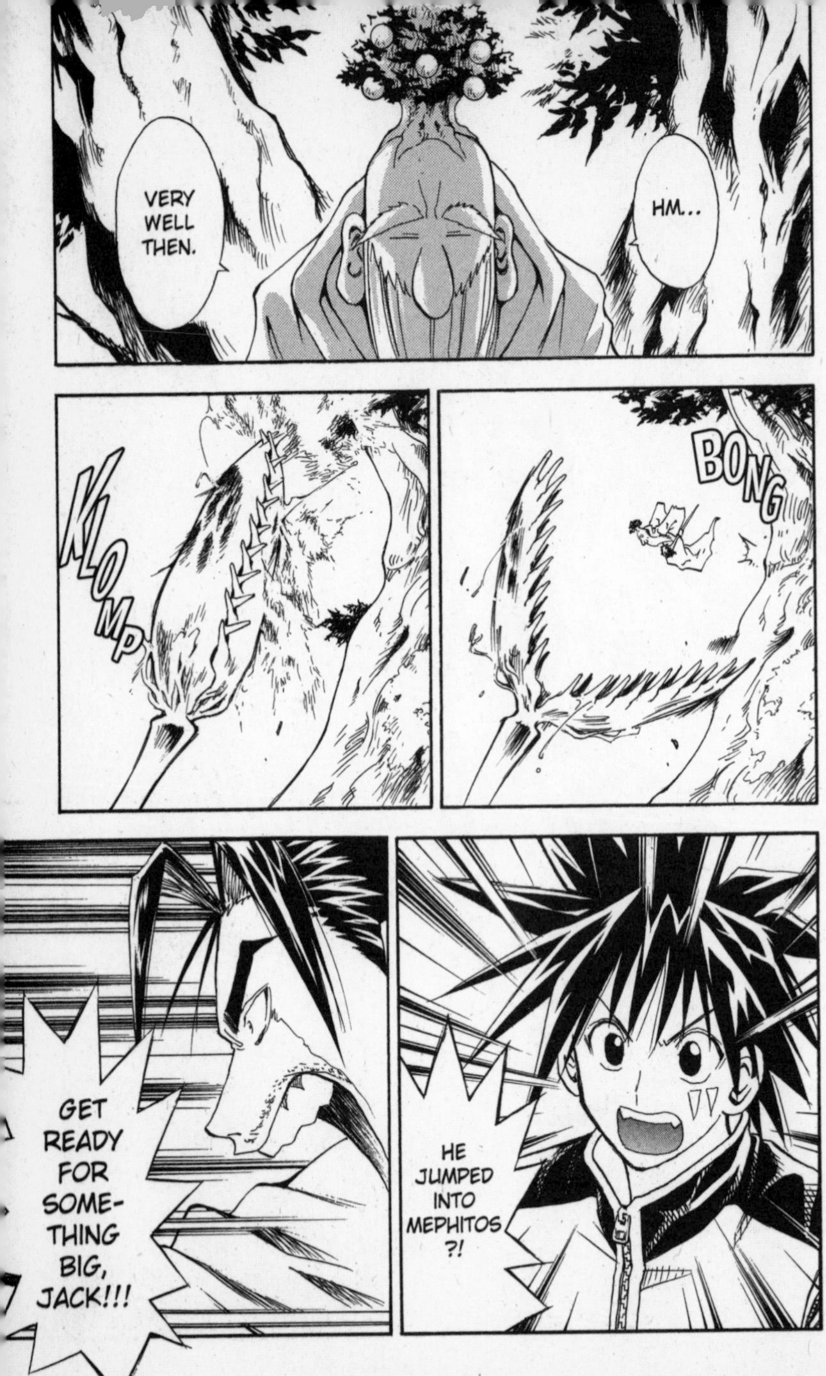
HM...
VERY WELL THEN.
BONG
KLOMP
HE JUMPED INTO MEPHITOS?!
GET READY FOR SOME-THING BIG, JACK!!!

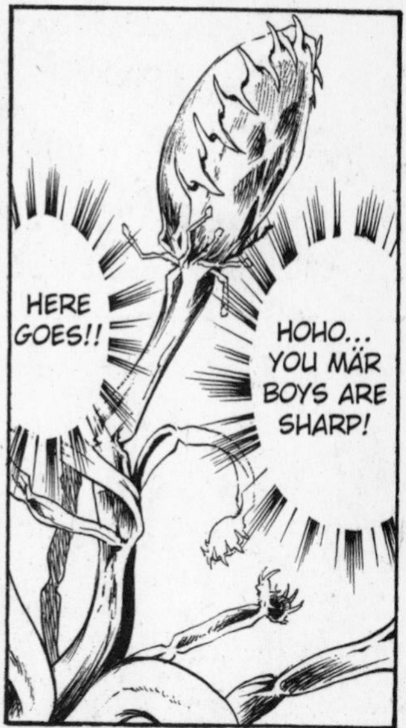
HOHO... YOU MÄR BOYS ARE SHARP!
HERE GOES!!
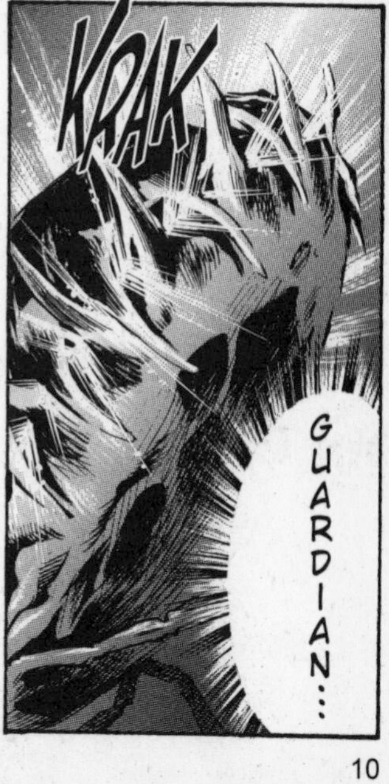
KRAK
GUARDIAN...
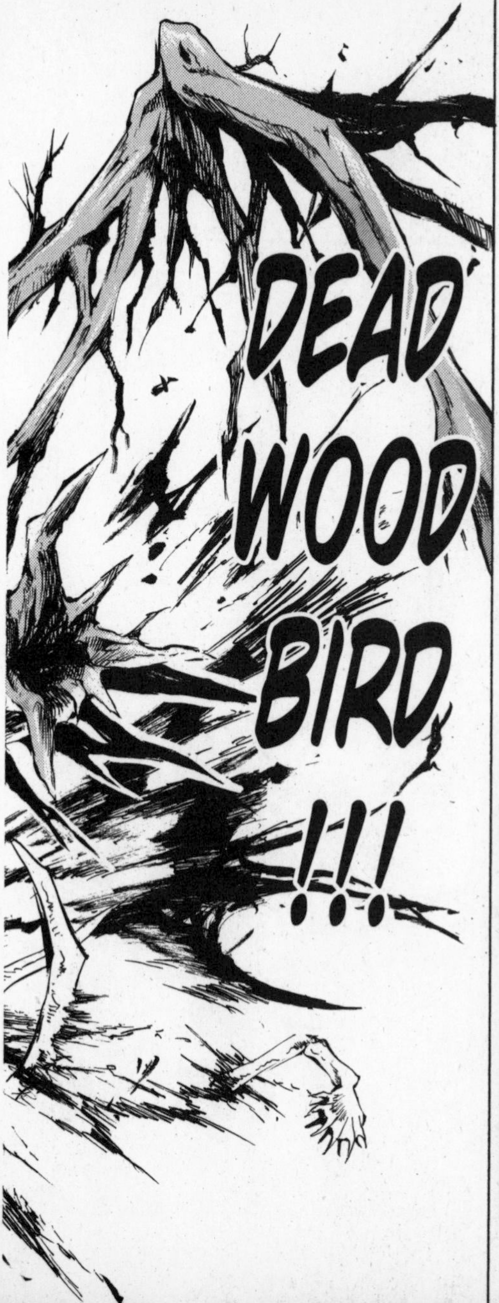
DEAD WOOD BIRD!!!

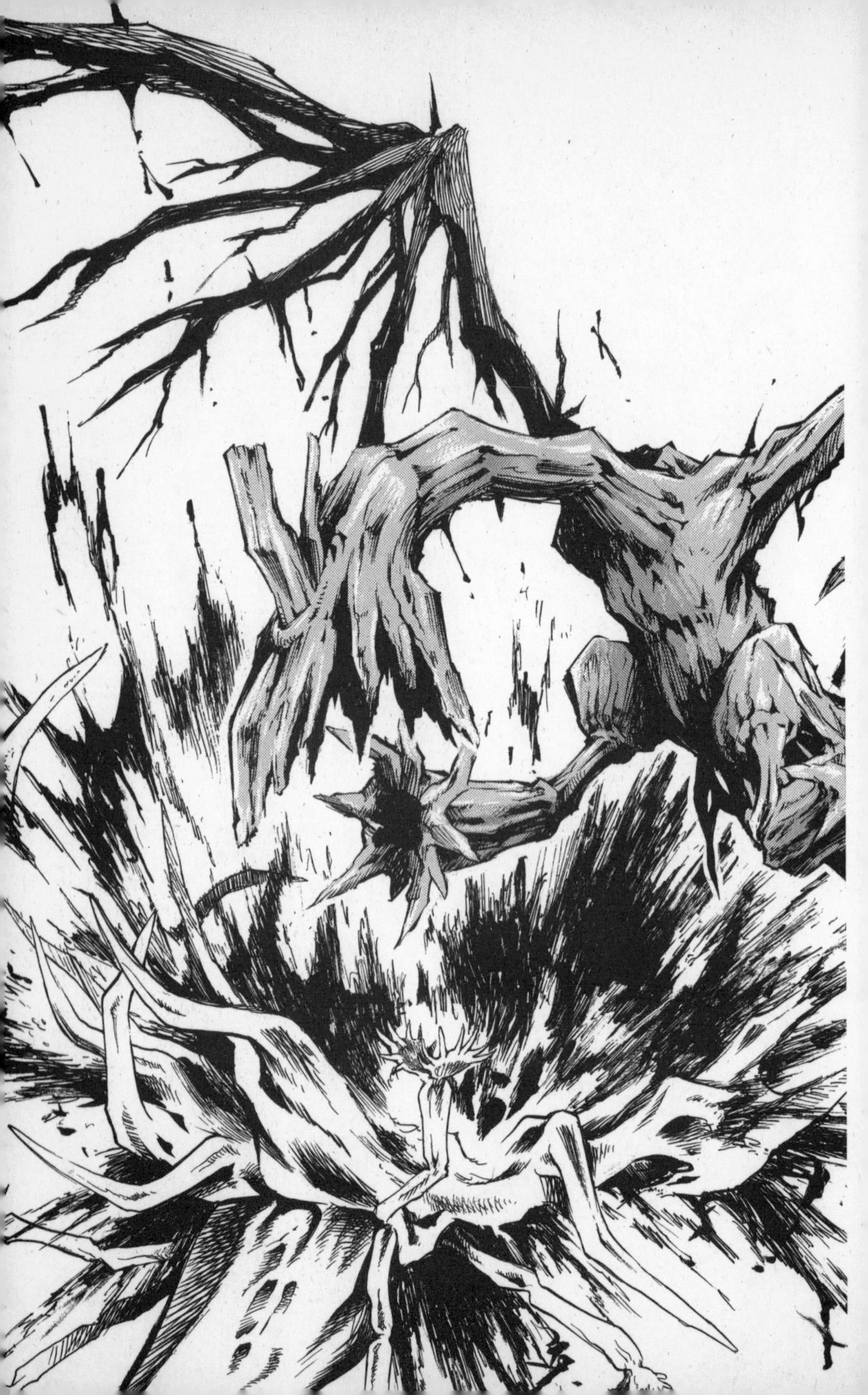

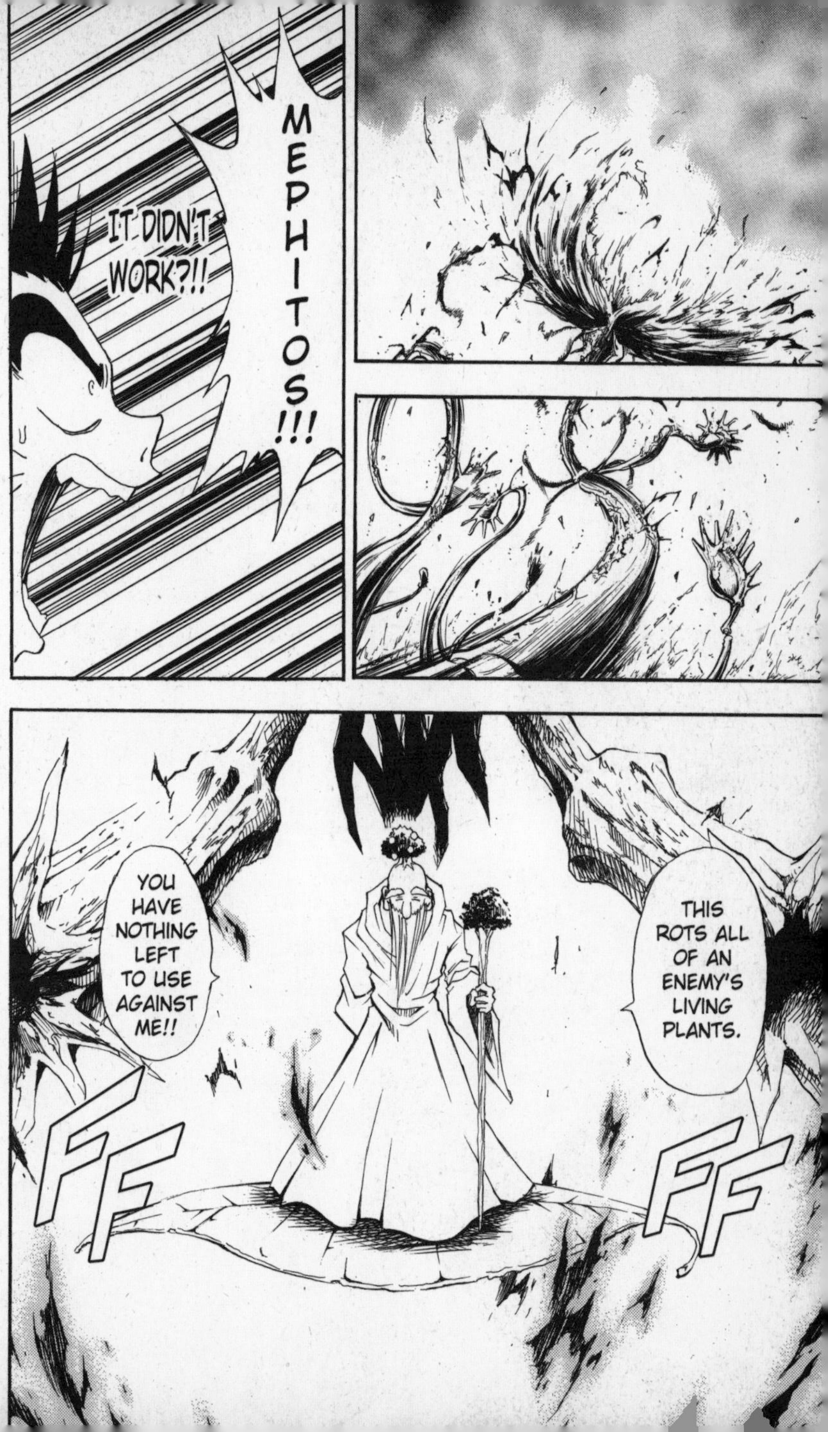
MEPHITOS!!!
IT DIDN'T WORK?!!
THIS ROTS ALL OF AN ENEMY'S LIVING PLANTS.
YOU HAVE NOTHING LEFT TO USE AGAINST ME!!
FF
FF

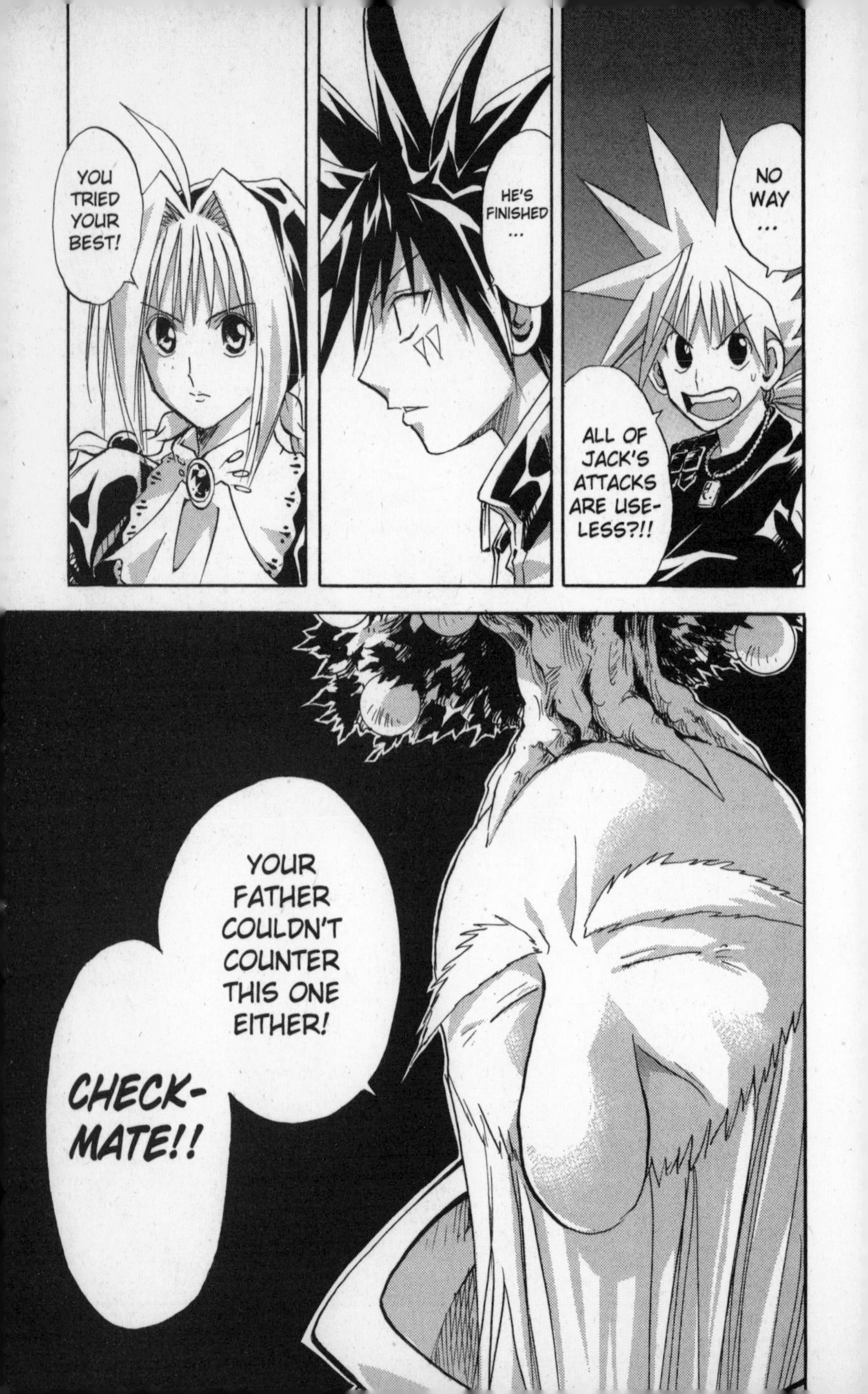
NO WAY ...
ALL OF JACK'S ATTACKS ARE USE-LESS?!!
HE'S FINISHED ...
YOU TRIED YOUR BEST!
YOUR FATHER COULDN'T COUNTER THIS ONE EITHER!
CHECK-MATE!!

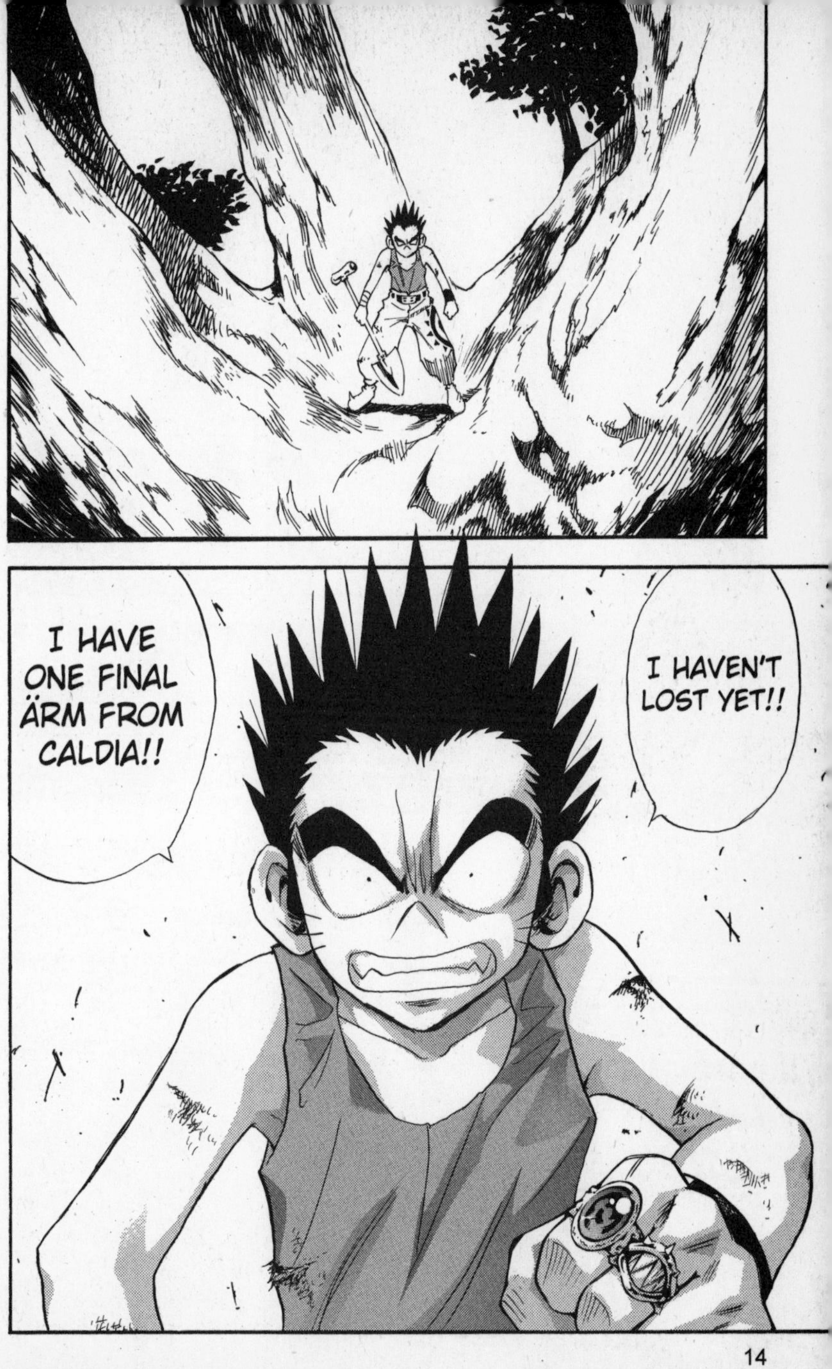
I HAVEN'T LOST YET!!
I HAVE ONE FINAL ÄRM FROM CALDIA!!

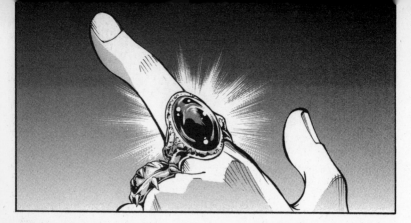

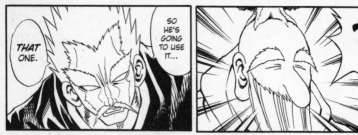

THAT ONE.

SO HE'S GOING TO USE IT...

?

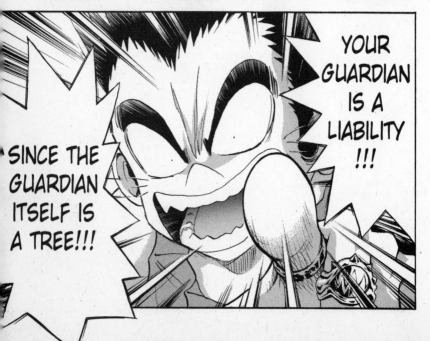

YOUR GUARDIAN IS A LIABILITY!!!

SINCE THE GUARDIAN ITSELF IS A TREE!!!

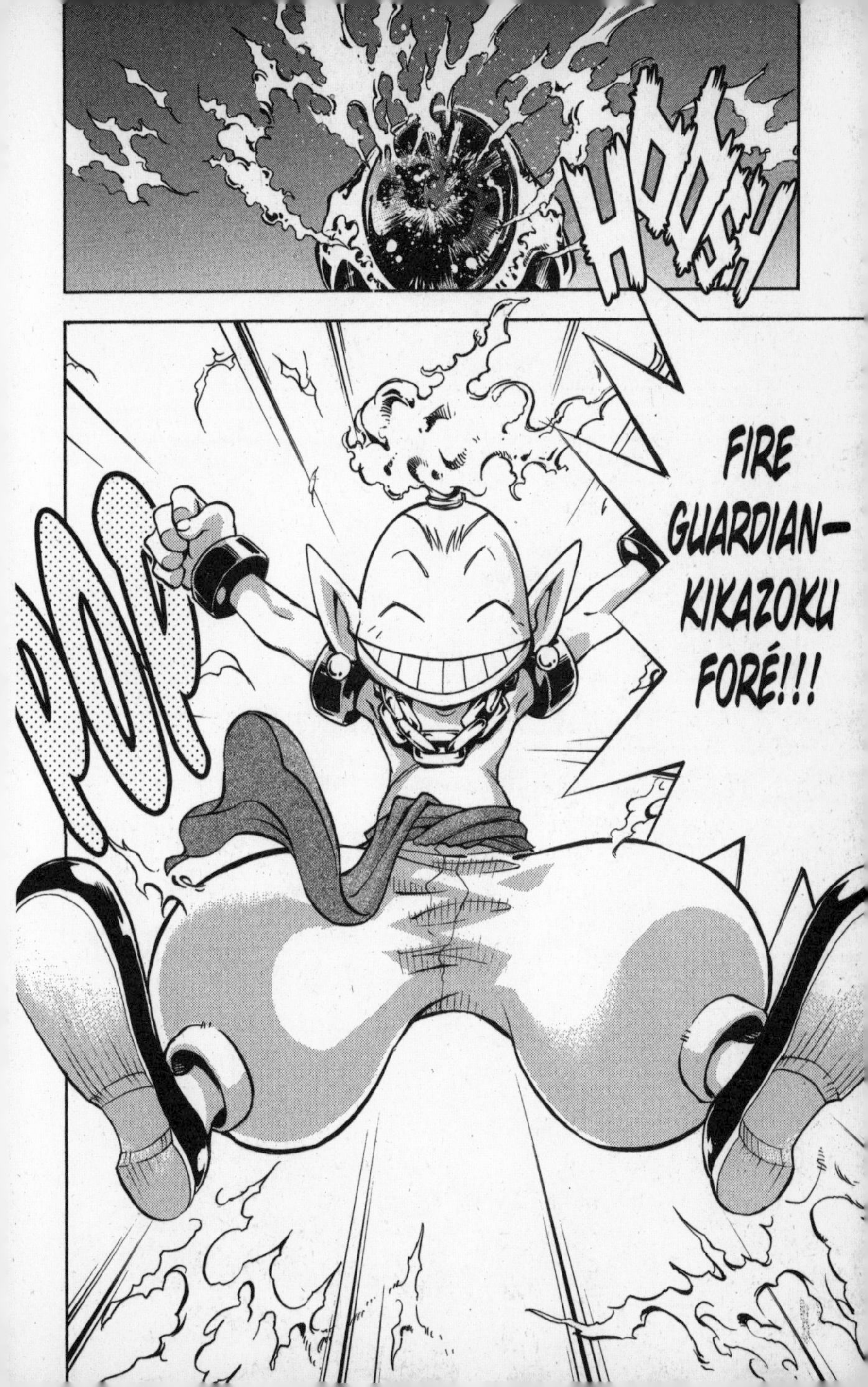
HOOSH
FIRE GUARDIAN-KIKAZOKU FORÉ!!!
POOF

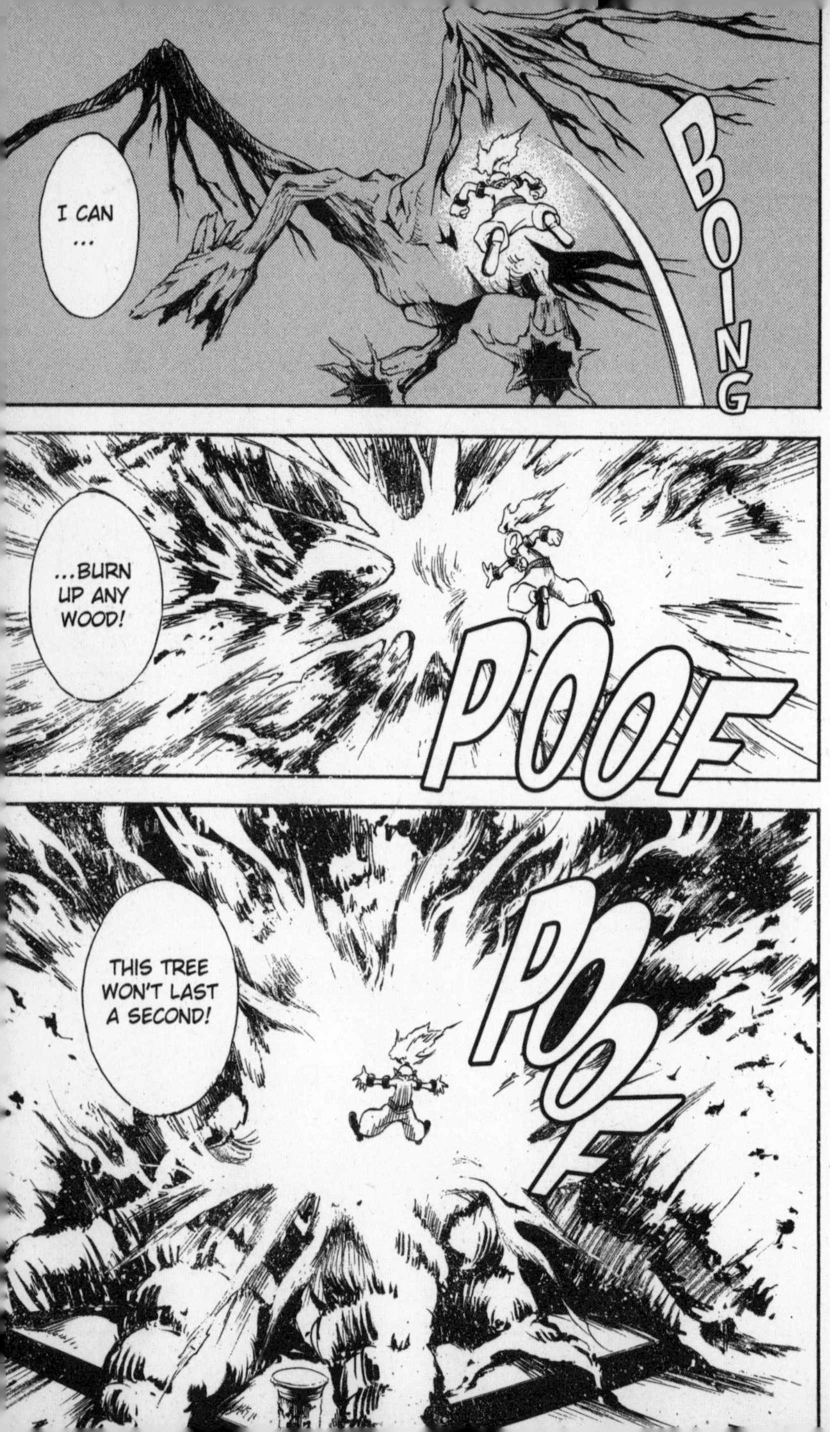
BOING
I CAN ...
...BURN UP ANY WOOD!
POOF
THIS TREE WON'T LAST A SECOND!
POOF

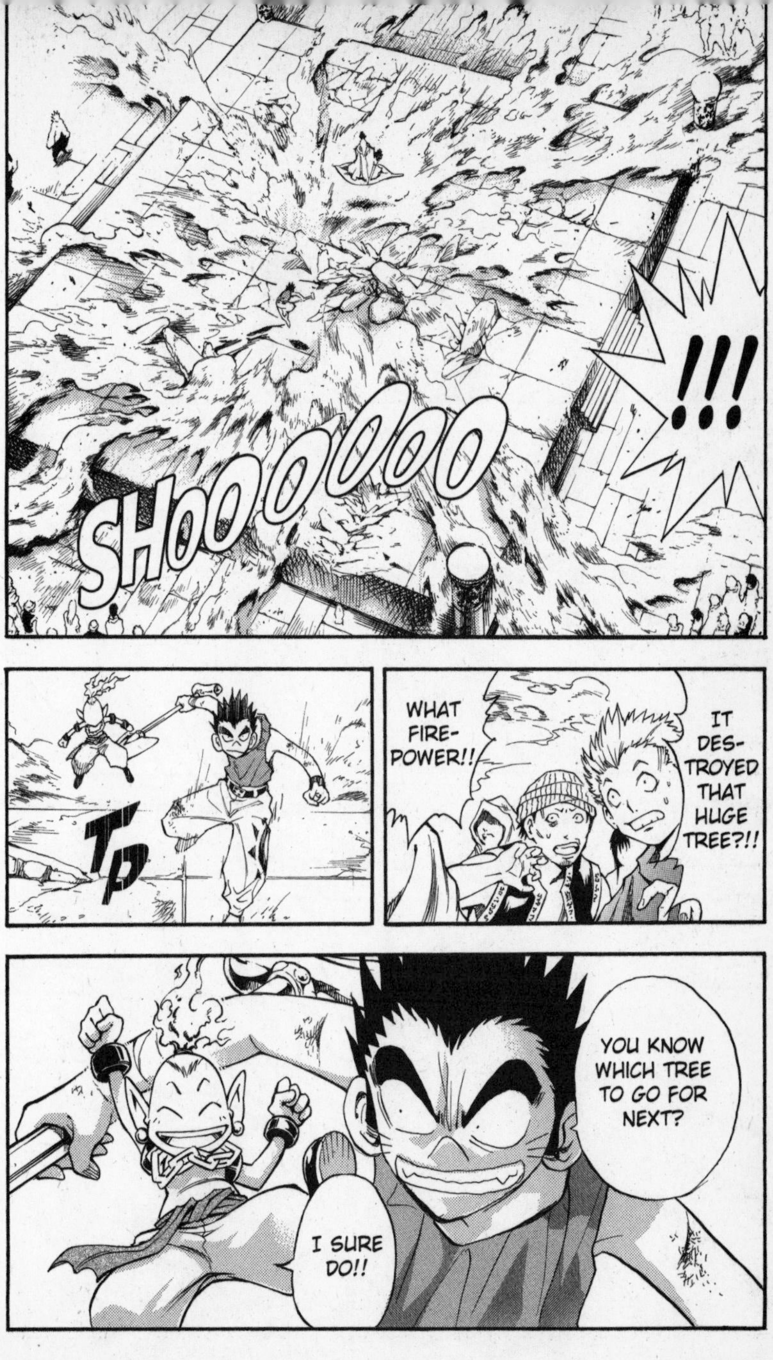
!!!
SHOOOOOO
IT DES-TROYED THAT HUGE TREE?!!
WHAT FIRE-POWER!!
TP
YOU KNOW WHICH TREE TO GO FOR NEXT?
I SURE DO!!

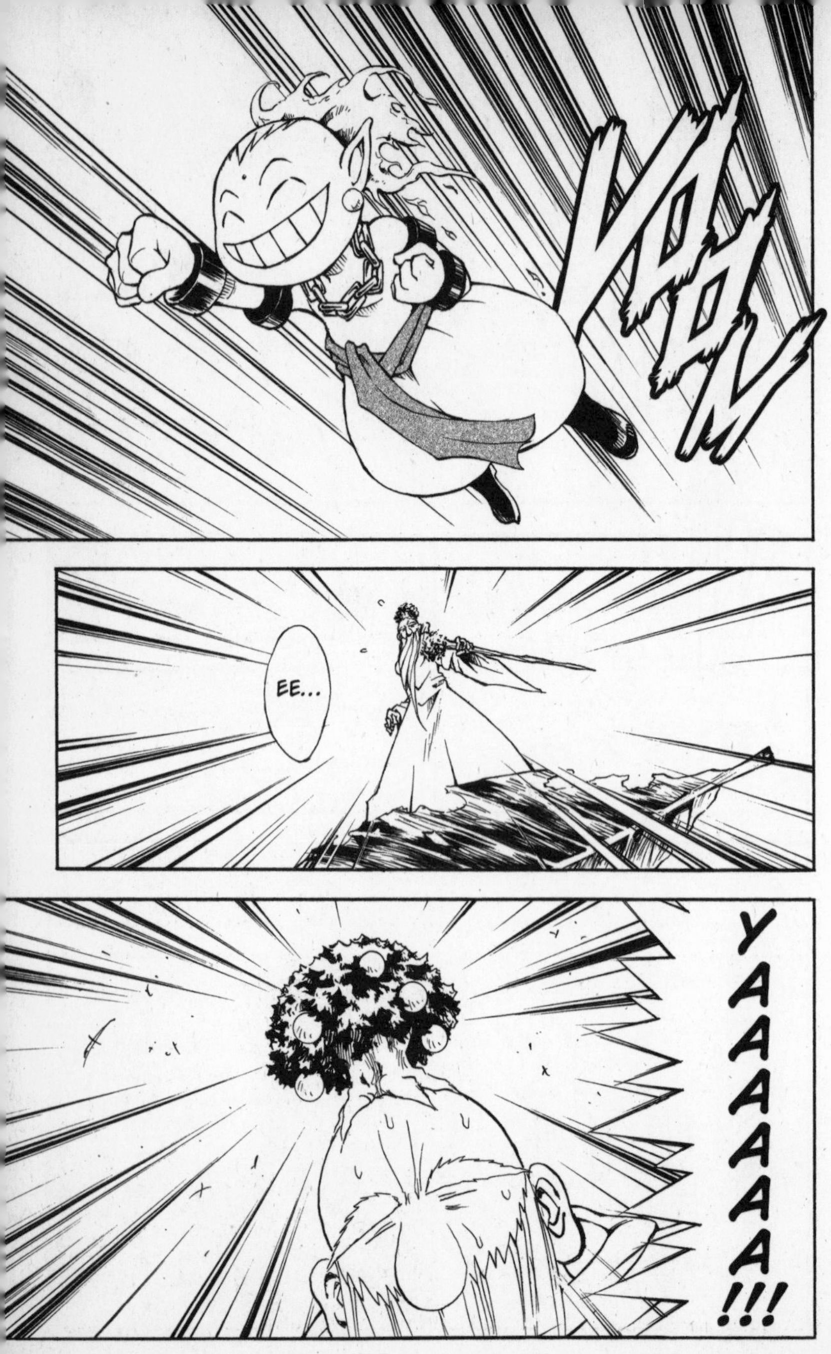
VAAN
EE...
YAAAAAAA!!!

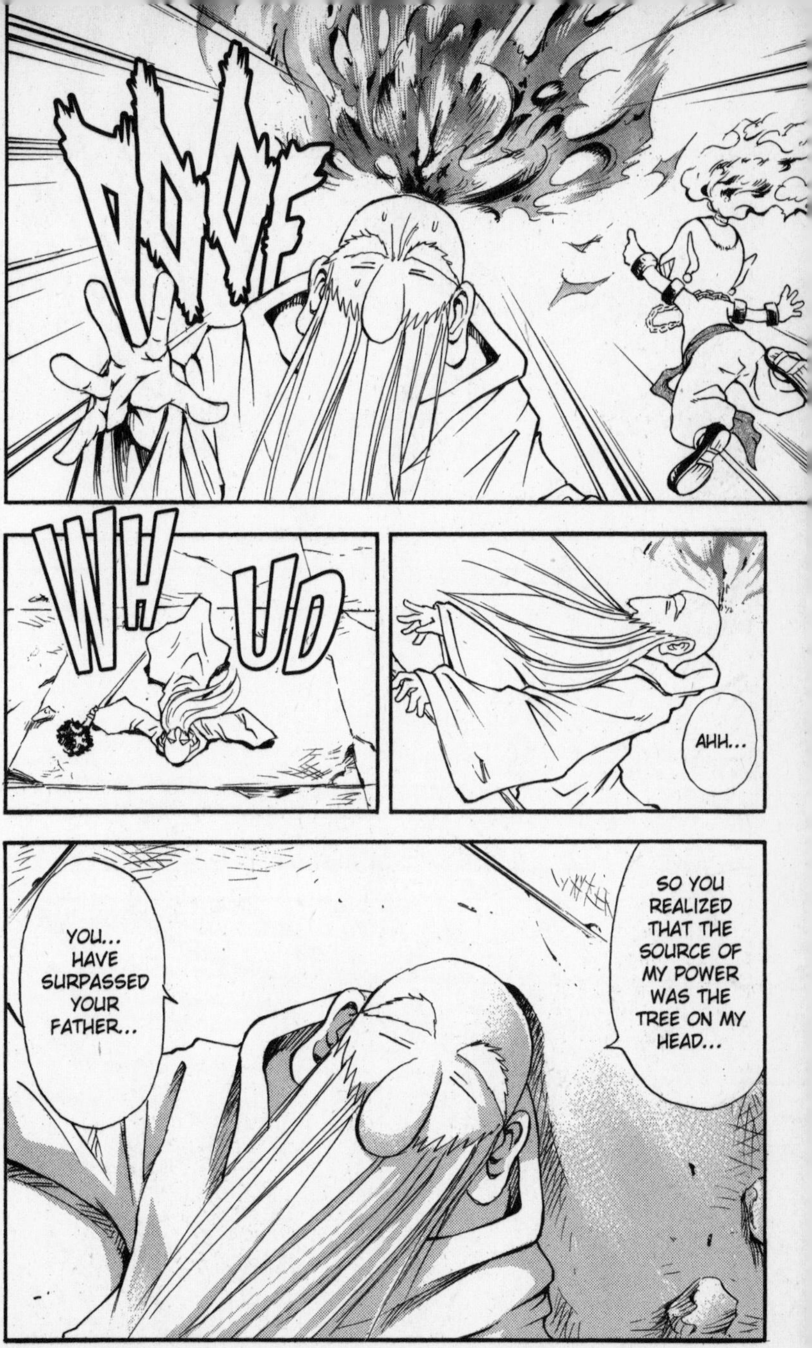
POOF
AHH...
WHUD
SO YOU REALIZED THAT THE SOURCE OF MY POWER WAS THE TREE ON MY HEAD...
YOU... HAVE SURPASSED YOUR FATHER...

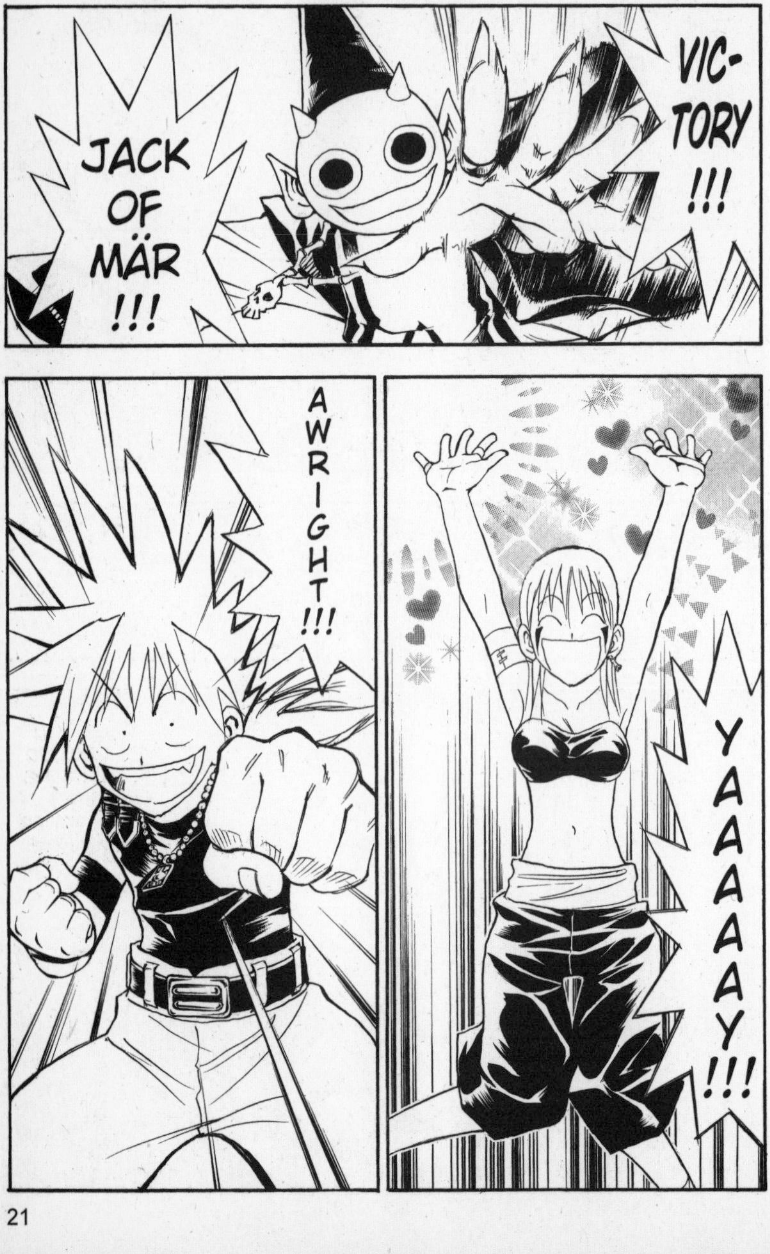
VIC-
TORY
!!!
JACK
OF
MÄR
!!!
YAAAAAAY!!!
AWRIGHT!!!

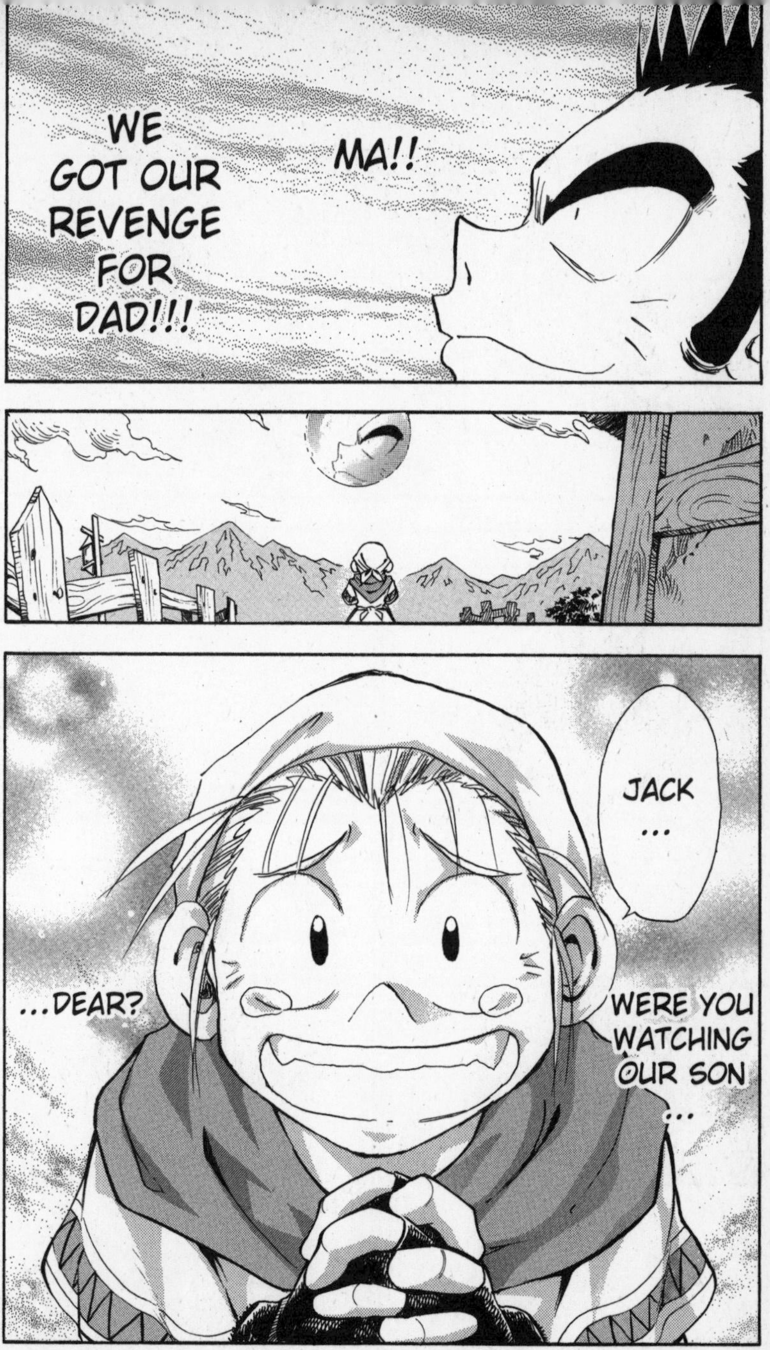
MA!!
WE GOT OUR REVENGE FOR DAD!!!
JACK ...
WERE YOU WATCHING OUR SON ...
...DEAR?

AKT.131/ FINAL BATTLE OF THE WAR GAMES: ALVISS VS. ROLAN ①

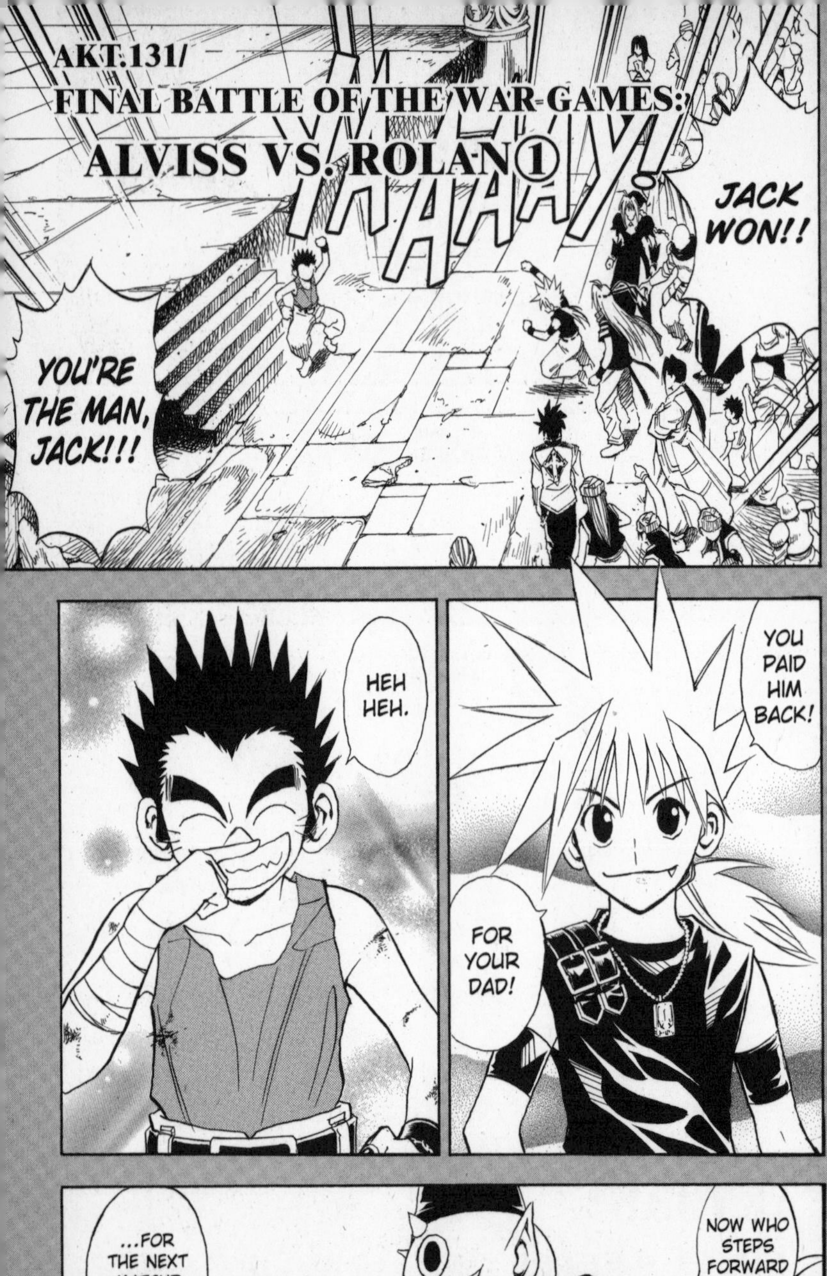

JACK WON!!
YOU'RE THE MAN, JACK!!!
YOU PAID HIM BACK!
FOR YOUR DAD!
HEH HEH.
NOW WHO STEPS FORWARD ...
...FOR THE NEXT MATCH?

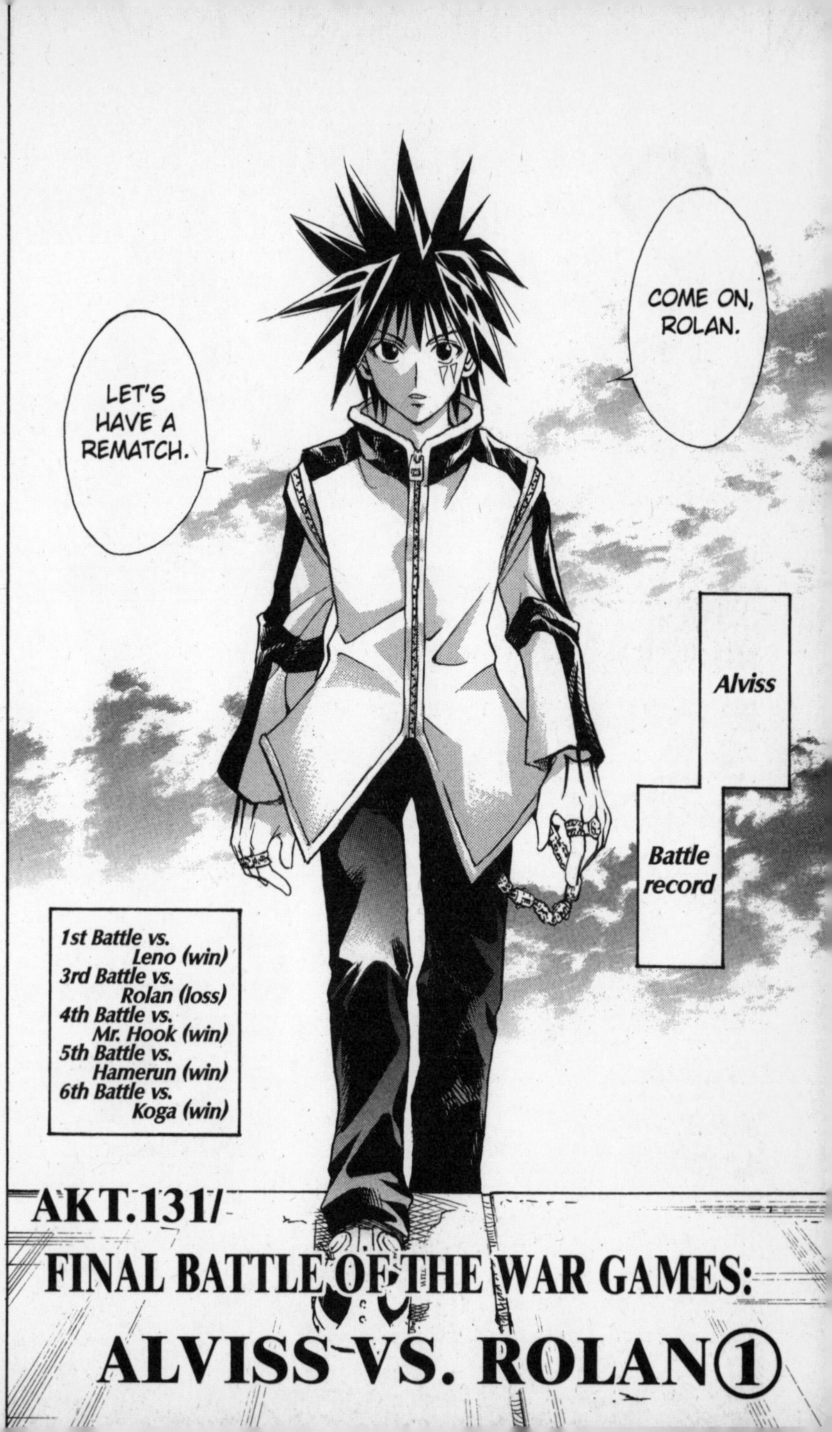
COME ON, ROLAN.
LET'S HAVE A REMATCH.
Alviss
Battle record
1st Battle vs. Leno (win)
3rd Battle vs. Rolan (loss)
4th Battle vs. Mr. Hook (win)
5th Battle vs. Hamerun (win)
6th Battle vs. Koga (win)

AKT.131/ FINAL BATTLE OF THE WAR GAMES: ALVISS VS. ROLAN ①

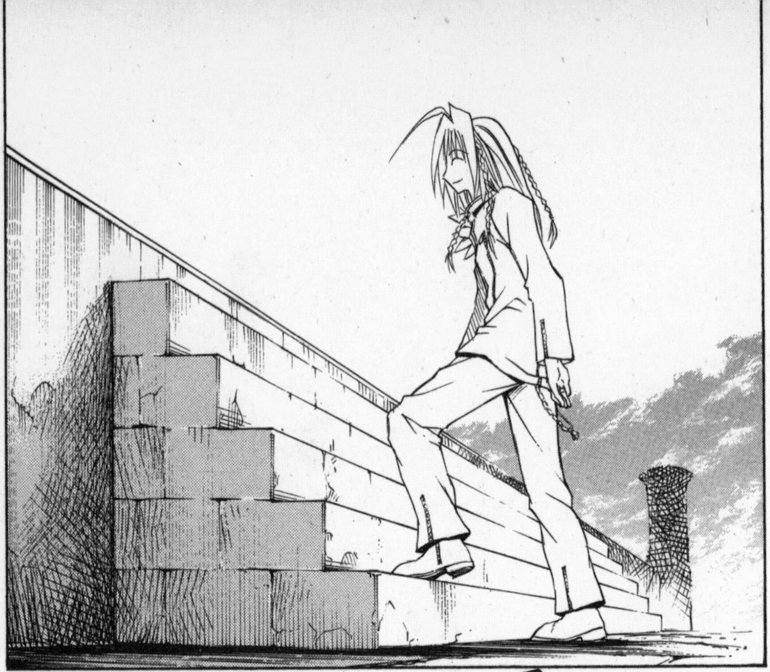

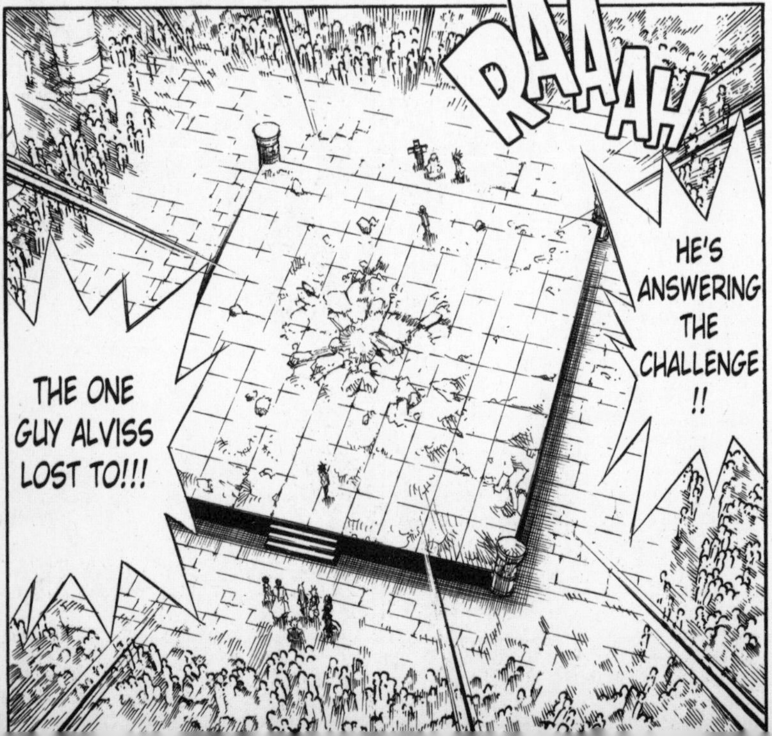
RAAAAH
HE'S ANSWERING THE CHALLENGE !!
THE ONE GUY ALVISS LOST TO!!!

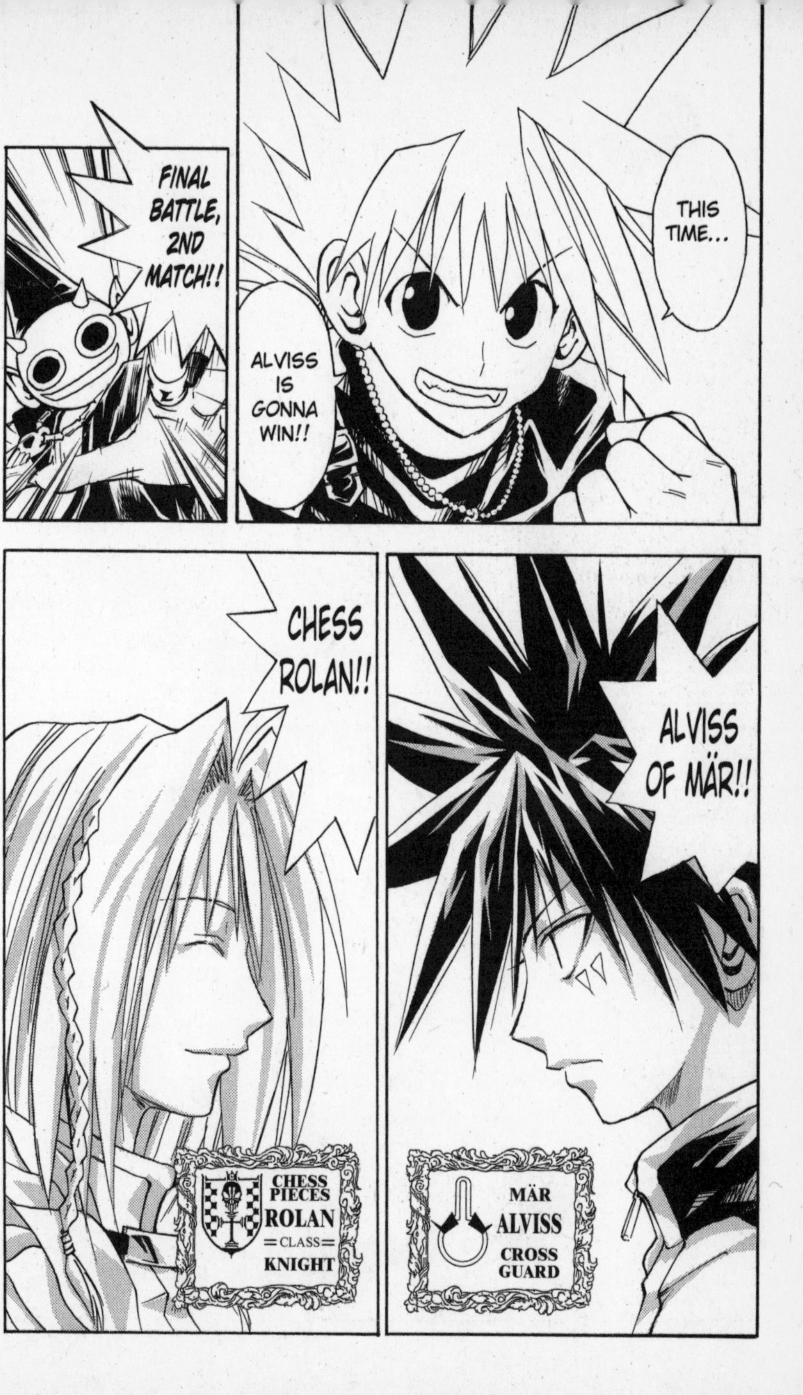
THIS TIME...
ALVISS IS GONNA WIN!!
FINAL BATTLE, 2ND MATCH!!
ALVISS OF MÄR!!
MÄR
ALVISS
CROSS GUARD
CHESS ROLAN!!
CHESS PIECES
ROLAN
=CLASS=
KNIGHT

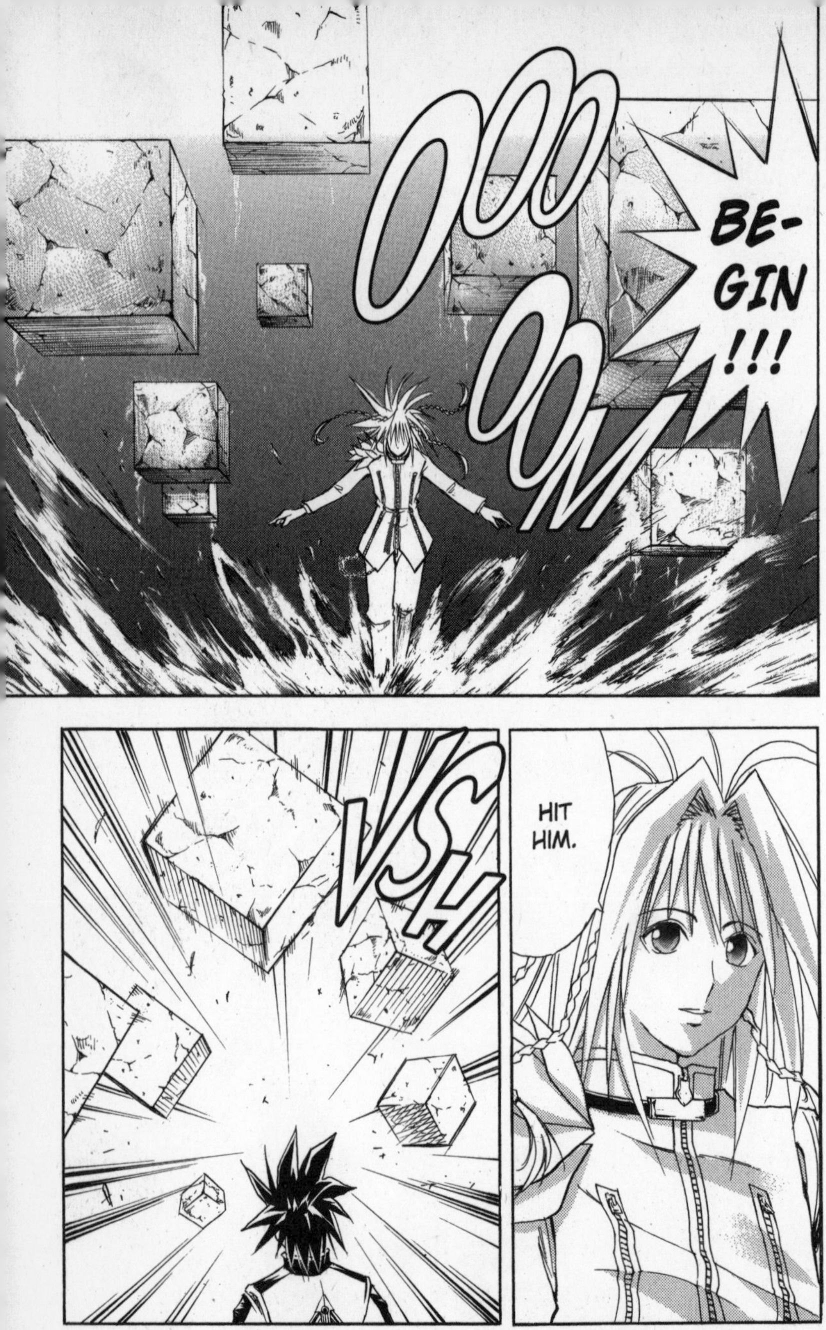
OOOOOOOOM
BE-
GIN
!!!
HIT
HIM.
VSH

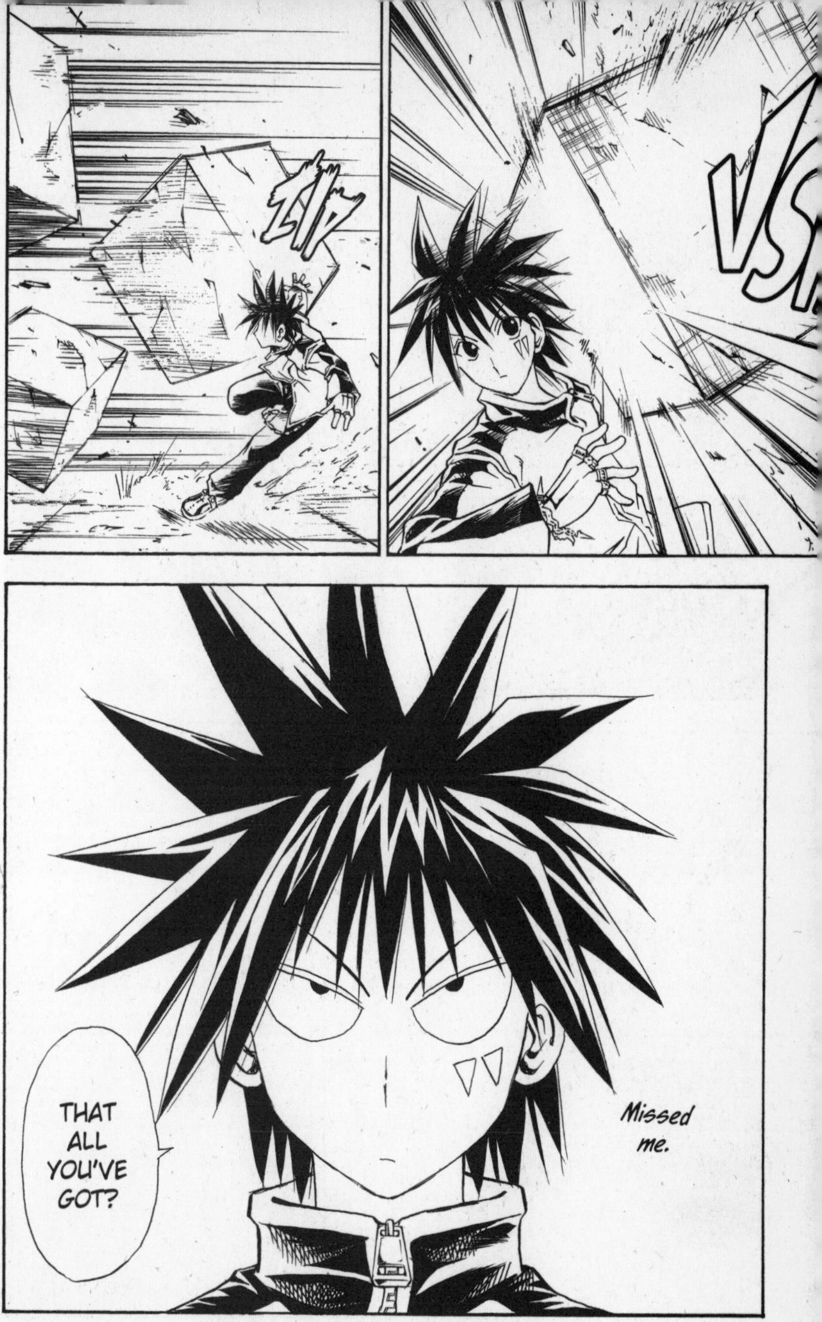
Missed me.
THAT ALL YOU'VE GOT?

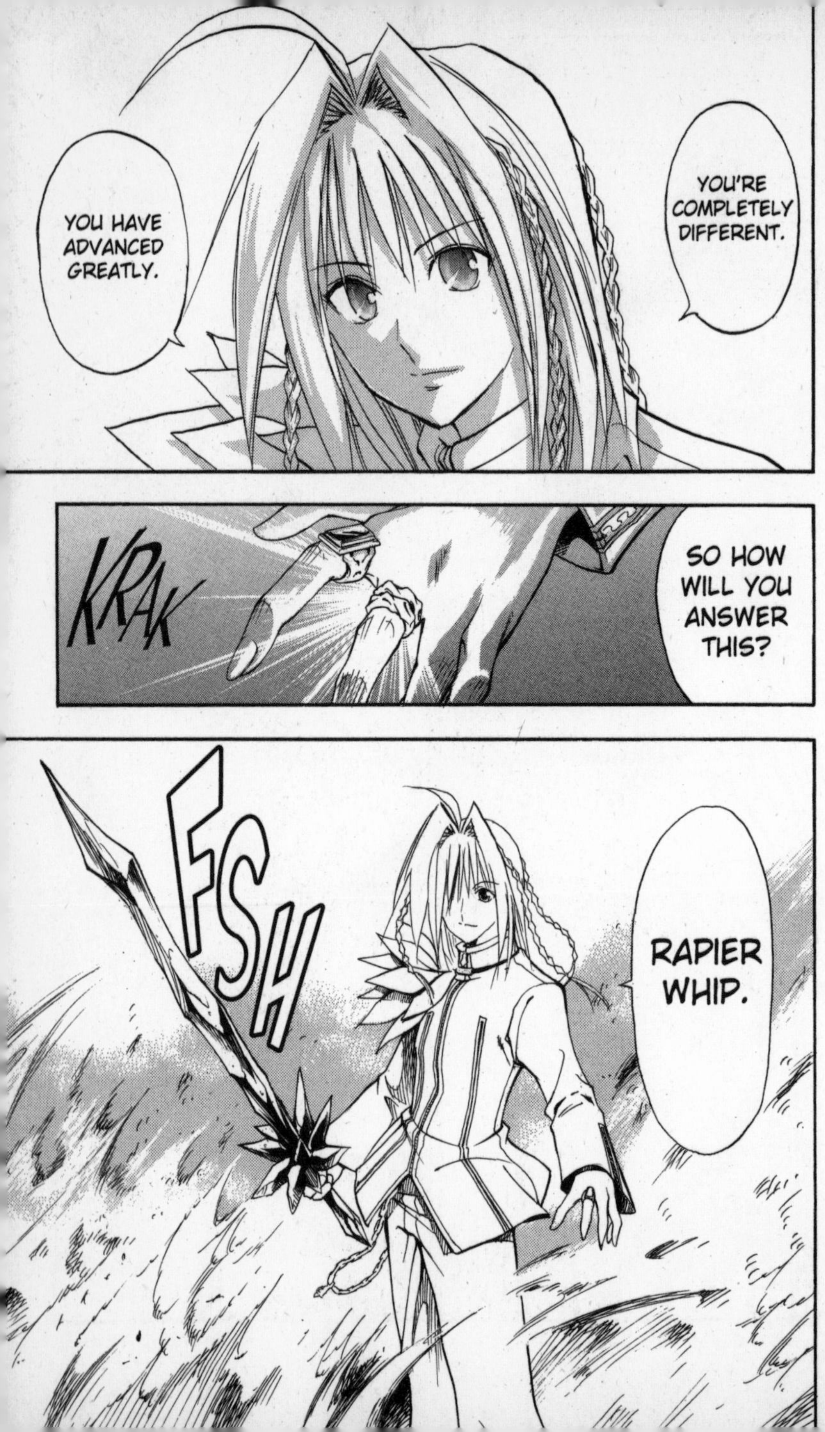
YOU'RE COMPLETELY DIFFERENT.
YOU HAVE ADVANCED GREATLY.
SO HOW WILL YOU ANSWER THIS?
KRAK
RAPIER WHIP.
FSH

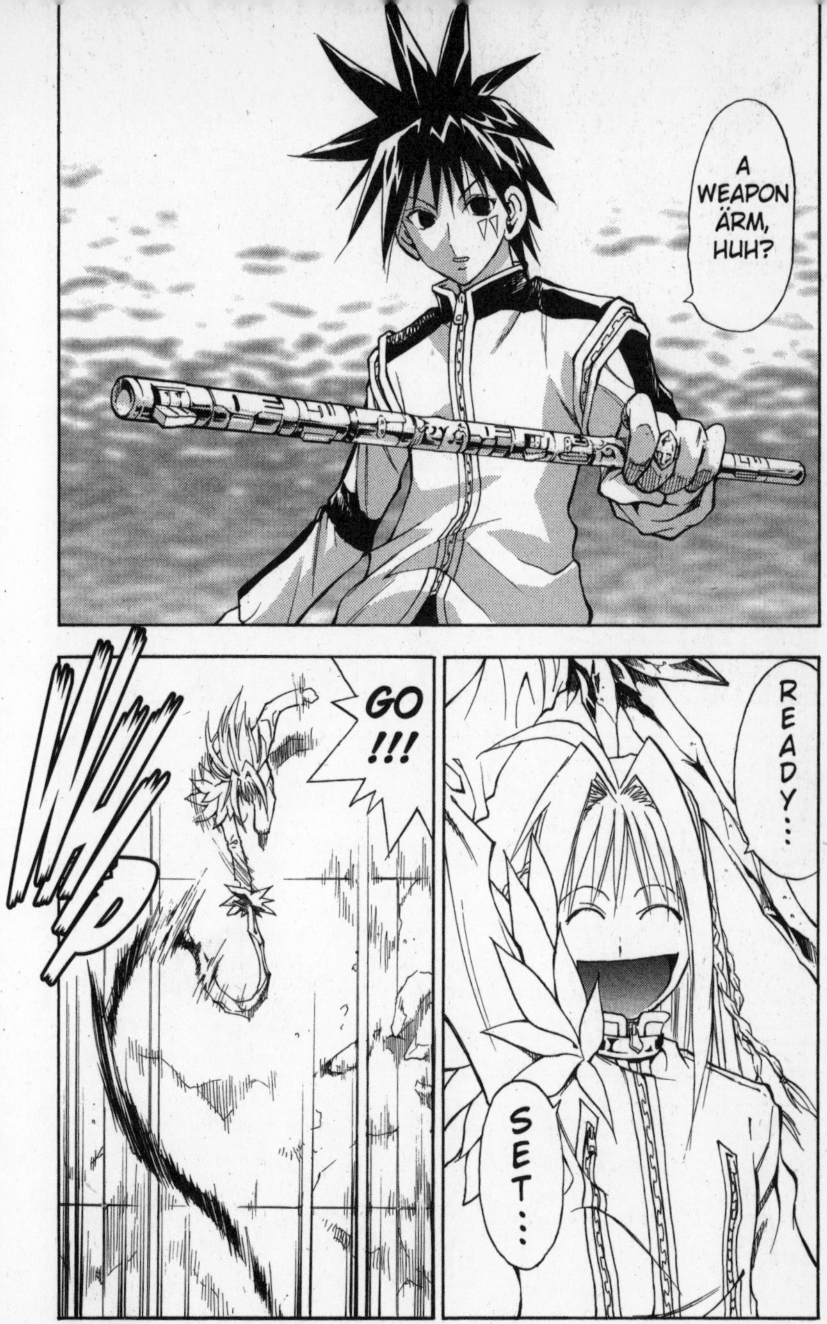
A WEAPON ÄRM, HUH?
READY...
SET...
GO!!!
WHAP

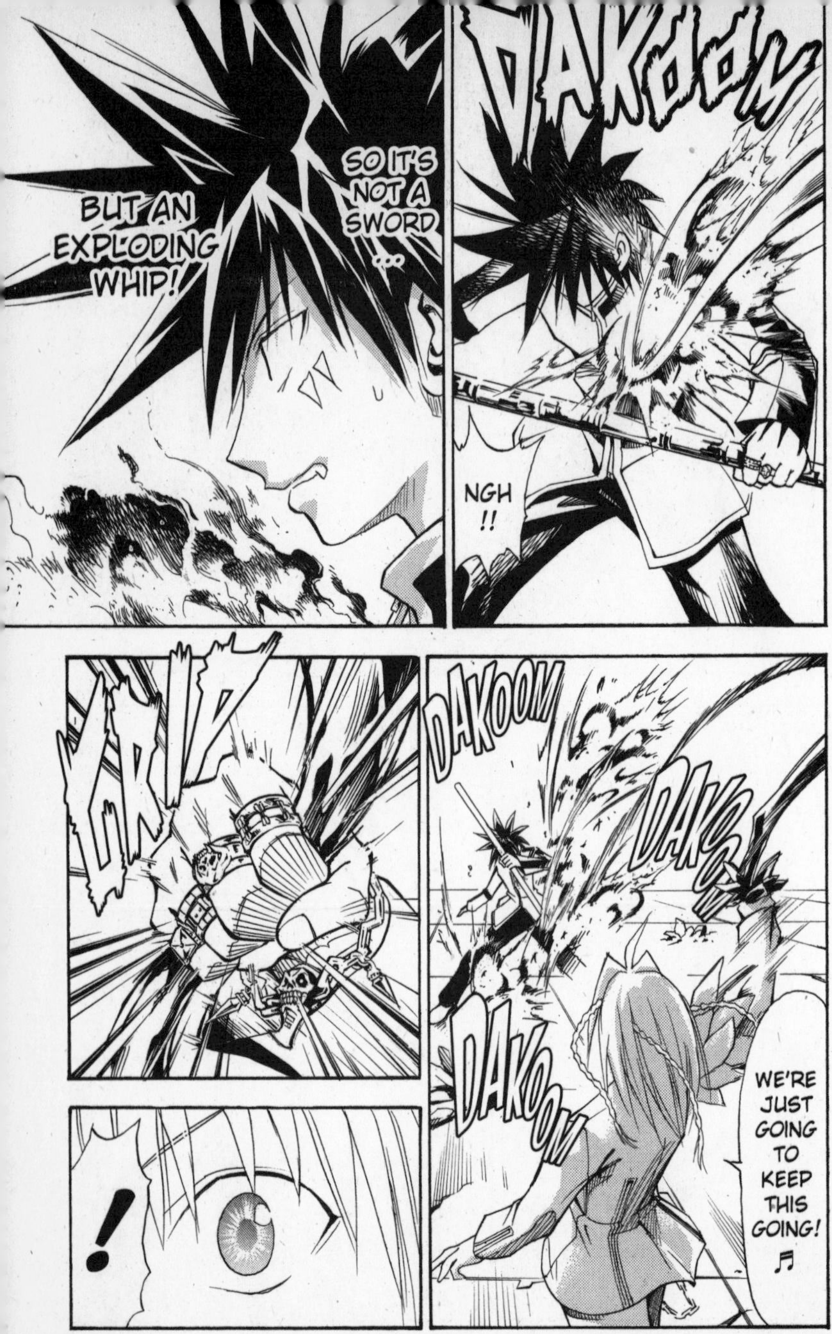
DAKOOM
NGH !!
SO IT'S NOT A SWORD...
BUT AN EXPLODING WHIP!
DAKOOM
WE'RE JUST GOING TO KEEP THIS GOING! ♬
!

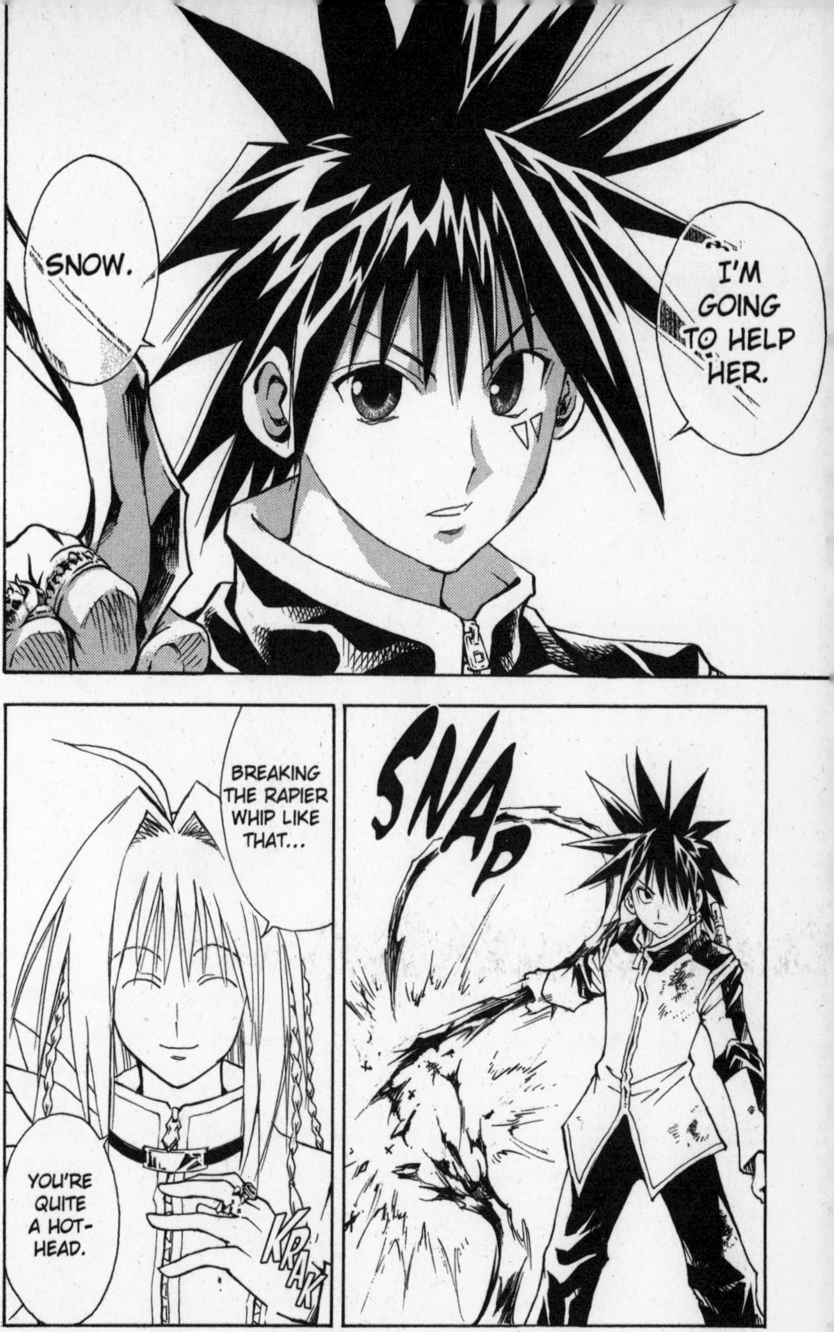
I'M GOING TO HELP HER.
SNOW.
SNAP
BREAKING THE RAPIER WHIP LIKE THAT...
YOU'RE QUITE A HOT-HEAD.
KRAK

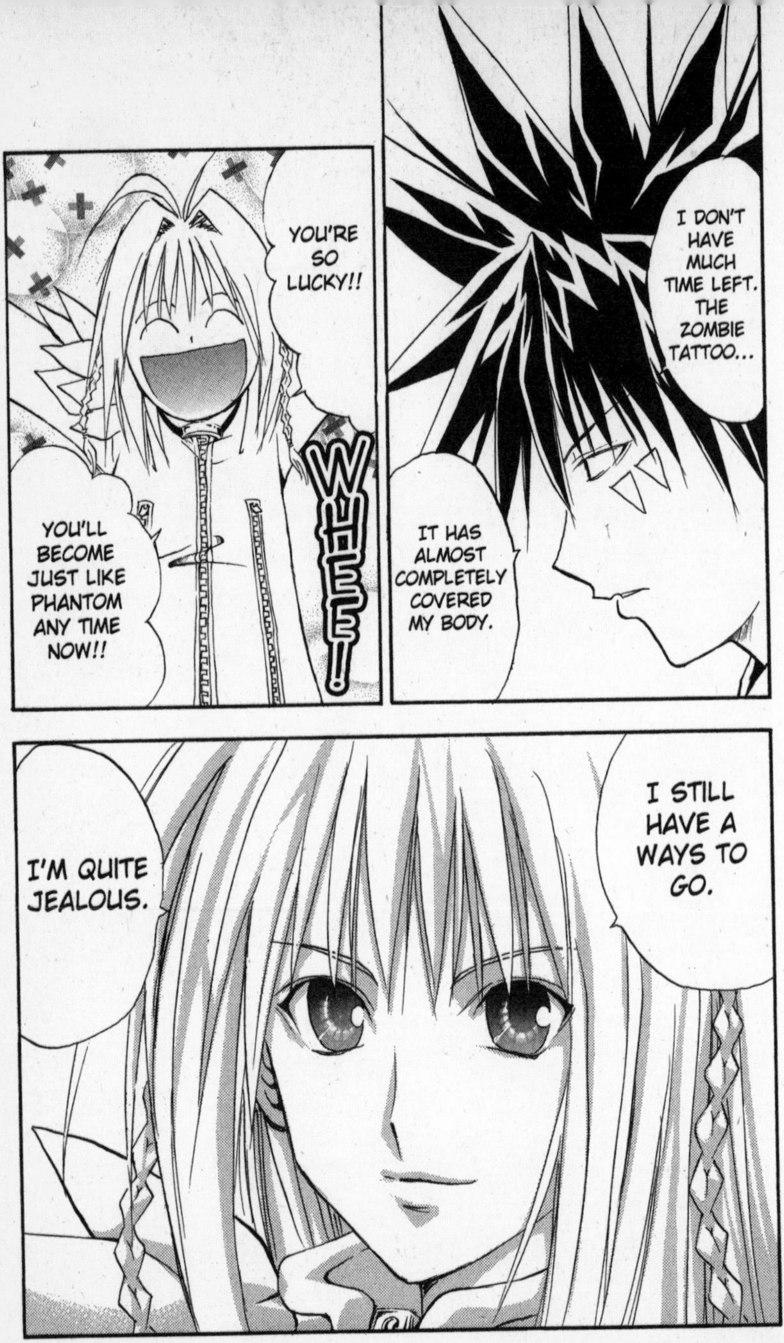
I DON'T HAVE MUCH TIME LEFT. THE ZOMBIE TATTOO...
IT HAS ALMOST COMPLETELY COVERED MY BODY.
YOU'RE SO LUCKY!!
WHEE!
YOU'LL BECOME JUST LIKE PHANTOM ANY TIME NOW!!
I STILL HAVE A WAYS TO GO.
I'M QUITE JEALOUS.

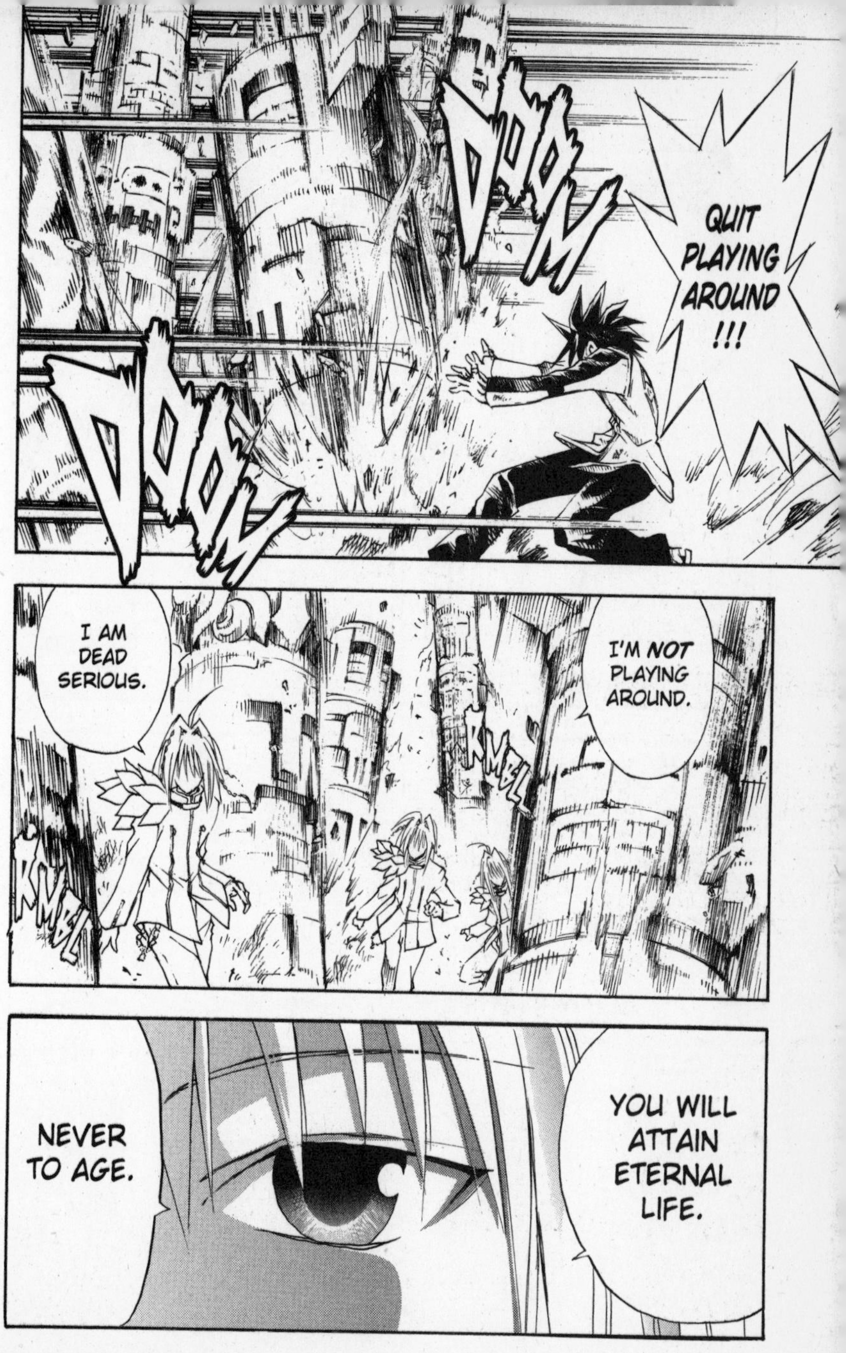
DOOM
QUIT PLAYING AROUND!!!
DOOM
I'M *NOT* PLAYING AROUND.
RMBL
I AM DEAD SERIOUS.
RMBL
YOU WILL ATTAIN ETERNAL LIFE.
NEVER TO AGE.

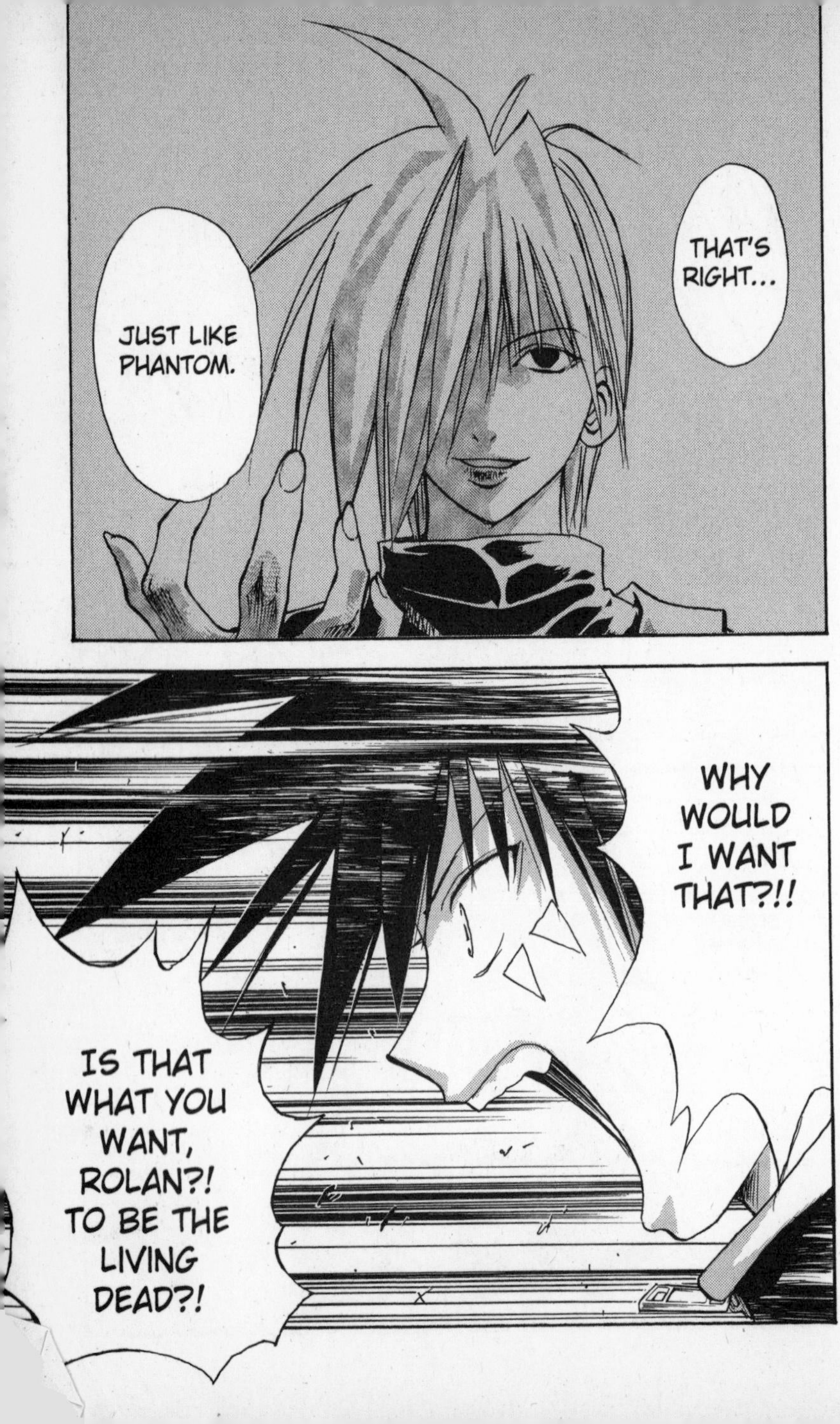
THAT'S RIGHT...
JUST LIKE PHANTOM.
WHY WOULD I WANT THAT?!!
IS THAT WHAT YOU WANT, ROLAN?! TO BE THE LIVING DEAD?!

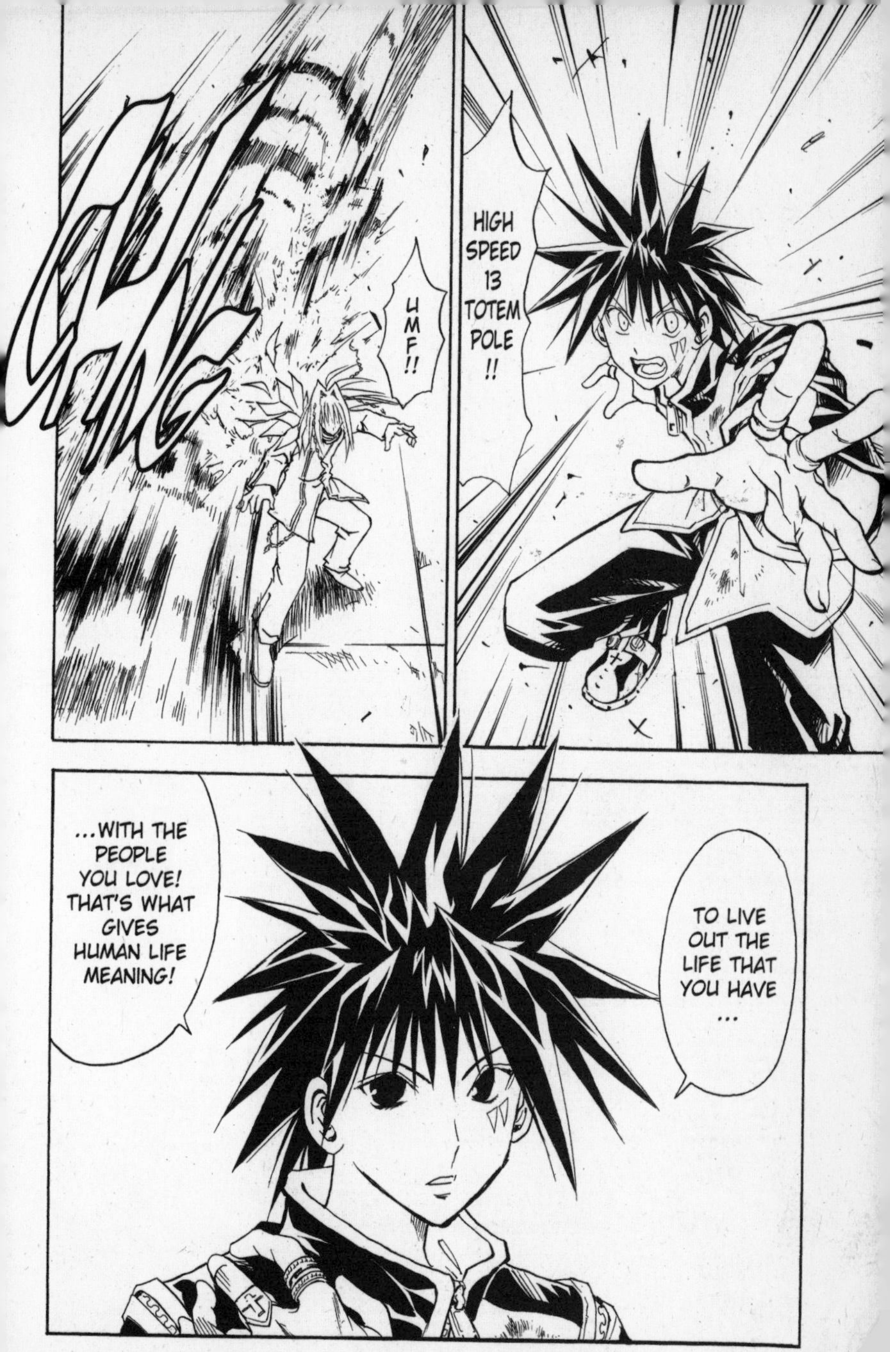
HIGH SPEED 13 TOTEM POLE !!
UMF!!
TO LIVE OUT THE LIFE THAT YOU HAVE ...
...WITH THE PEOPLE YOU LOVE! THAT'S WHAT GIVES HUMAN LIFE MEANING!

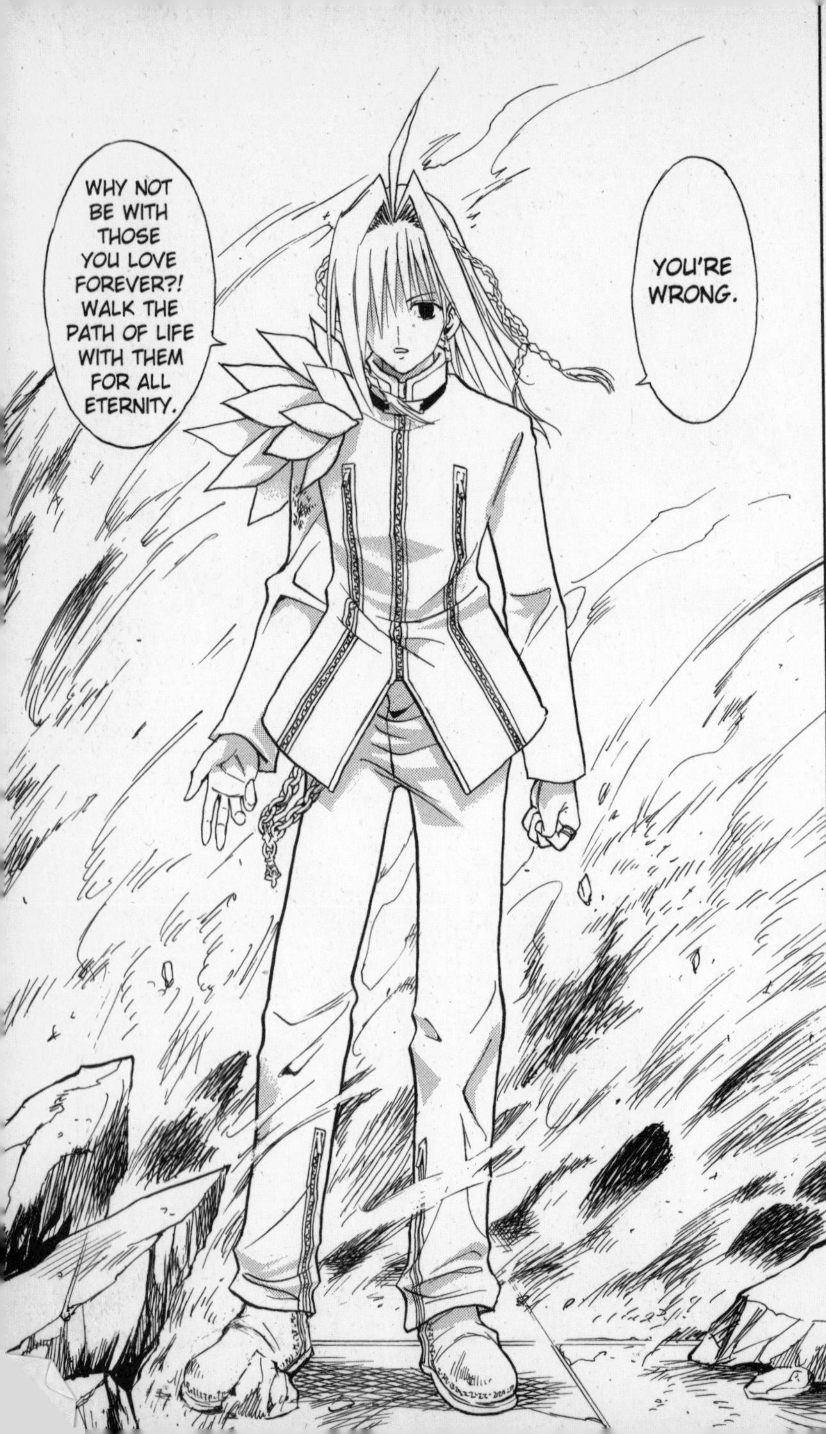
WHY NOT BE WITH THOSE YOU LOVE FOREVER?! WALK THE PATH OF LIFE WITH THEM FOR ALL ETERNITY.
YOU'RE WRONG.

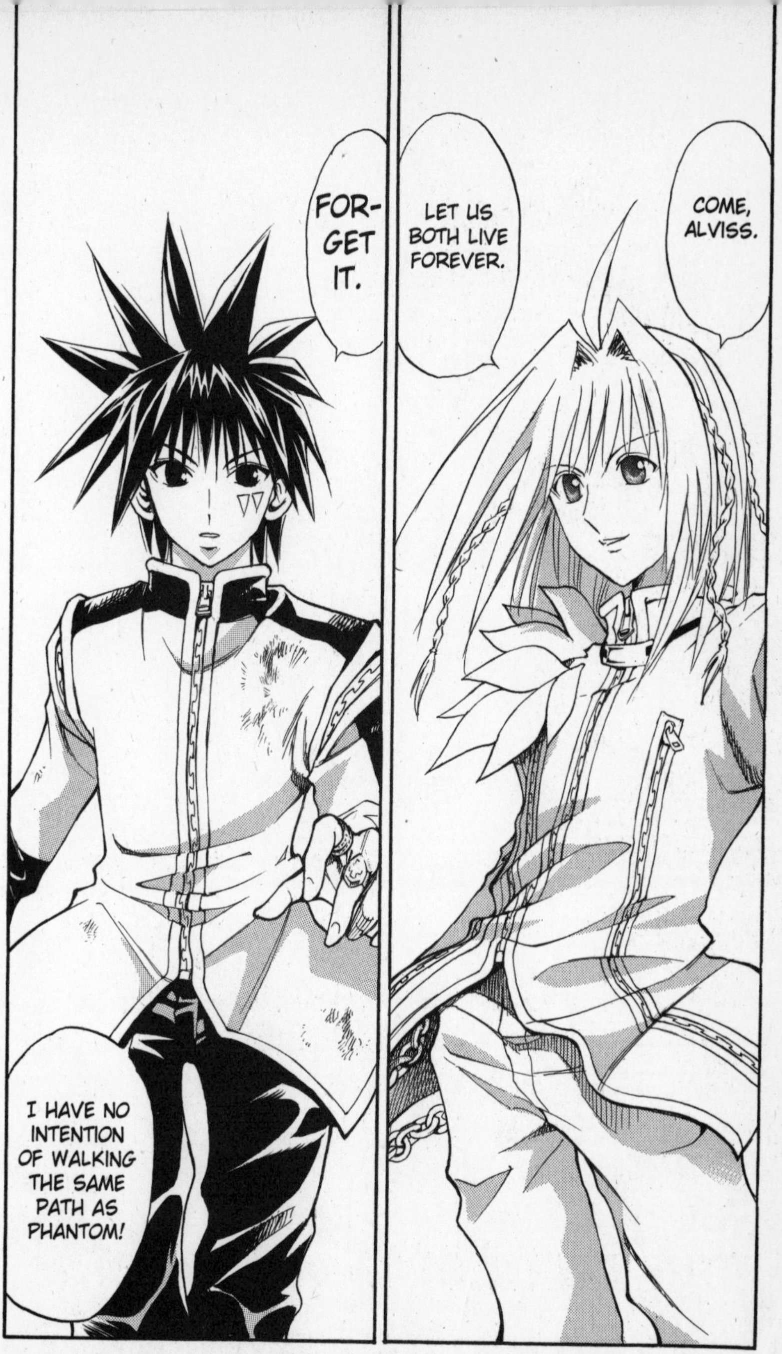
COME, ALVISS.
LET US BOTH LIVE FOREVER.
FOR-GET IT.
I HAVE NO INTENTION OF WALKING THE SAME PATH AS PHANTOM!

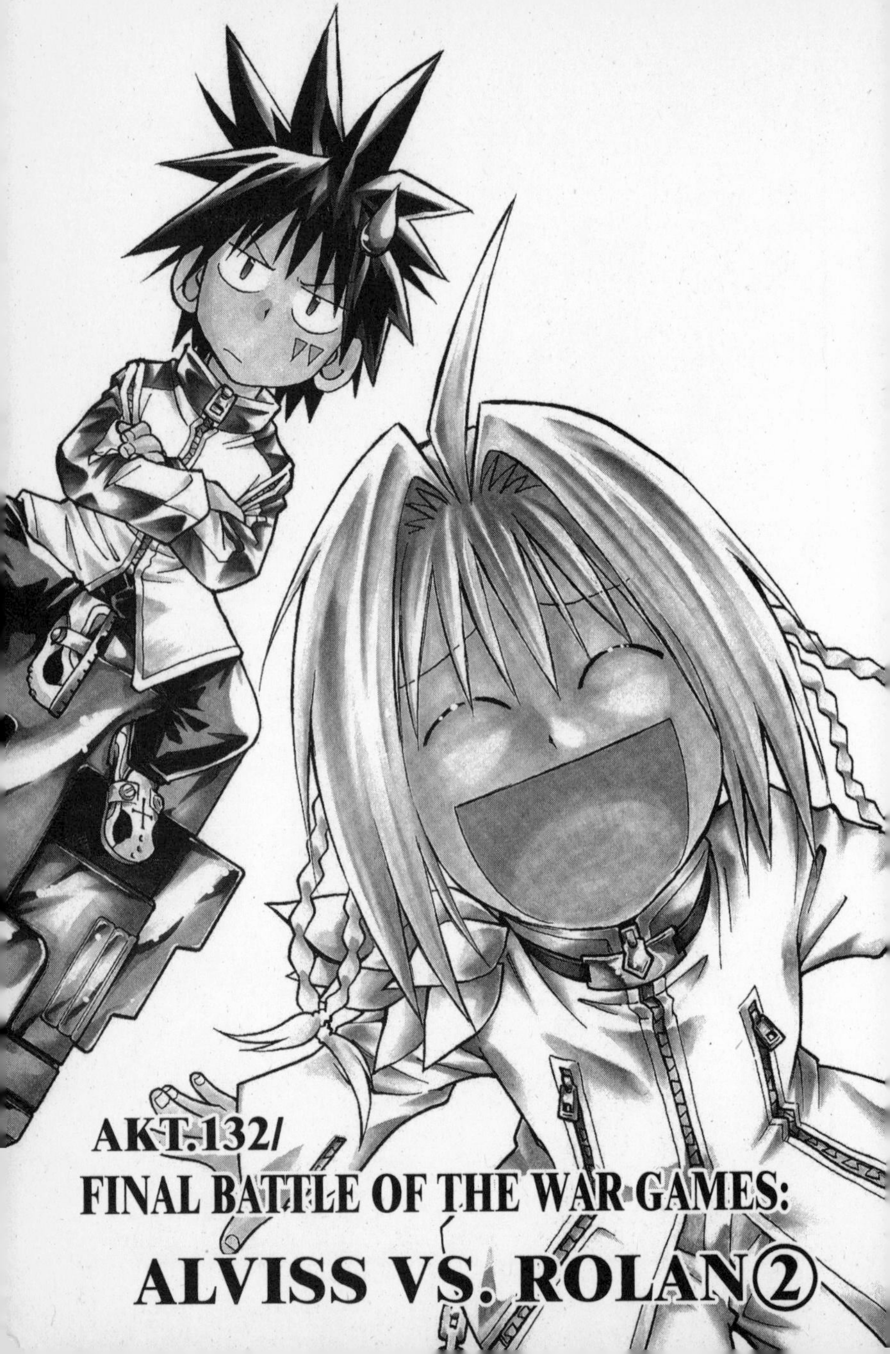

AKT.132/ FINAL BATTLE OF THE WAR GAMES: ALVISS VS. ROLAN②

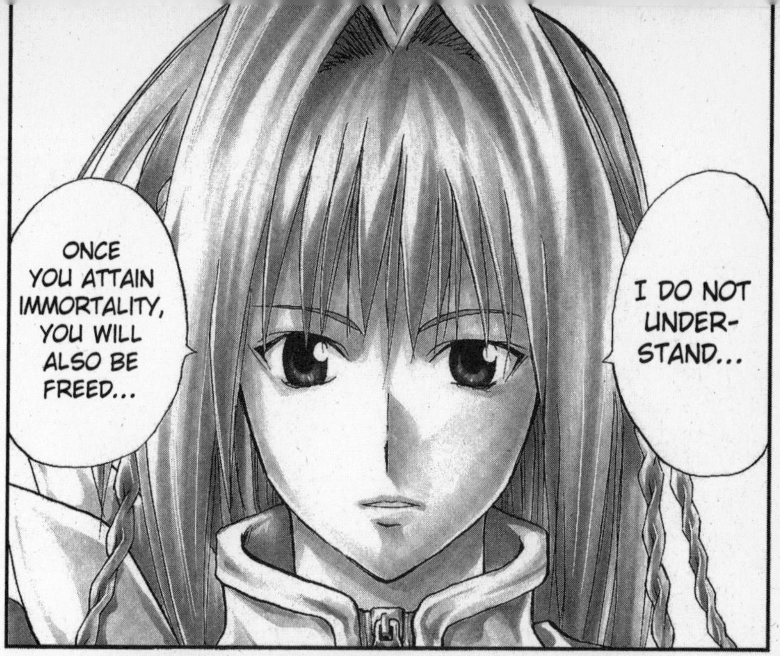
I DO NOT UNDER-STAND...
ONCE YOU ATTAIN IMMORTALITY, YOU WILL ALSO BE FREED...
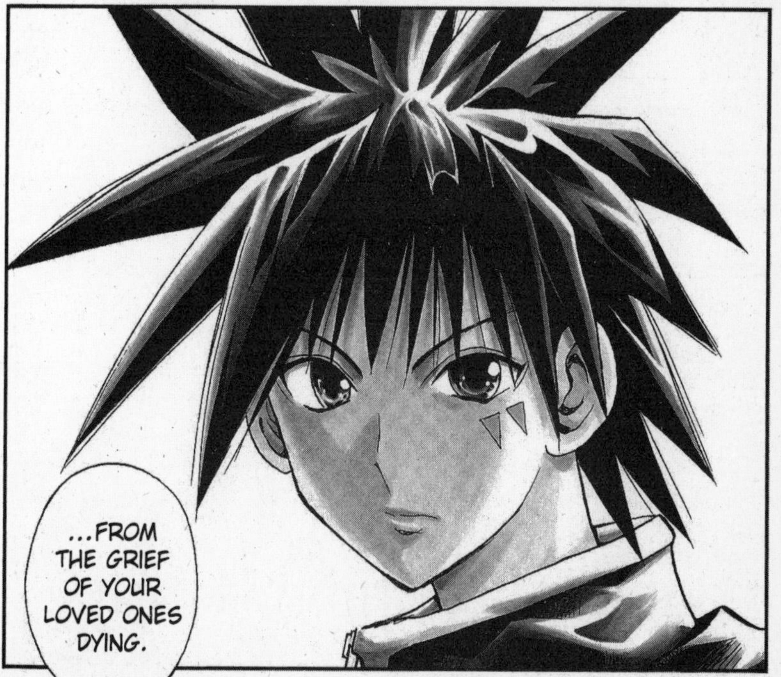
...FROM THE GRIEF OF YOUR LOVED ONES DYING.

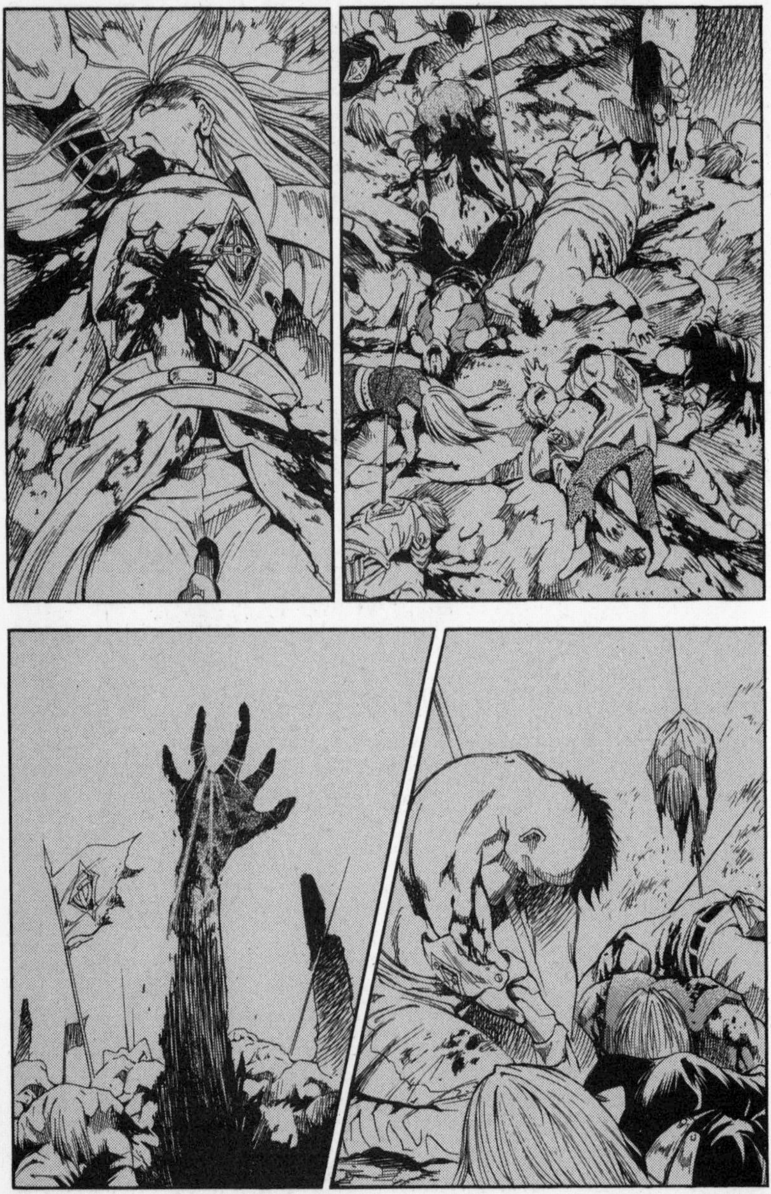

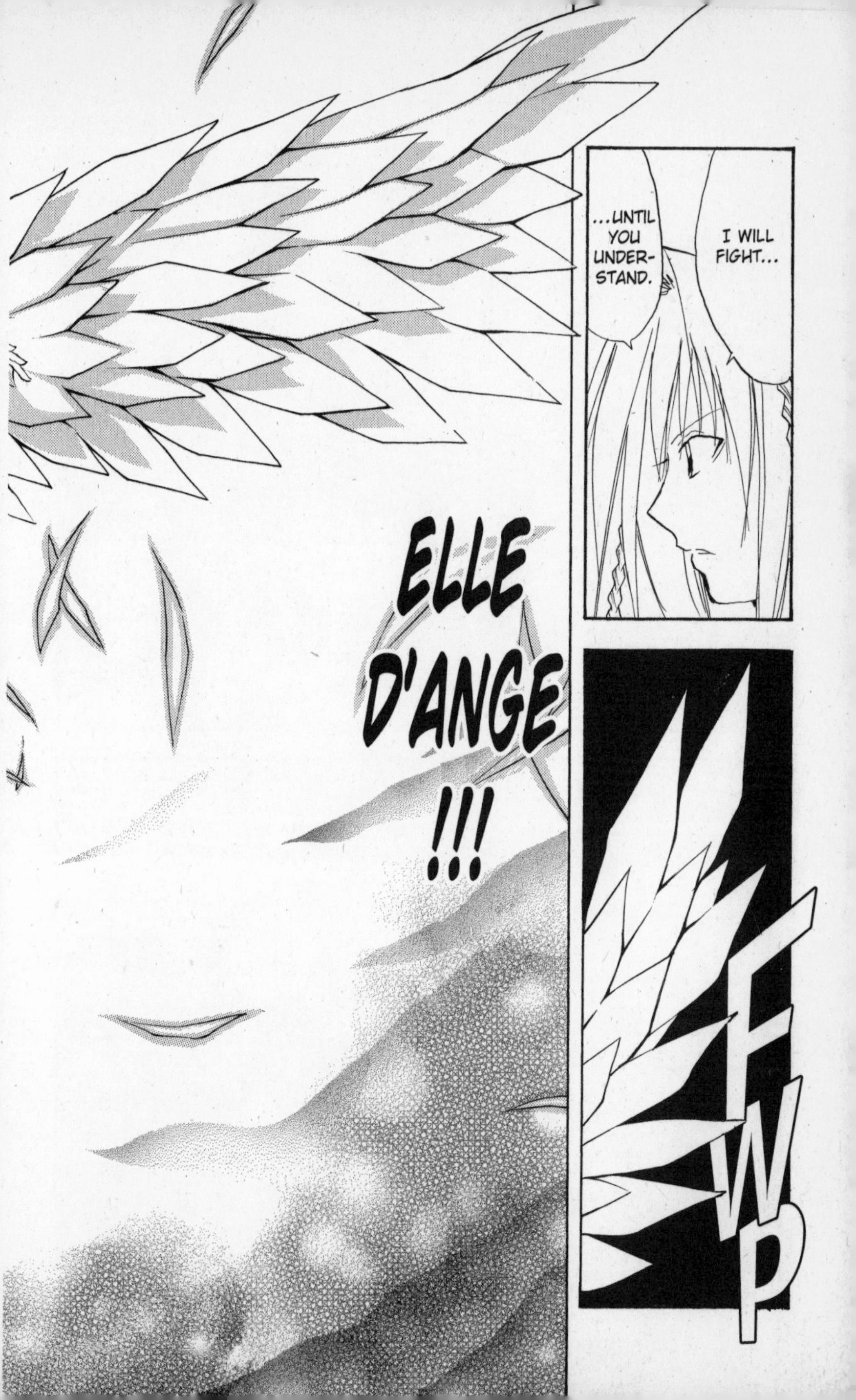
I WILL FIGHT...
...UNTIL YOU UNDER-STAND.
FWP
ELLE D'ANGE!!!

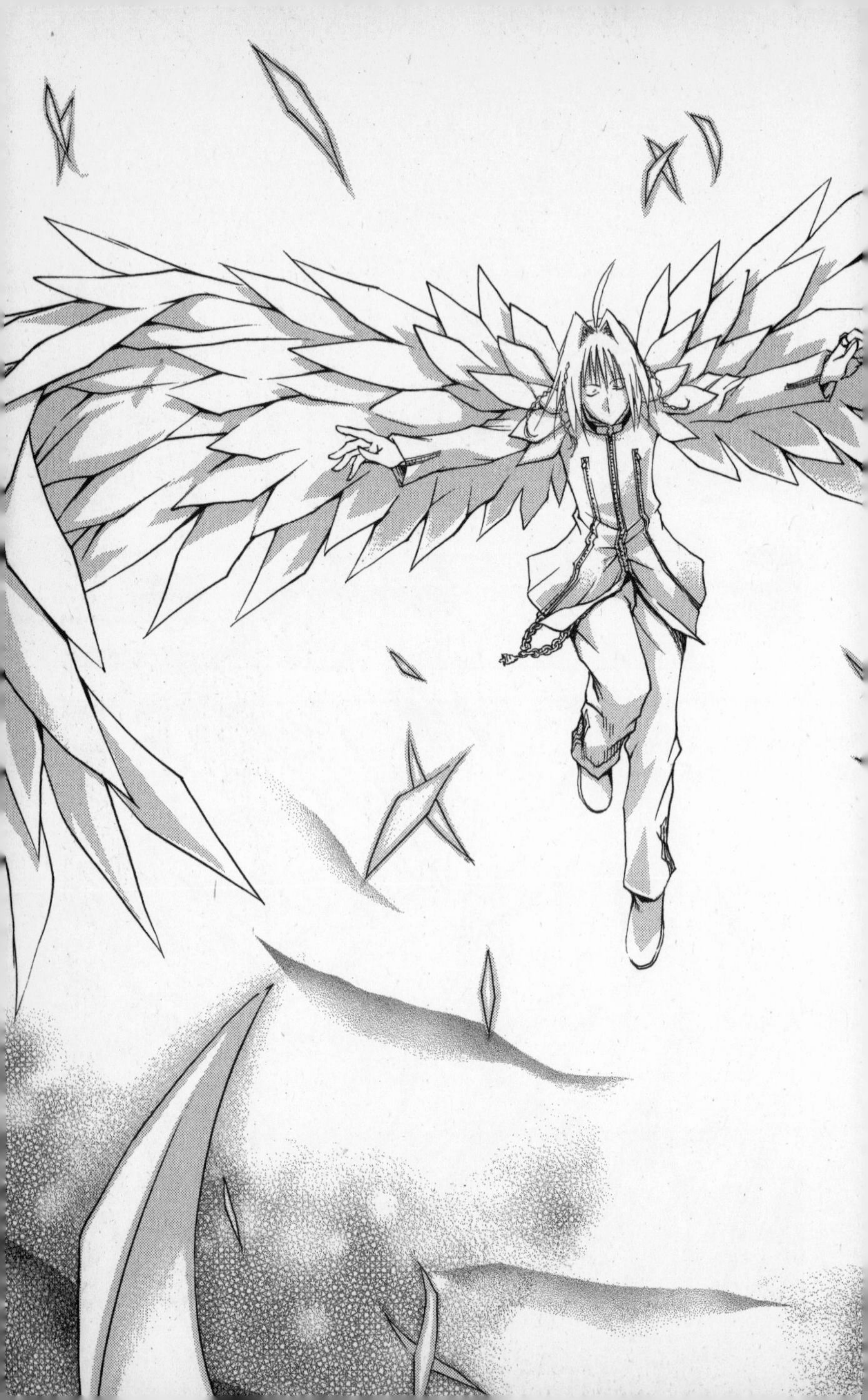

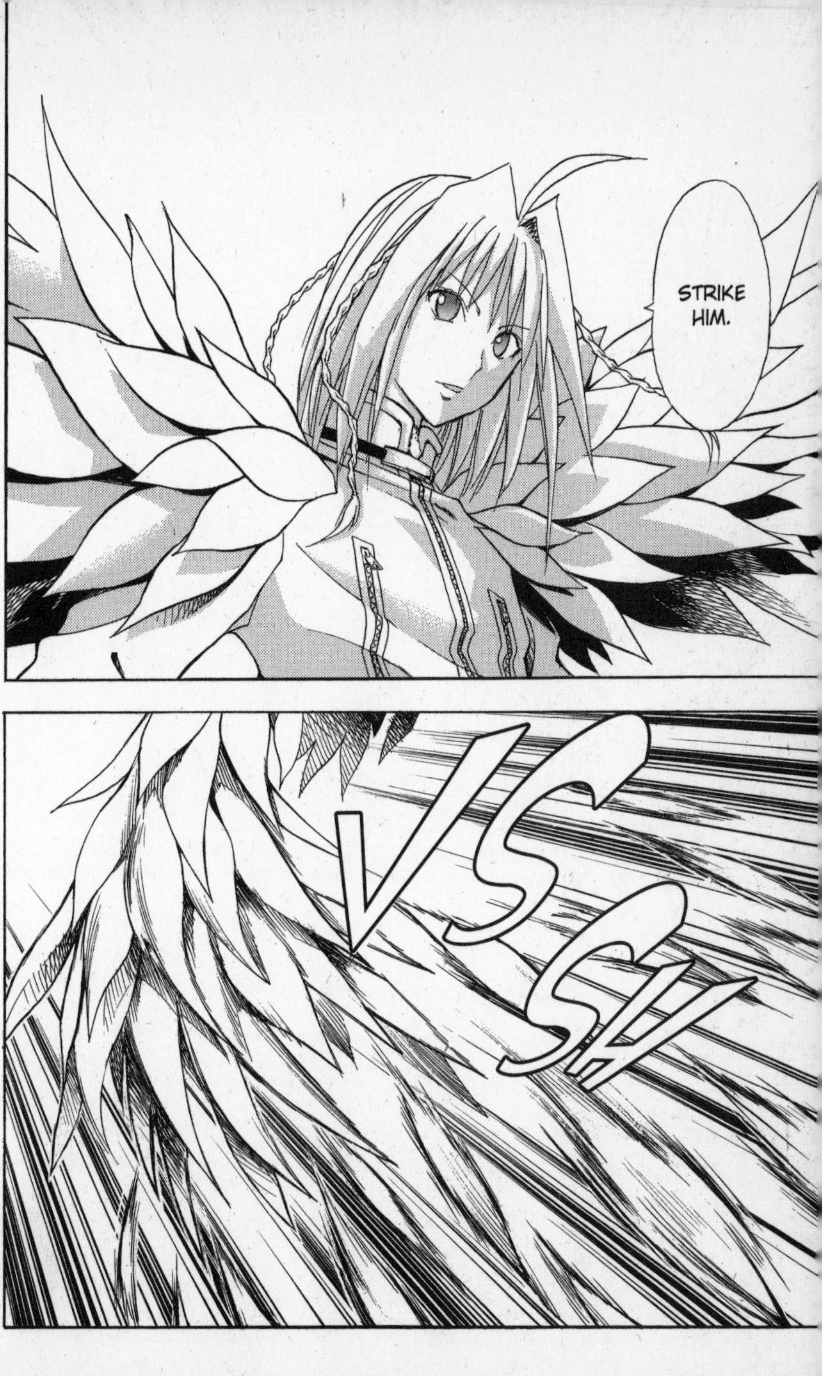
STRIKE HIM.
VSSH

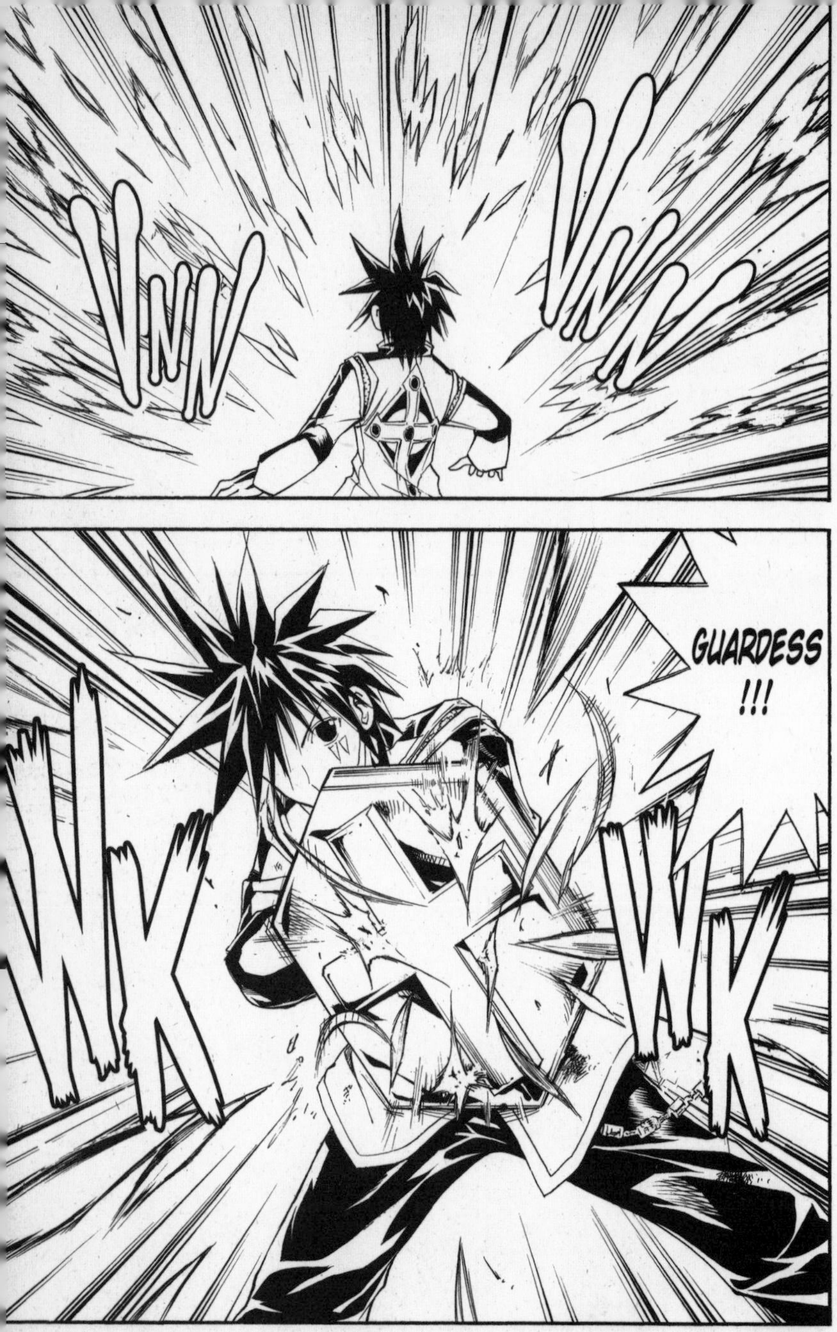
GUARDESS
!!!

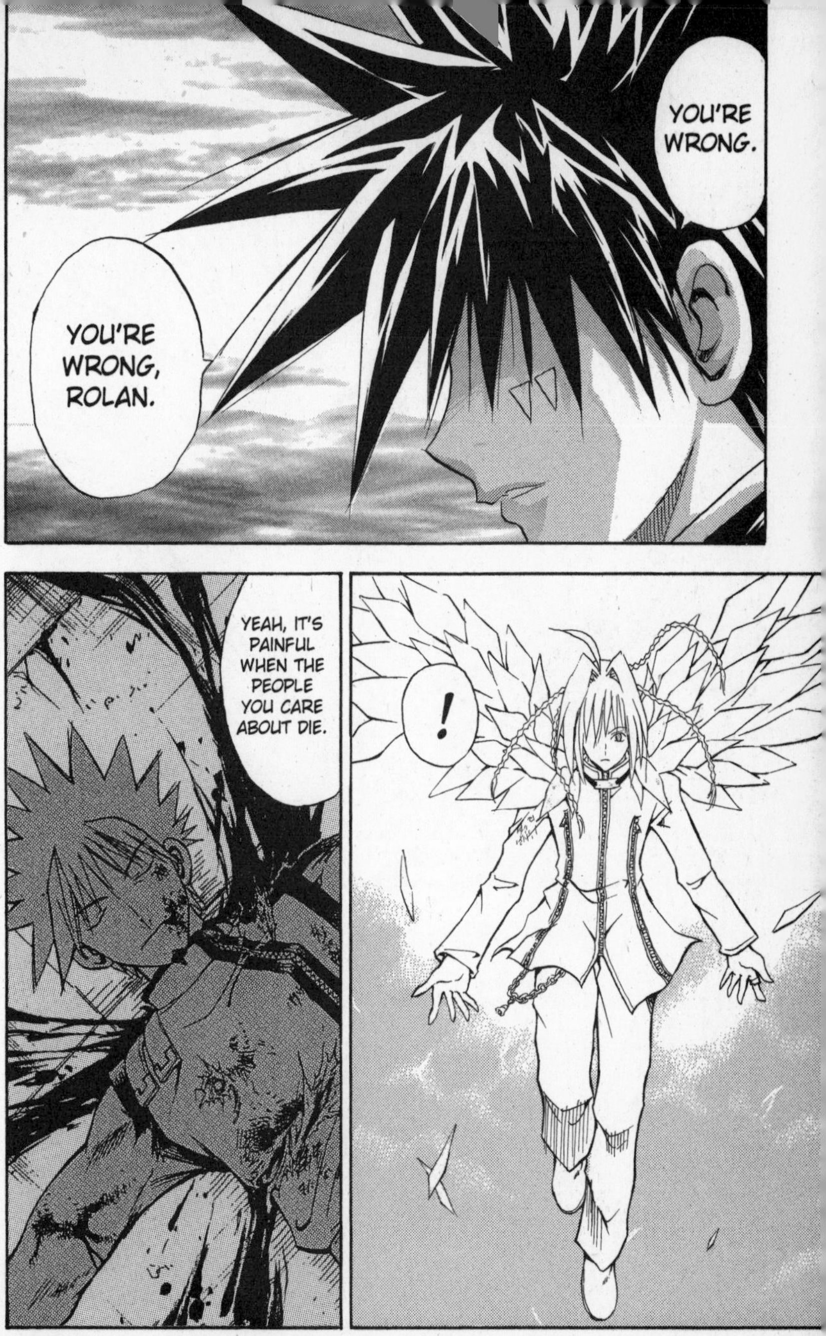
YOU'RE WRONG.
YOU'RE WRONG, ROLAN.
!
YEAH, IT'S PAINFUL WHEN THE PEOPLE YOU CARE ABOUT DIE.

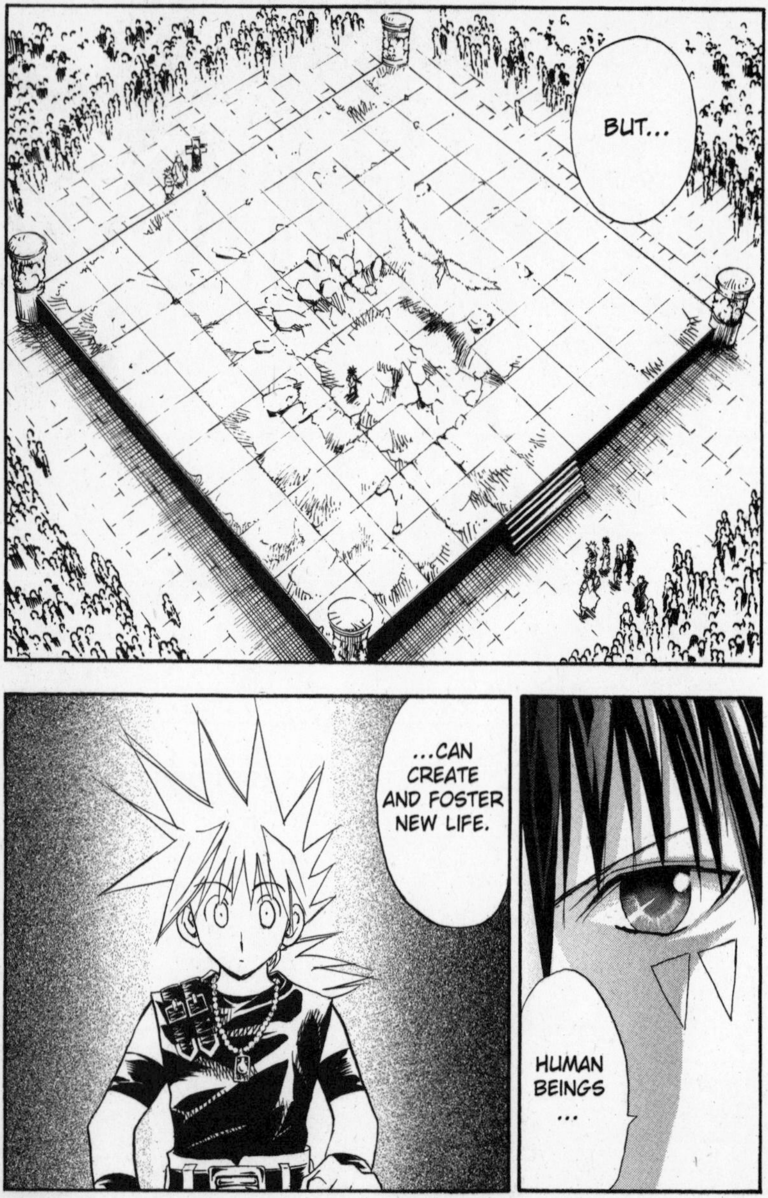
BUT...
HUMAN BEINGS ...
...CAN CREATE AND FOSTER NEW LIFE.

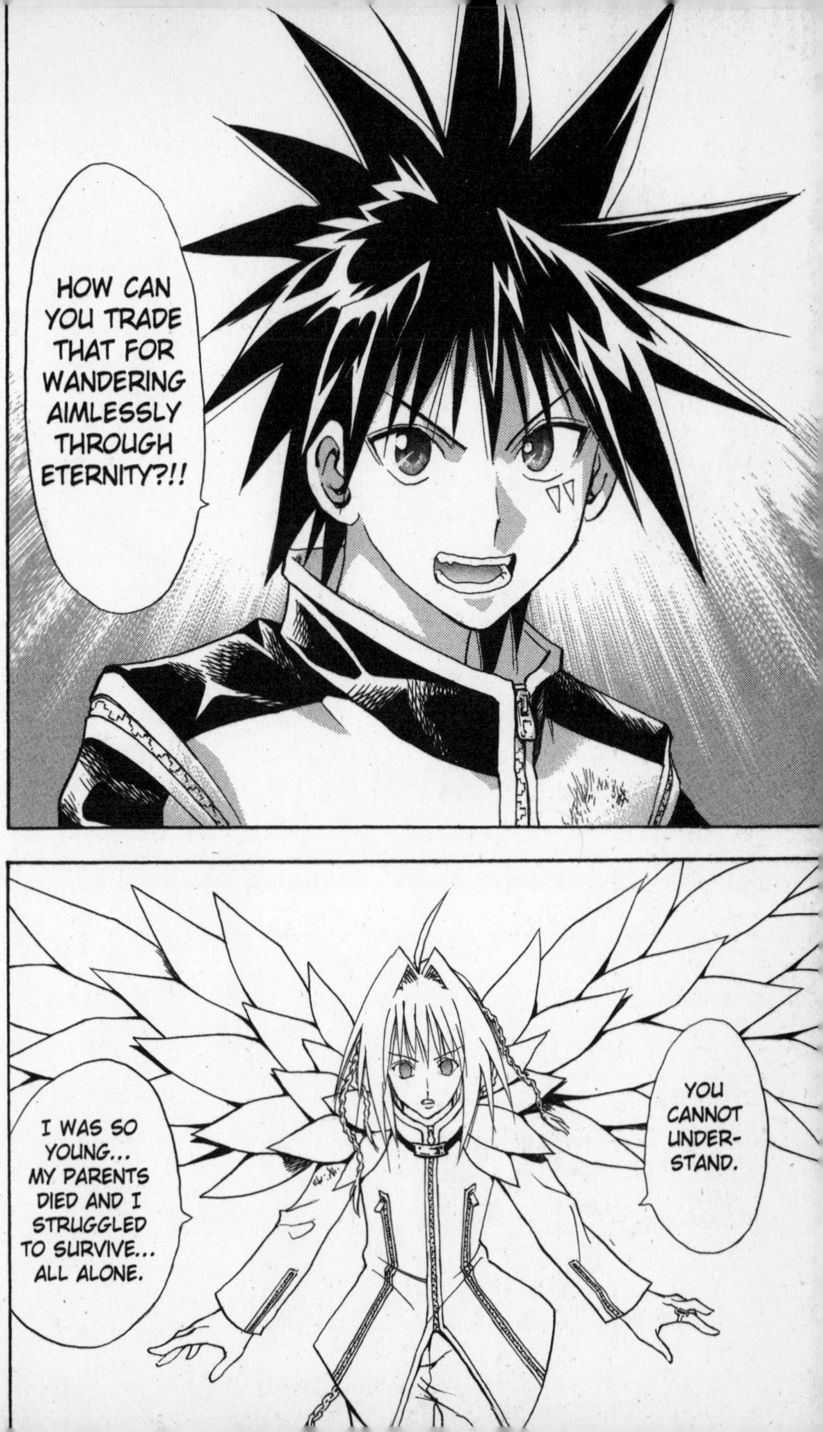
HOW CAN YOU TRADE THAT FOR WANDERING AIMLESSLY THROUGH ETERNITY?!!
YOU CANNOT UNDER-STAND.
I WAS SO YOUNG... MY PARENTS DIED AND I STRUGGLED TO SURVIVE... ALL ALONE.

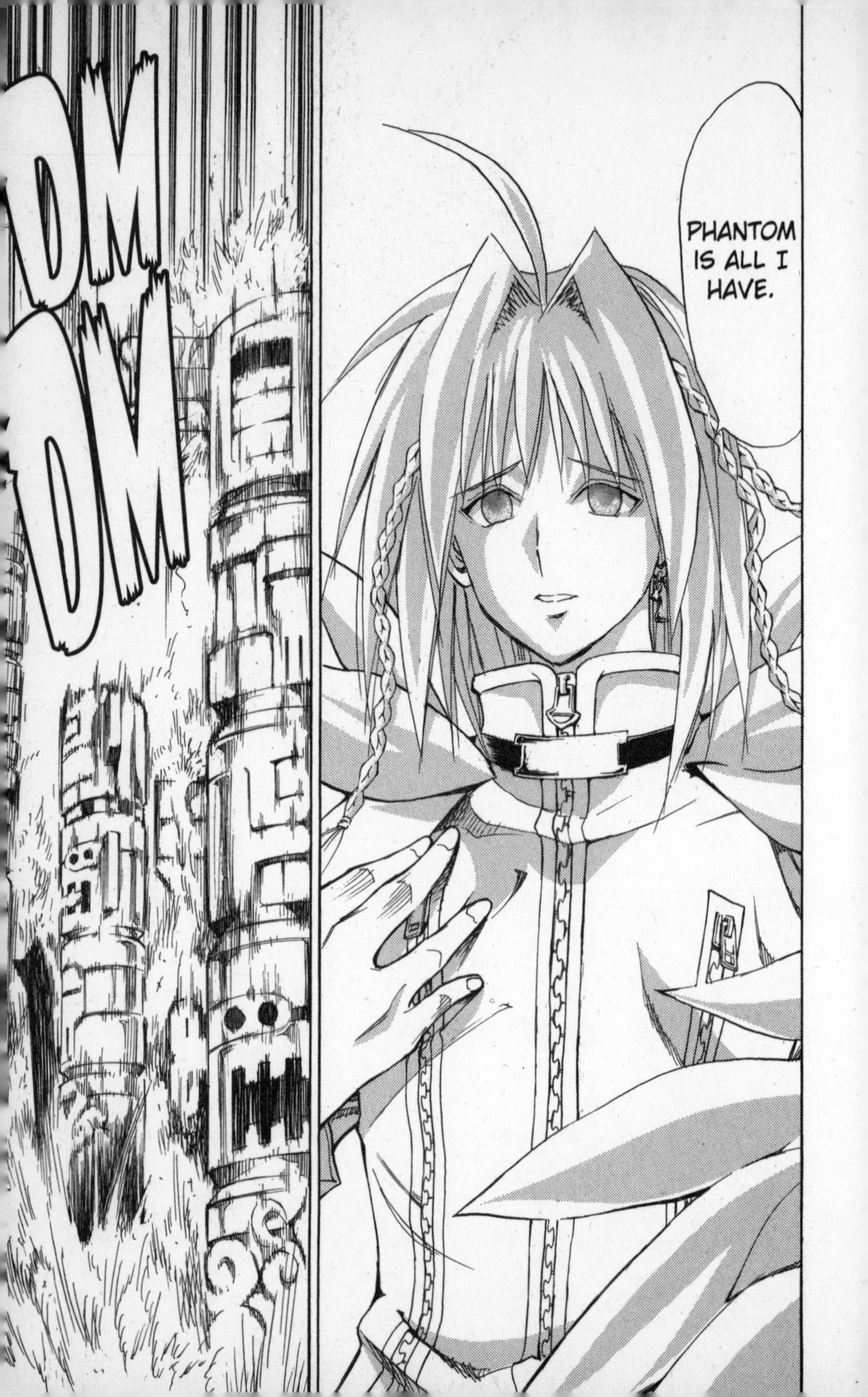
PHANTOM IS ALL I HAVE.

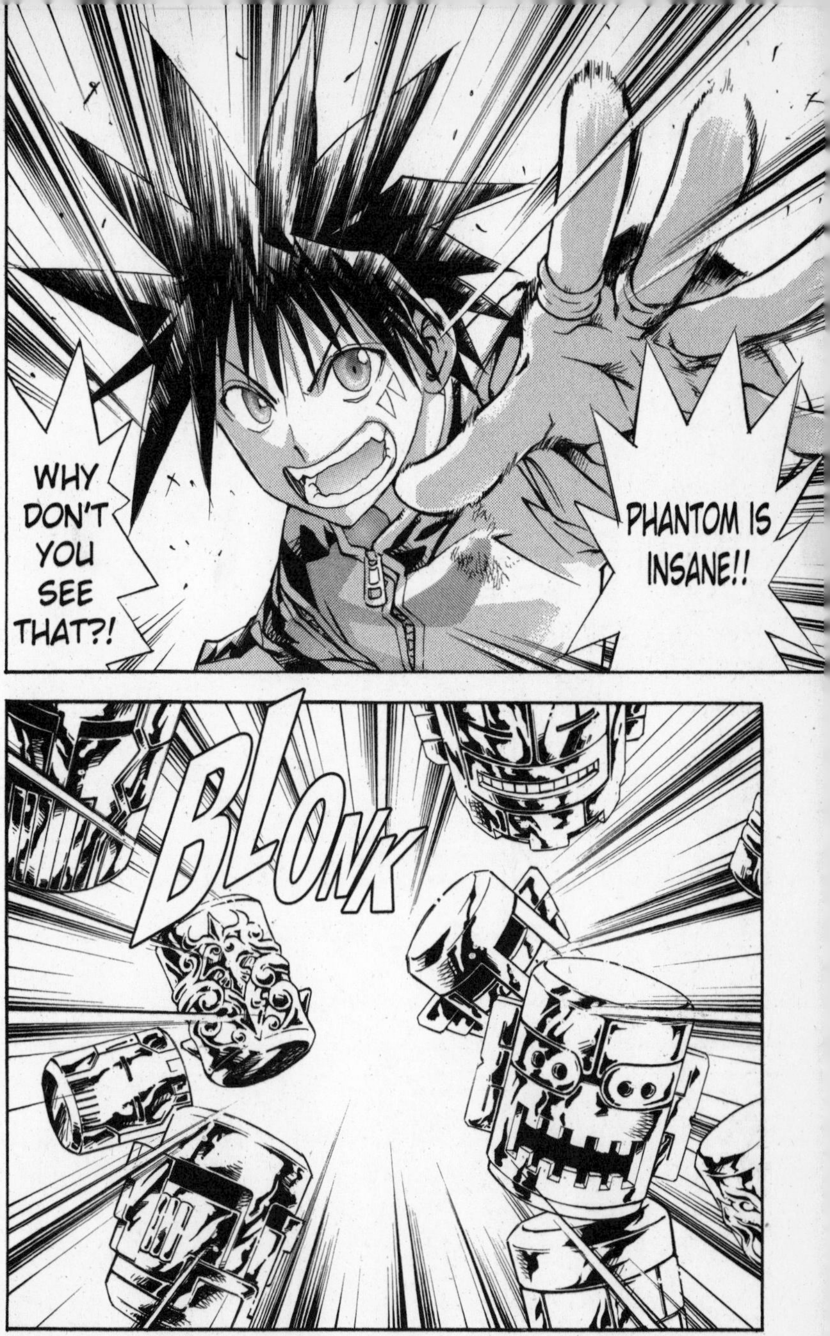
PHANTOM IS INSANE!!
WHY DON'T YOU SEE THAT?!
BLONK

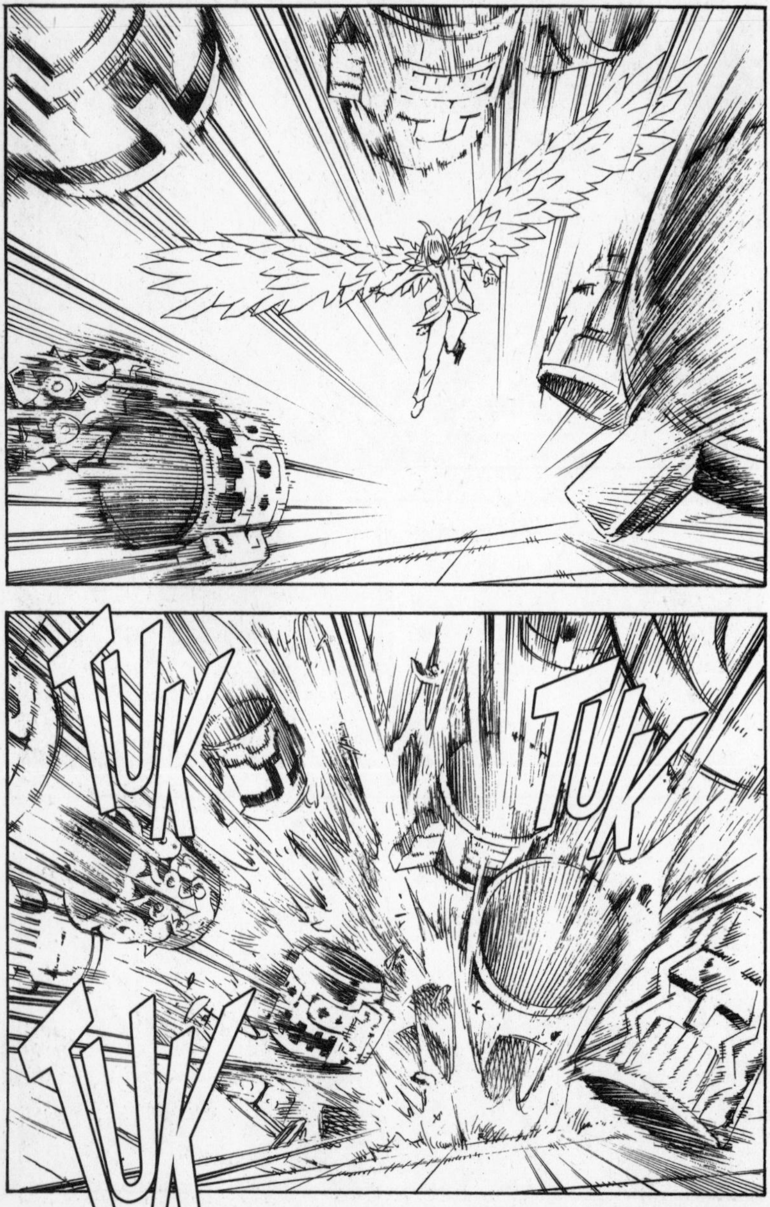
TUK
TUK
TUK

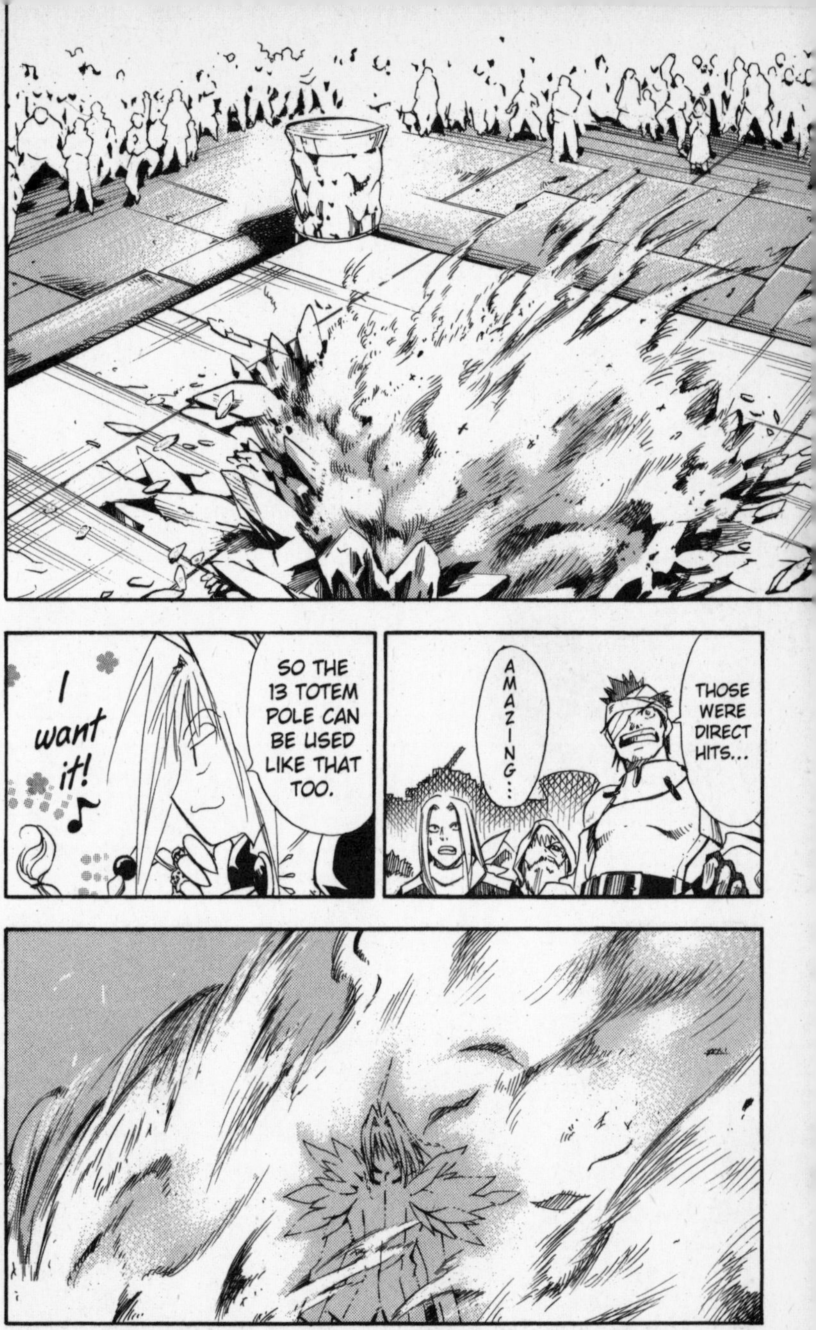
THOSE WERE DIRECT HITS...
AMAZING...
SO THE 13 TOTEM POLE CAN BE USED LIKE THAT TOO.
I want it! ♪

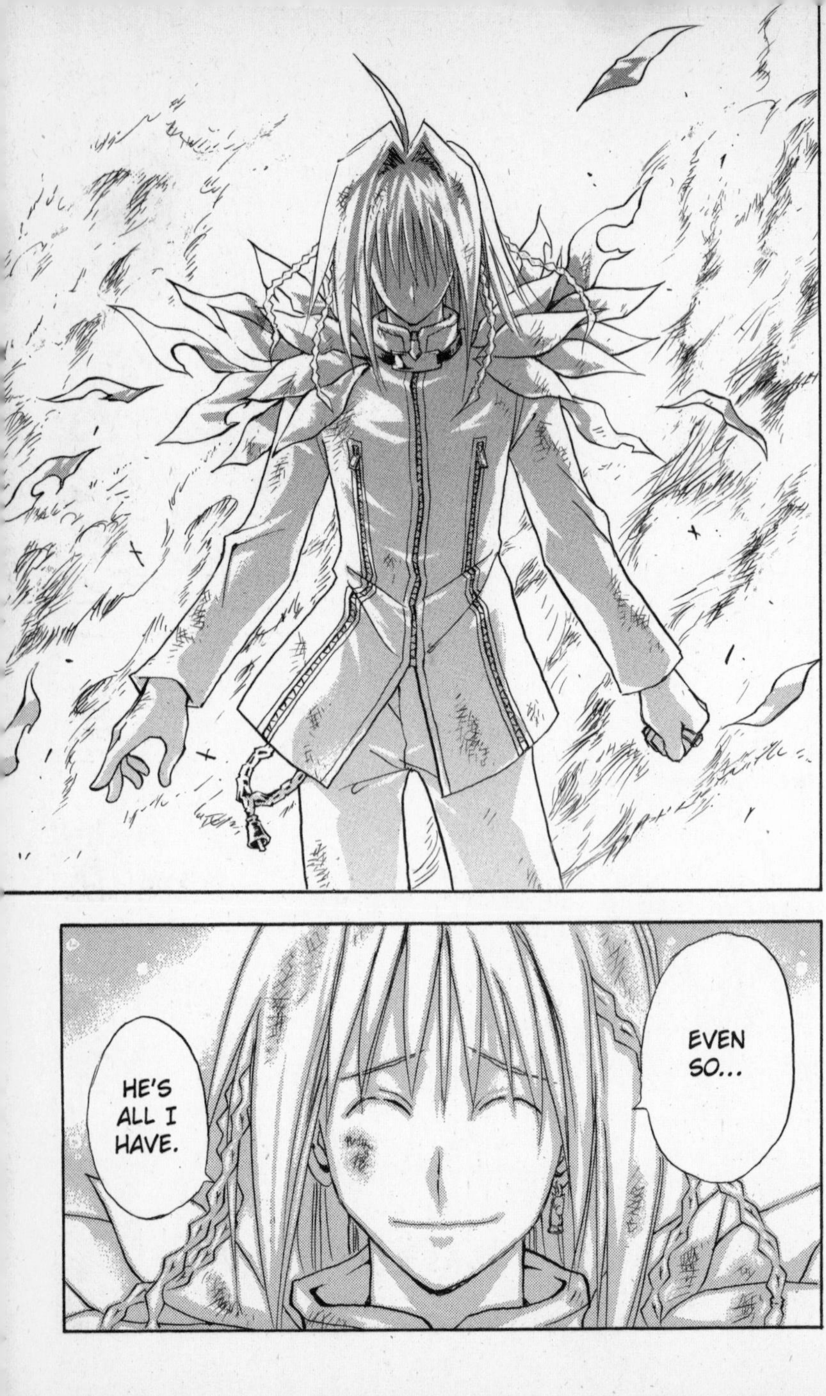
EVEN SO...
HE'S ALL I HAVE.

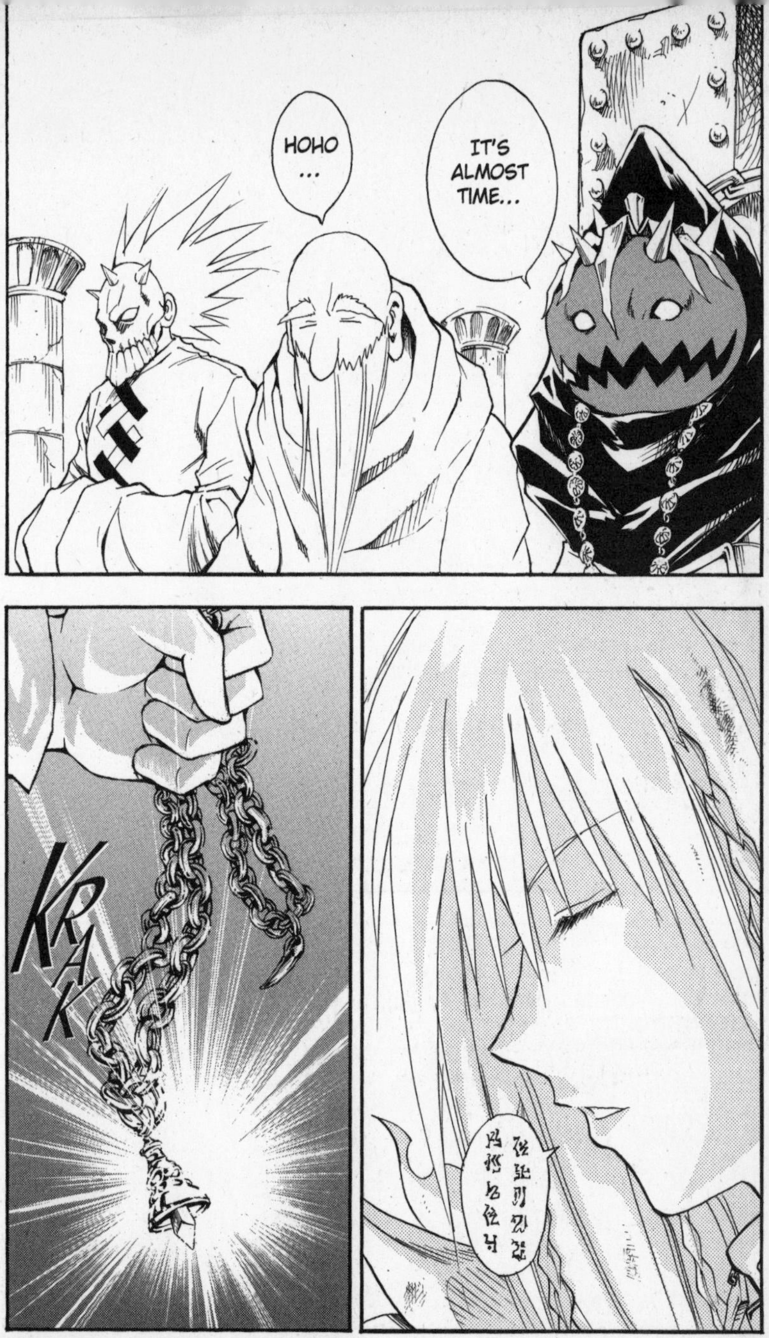
IT'S ALMOST TIME...
HOHO ...
KRAK

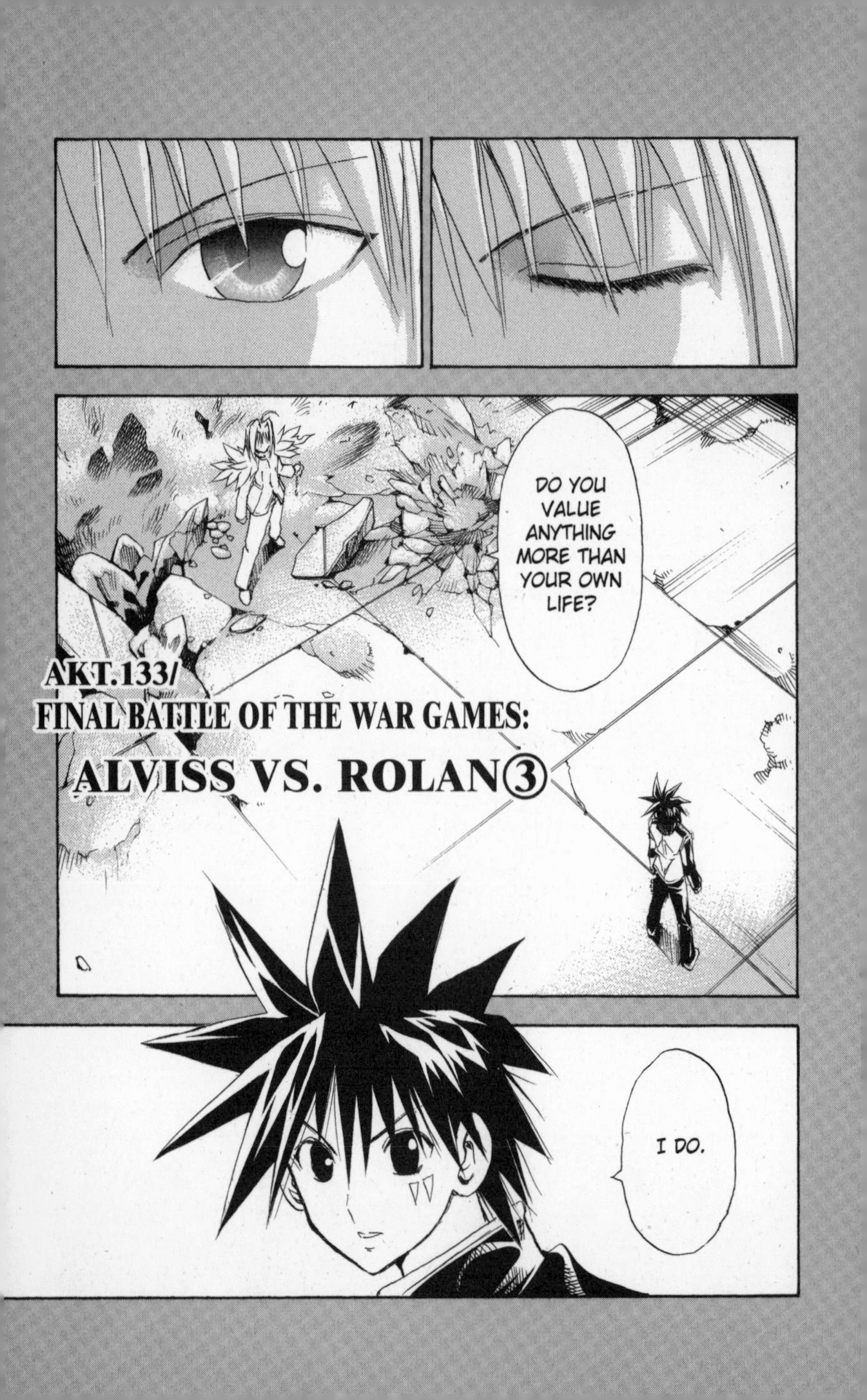
DO YOU VALUE ANYTHING MORE THAN YOUR OWN LIFE?
AKT.133/
FINAL BATTLE OF THE WAR GAMES:
ALVISS VS. ROLAN③
I DO.

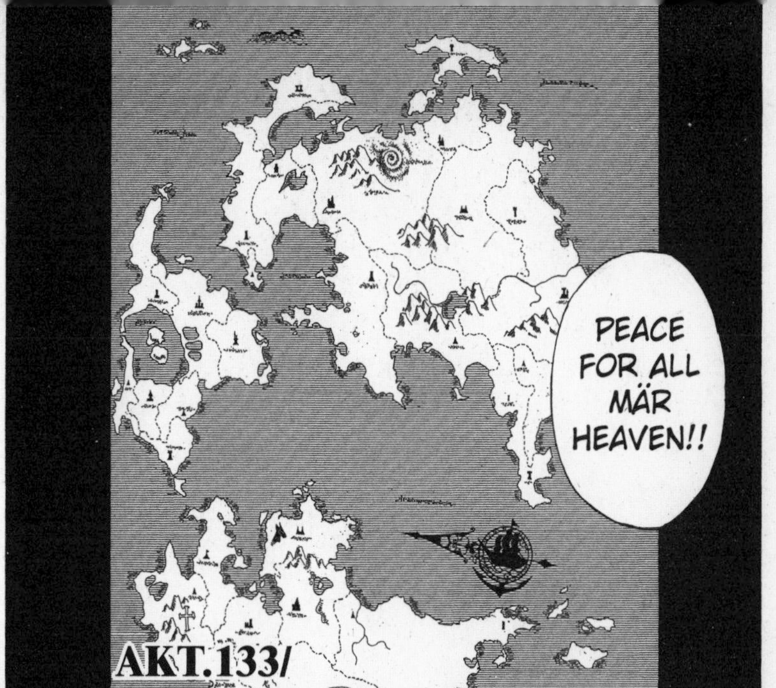
PEACE FOR ALL MÄR HEAVEN!!
AKT.133/
FINAL BATTLE OF THE WAR GAMES:
ALVISS VS. ROLAN③

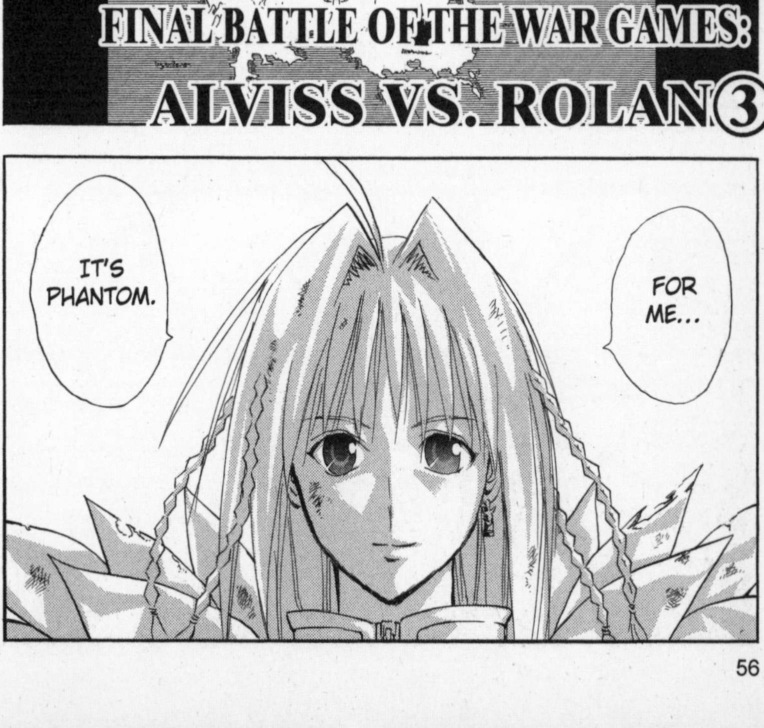
FOR ME...
IT'S PHANTOM.

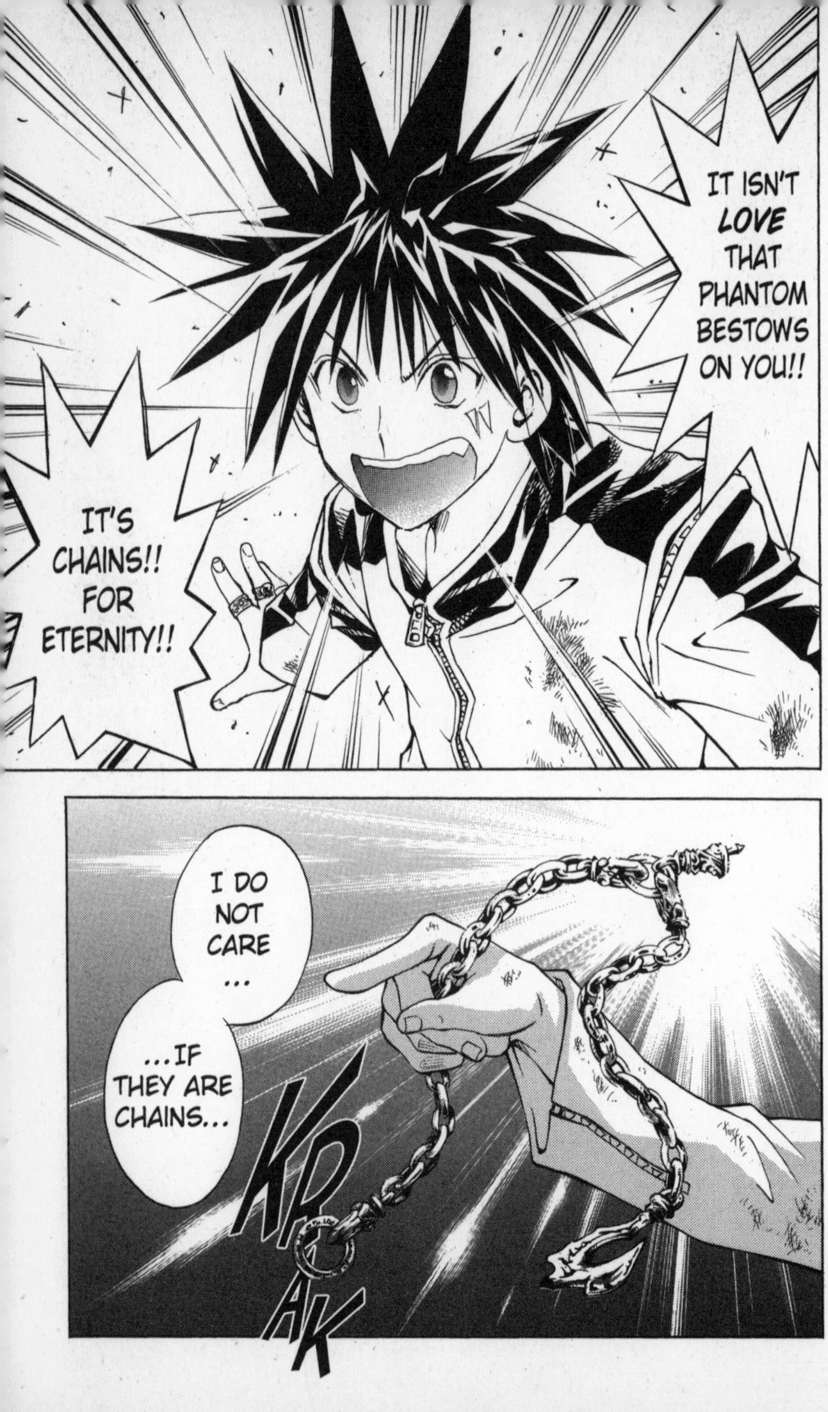

IT ISN'T LOVE THAT PHANTOM BESTOWS ON YOU!!
IT'S CHAINS!! FOR ETERNITY!!
I DO NOT CARE ...
...IF THEY ARE CHAINS...
KRAK

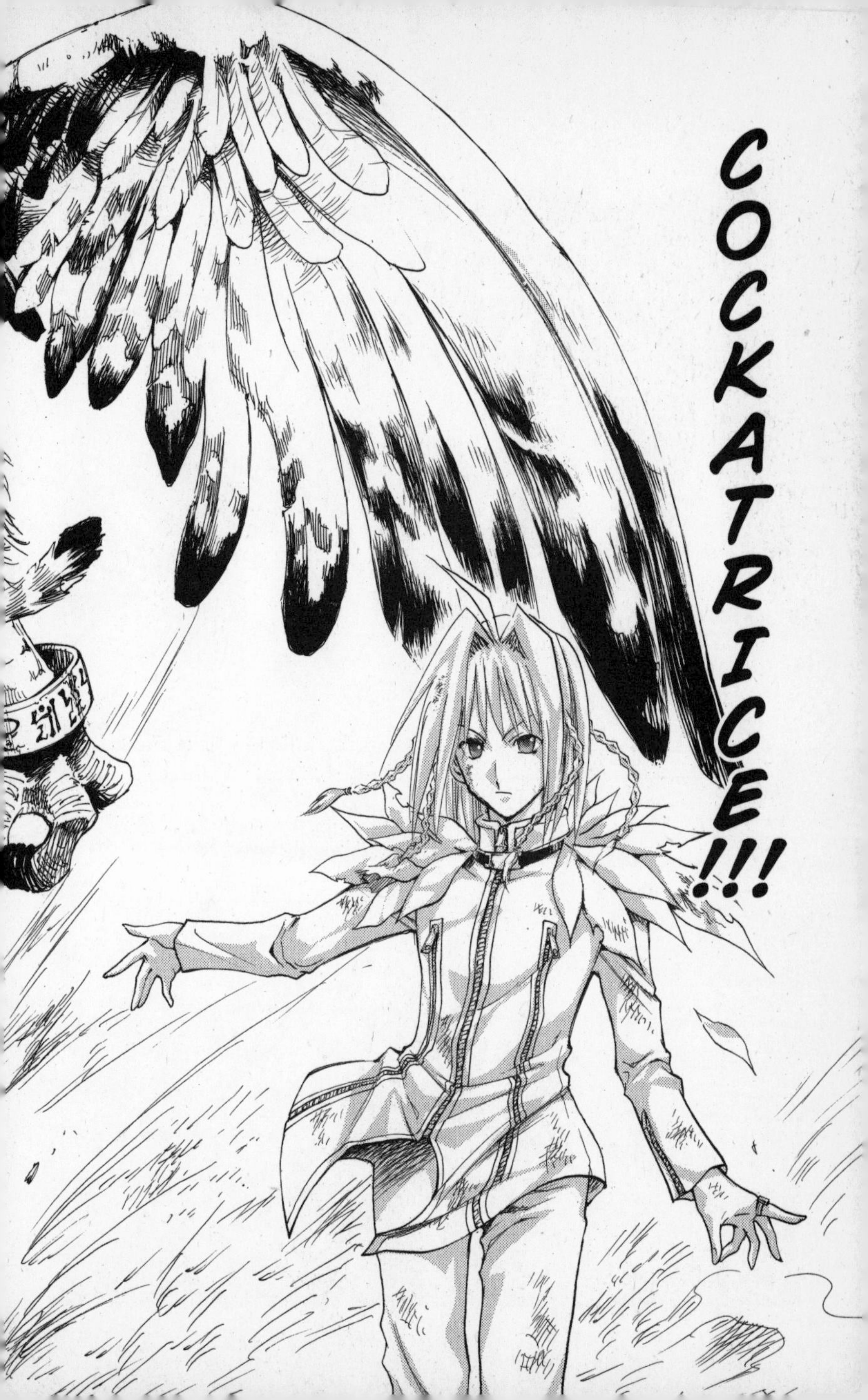
COCKATRICE!!!

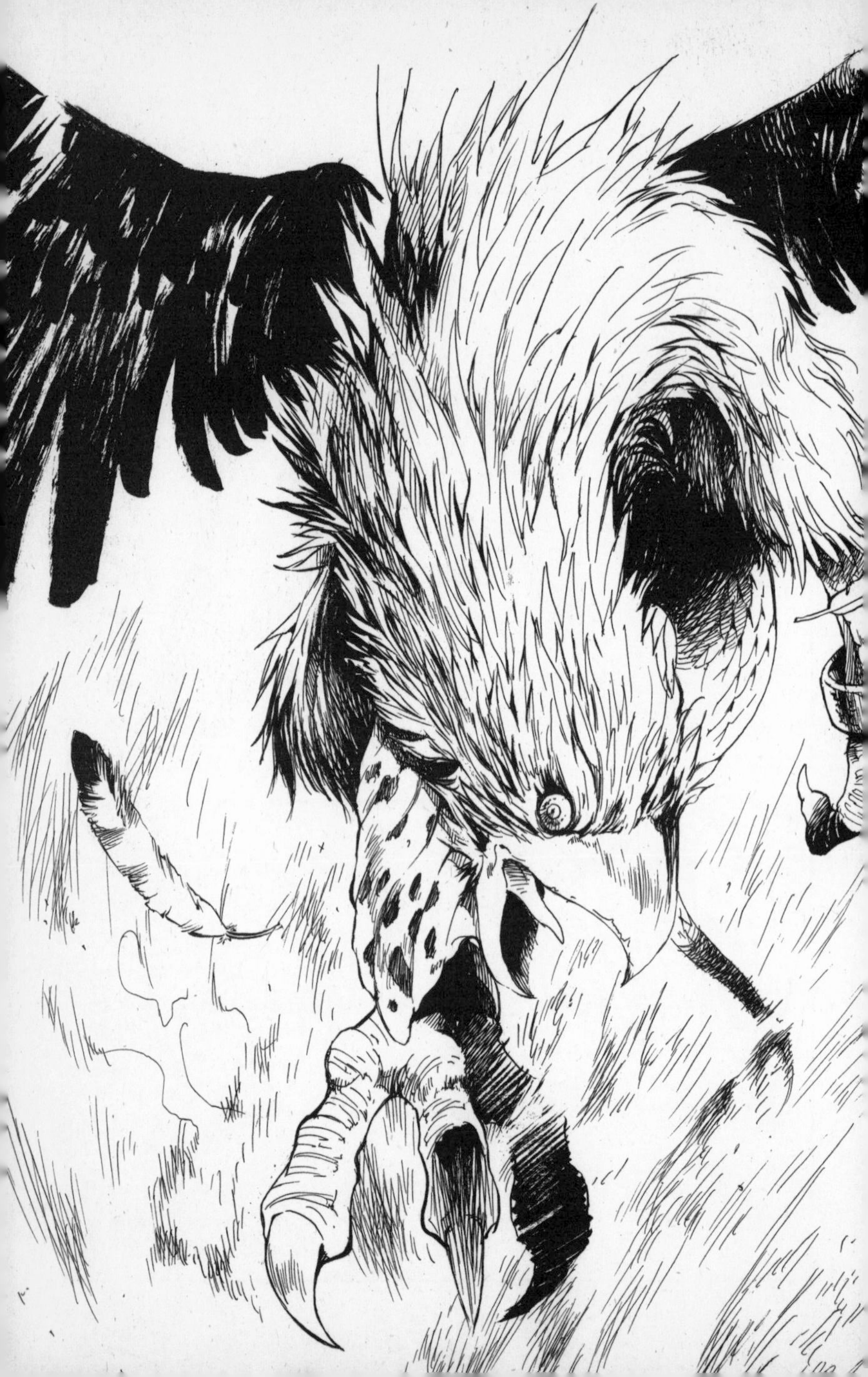

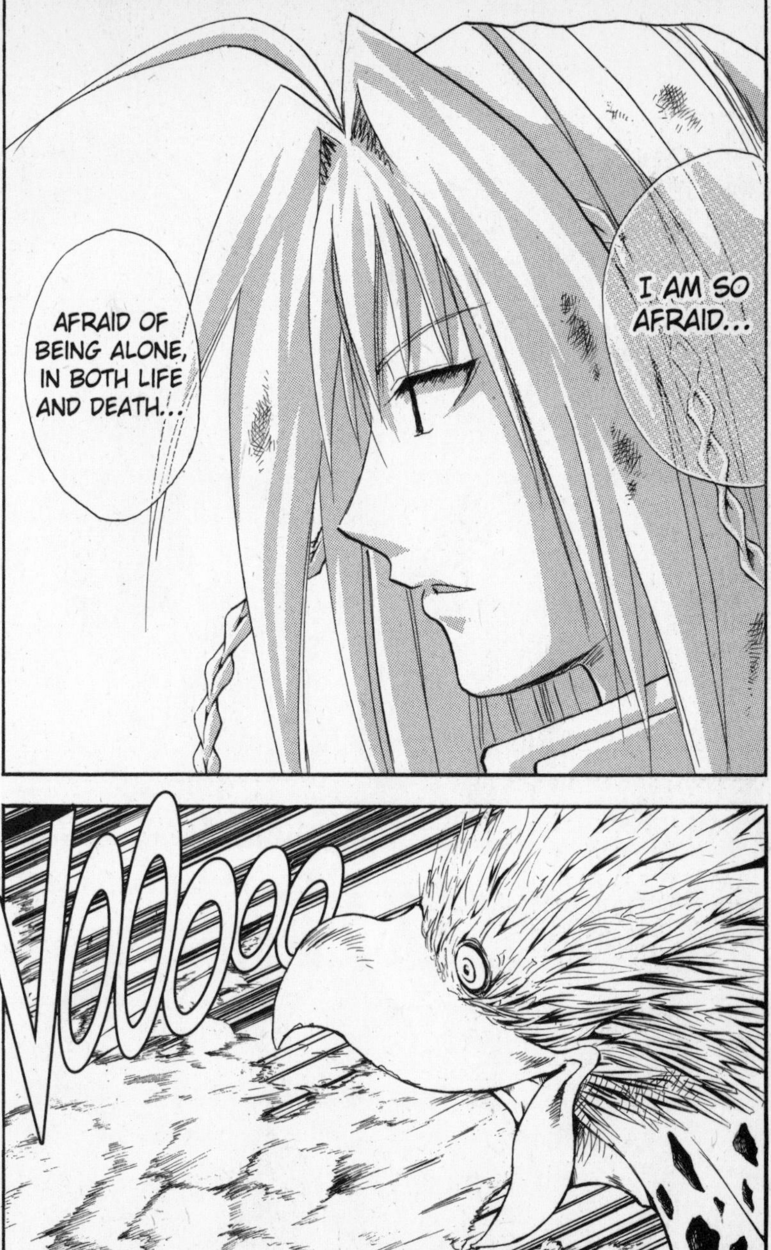
I AM SO AFRAID...
AFRAID OF BEING ALONE, IN BOTH LIFE AND DEATH...
VOOOOOO

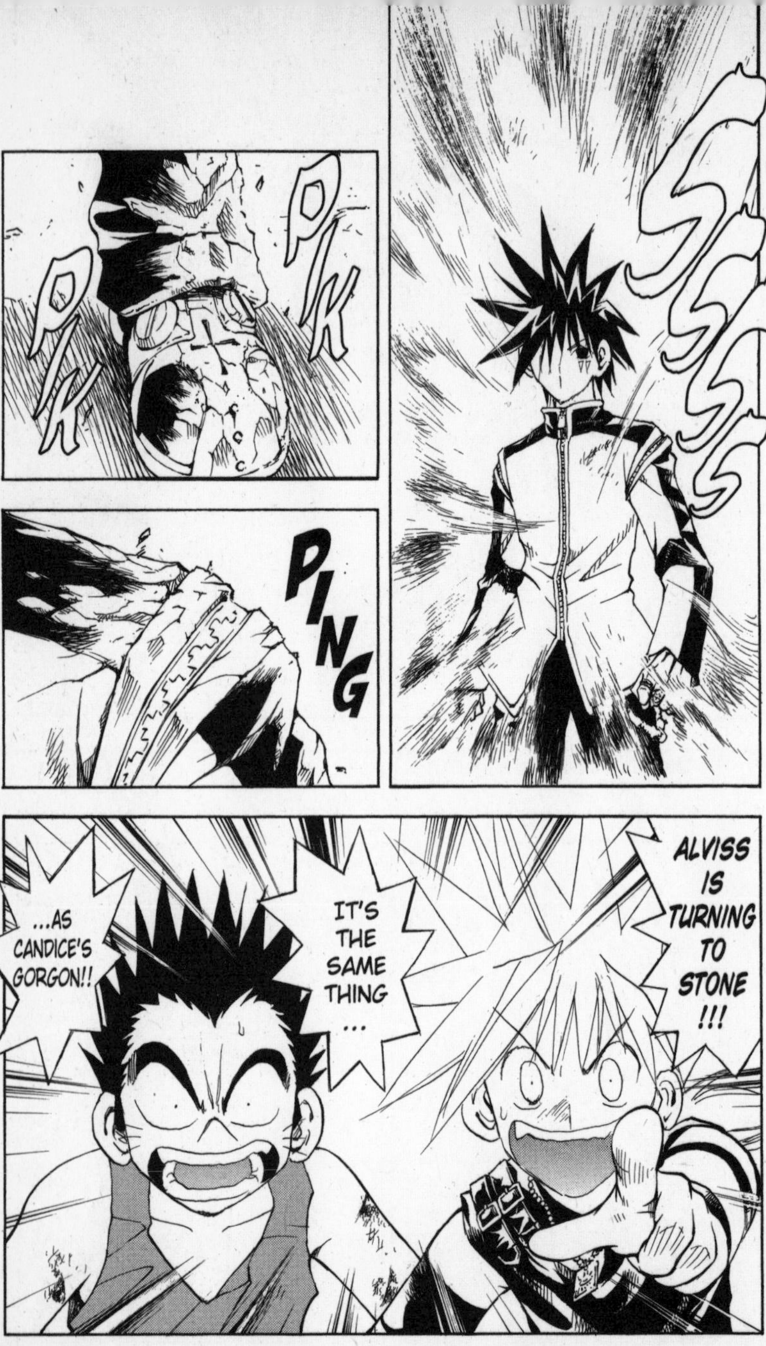
SSSSS
PIK
PIK
PING
ALVISS IS TURNING TO STONE!!!
IT'S THE SAME THING...
...AS CANDICE'S GORGON!!

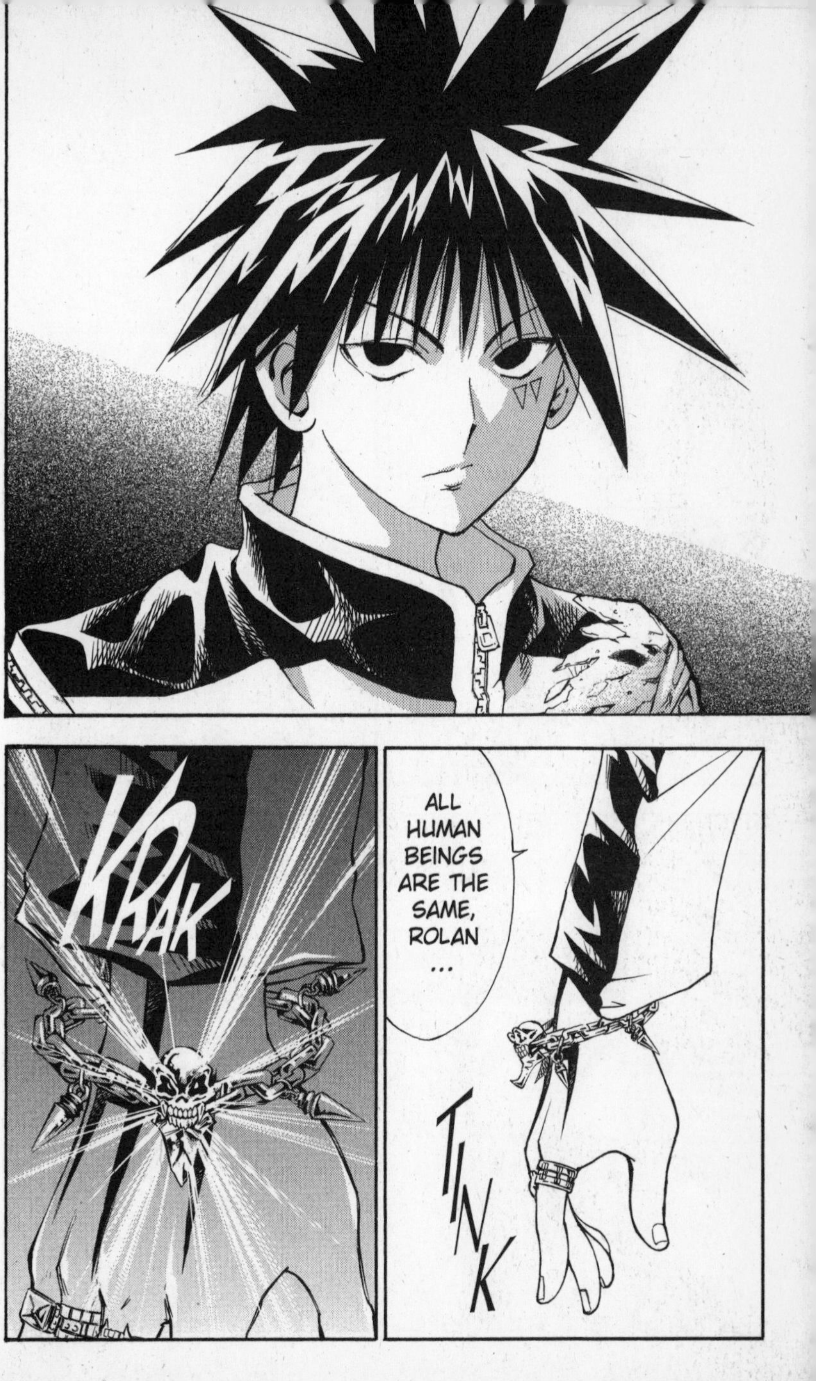
ALL HUMAN BEINGS ARE THE SAME, ROLAN ...
TINK
KRAK

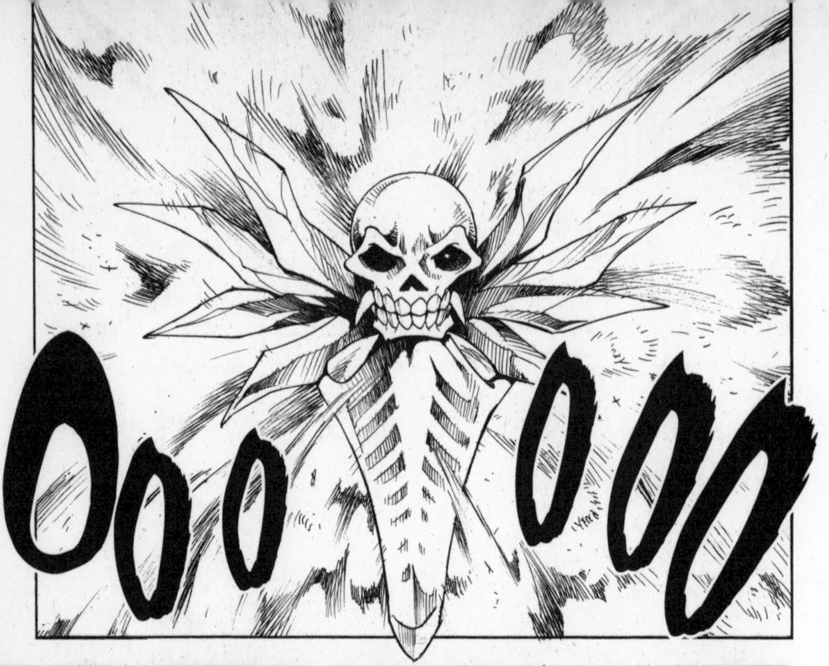
OOOOOOO
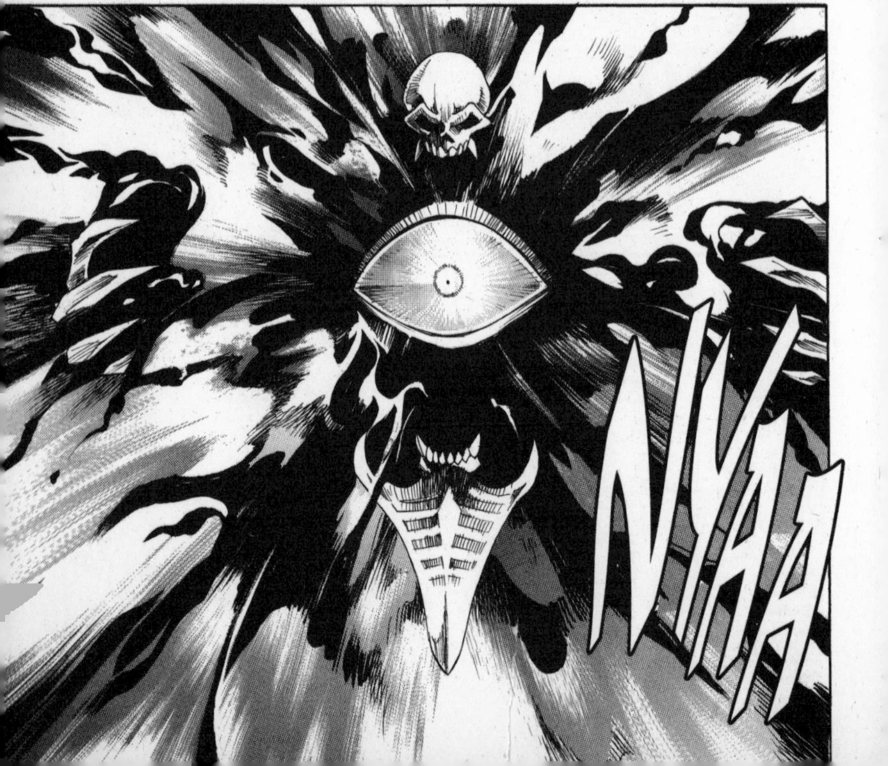
NYAA

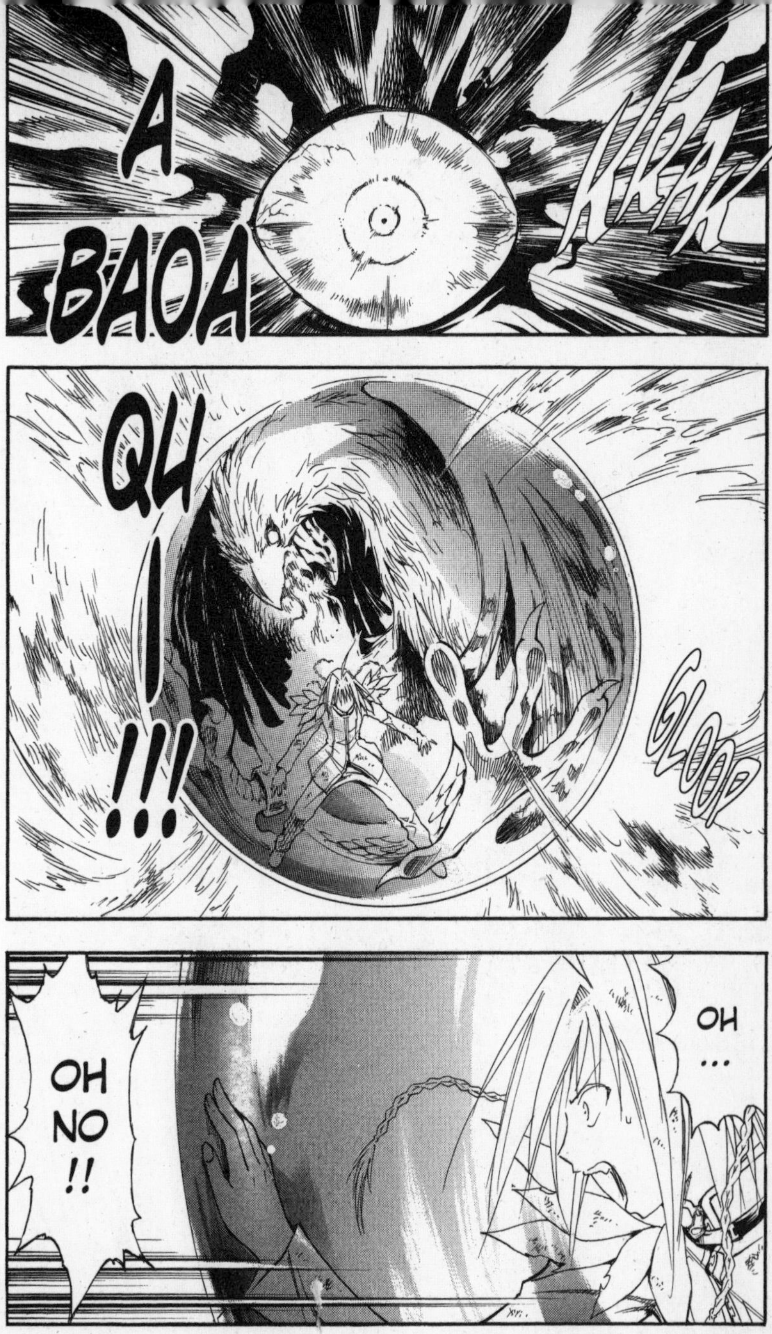
KRAK!
A BAOA
QUI!!!
GLOOP
OH ...
OH NO !!

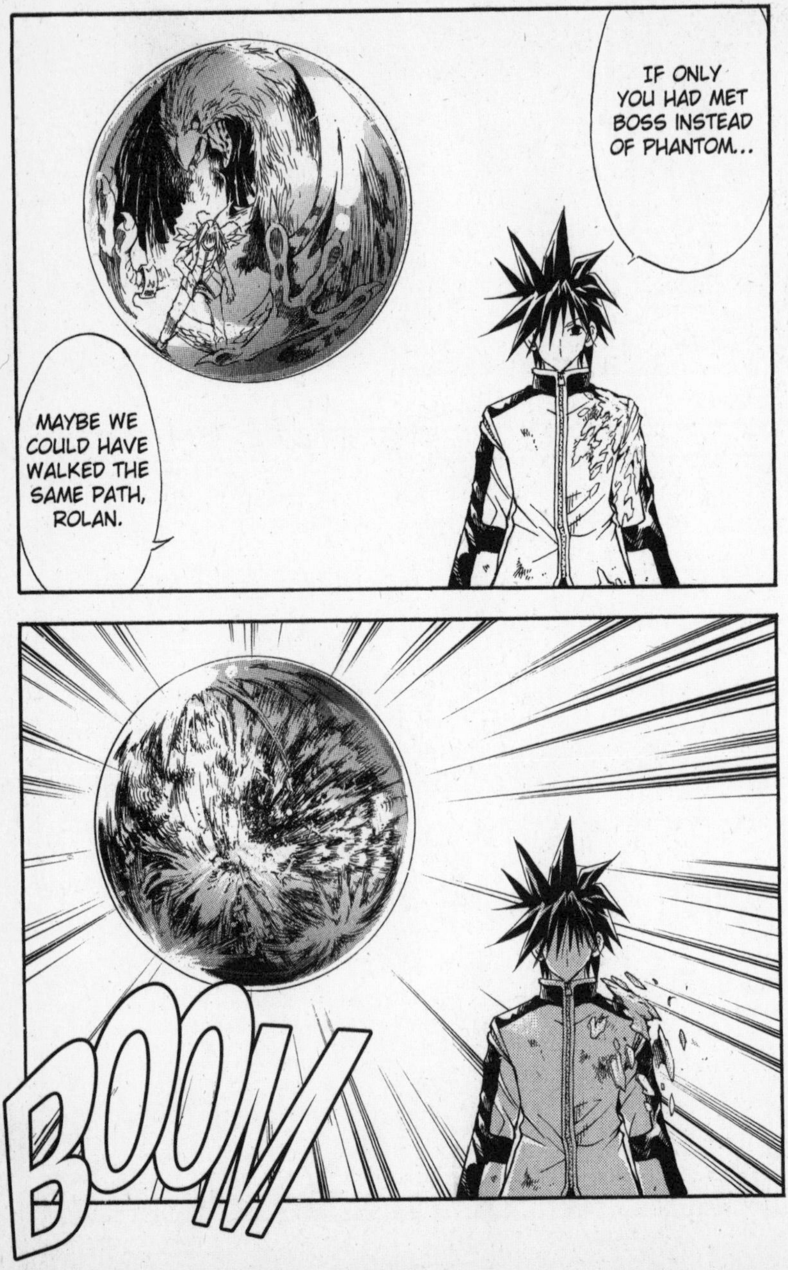
IF ONLY YOU HAD MET BOSS INSTEAD OF PHANTOM...
MAYBE WE COULD HAVE WALKED THE SAME PATH, ROLAN.
BOOM

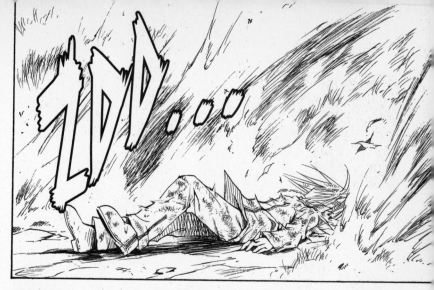

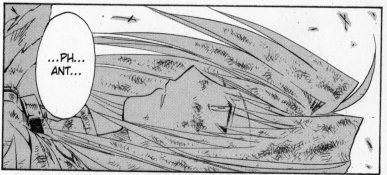

...PH...
ANT...

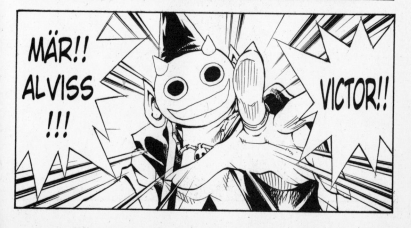

MÄR!!
ALVISS!!!

VICTOR!!

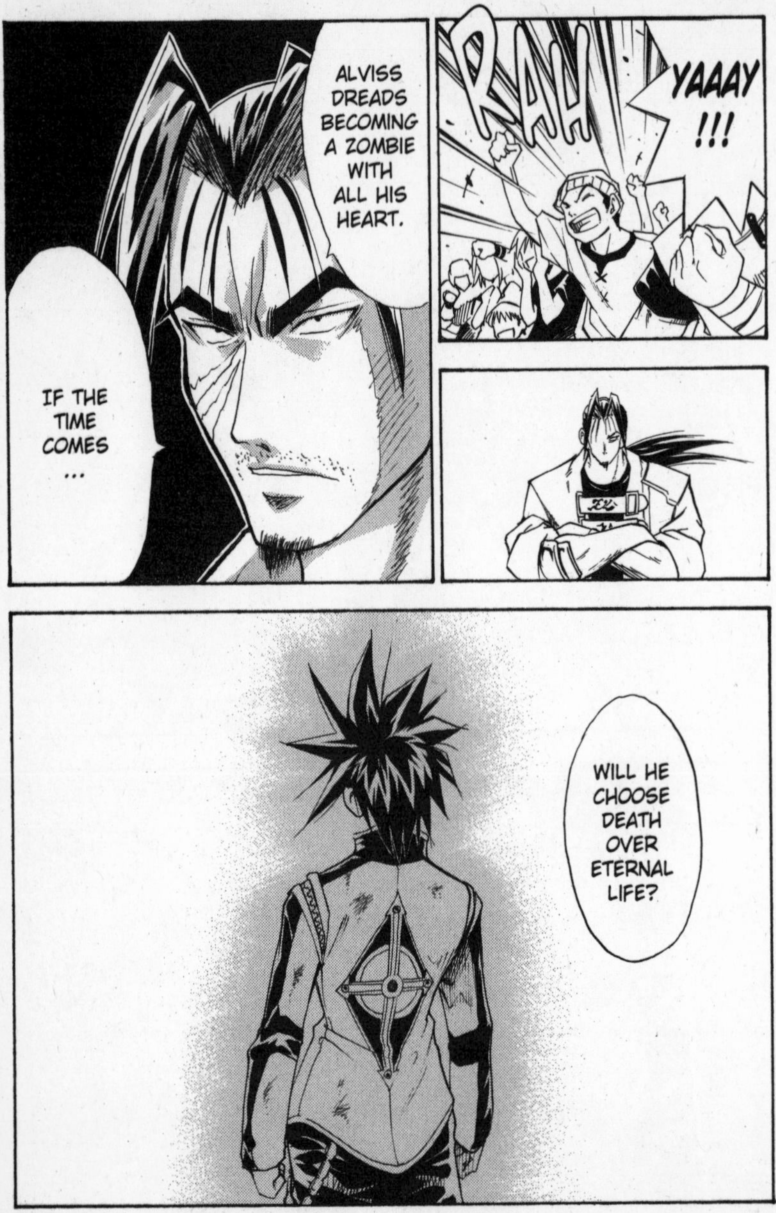
RAH
YAAAY !!!
ALVISS DREADS BECOMING A ZOMBIE WITH ALL HIS HEART.
IF THE TIME COMES ...
WILL HE CHOOSE DEATH OVER ETERNAL LIFE?

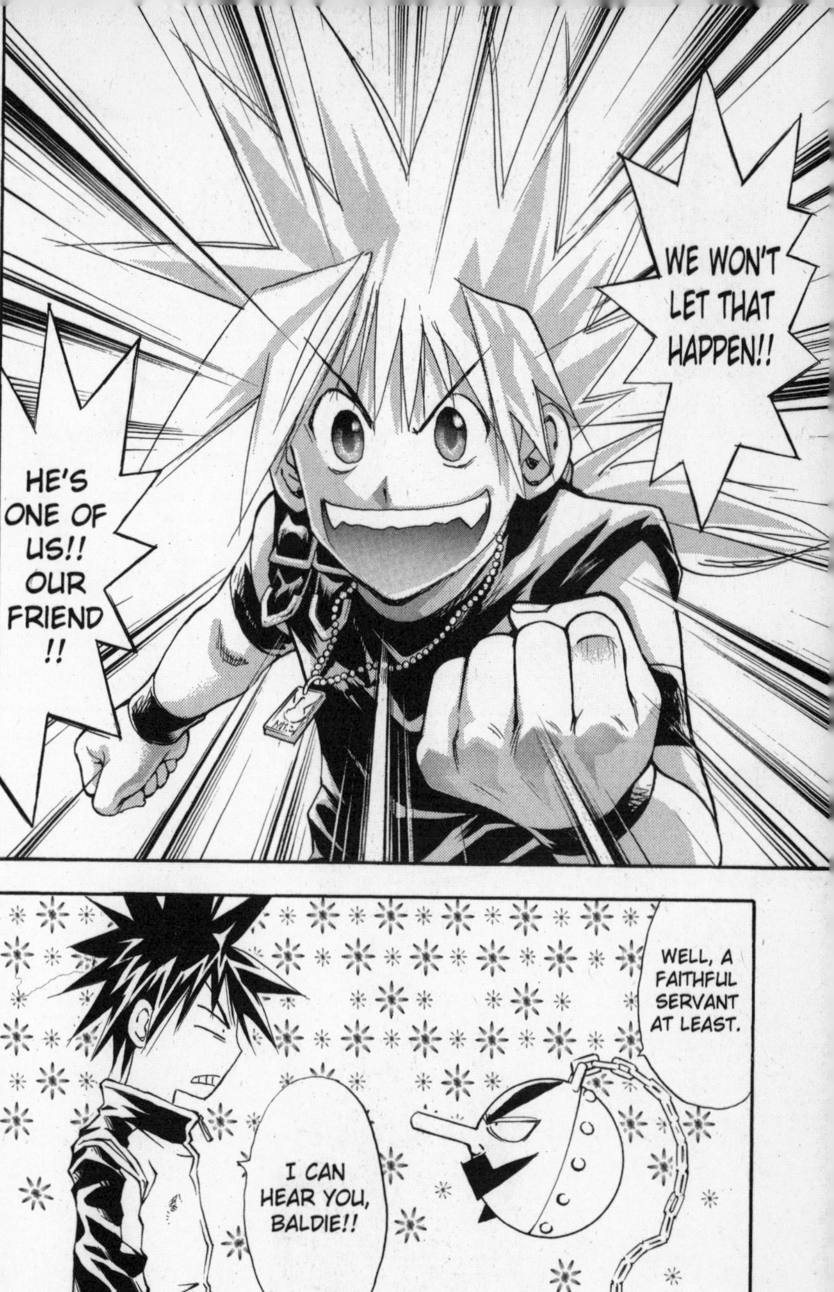
WE WON'T LET THAT HAPPEN!!
HE'S ONE OF US!! OUR FRIEND!!
WELL, A FAITHFUL SERVANT AT LEAST.
I CAN HEAR YOU, BALDIE!!

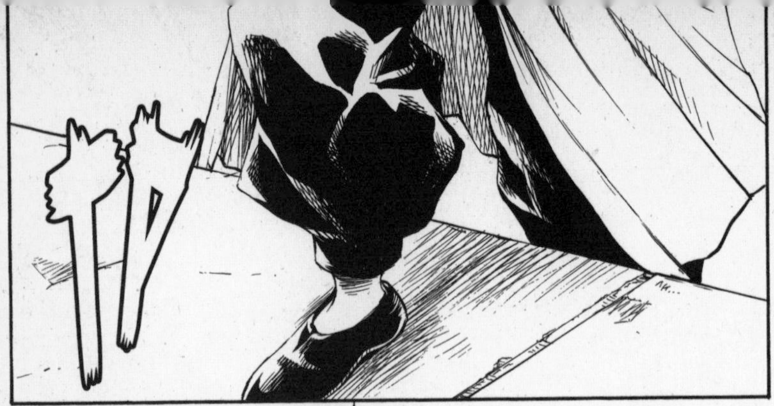
AH...
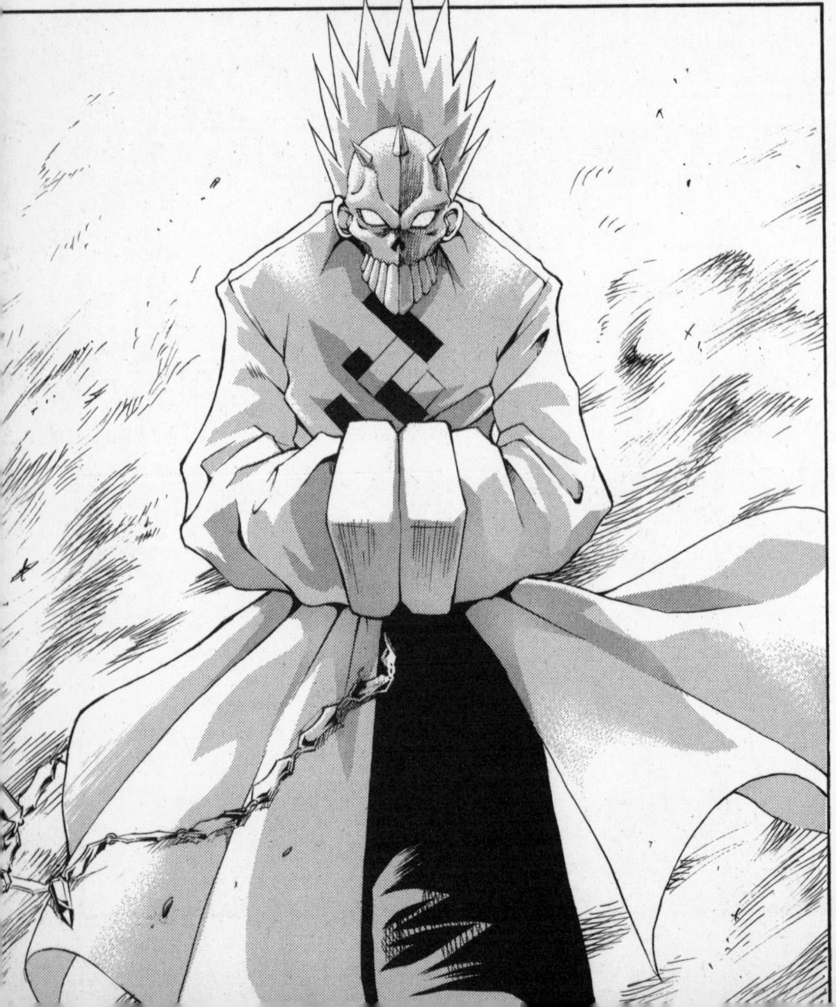

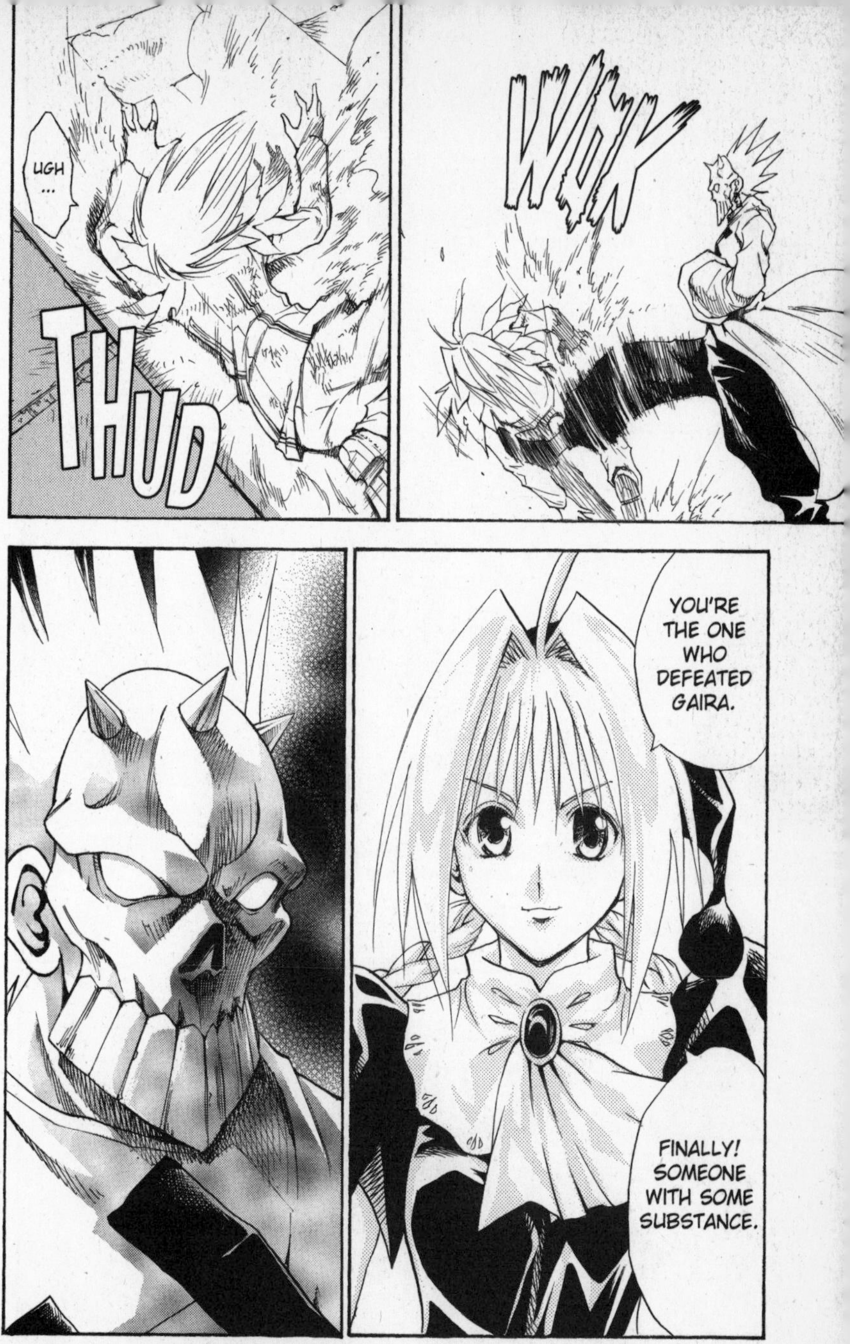
WOK
UGH ...
THUD
YOU'RE THE ONE WHO DEFEATED GAIRA.
FINALLY! SOMEONE WITH SOME SUBSTANCE.

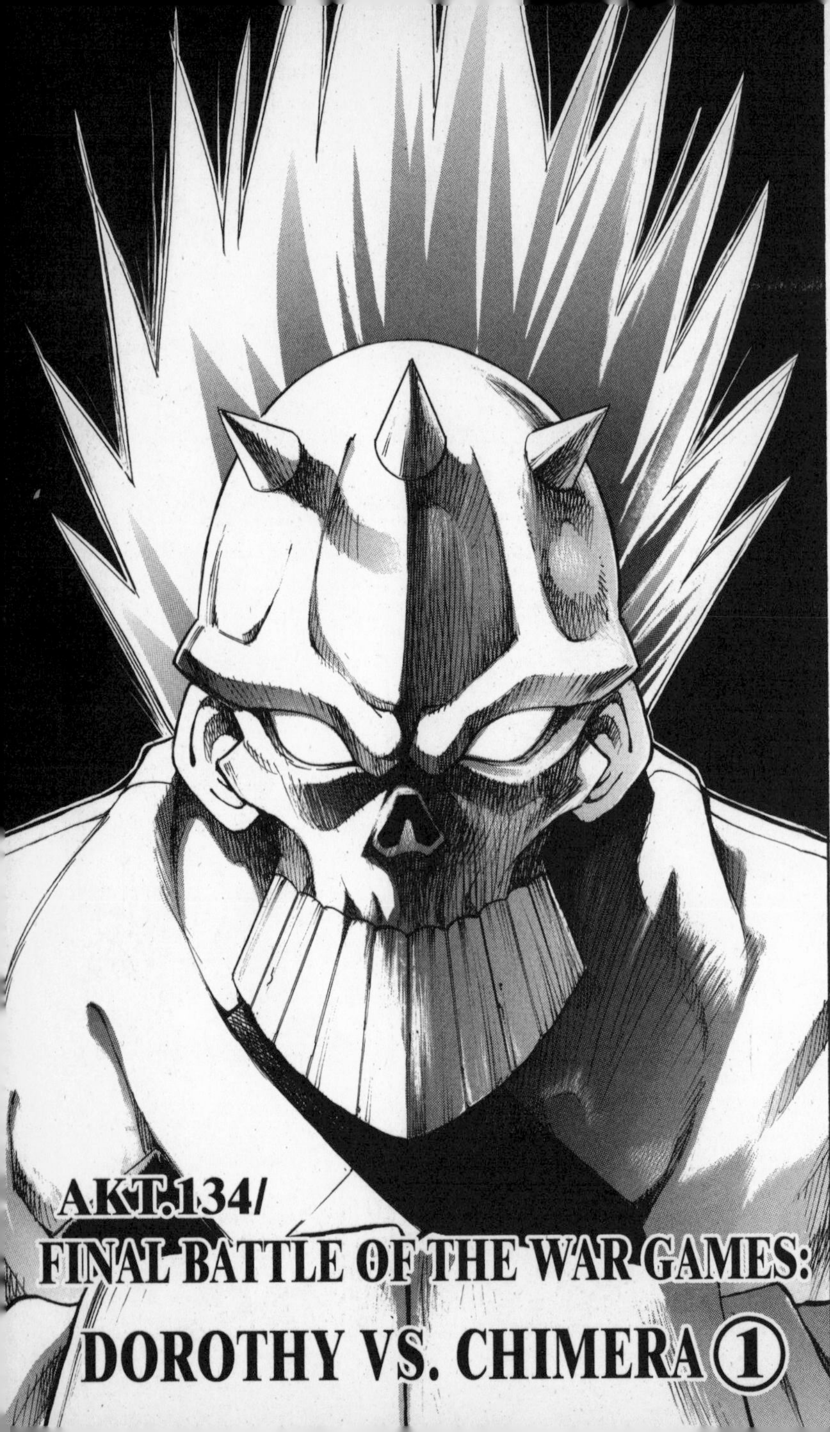
AKT.134/
FINAL BATTLE OF THE WAR GAMES:
DOROTHY VS. CHIMERA ①

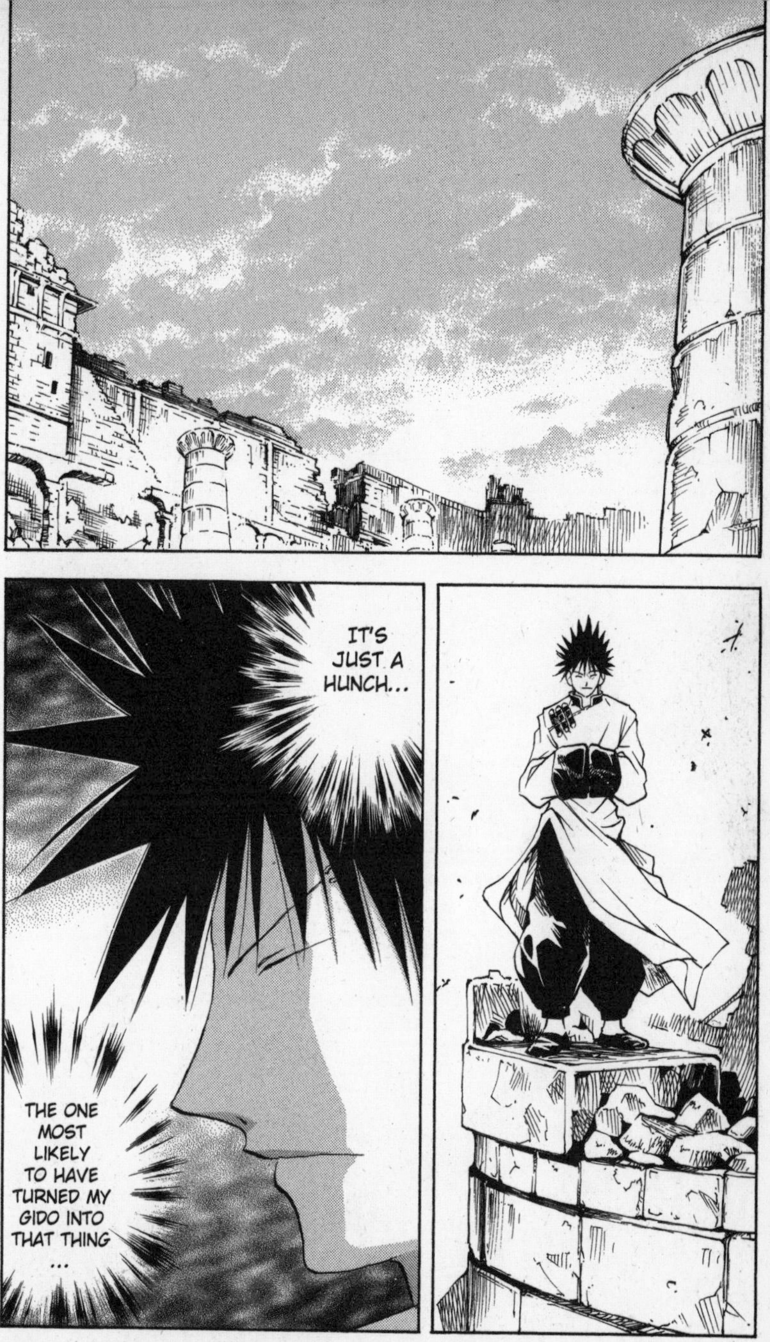
IT'S JUST A HUNCH...
THE ONE MOST LIKELY TO HAVE TURNED MY GIDO INTO THAT THING ...

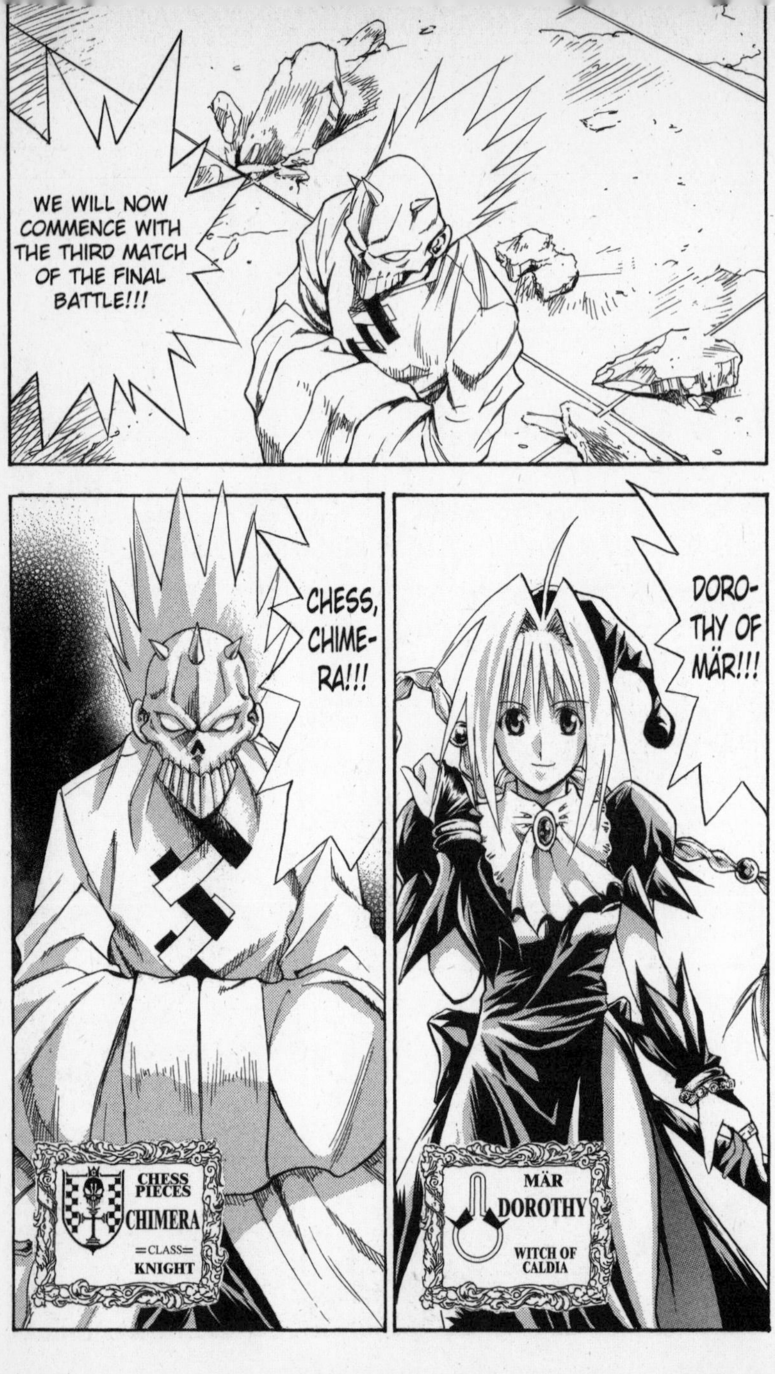
WE WILL NOW COMMENCE WITH THE THIRD MATCH OF THE FINAL BATTLE!!!
DORO-THY OF MÄR!!!
MÄR
DOROTHY
WITCH OF CALDIA
CHESS, CHIME-RA!!!
CHESS PIECES
CHIMERA
=CLASS=
KNIGHT

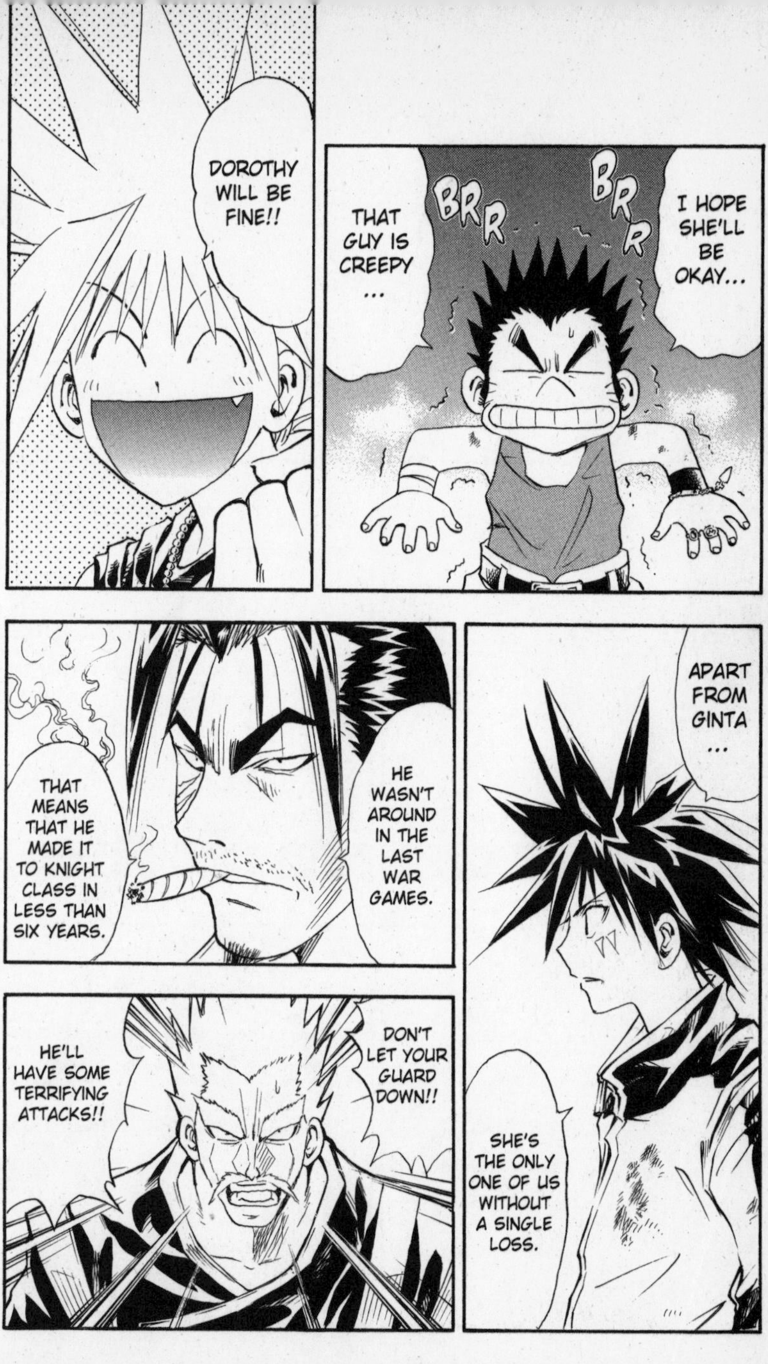
I HOPE SHE'LL BE OKAY...
BRRR
BRRR
THAT GUY IS CREEPY ...
DOROTHY WILL BE FINE!!
APART FROM GINTA ...
SHE'S THE ONLY ONE OF US WITHOUT A SINGLE LOSS.
HE WASN'T AROUND IN THE LAST WAR GAMES.
THAT MEANS THAT HE MADE IT TO KNIGHT CLASS IN LESS THAN SIX YEARS.
DON'T LET YOUR GUARD DOWN!!
HE'LL HAVE SOME TERRIFYING ATTACKS!!

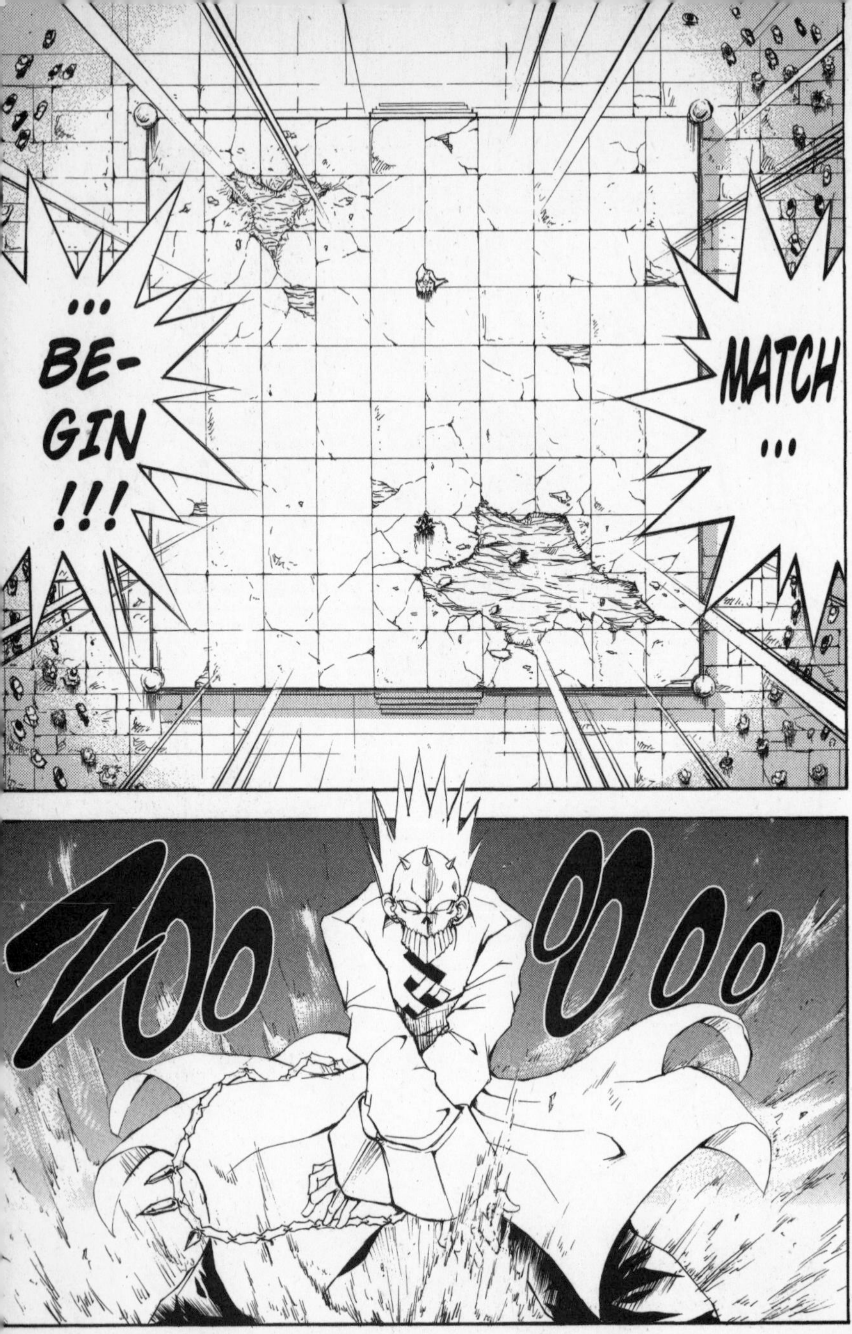
MATCH ...
... BE-GIN !!!
ZOOOOOO

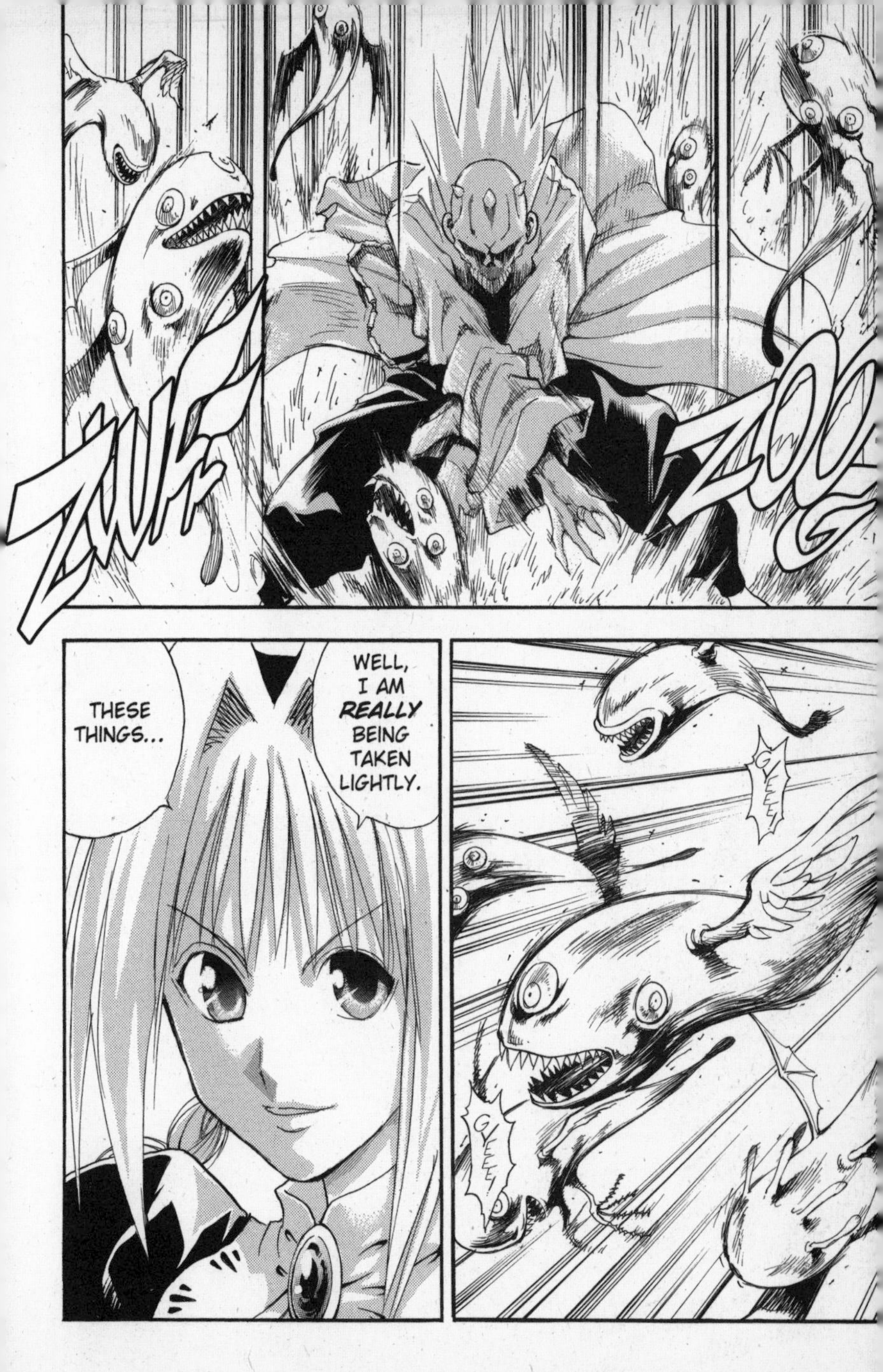
ZOOG
ZUK
GYEEE!
GYEEE!
WELL, I AM *REALLY* BEING TAKEN LIGHTLY.
THESE THINGS...

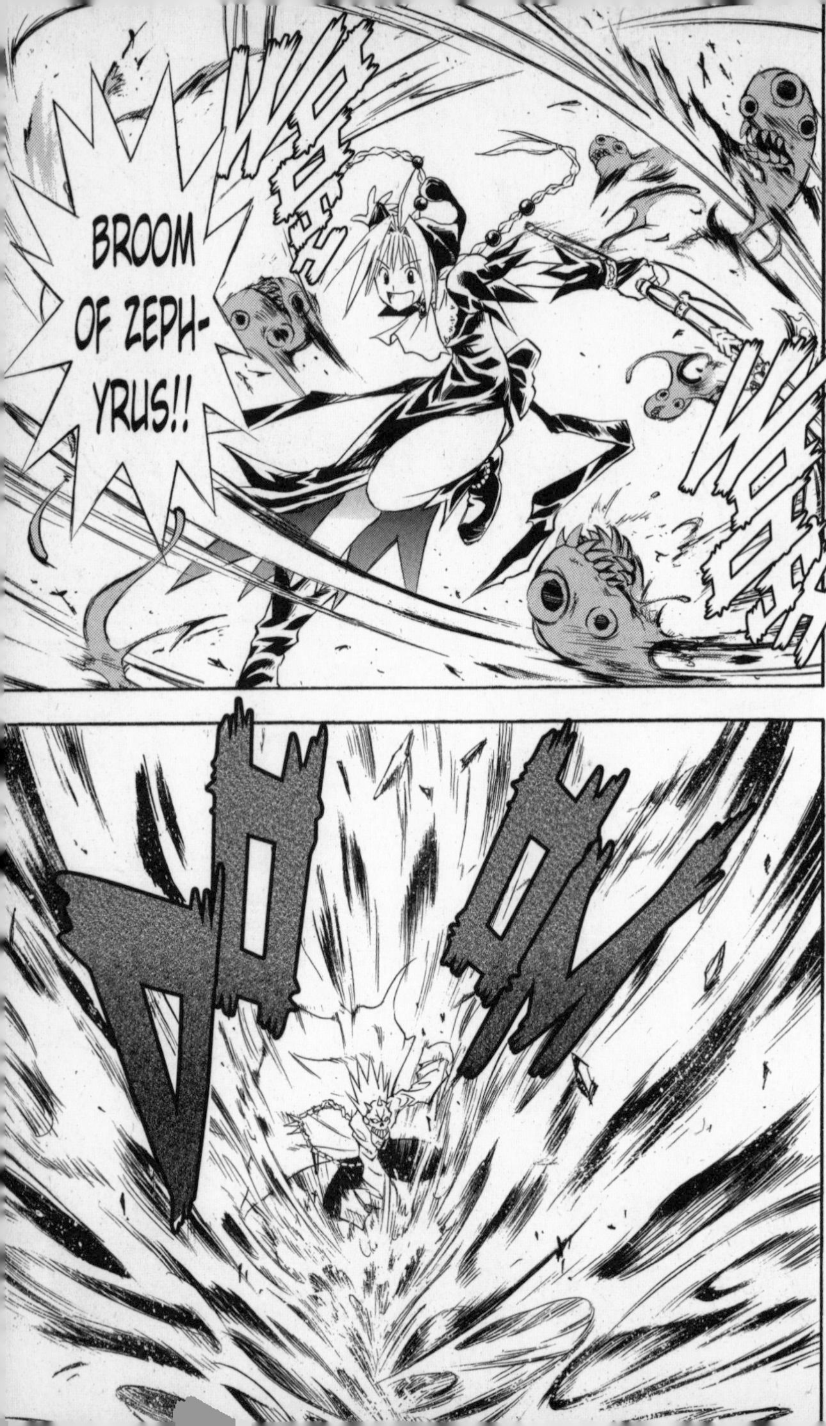
BROOM OF ZEPH-YRUS!!

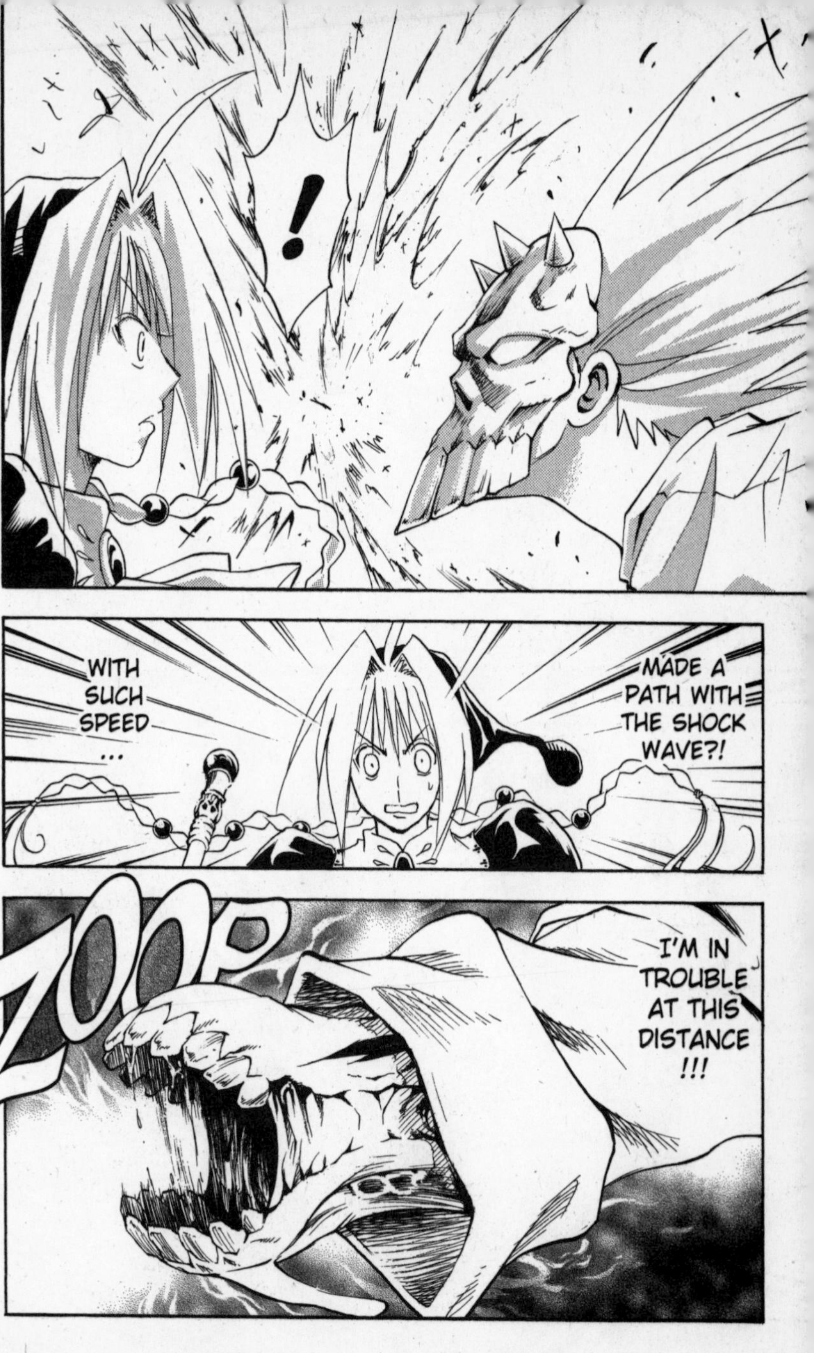
!
MADE A PATH WITH THE SHOCK WAVE?!
WITH SUCH SPEED...
I'M IN TROUBLE AT THIS DISTANCE!!!
ZOOP

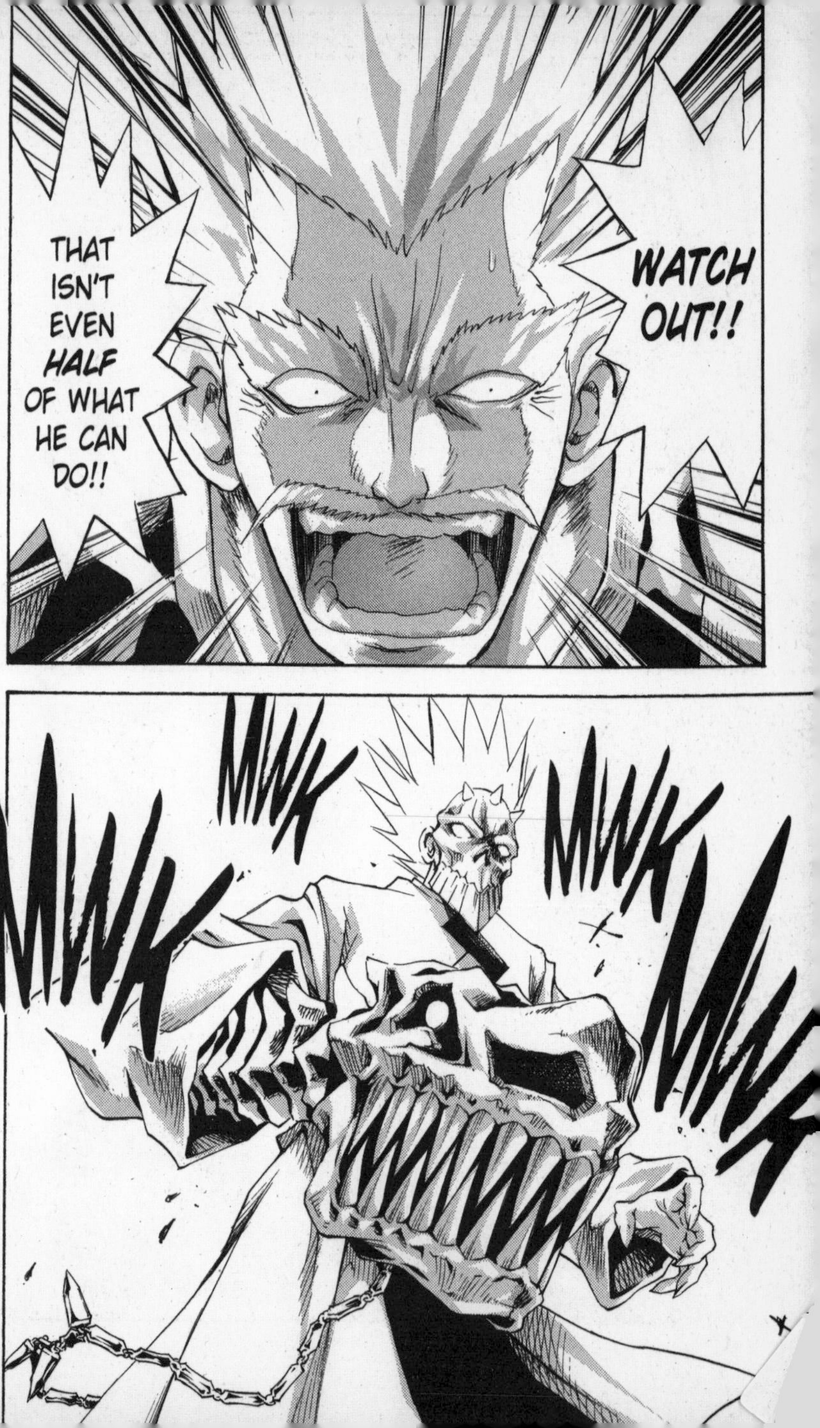
WATCH OUT!!
THAT ISN'T EVEN *HALF* OF WHAT HE CAN DO!!
MWK
MWK
MWK
MWK

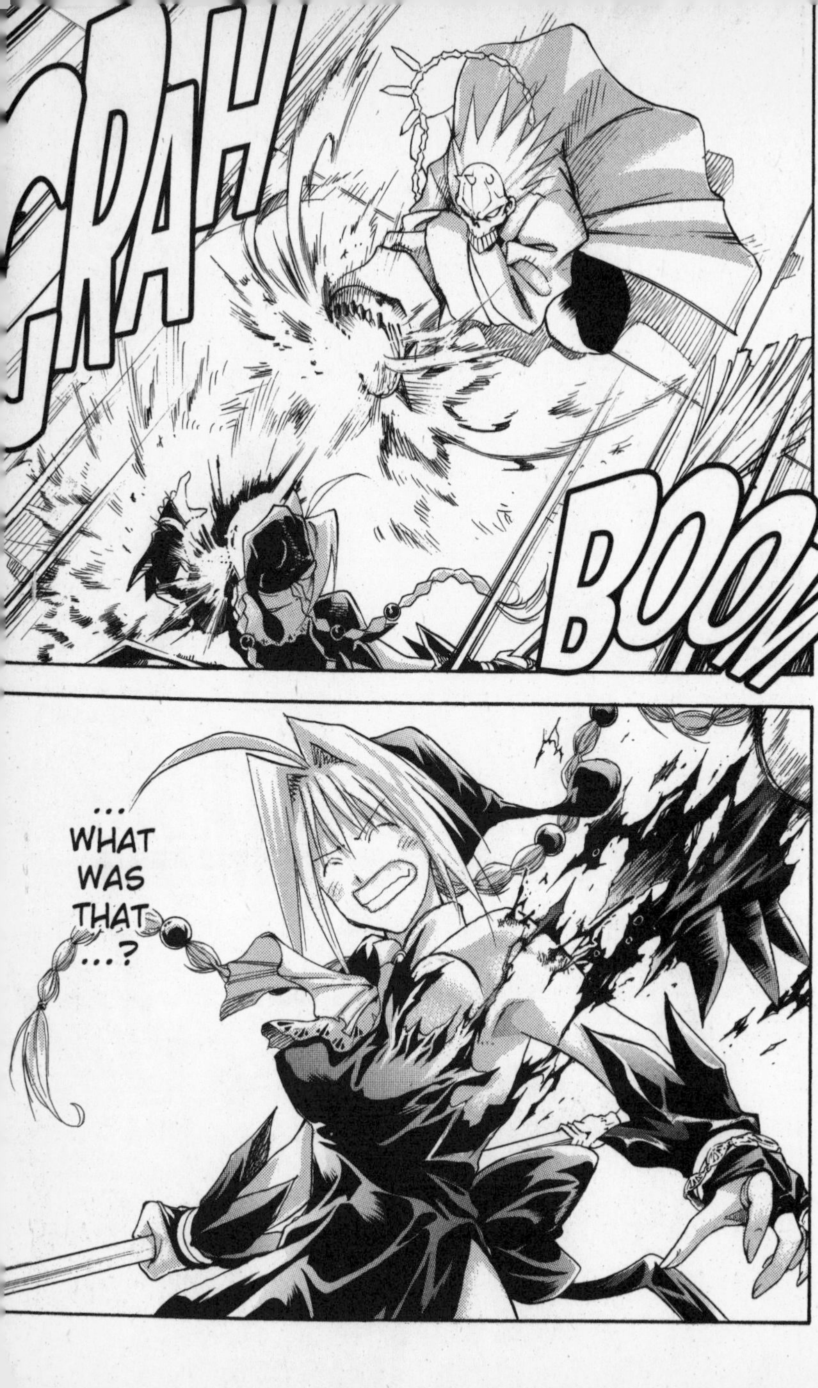
CRAH
BOOM
...WHAT WAS THAT...?

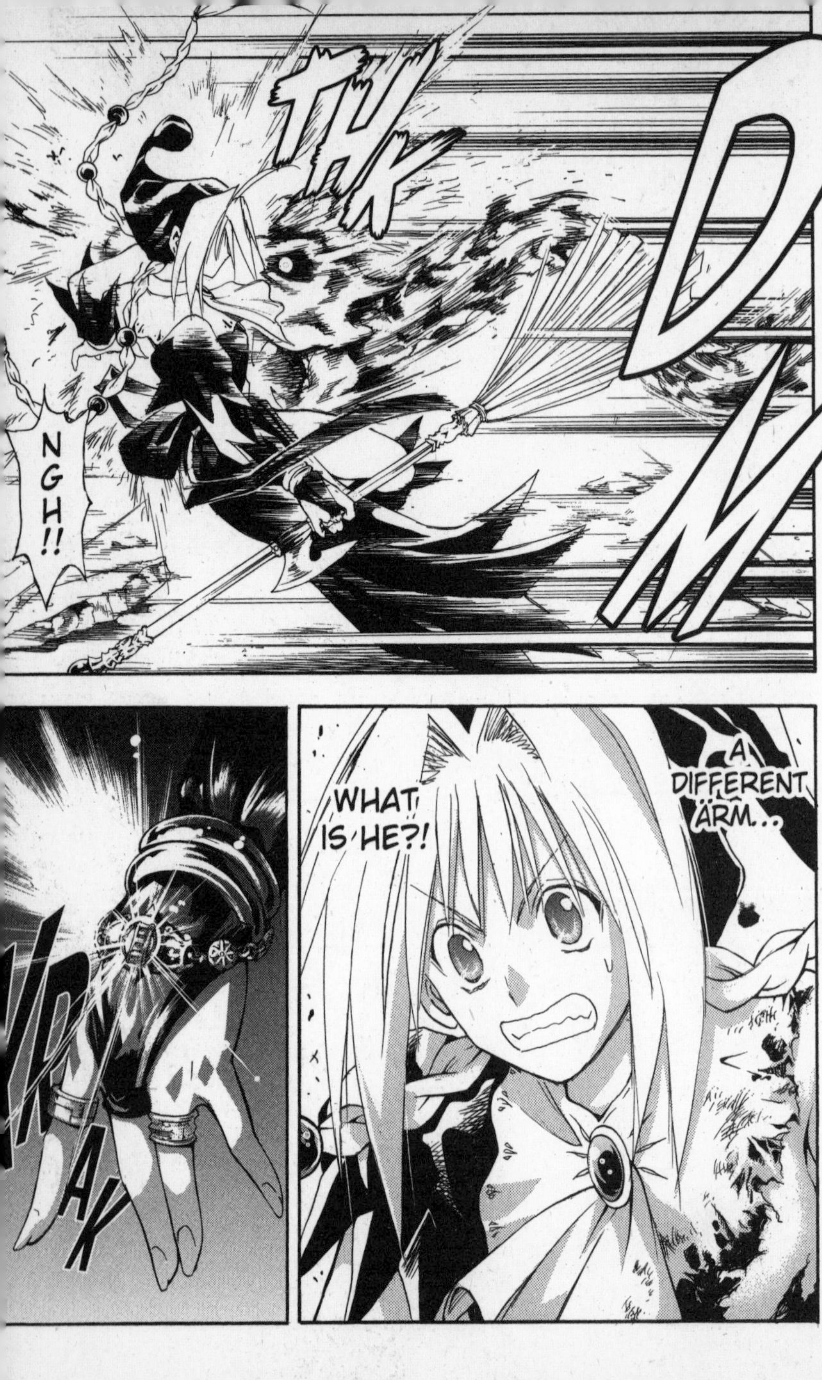
THK
NGH!!
A DIFFERENT ARM...
WHAT IS HE?!

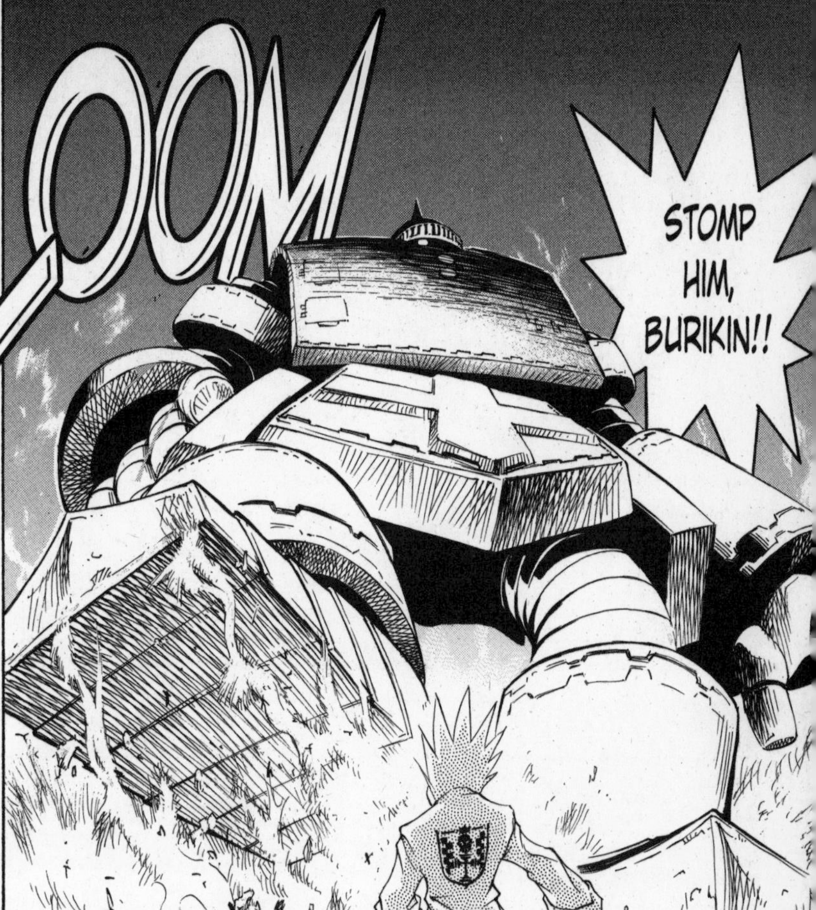
STOMP HIM, BURIKIN!!
LOOM
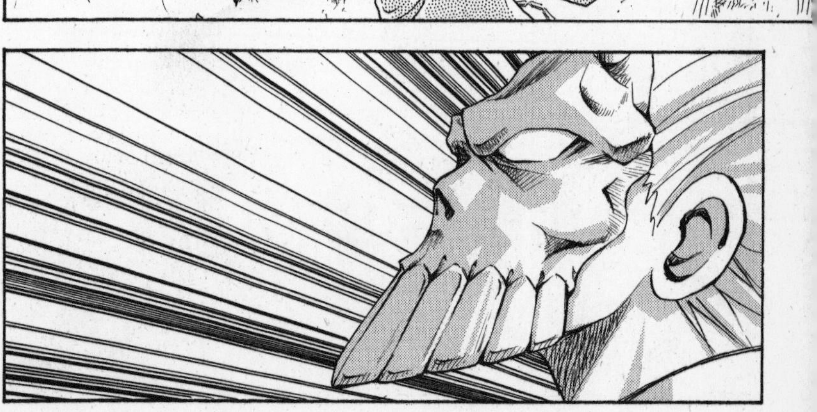

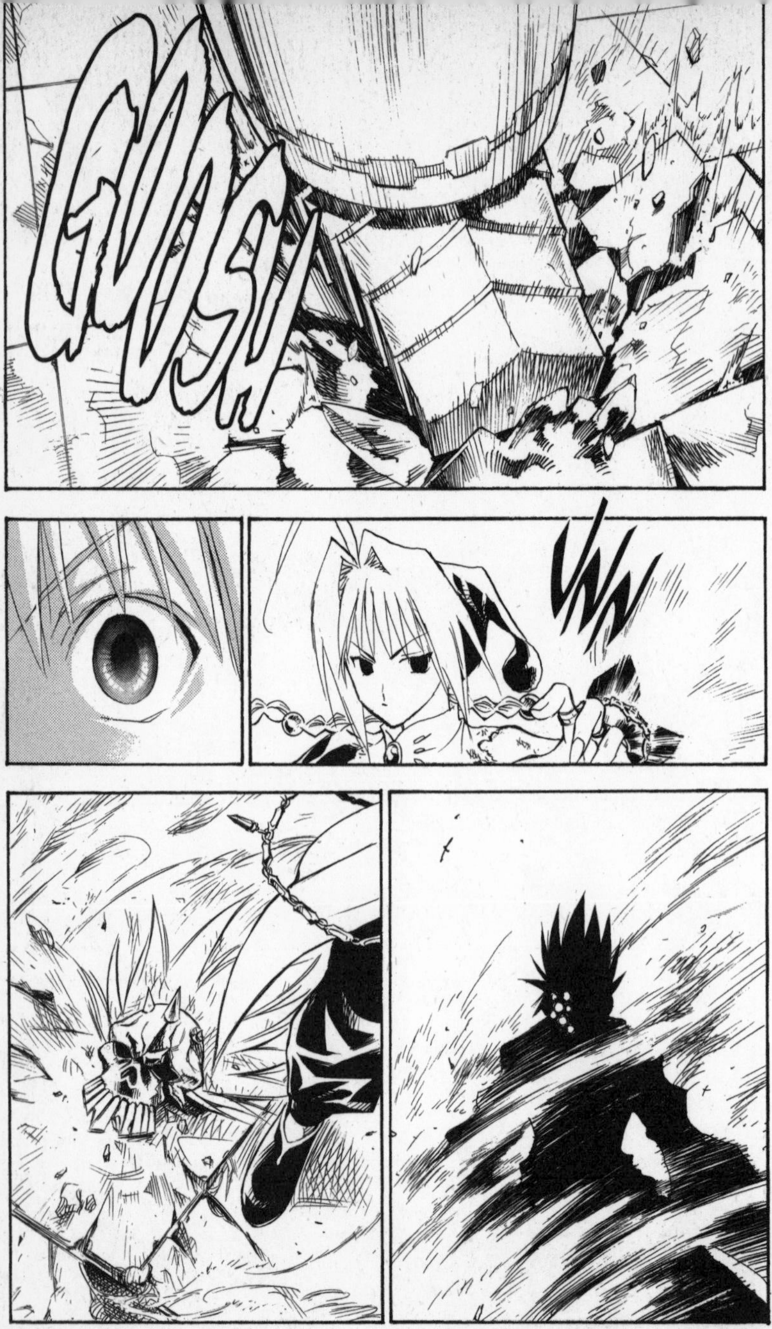
GOSH

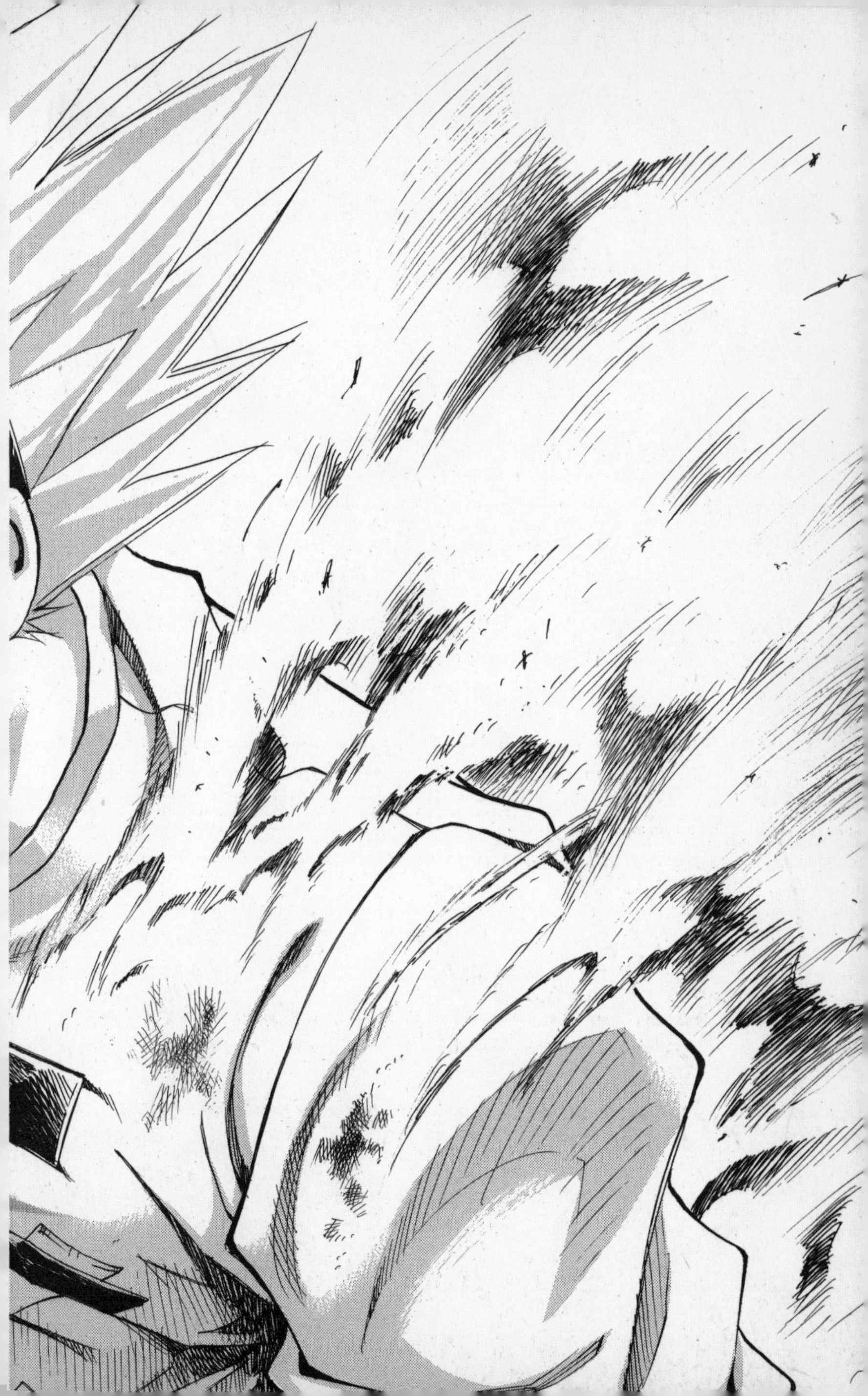

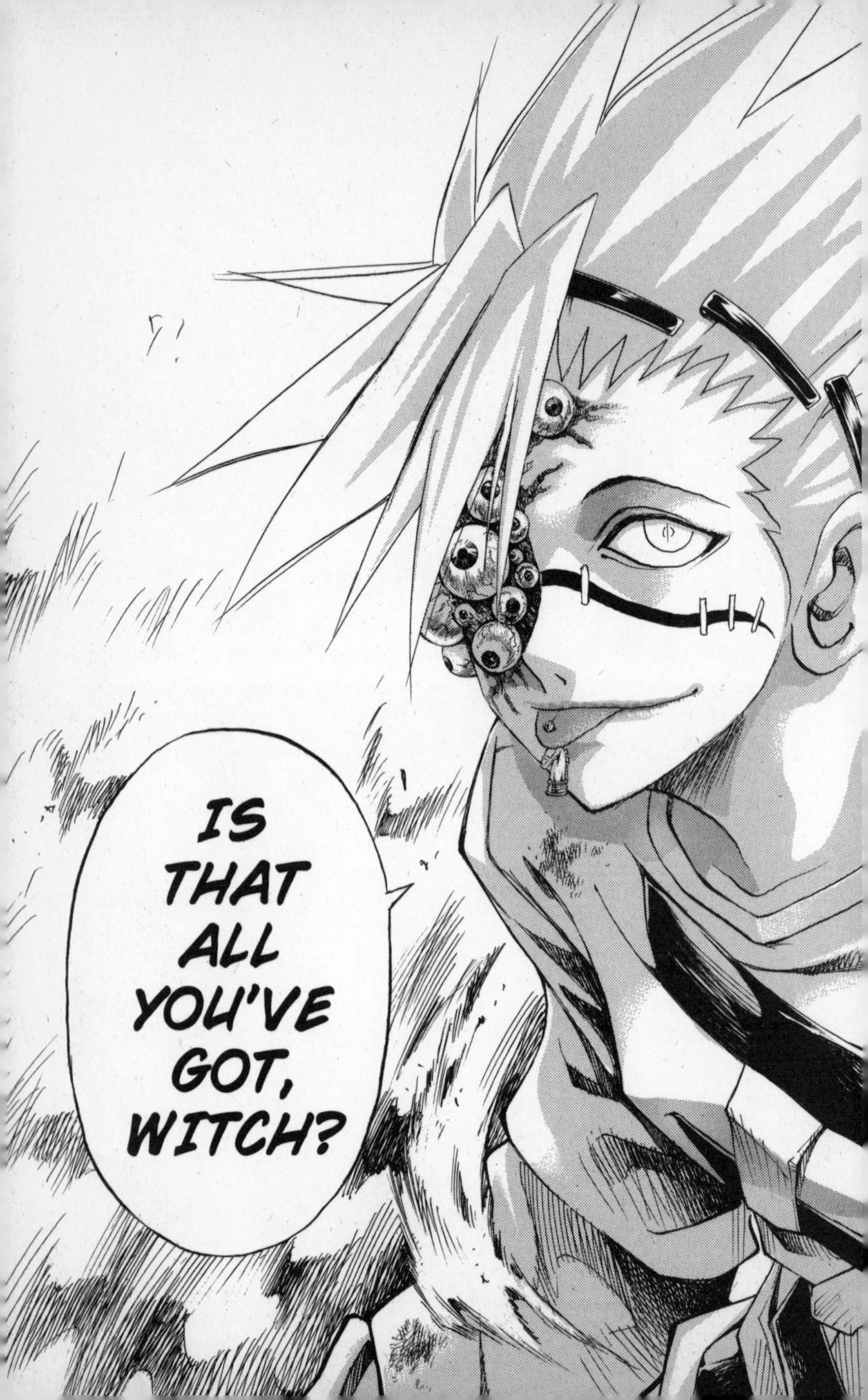
IS THAT ALL YOU'VE GOT, WITCH?

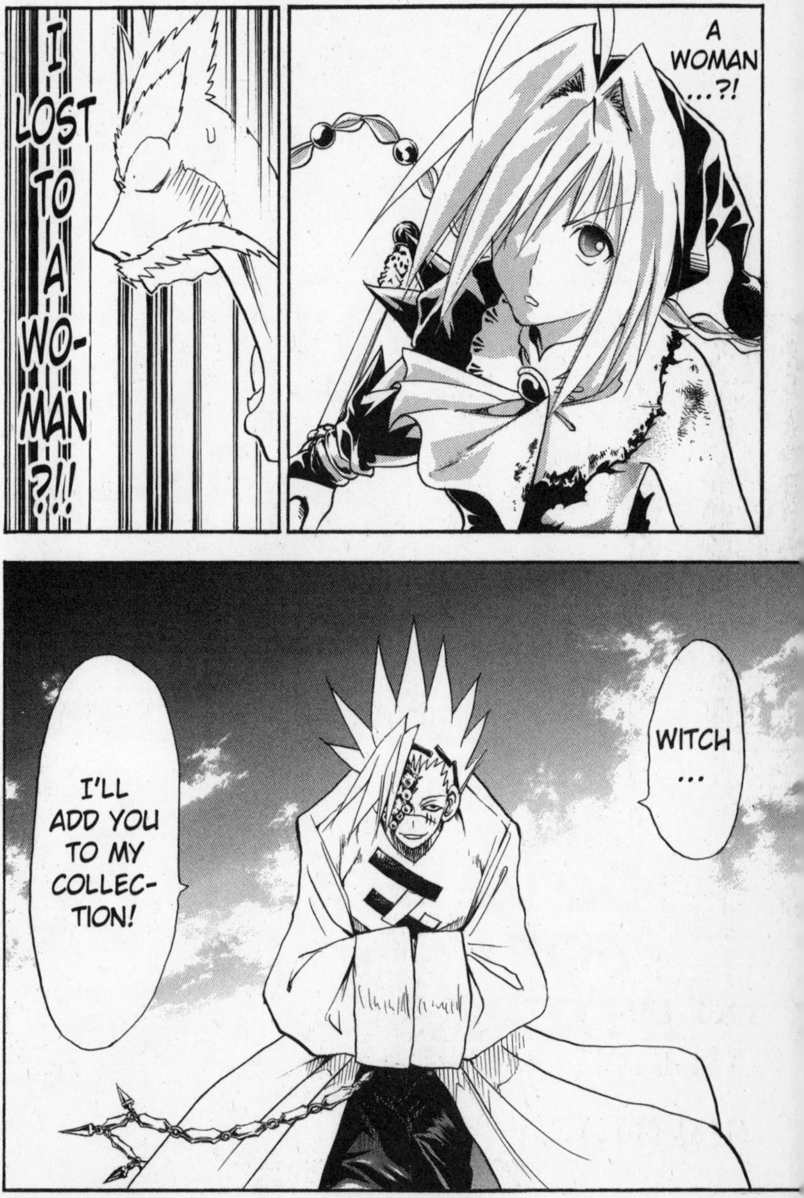
A WOMAN ...?!
I LOST TO A WO-MAN ?!!
WITCH ...
I'LL ADD YOU TO MY COLLEC-TION!

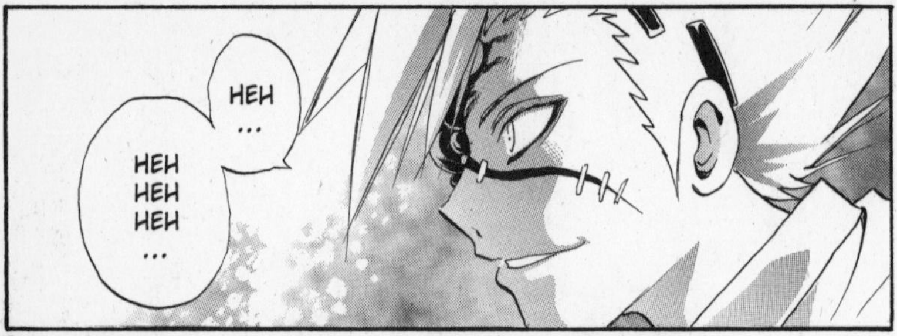
HEH ... HEH HEH HEH ...

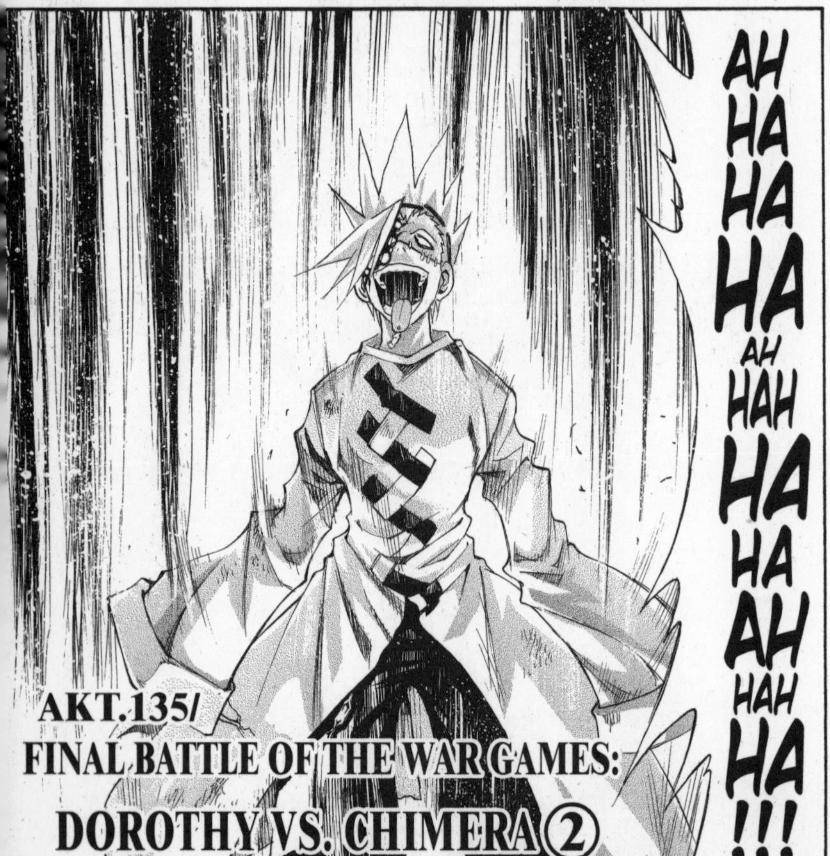
AH HA HA HA HA AH HAH HA HA AH HAH HA!!!

AKT.135/ FINAL BATTLE OF THE WAR GAMES: DOROTHY VS. CHIMERA ②

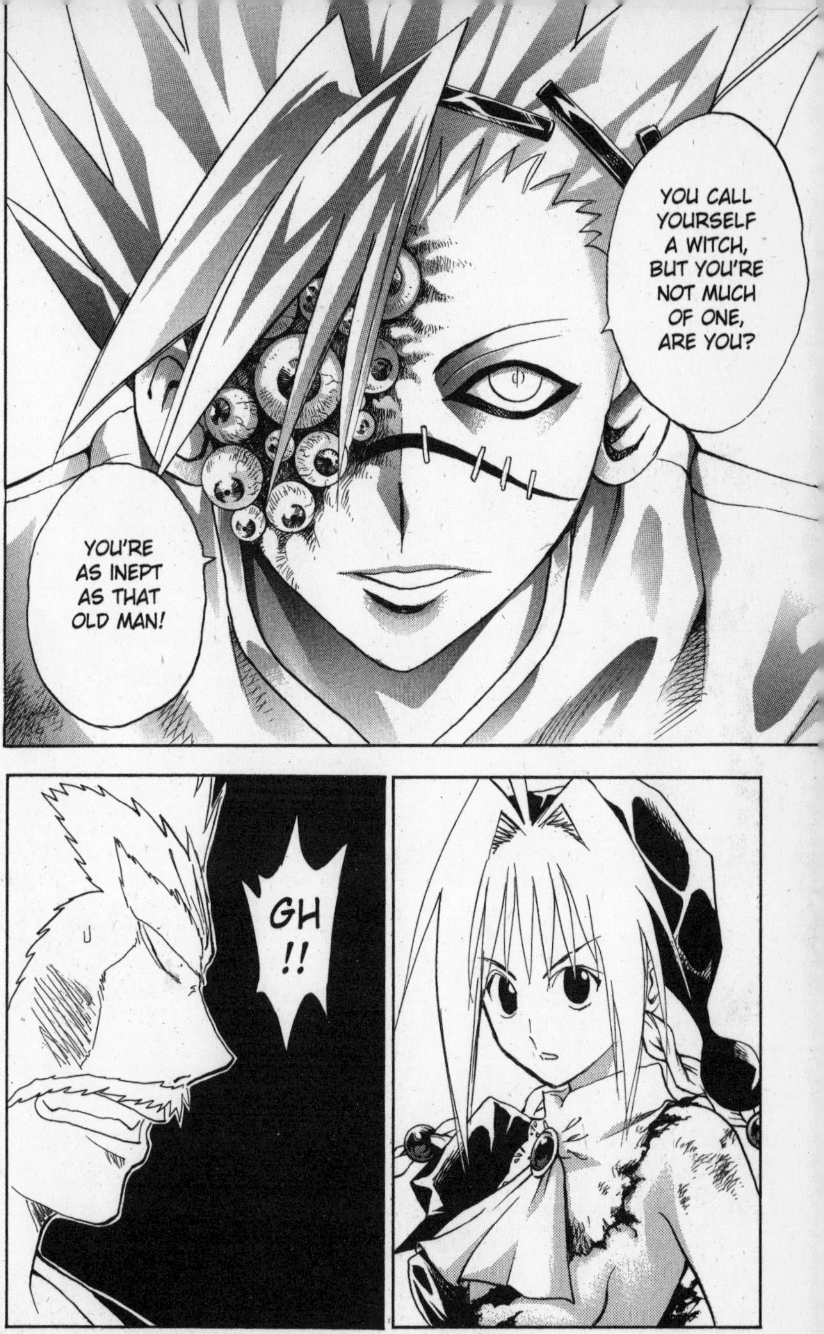
YOU CALL YOURSELF A WITCH, BUT YOU'RE NOT MUCH OF ONE, ARE YOU?
YOU'RE AS INEPT AS THAT OLD MAN!
GH !!

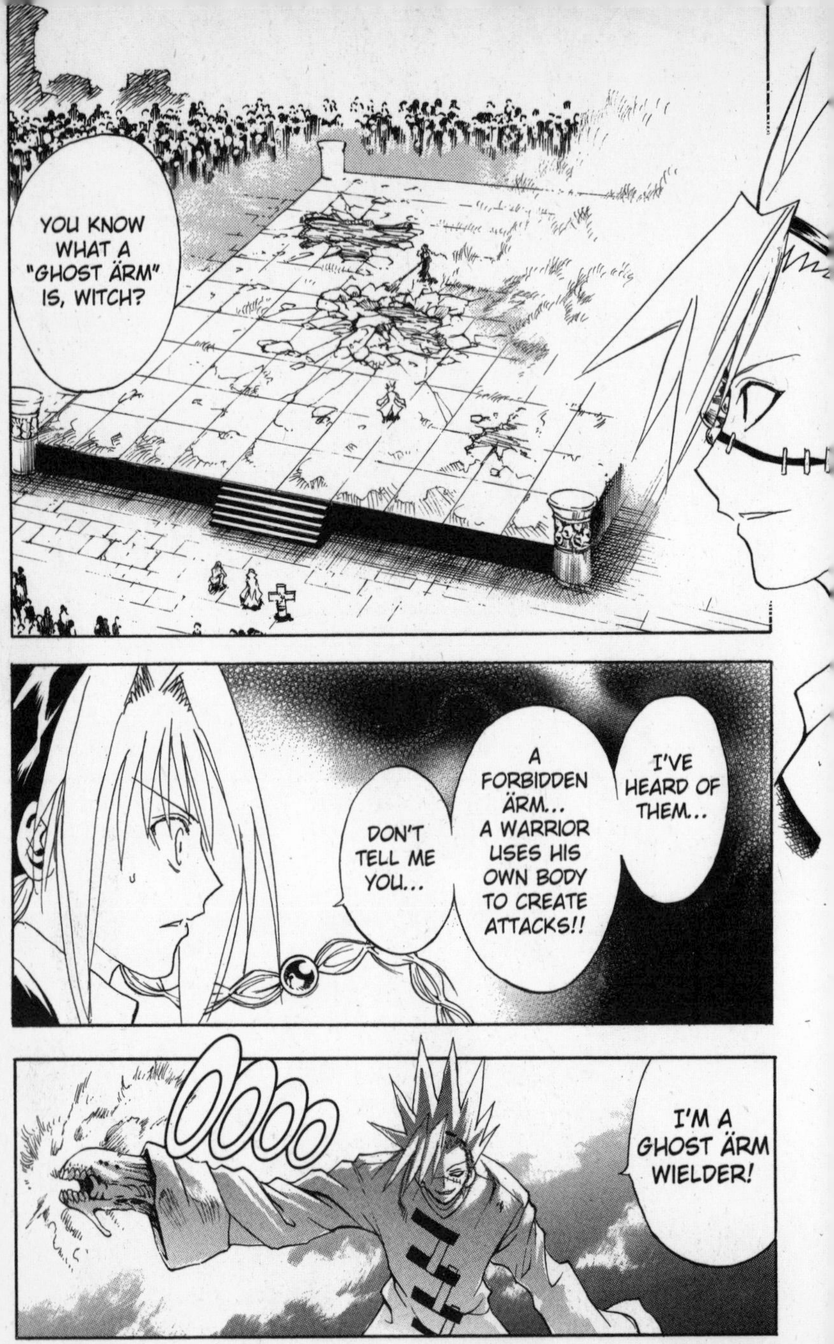
YOU KNOW WHAT A "GHOST ÄRM" IS, WITCH?
I'VE HEARD OF THEM...
A FORBIDDEN ÄRM... A WARRIOR USES HIS OWN BODY TO CREATE ATTACKS!!
DON'T TELL ME YOU...
I'M A GHOST ÄRM WIELDER!

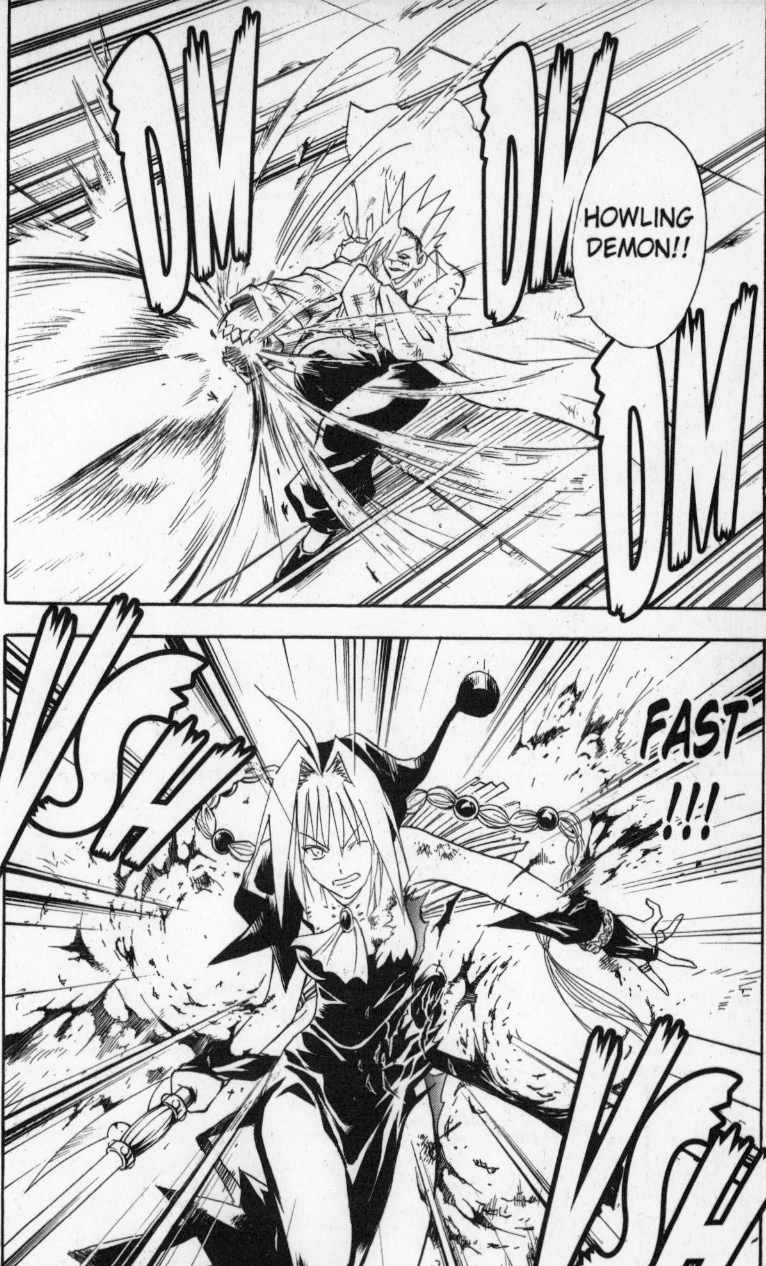
HOWLING DEMON!!
DOM
FAST-!!!
VSH
VSH

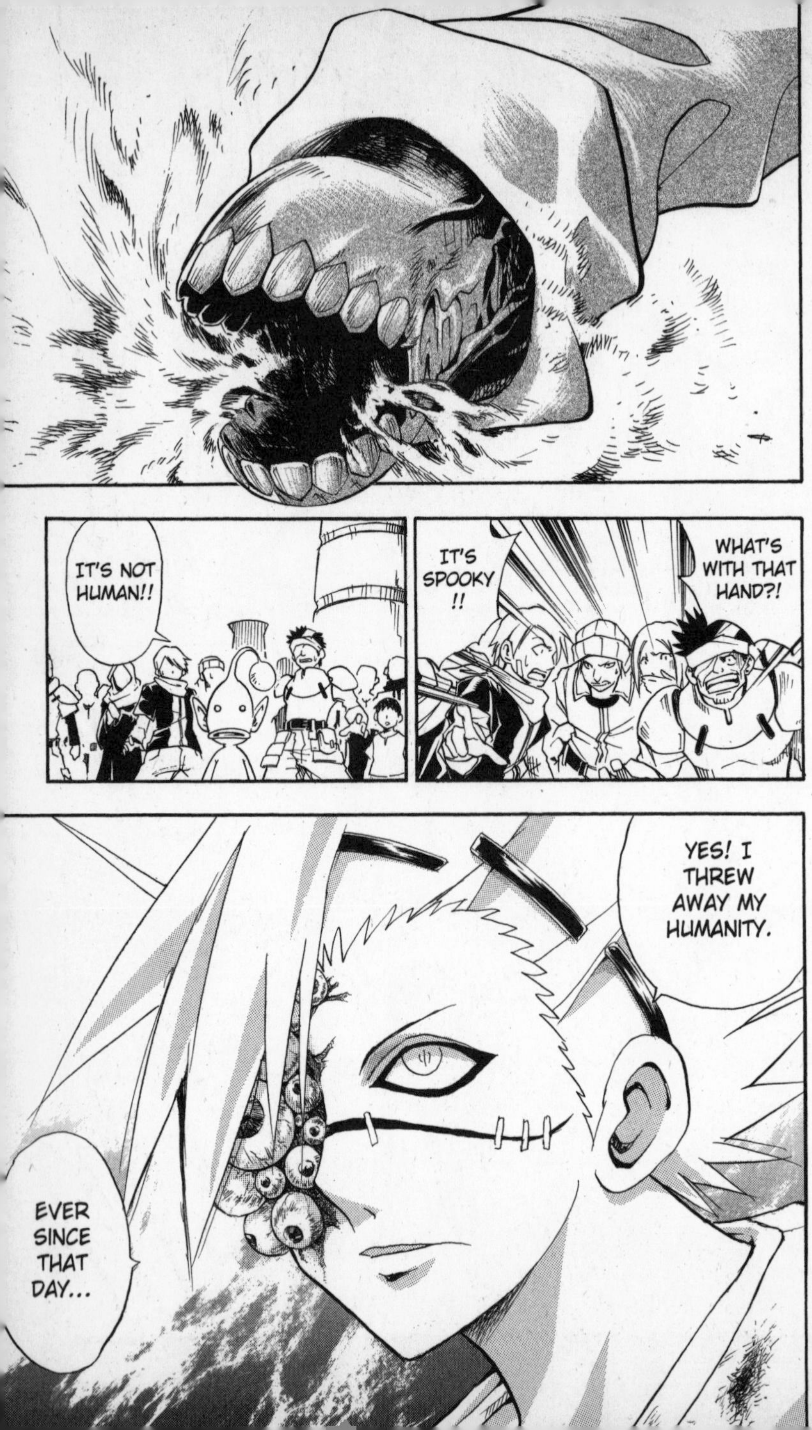
WHAT'S WITH THAT HAND?!
IT'S SPOOKY!!
IT'S NOT HUMAN!!
YES! I THREW AWAY MY HUMANITY.
EVER SINCE THAT DAY...

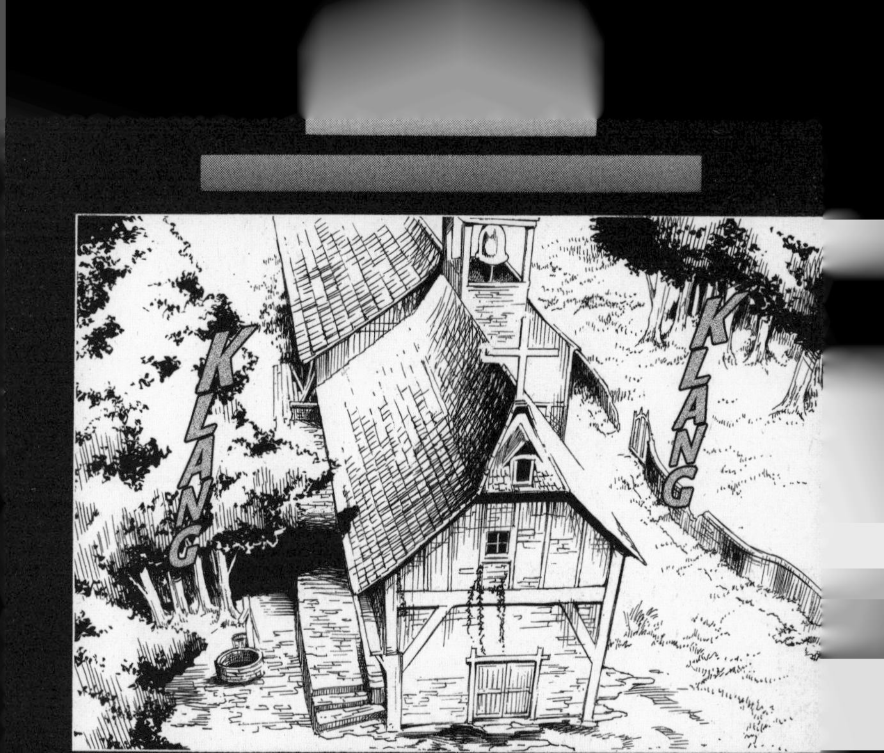
KLANG
KLANG

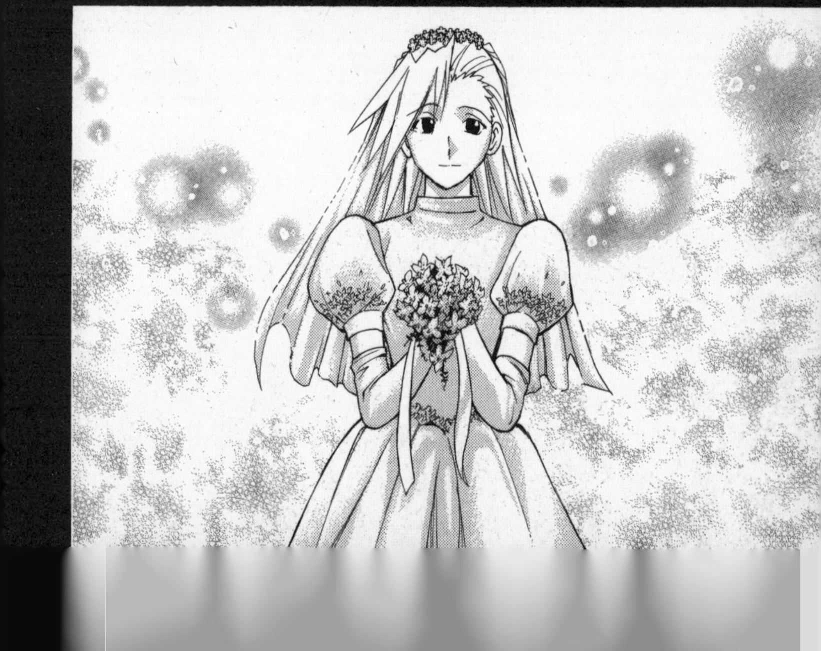

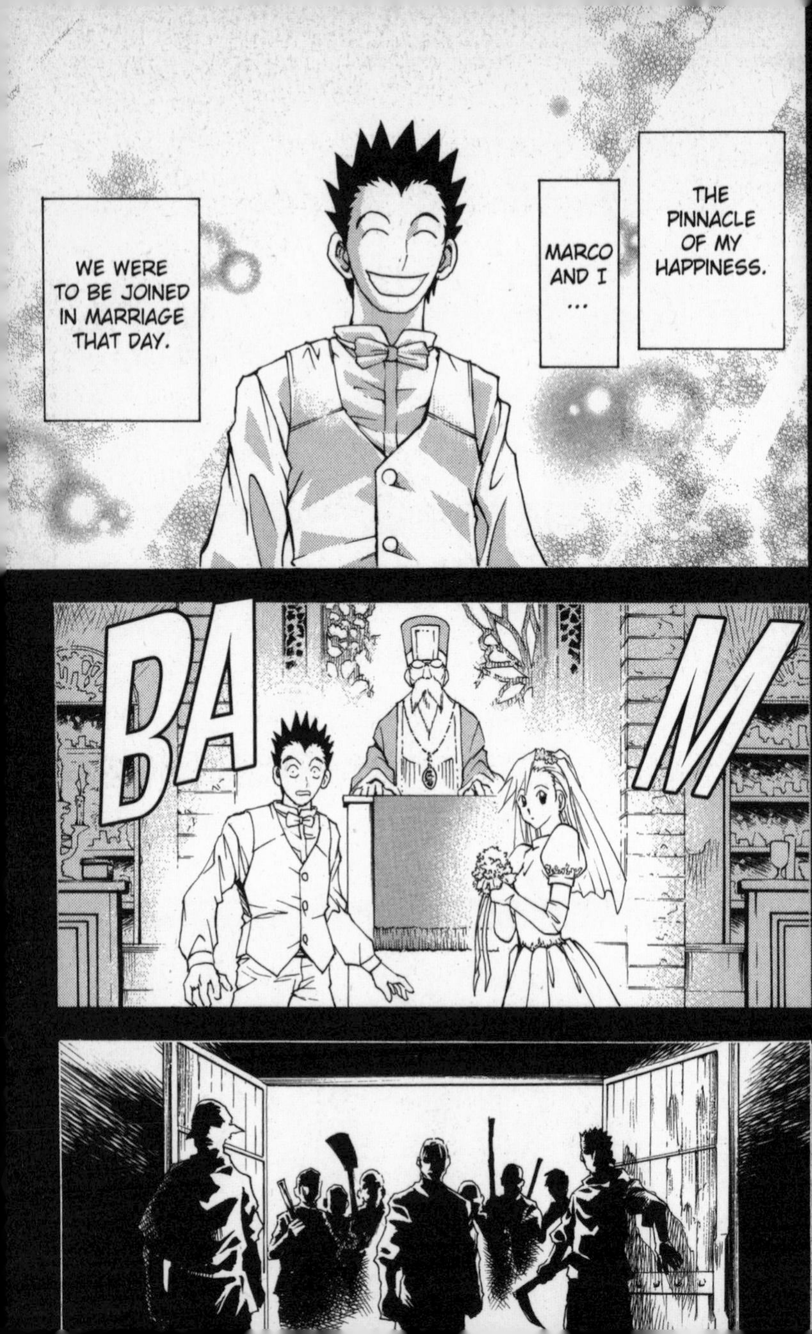
THE PINNACLE OF MY HAPPINESS.
MARCO AND I ...
WE WERE TO BE JOINED IN MARRIAGE THAT DAY.
BAM

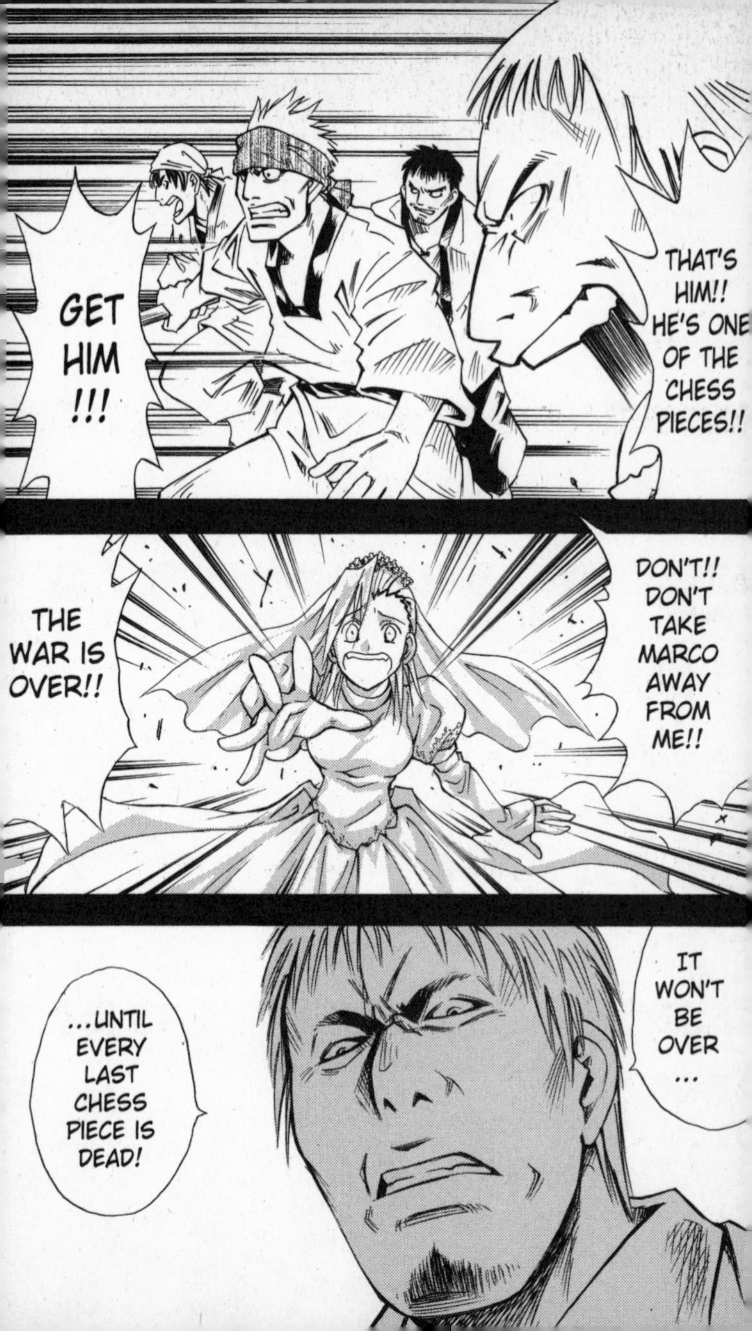
THAT'S HIM!! HE'S ONE OF THE CHESS PIECES!!
GET HIM !!!
DON'T!! DON'T TAKE MARCO AWAY FROM ME!!
THE WAR IS OVER!!
IT WON'T BE OVER ...
...UNTIL EVERY LAST CHESS PIECE IS DEAD!

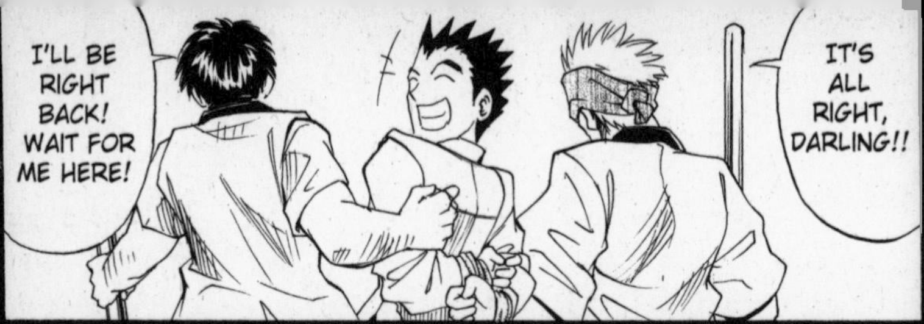
IT'S ALL RIGHT, DARLING!!
I'LL BE RIGHT BACK! WAIT FOR ME HERE!

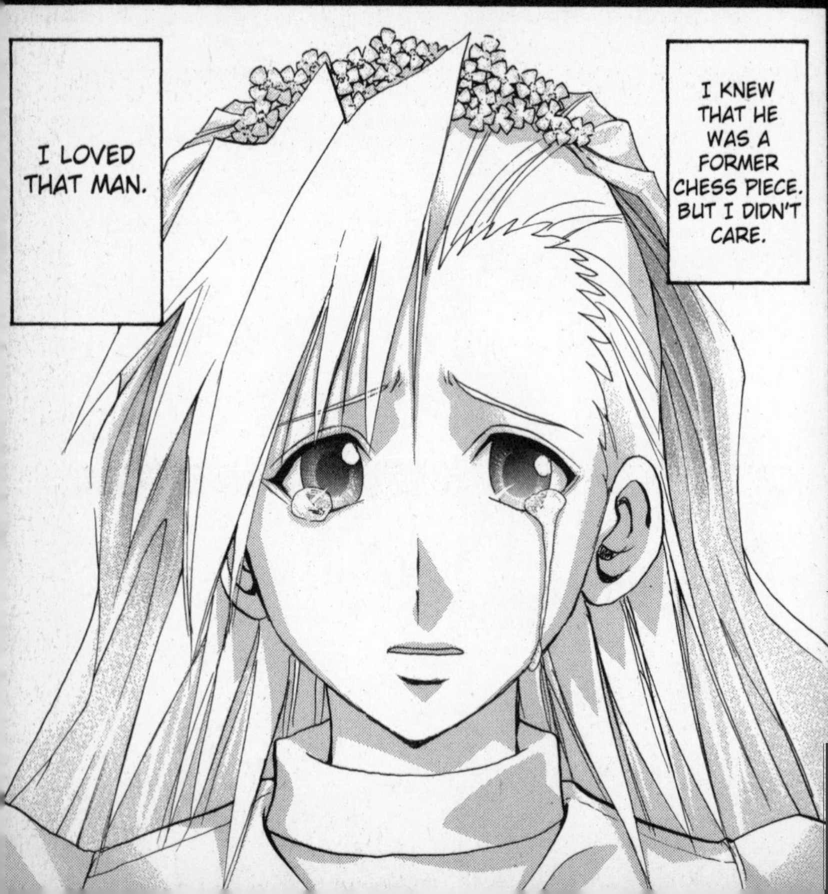
I KNEW THAT HE WAS A FORMER CHESS PIECE. BUT I DIDN'T CARE.
I LOVED THAT MAN.

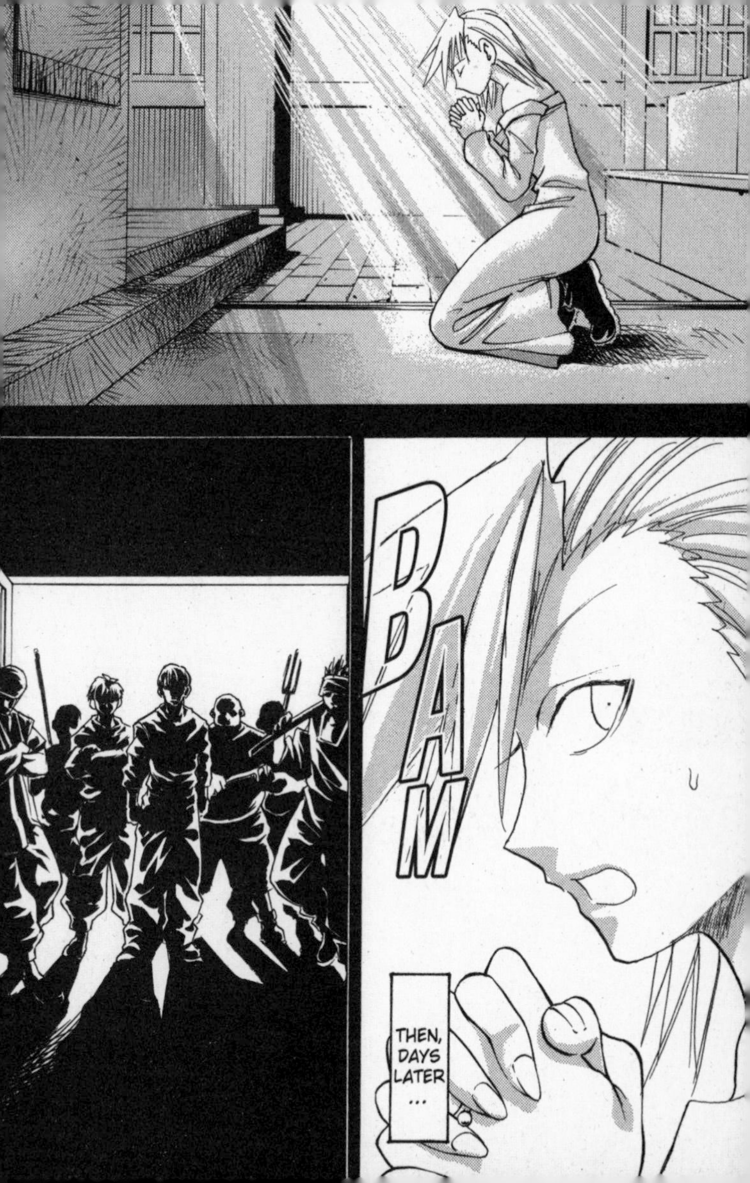
BAM
THEN, DAYS LATER...

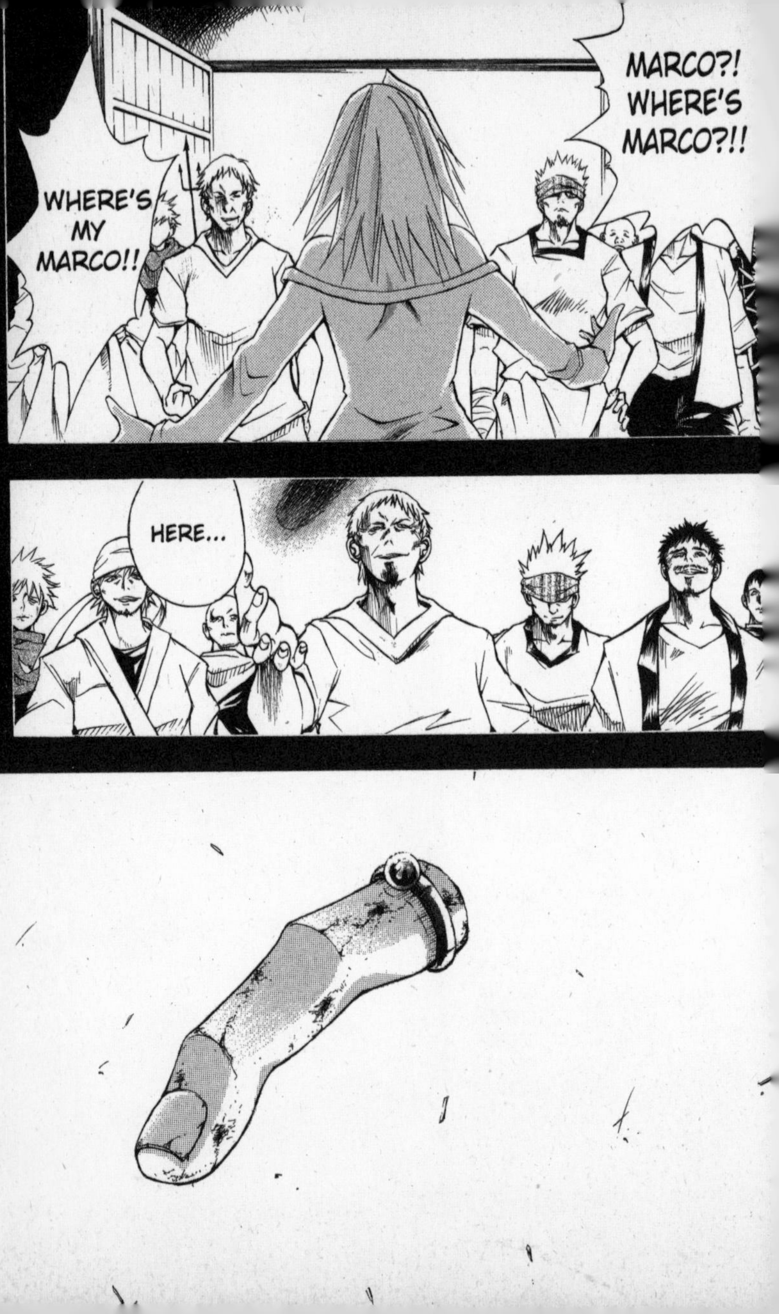
MARCO?! WHERE'S MARCO?!!
WHERE'S MY MARCO!!
HERE...

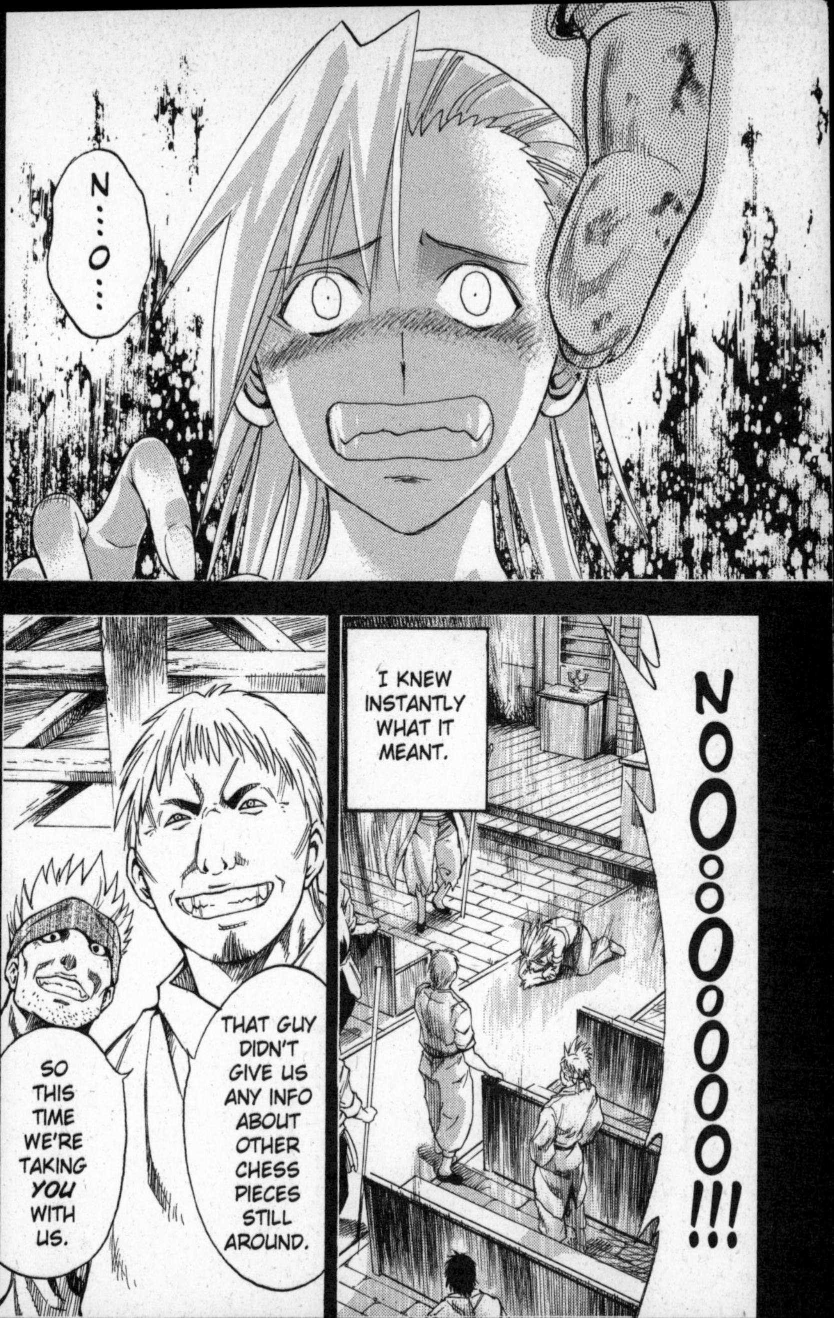
N...O...
I KNEW INSTANTLY WHAT IT MEANT.
NOOOOOOOO!!!
THAT GUY DIDN'T GIVE US ANY INFO ABOUT OTHER CHESS PIECES STILL AROUND.
SO THIS TIME WE'RE TAKING *YOU* WITH US.

WHAT
FOLLOWED
WAS...
A LIVING
HELL FOR
ME...

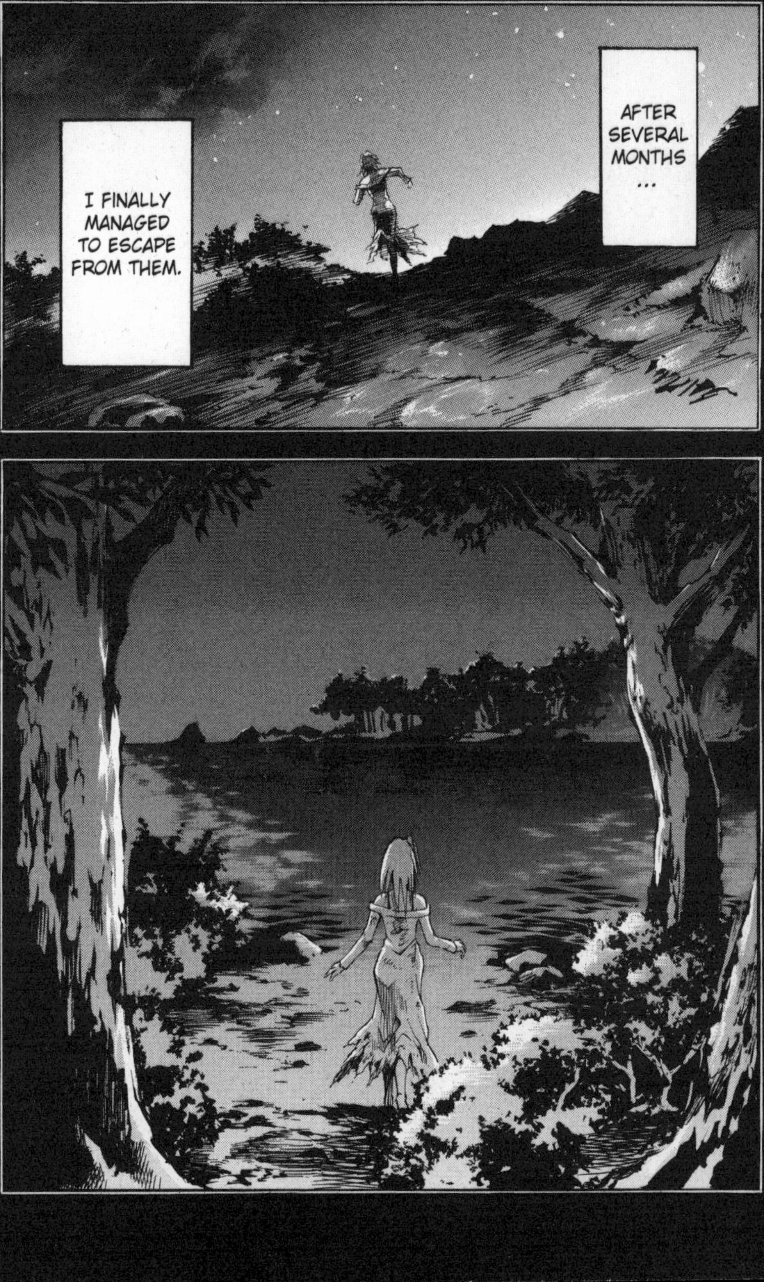
AFTER SEVERAL MONTHS ...
I FINALLY MANAGED TO ESCAPE FROM THEM.

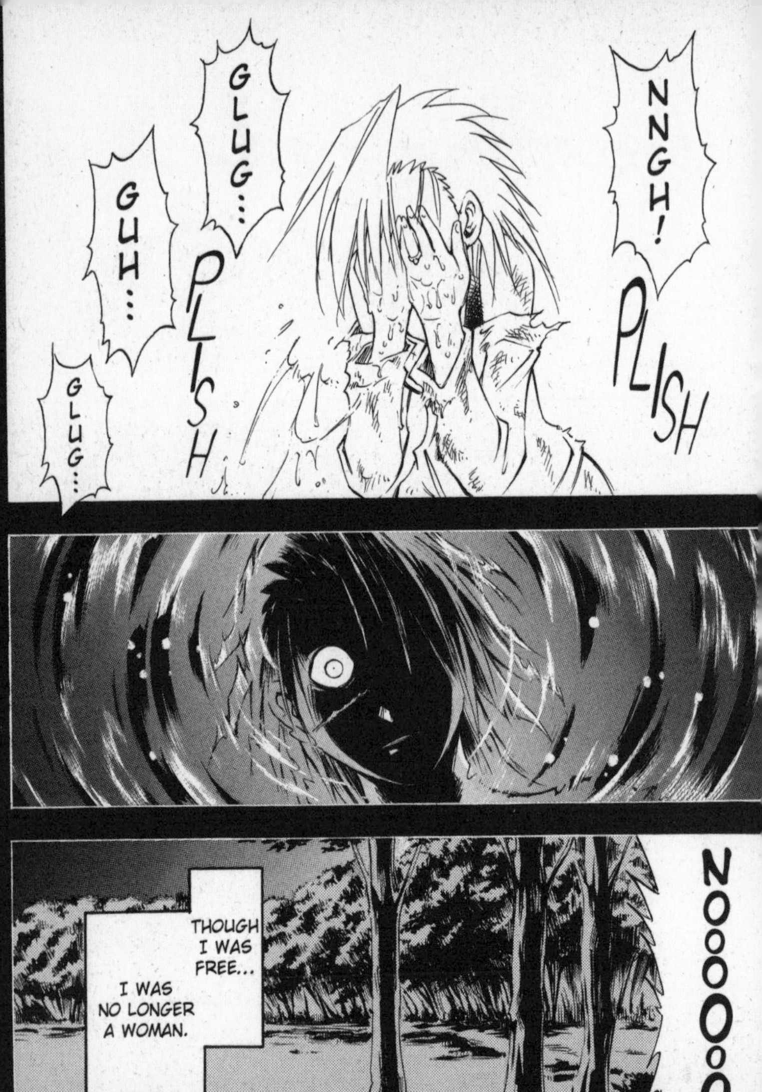
NNGH!
PLISH
GLUG...
GUH...
PLISH
GLUG...
NOOOOOO!!
THOUGH I WAS FREE...
I WAS NO LONGER A WOMAN.

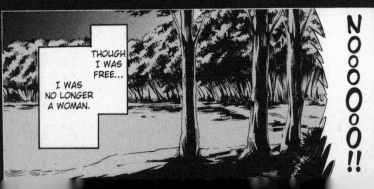

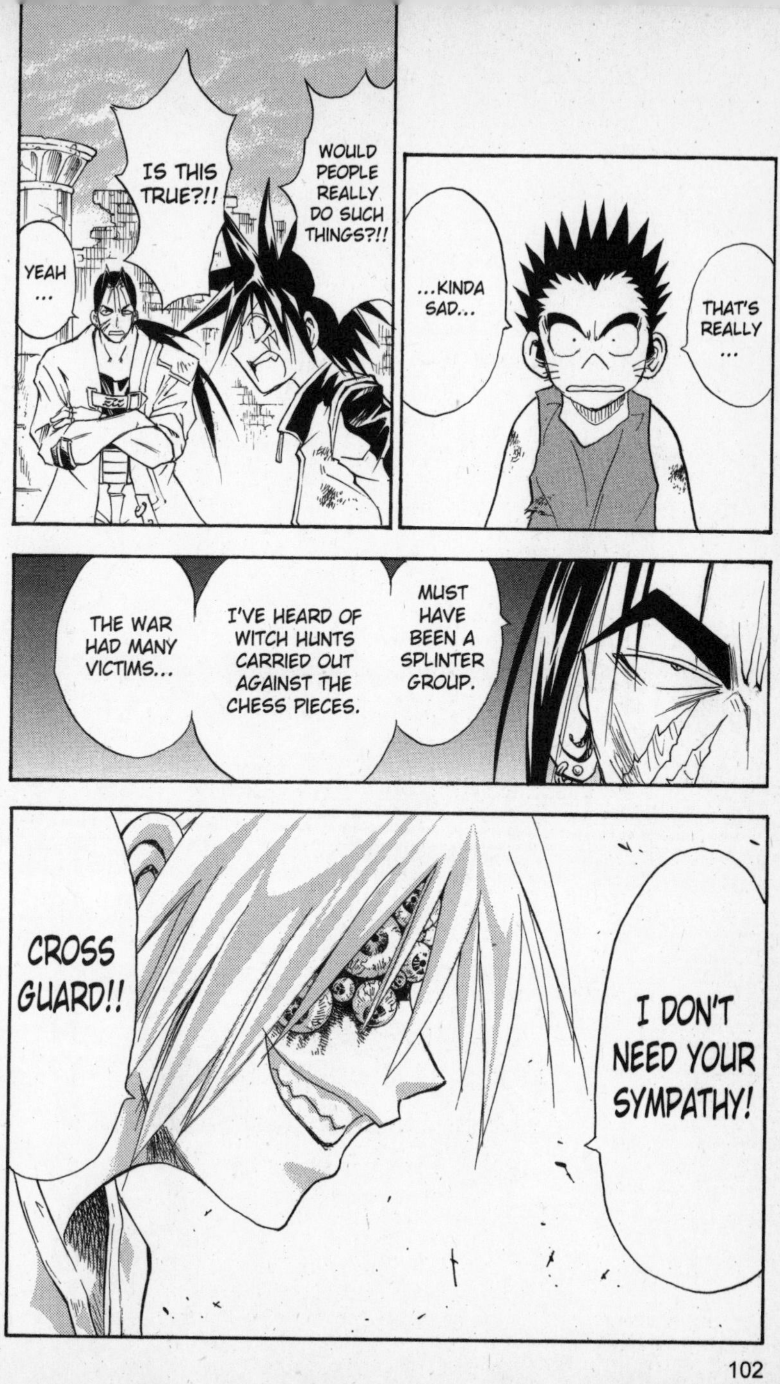
THAT'S REALLY ...
...KINDA SAD...
WOULD PEOPLE REALLY DO SUCH THINGS?!!
IS THIS TRUE?!!
YEAH ...
MUST HAVE BEEN A SPLINTER GROUP.
I'VE HEARD OF WITCH HUNTS CARRIED OUT AGAINST THE CHESS PIECES.
THE WAR HAD MANY VICTIMS...
I DON'T NEED YOUR SYMPATHY!
CROSS GUARD!!

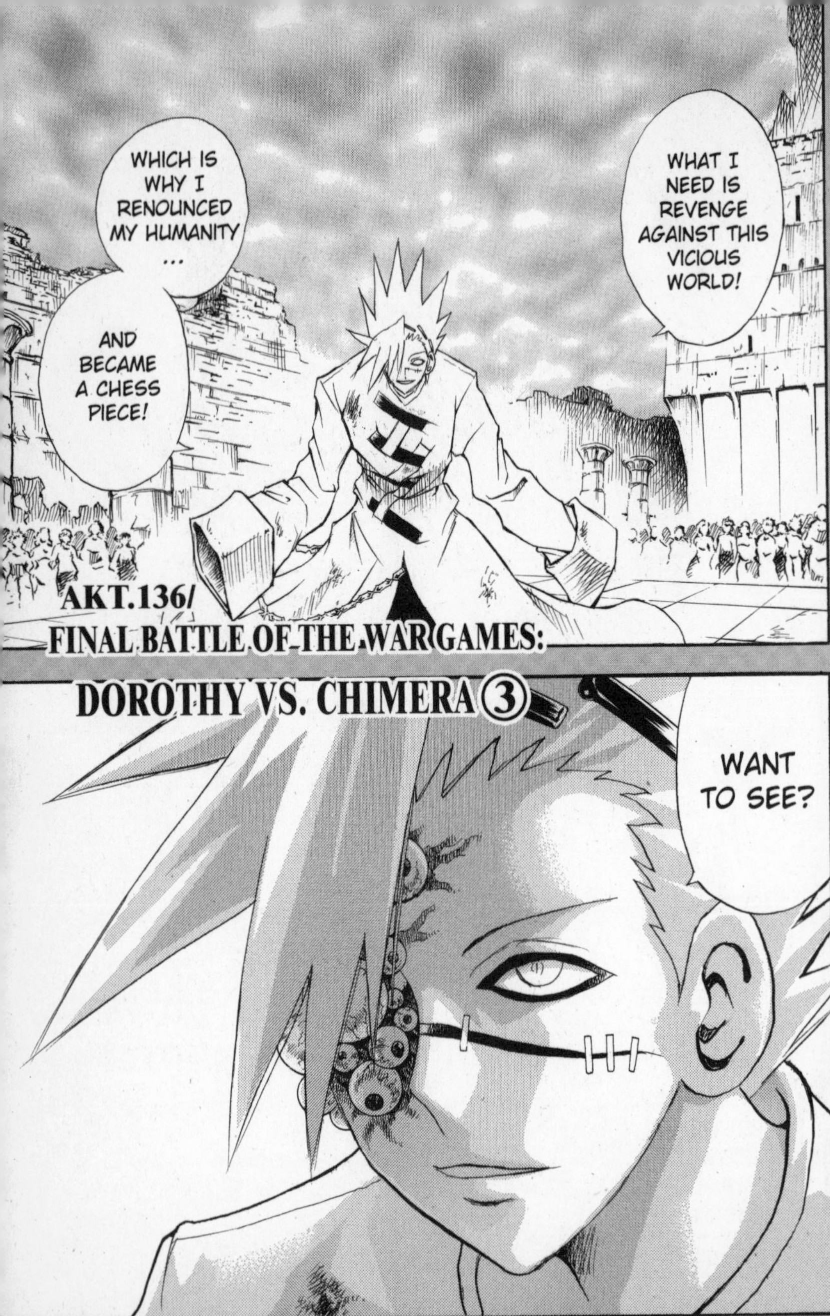
WHAT I NEED IS REVENGE AGAINST THIS VICIOUS WORLD!
WHICH IS WHY I RENOUNCED MY HUMANITY ...
AND BECAME A CHESS PIECE!
AKT.136/
FINAL BATTLE OF THE WAR GAMES:
DOROTHY VS. CHIMERA ③
WANT TO SEE?

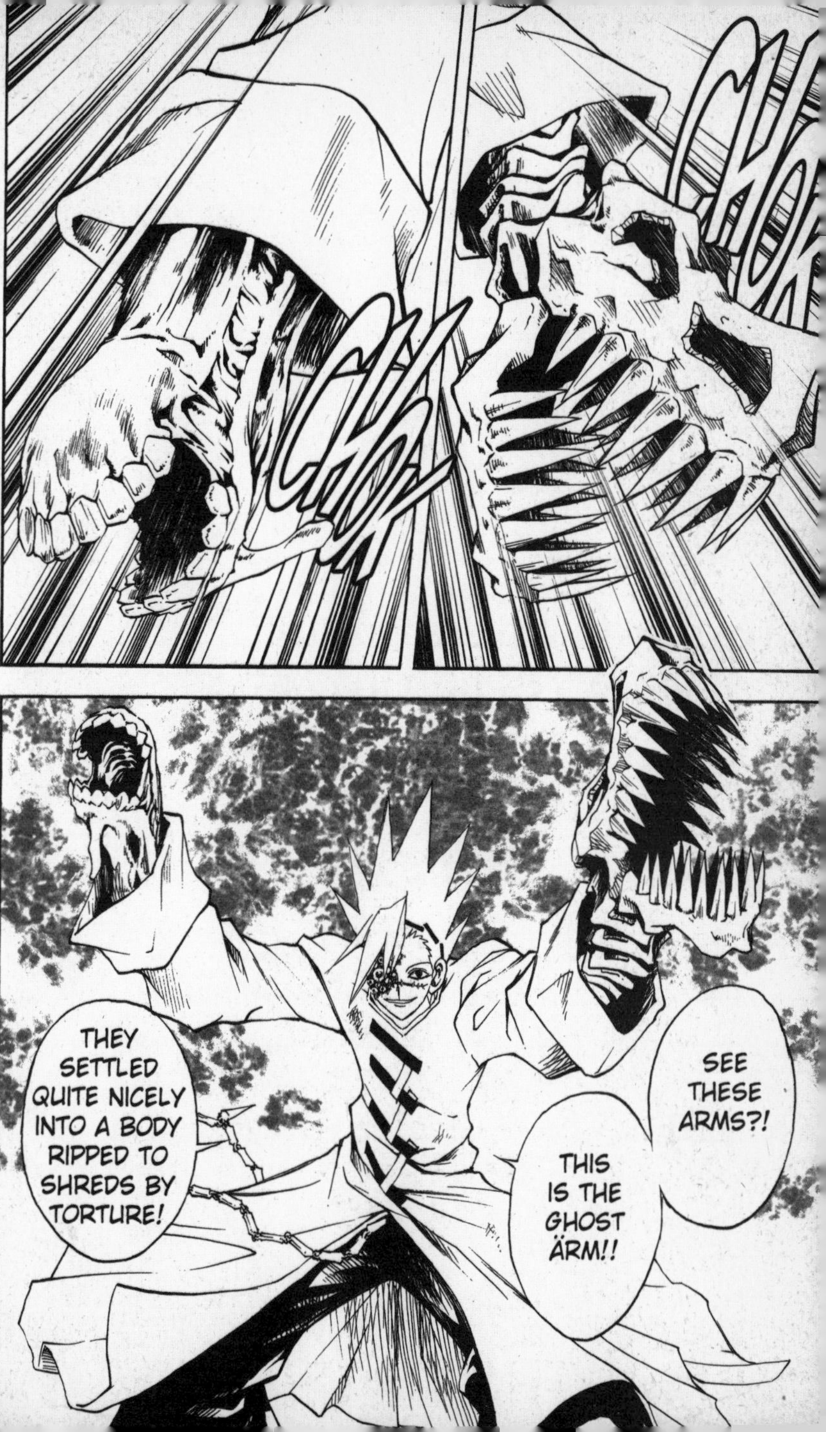
CHOK
CHOK
SEE THESE ARMS?!
THIS IS THE GHOST ÄRM!!
THEY SETTLED QUITE NICELY INTO A BODY RIPPED TO SHREDS BY TORTURE!

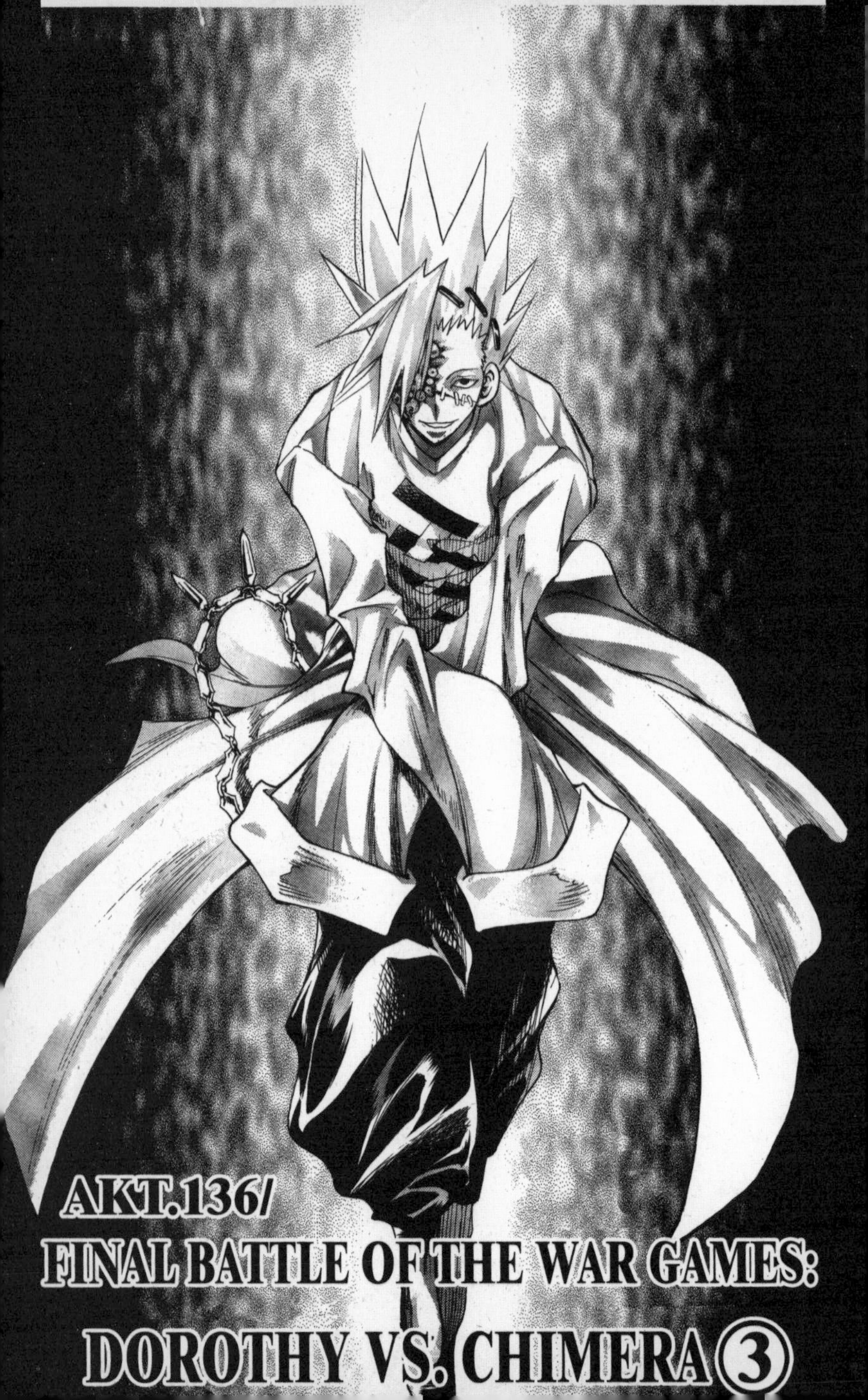
AKT.136/
FINAL BATTLE OF THE WAR GAMES:
DOROTHY VS. CHIMERA ③

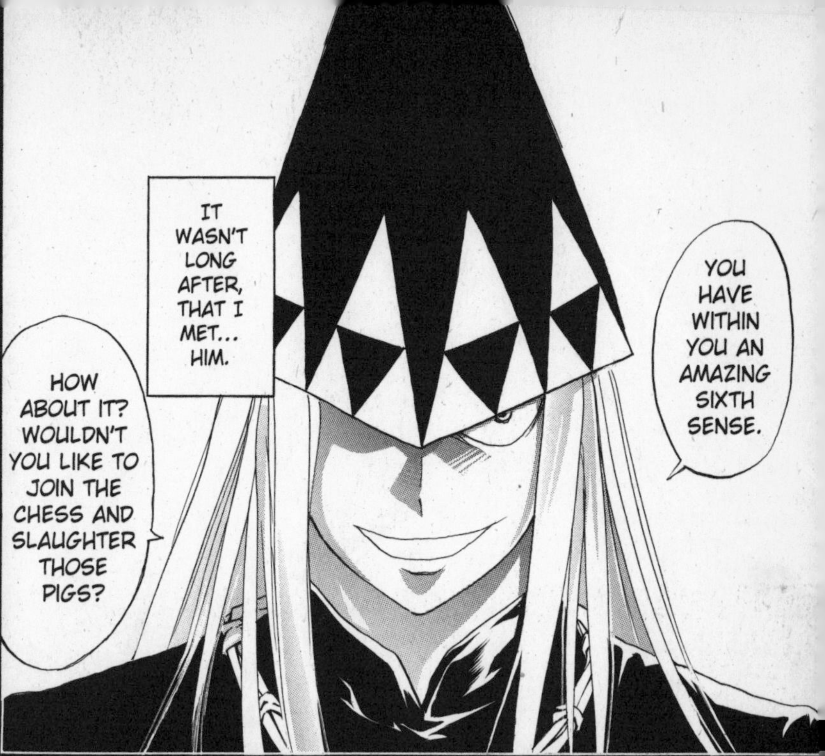
IT WASN'T LONG AFTER, THAT I MET... HIM.
YOU HAVE WITHIN YOU AN AMAZING SIXTH SENSE.
HOW ABOUT IT? WOULDN'T YOU LIKE TO JOIN THE CHESS AND SLAUGHTER THOSE PIGS?
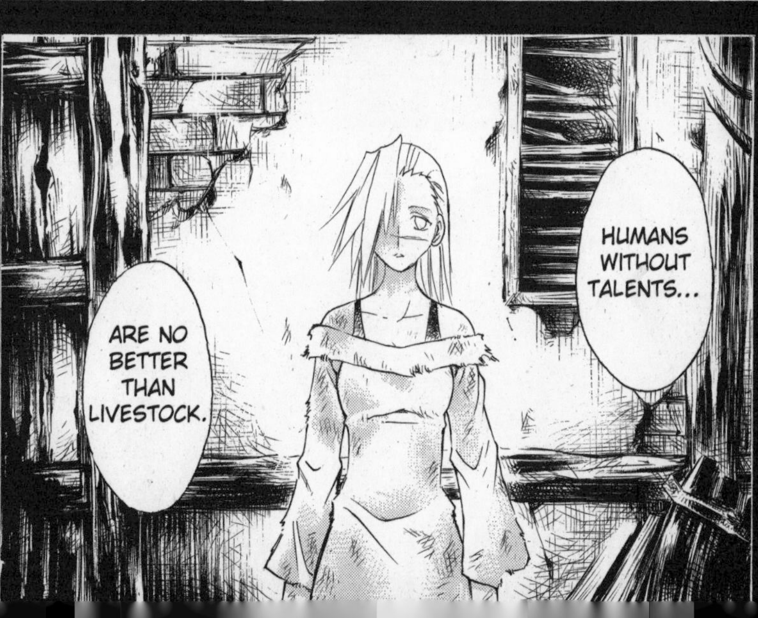
HUMANS WITHOUT TALENTS...
ARE NO BETTER THAN LIVESTOCK.

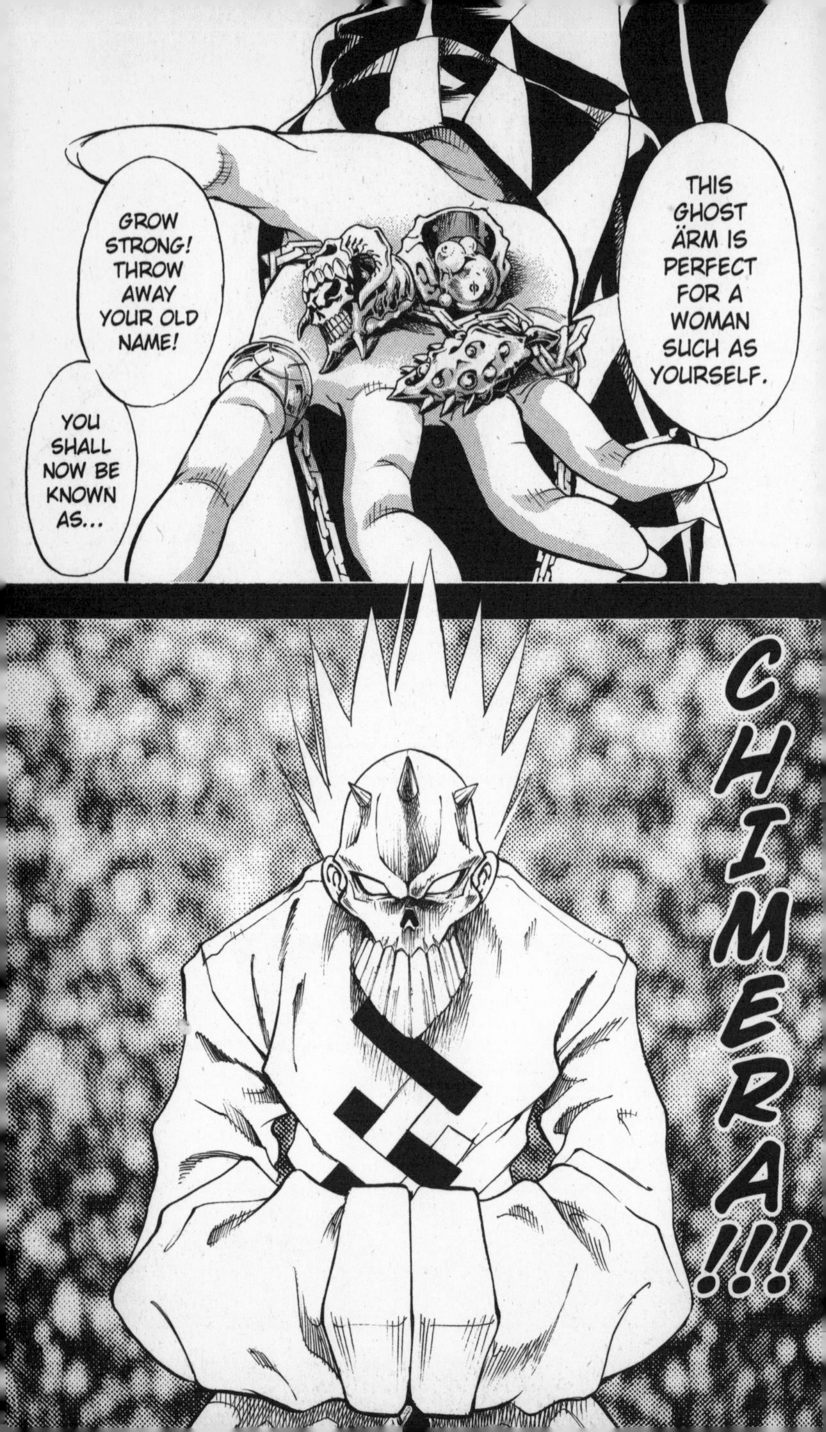
THIS GHOST ÄRM IS PERFECT FOR A WOMAN SUCH AS YOURSELF.
GROW STRONG! THROW AWAY YOUR OLD NAME!
YOU SHALL NOW BE KNOWN AS...
CHIMERA!!!

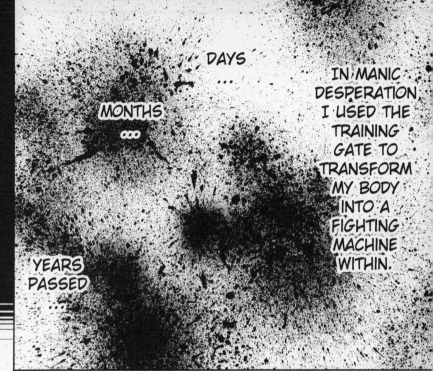

DAYS
...

MONTHS
...

YEARS
PASSED
...

IN MANIC
DESPERATION
I USED THE
TRAINING
GATE TO
TRANSFORM
MY BODY
INTO A
FIGHTING
MACHINE
WITHIN.

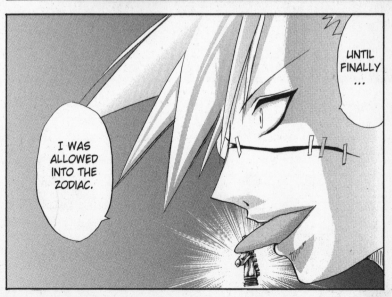

UNTIL
FINALLY
...

I WAS
ALLOWED
INTO THE
ZODIAC.

108

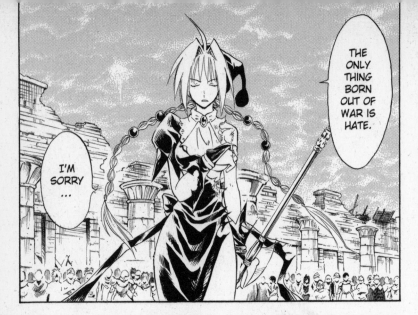

THE ONLY THING BORN OUT OF WAR IS HATE.

I'M SORRY...

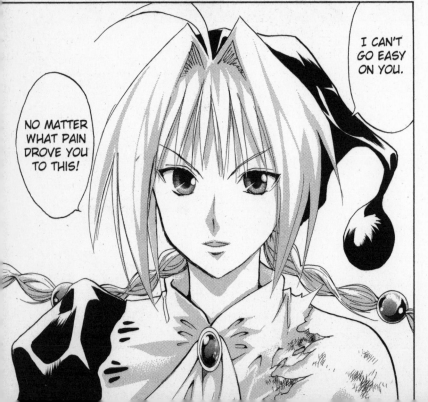

I CAN'T GO EASY ON YOU.

NO MATTER WHAT PAIN DROVE YOU TO THIS!

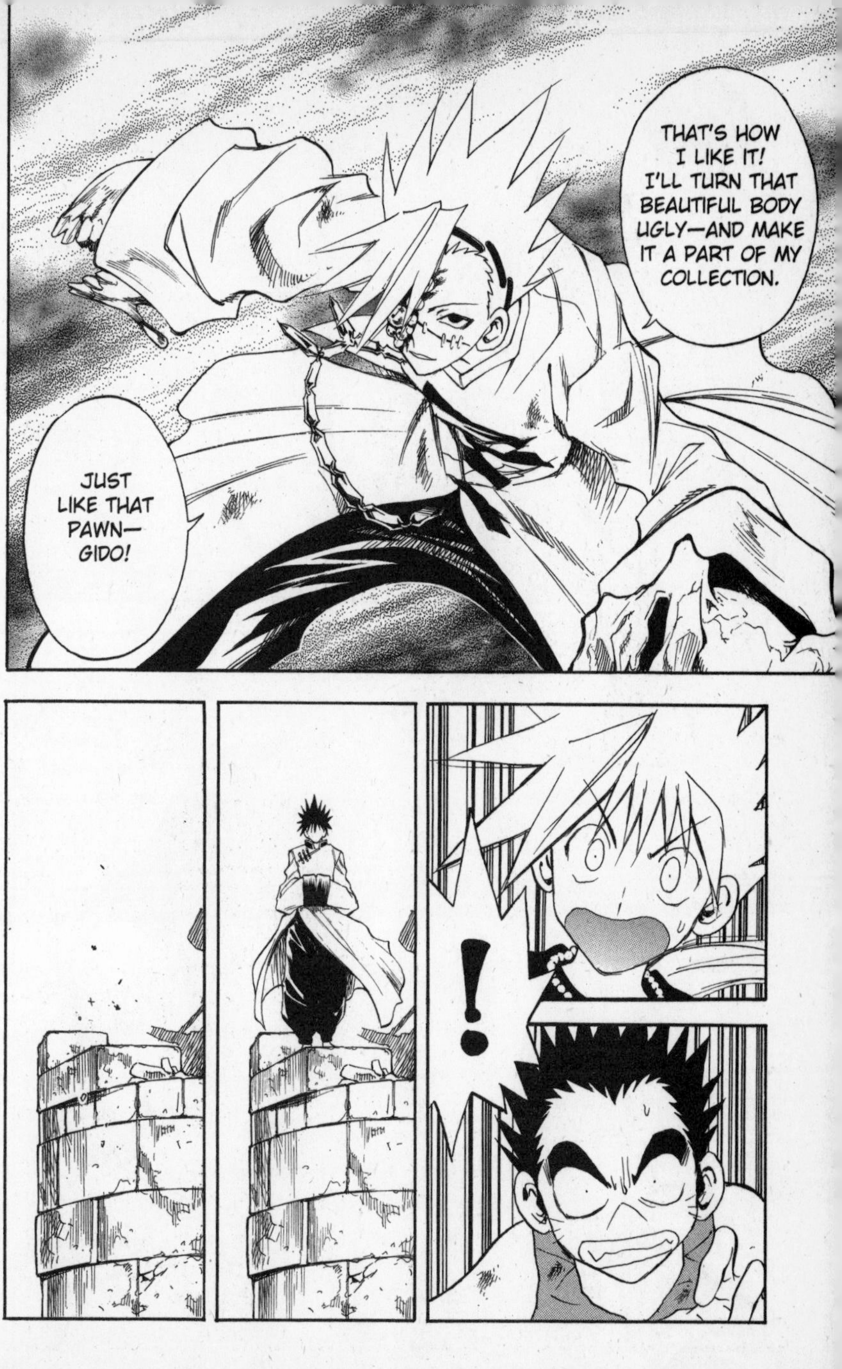
THAT'S HOW I LIKE IT! I'LL TURN THAT BEAUTIFUL BODY UGLY—AND MAKE IT A PART OF MY COLLECTION.
JUST LIKE THAT PAWN—GIDO!
!

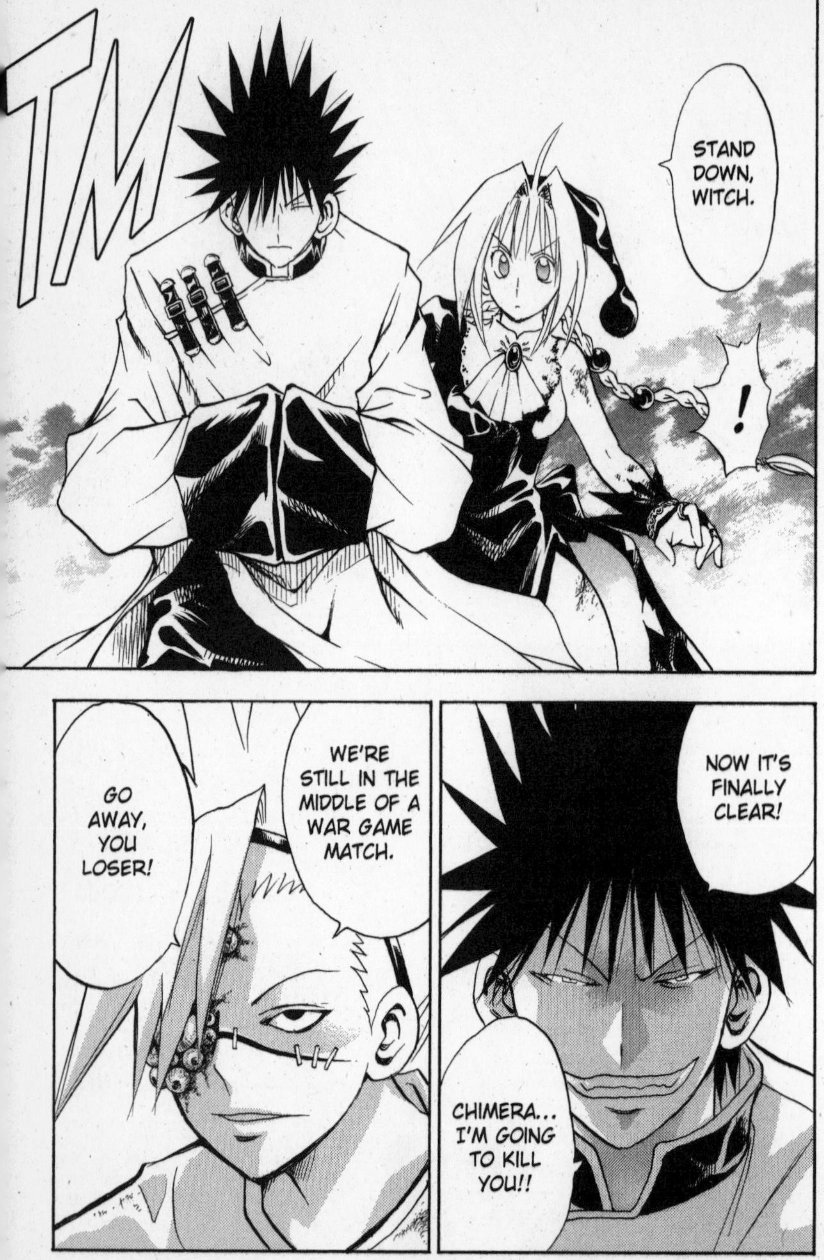
STAND DOWN, WITCH.
!
TM
NOW IT'S FINALLY CLEAR!
CHIMERA... I'M GOING TO KILL YOU!!
WE'RE STILL IN THE MIDDLE OF A WAR GAME MATCH.
GO AWAY, YOU LOSER!

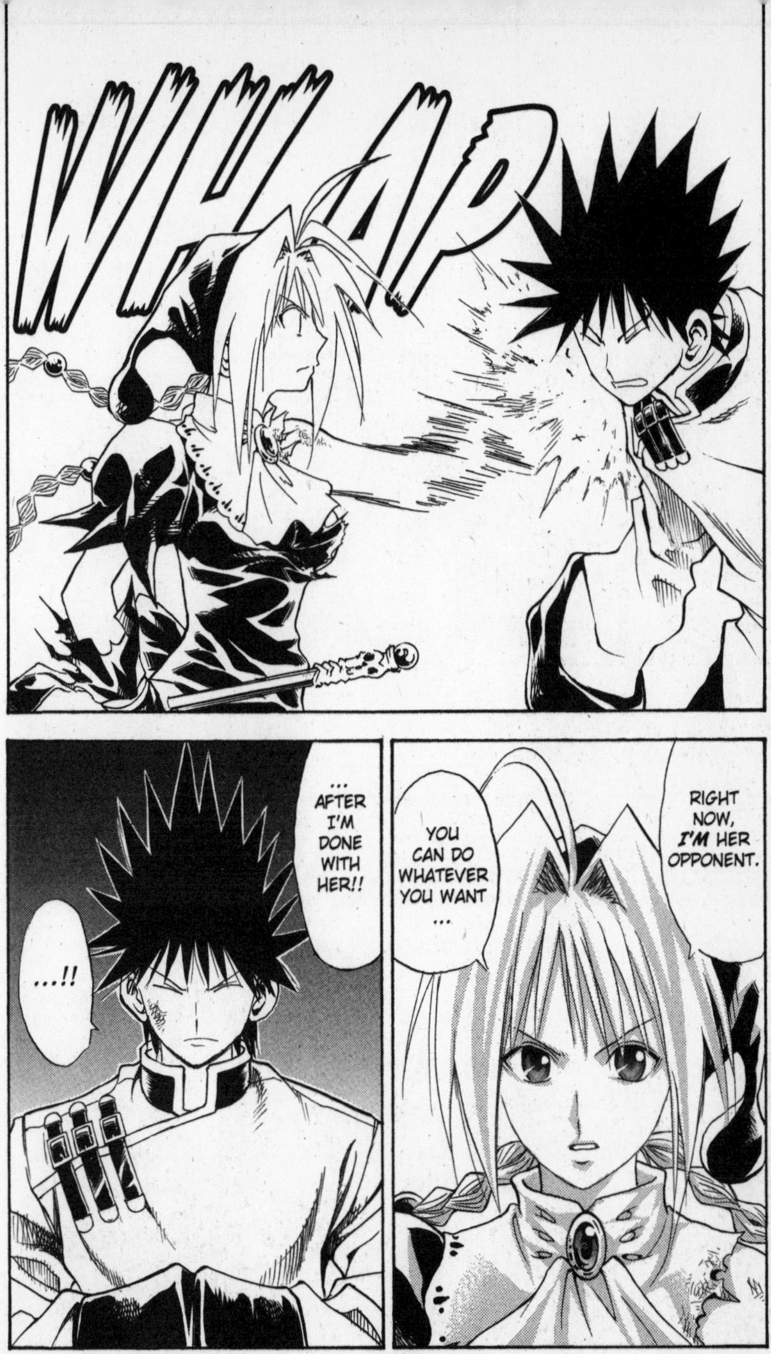
WHAP
RIGHT NOW, *I'M* HER OPPONENT.
YOU CAN DO WHATEVER YOU WANT ...
... AFTER I'M DONE WITH HER!!
...!!

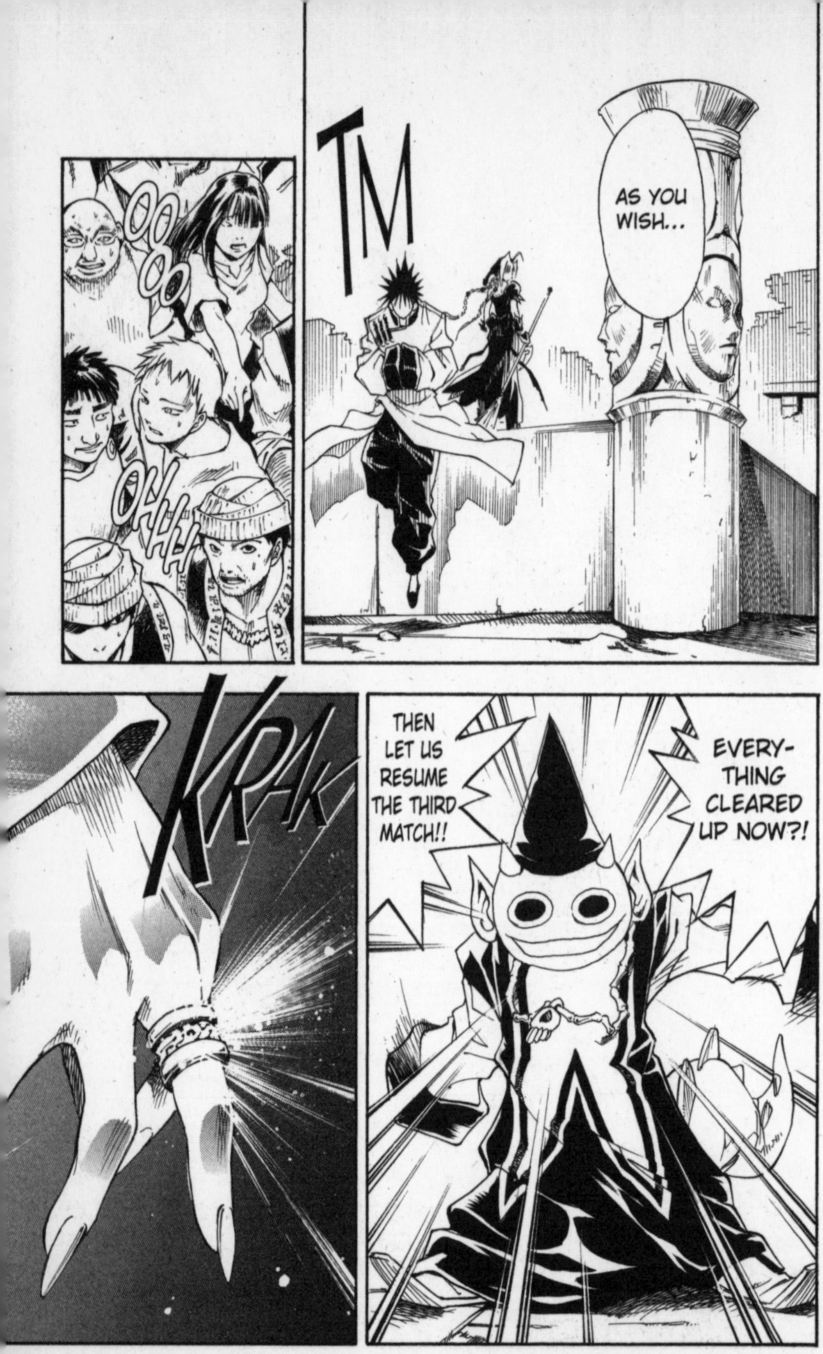
AS YOU WISH...
TM
OOOO
OHHH
EVERY-THING CLEARED UP NOW?!
THEN LET US RESUME THE THIRD MATCH!!
KRAK

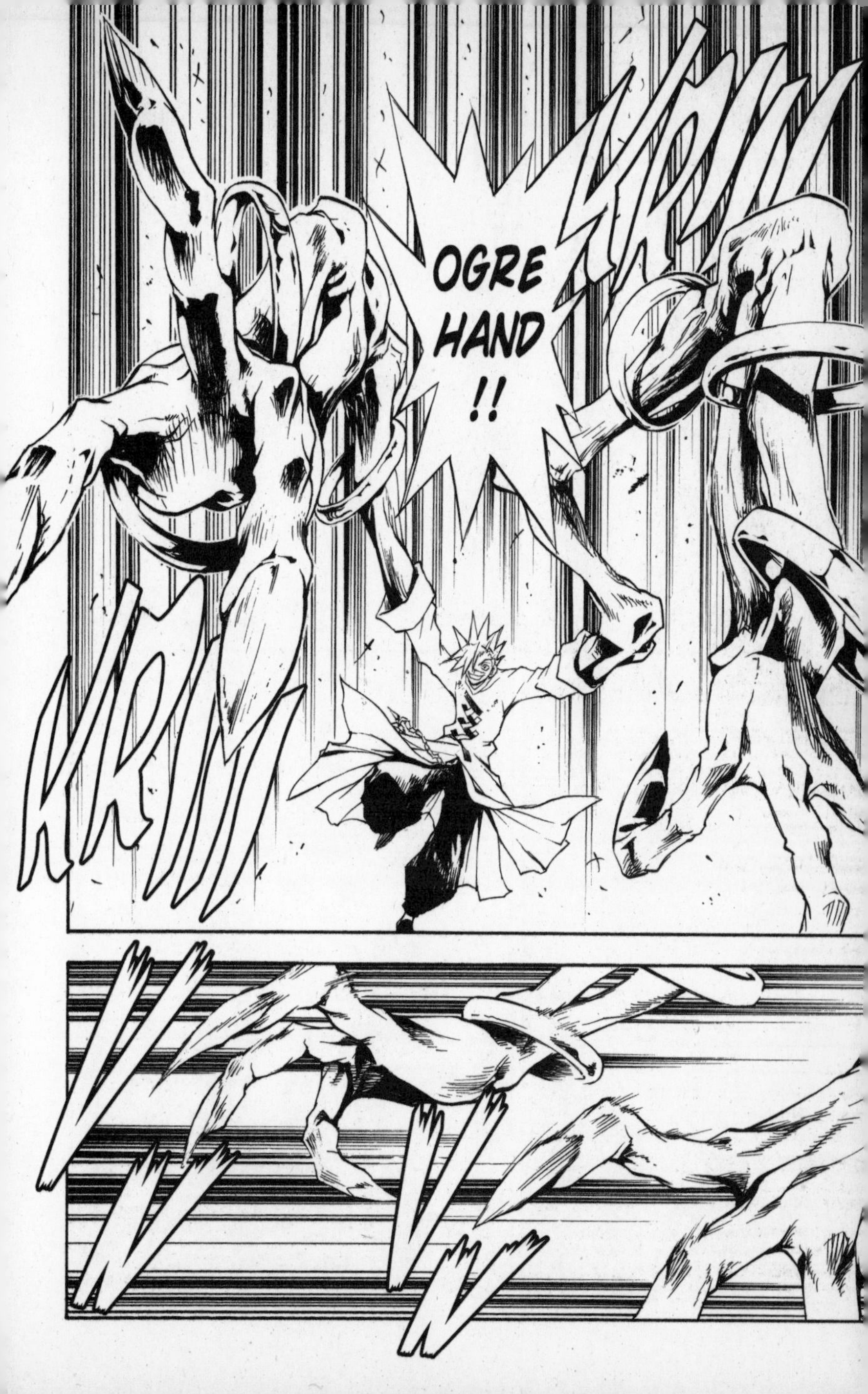
OGRE HAND !!

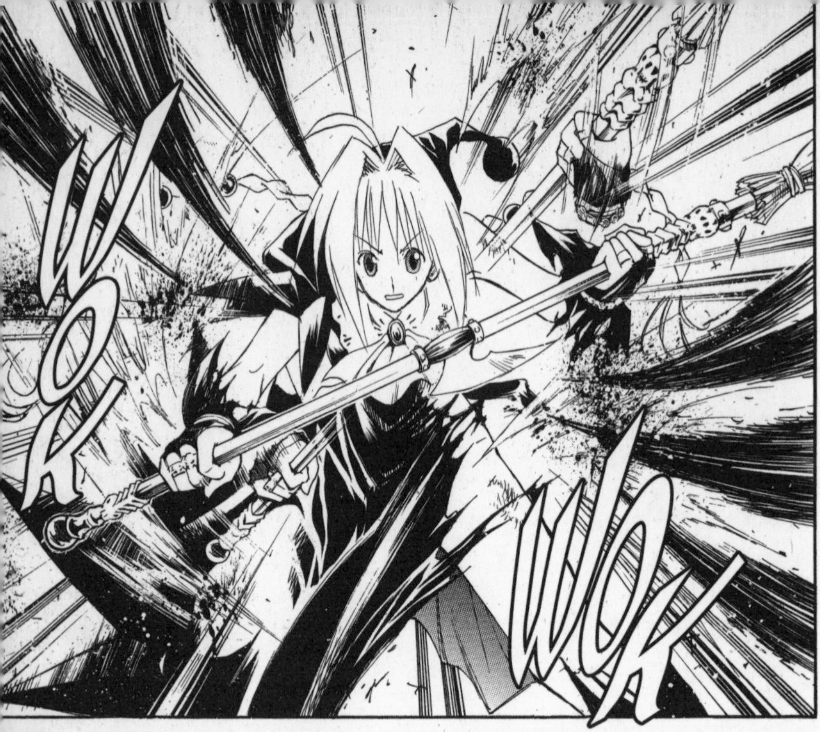
WOK
WOK
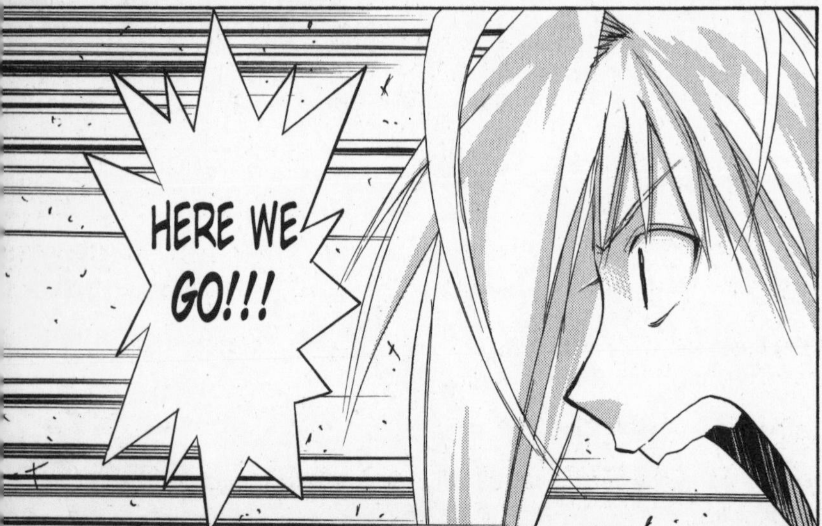
HERE WE GO!!!

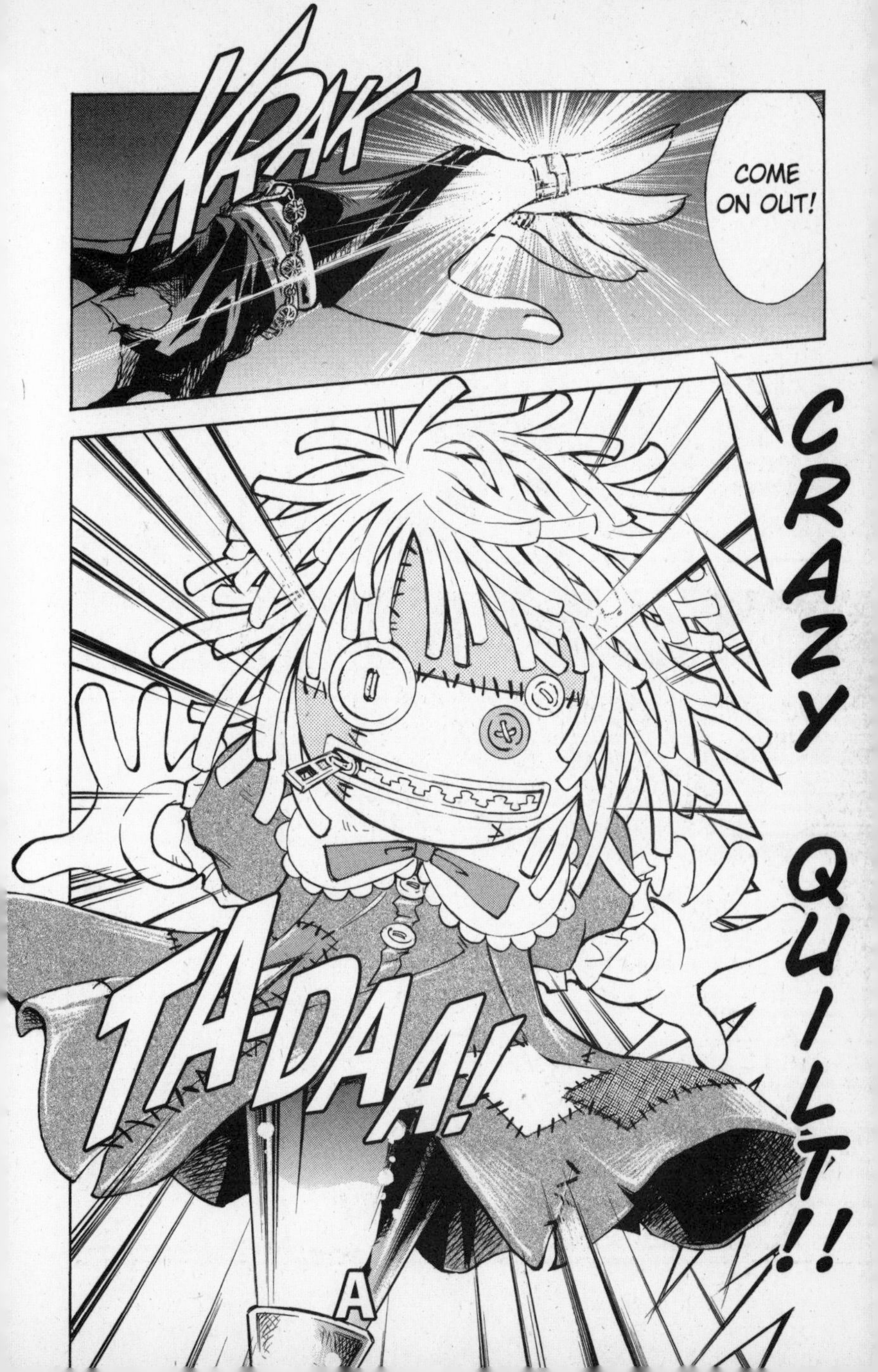
KRAK
COME ON OUT!
CRAZY QUILT!!
TA-DAA!
A

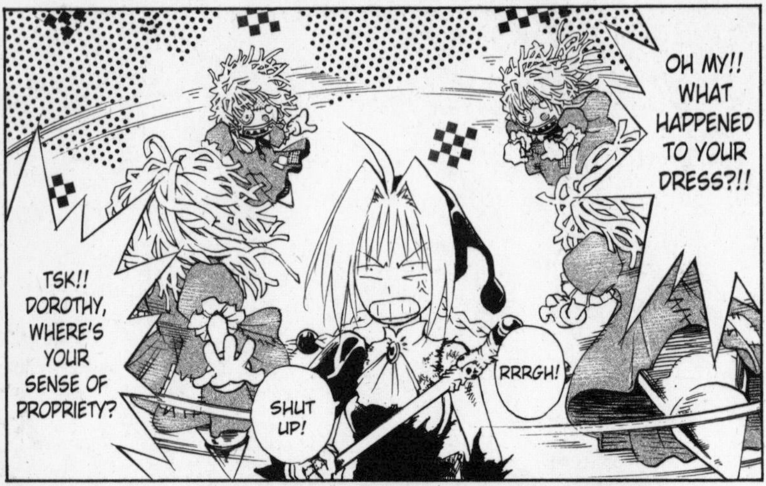
OH MY!! WHAT HAPPENED TO YOUR DRESS?!!
RRRGH!
TSK!! DOROTHY, WHERE'S YOUR SENSE OF PROPRIETY?
SHUT UP!

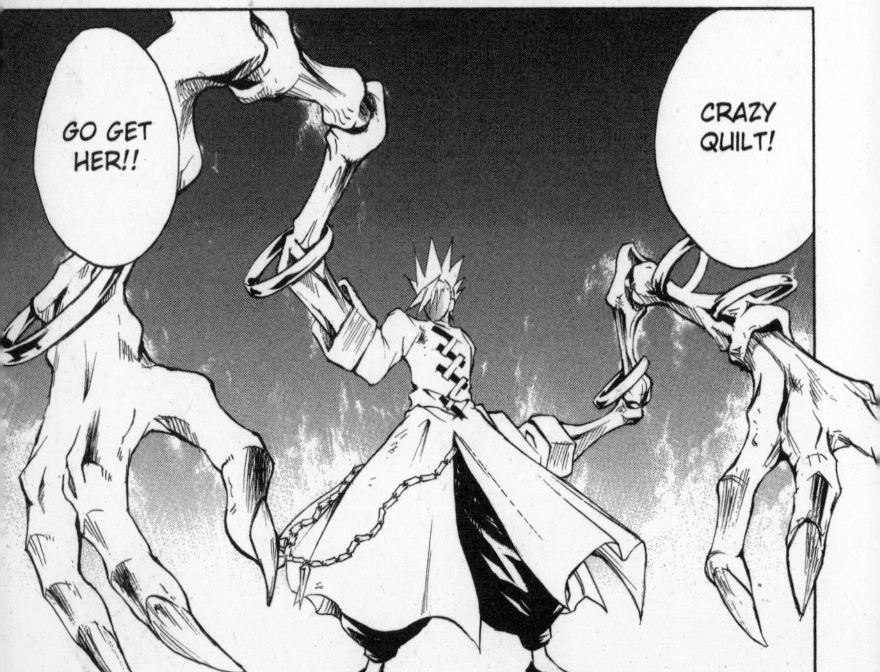
CRAZY QUILT!
GO GET HER!!

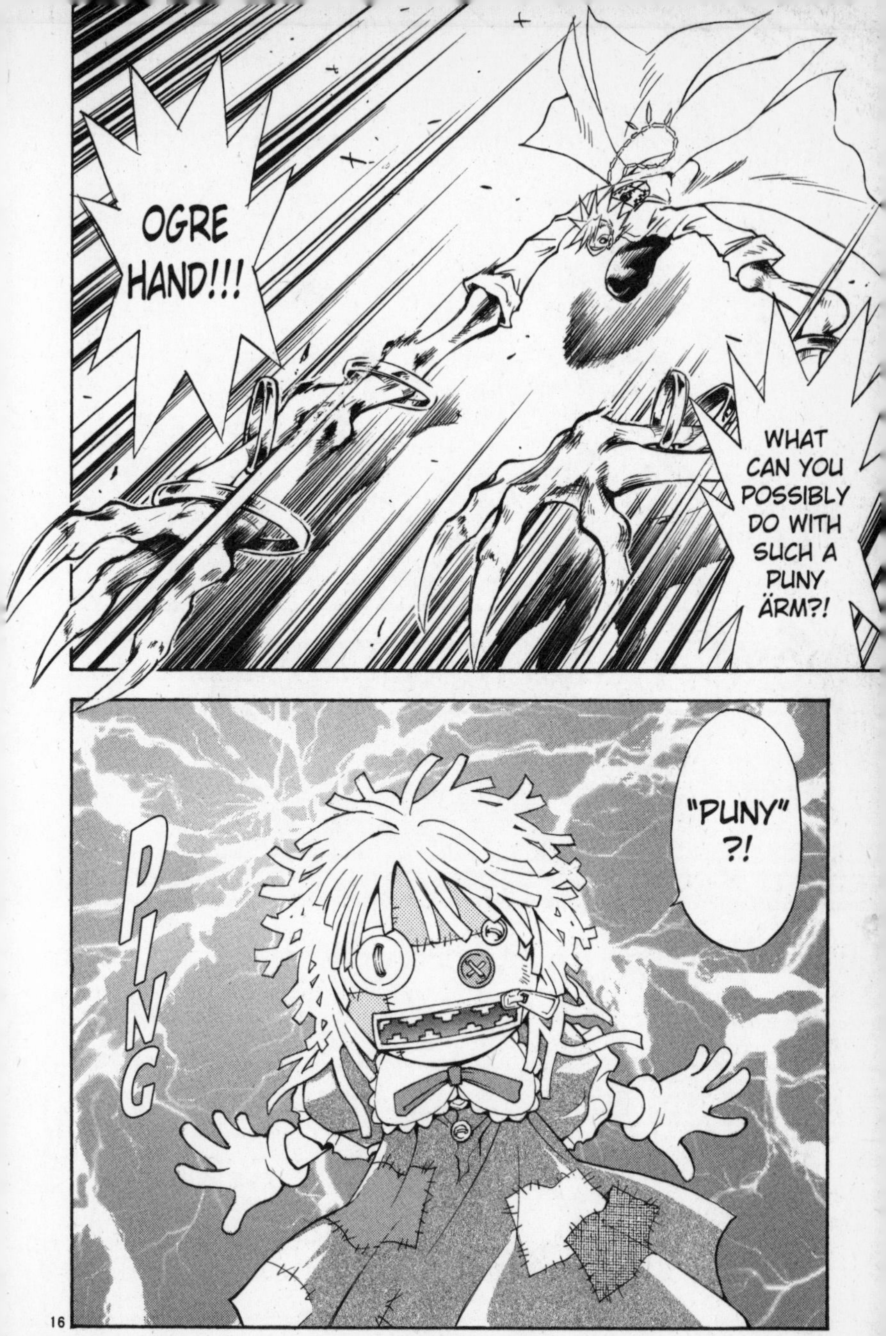
OGRE HAND!!!
WHAT CAN YOU POSSIBLY DO WITH SUCH A PUNY ÄRM?!
"PUNY" ?!
PING

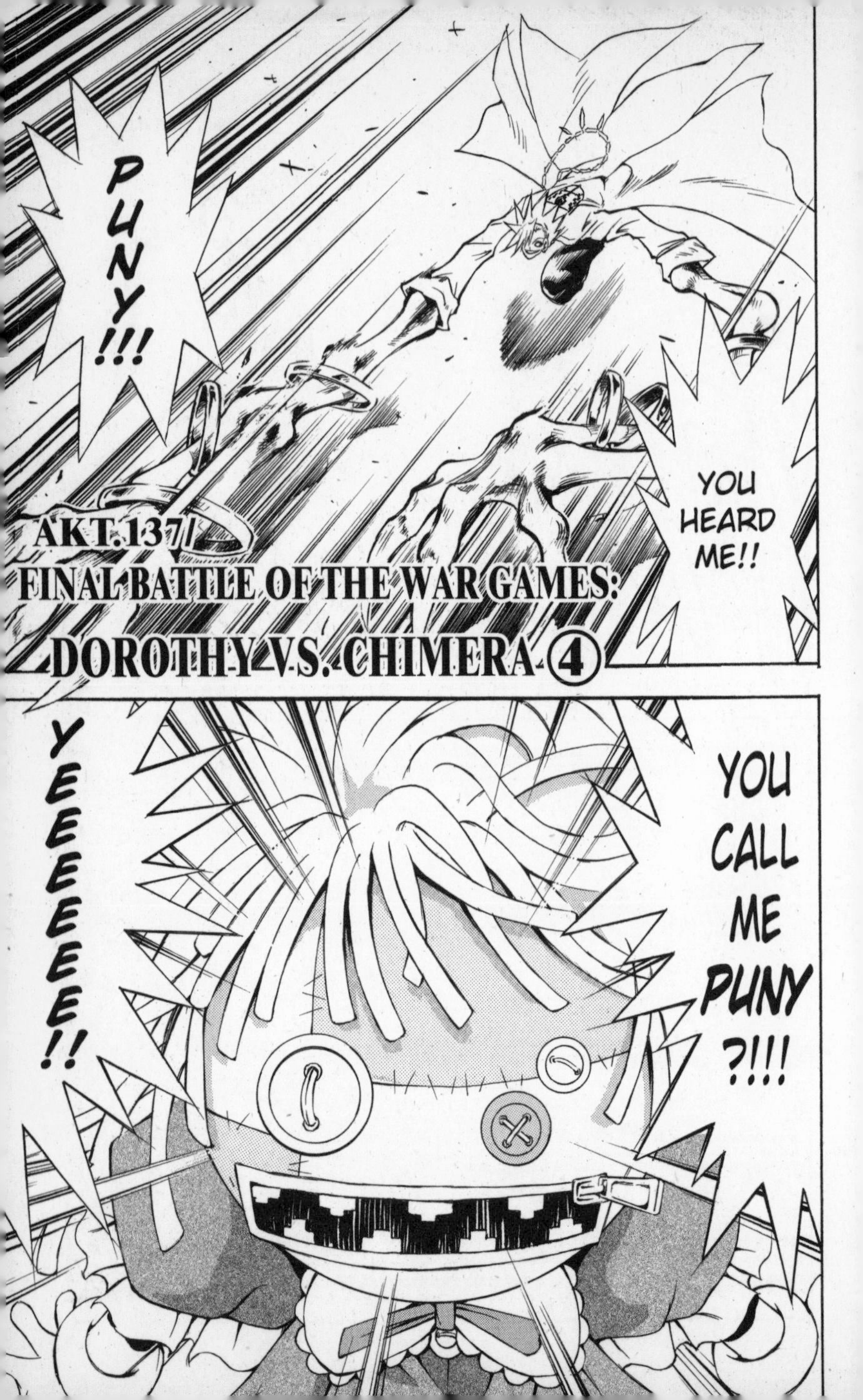
PUNY!!!
YOU HEARD ME!!
AKT.137/
FINAL BATTLE OF THE WAR GAMES:
DOROTHY VS. CHIMERA ④
YOU CALL ME PUNY?!!!
YEEEEEEE!!

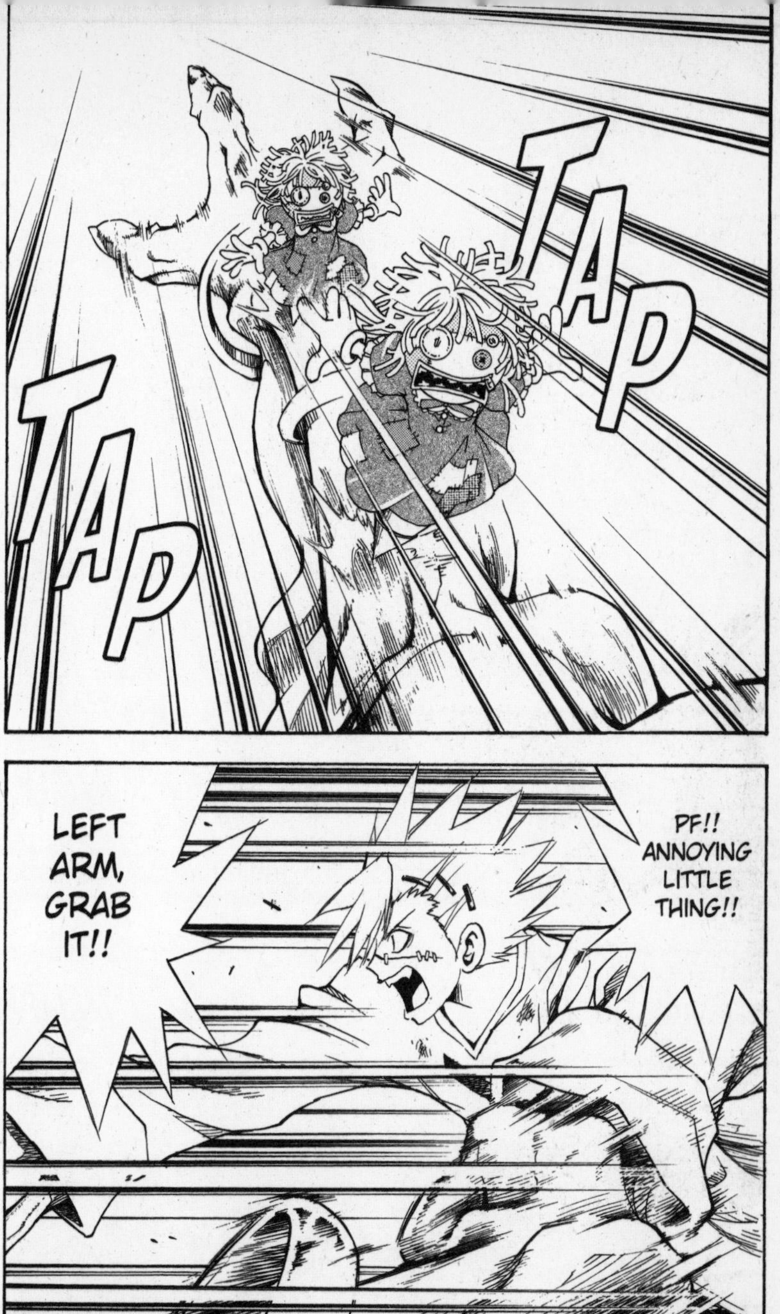

TAP
TAP
PF!! ANNOYING LITTLE THING!!
LEFT ARM, GRAB IT!!

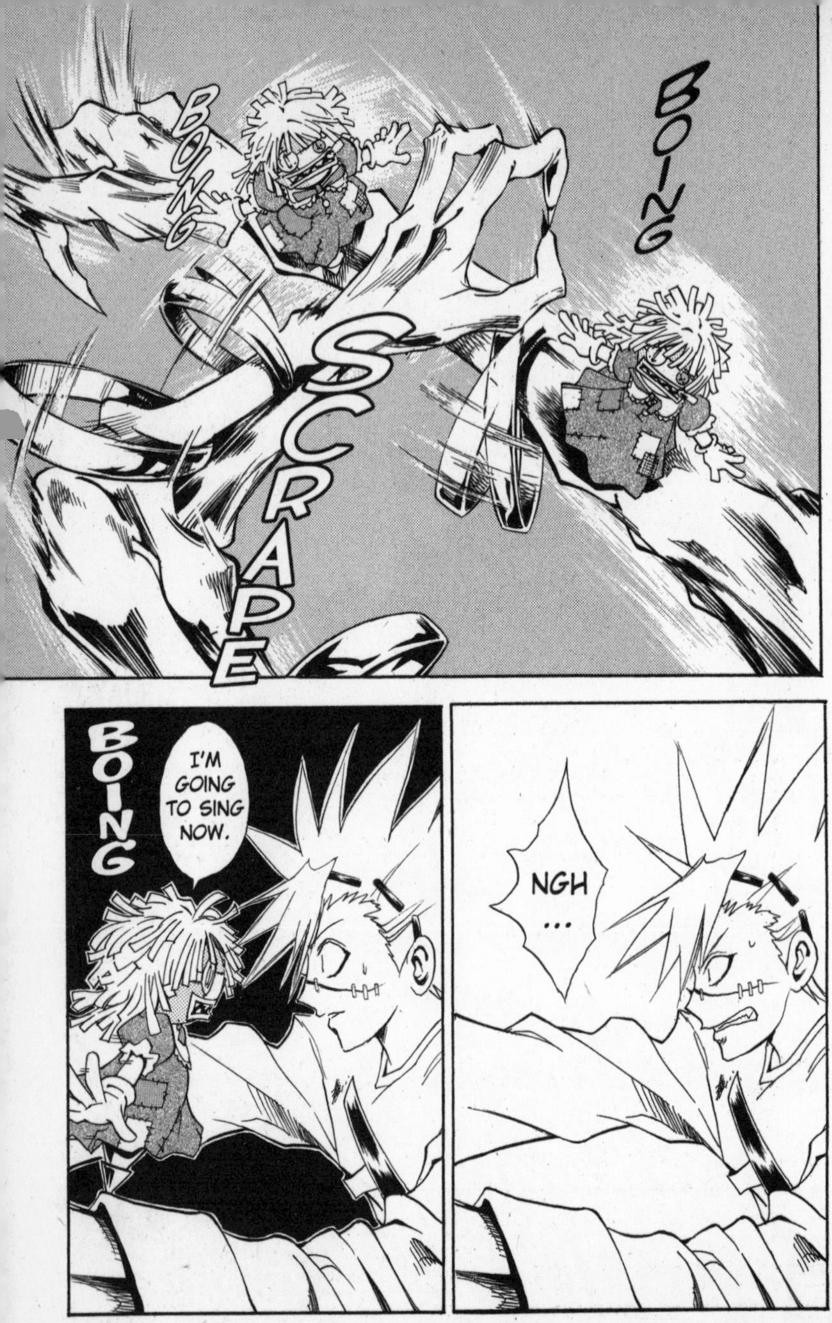
BOING
BOING
SCRAPE
NGH ...
BOING
I'M GOING TO SING NOW.

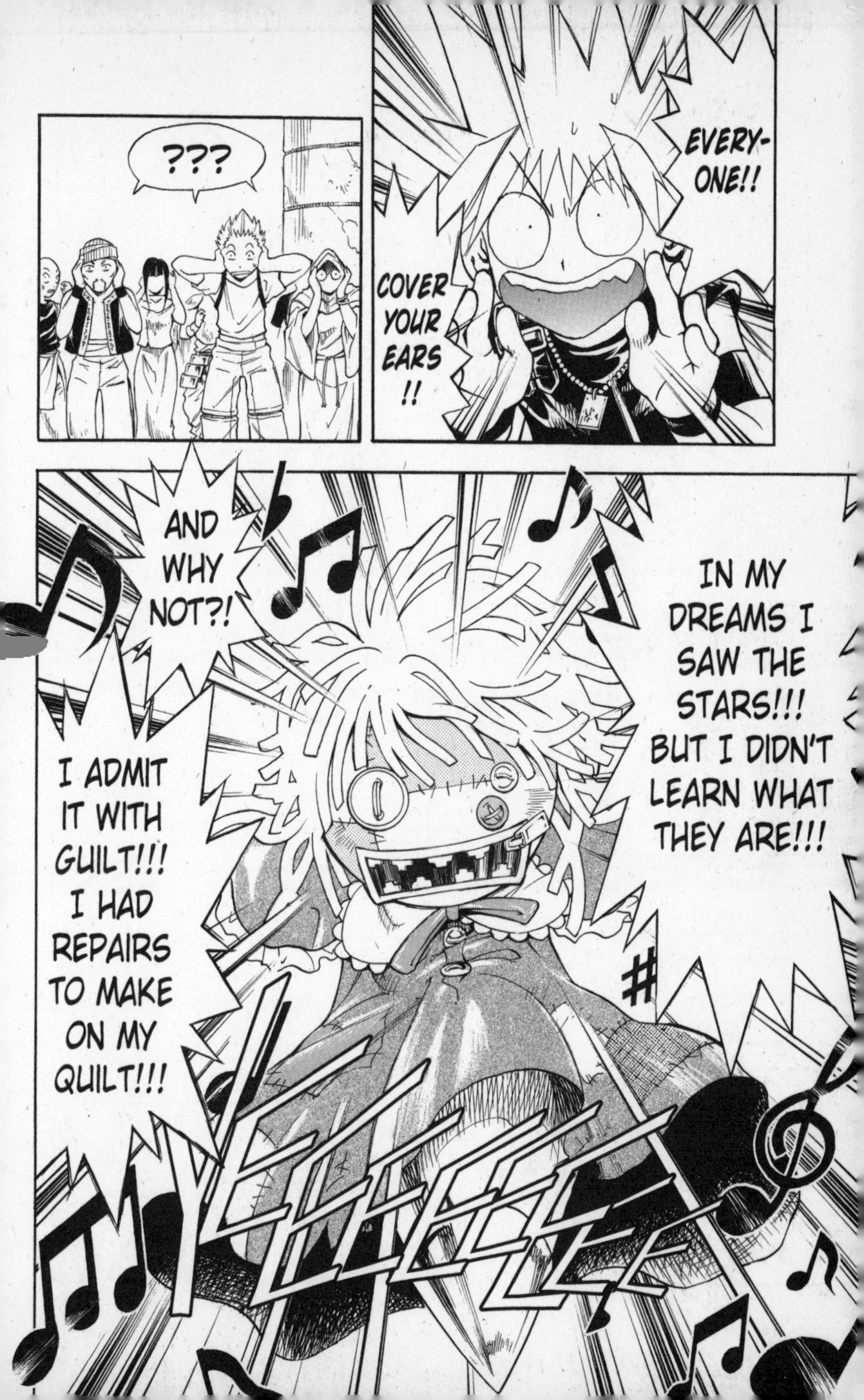
EVERY-ONE!!
COVER YOUR EARS !!
???
IN MY DREAMS I SAW THE STARS!!! BUT I DIDN'T LEARN WHAT THEY ARE!!!
AND WHY NOT?!
I ADMIT IT WITH GUILT!!! I HAD REPAIRS TO MAKE ON MY QUILT!!!

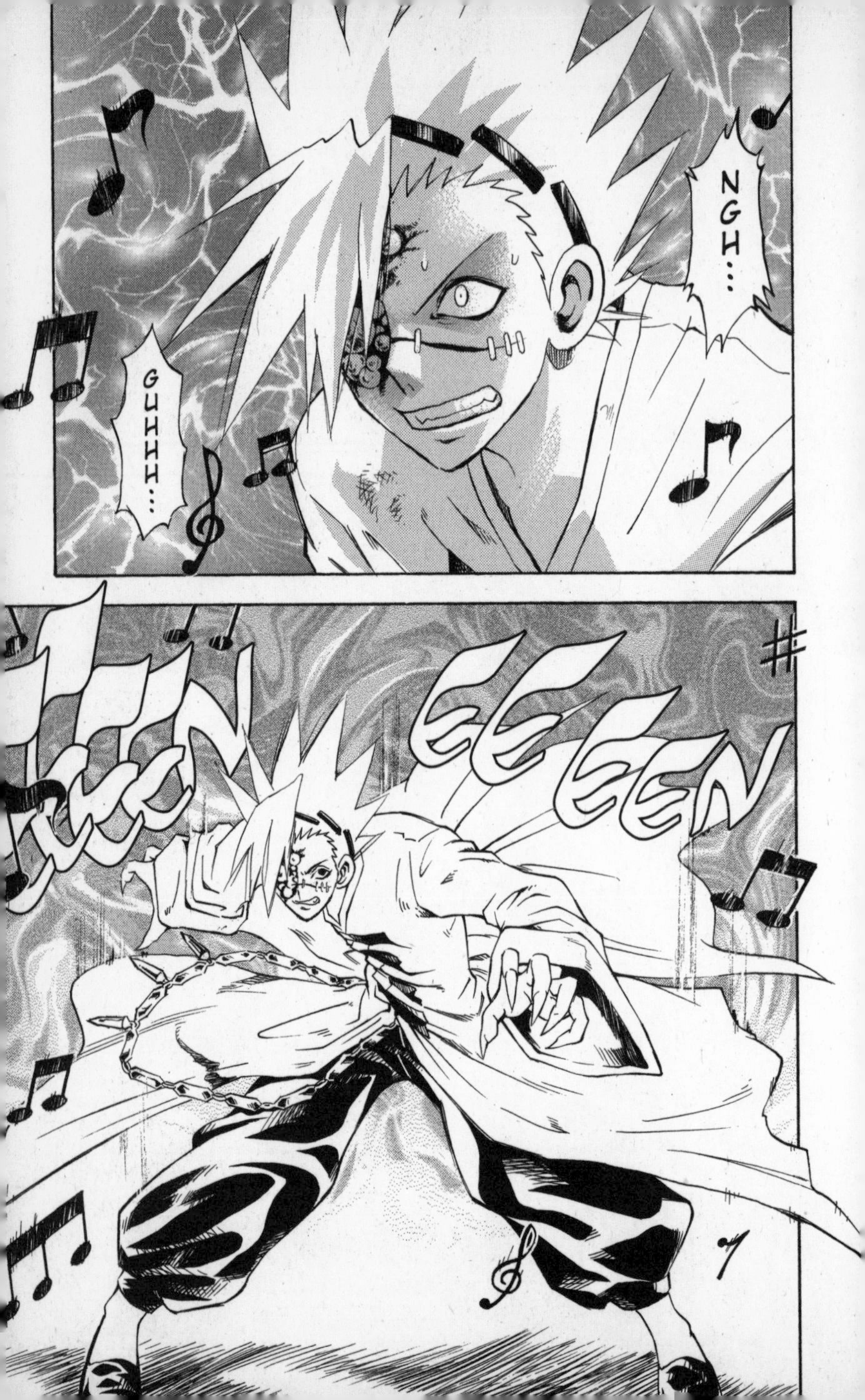
NGH...
GUHHH...

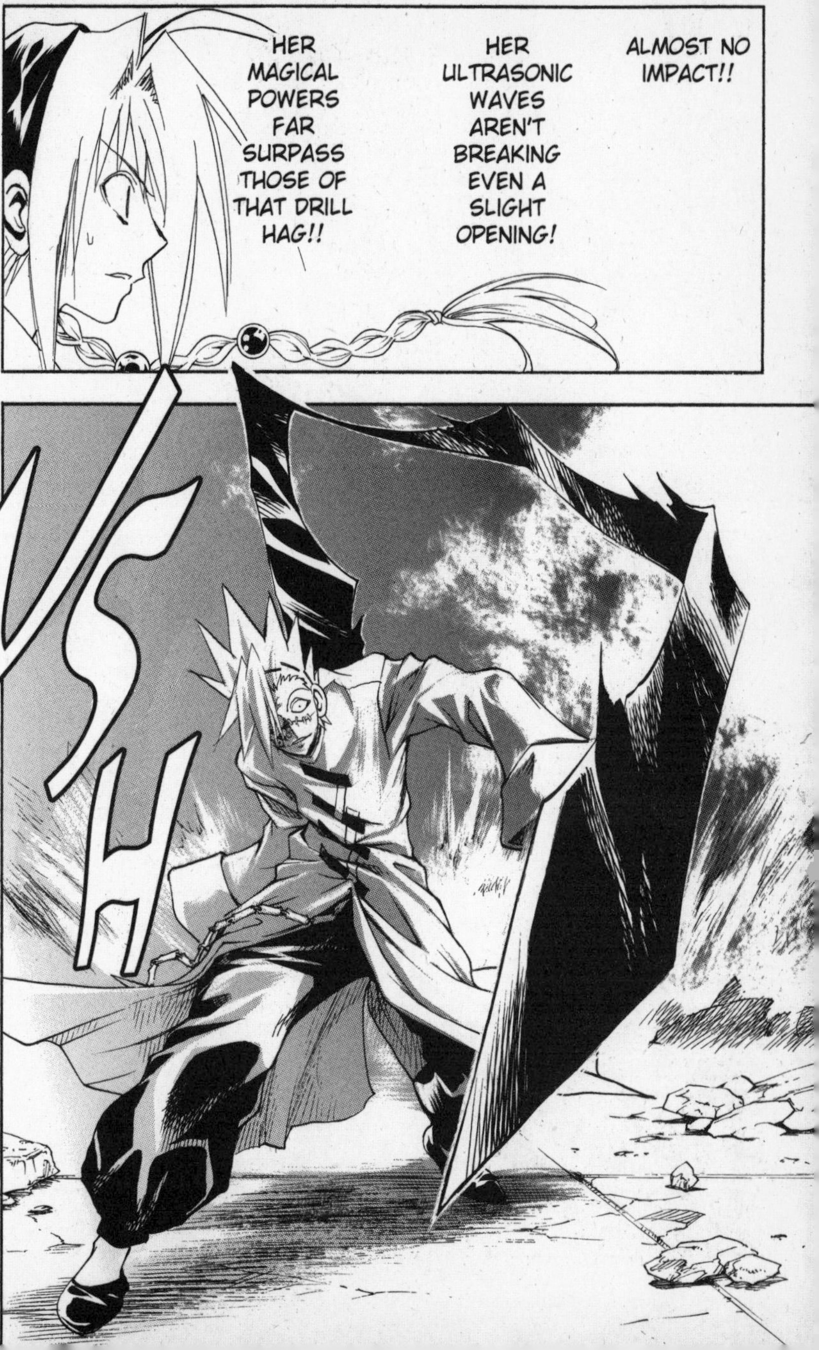
ALMOST NO IMPACT!!
HER ULTRASONIC WAVES AREN'T BREAKING EVEN A SLIGHT OPENING!
HER MAGICAL POWERS FAR SURPASS THOSE OF THAT DRILL HAG!!
VSH

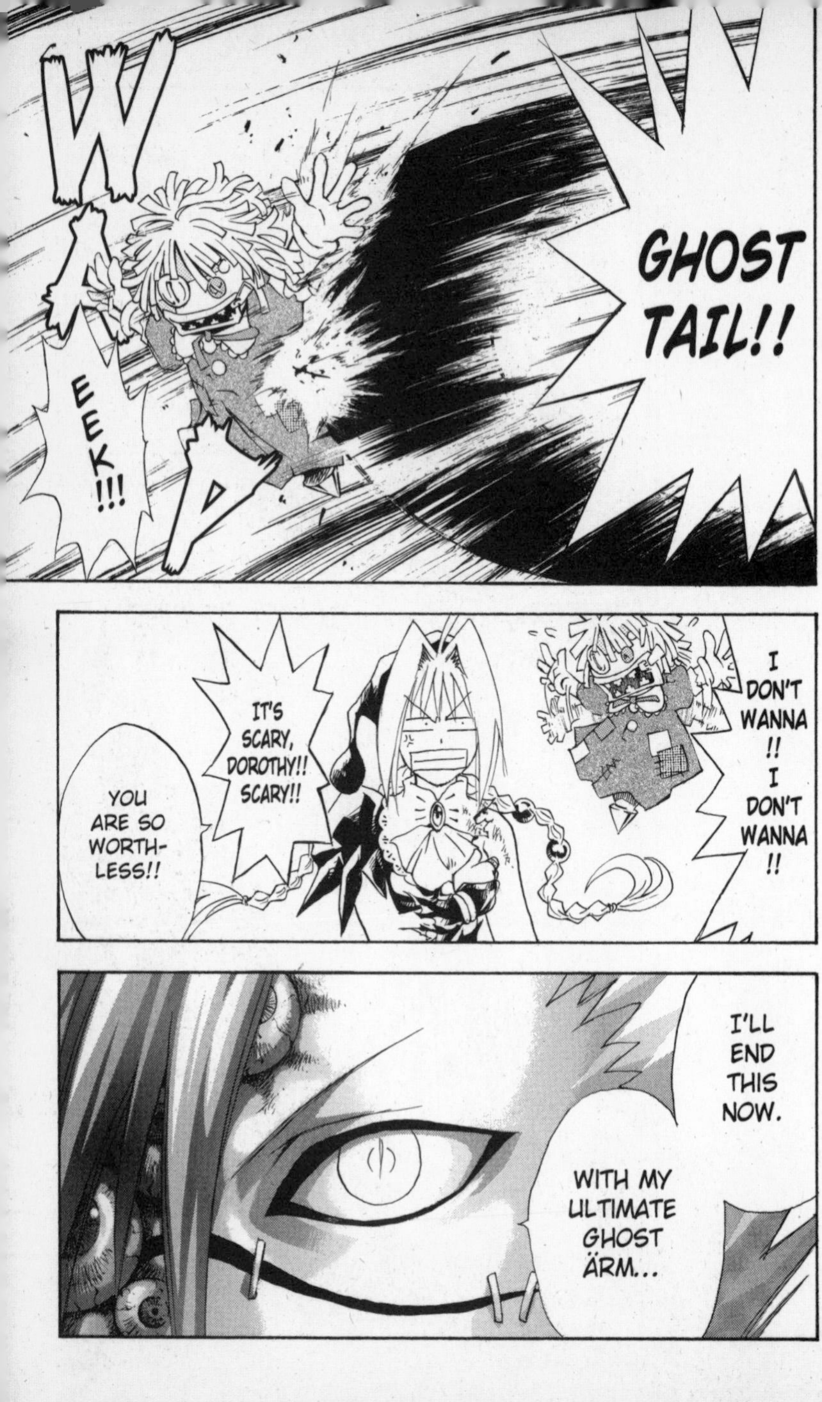
GHOST TAIL!!
WA
EEK!!!
I DON'T WANNA!! I DON'T WANNA!!
IT'S SCARY, DOROTHY!! SCARY!!
YOU ARE SO WORTH-LESS!!
I'LL END THIS NOW.
WITH MY ULTIMATE GHOST ÄRM...

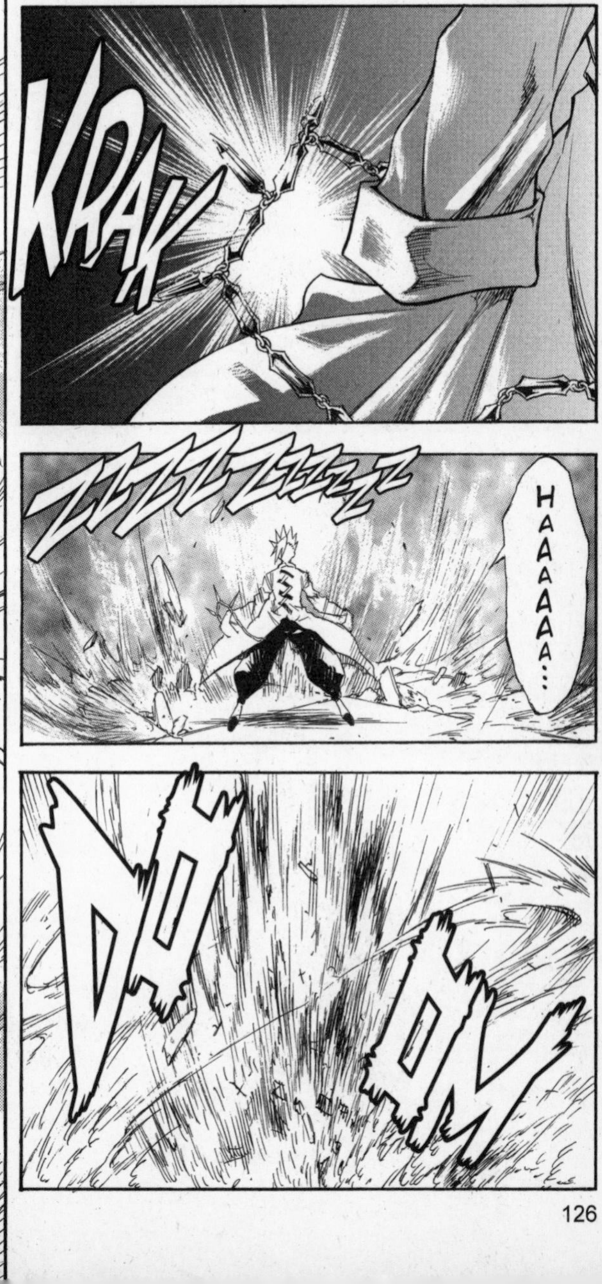
KRAK
ZZZZZZZZZZ
HAAAAAA...
DO
ON
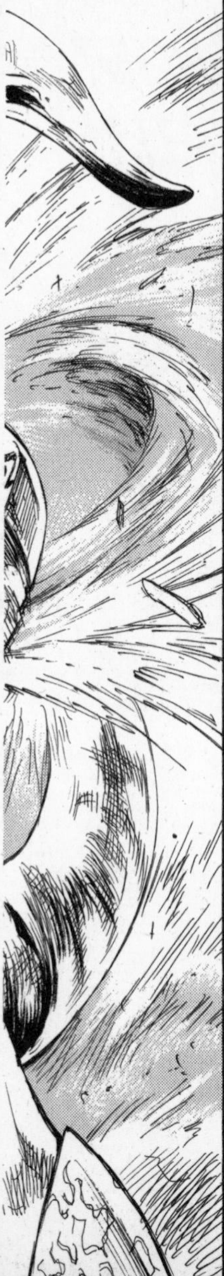

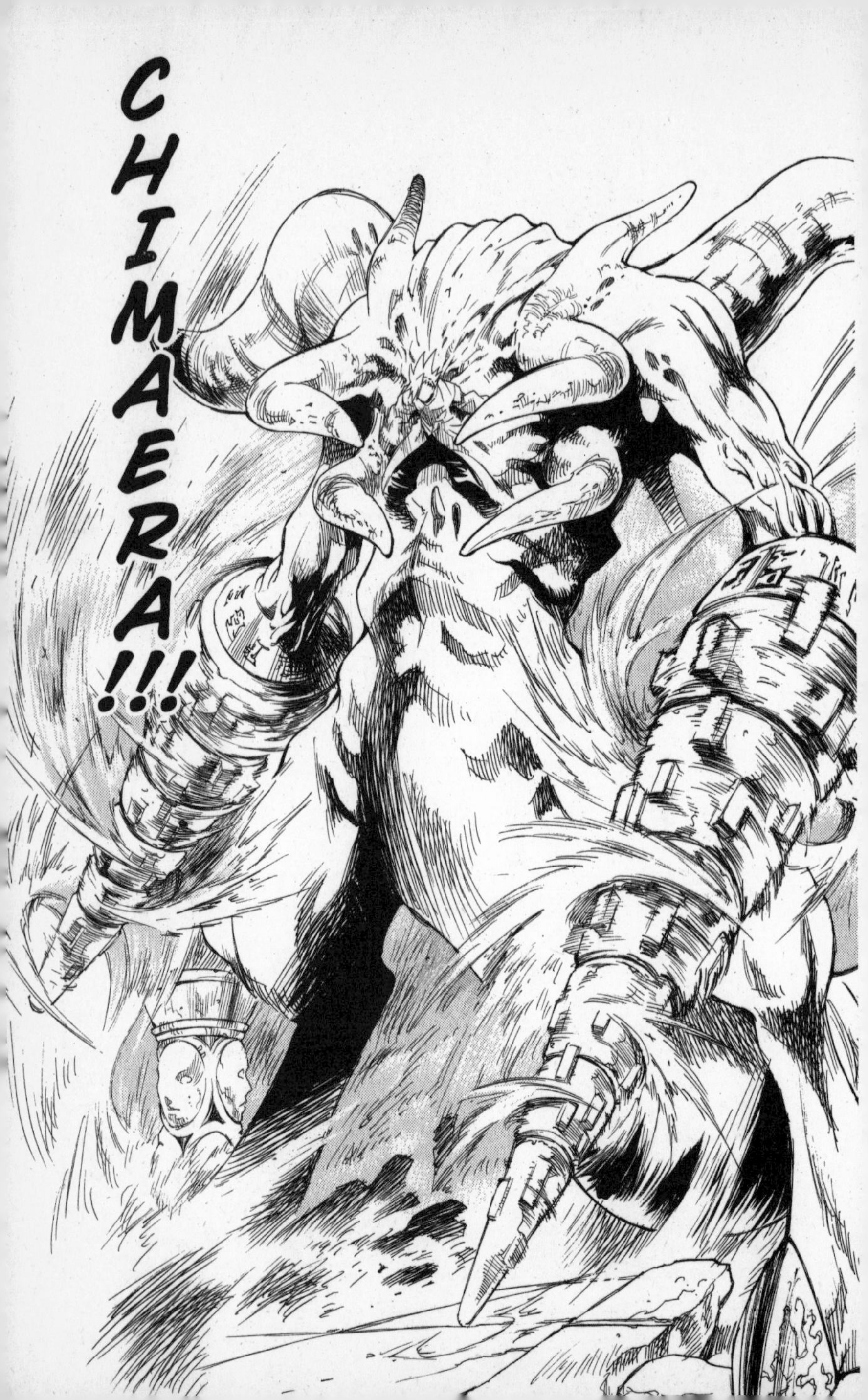
CHIMAERA!!!

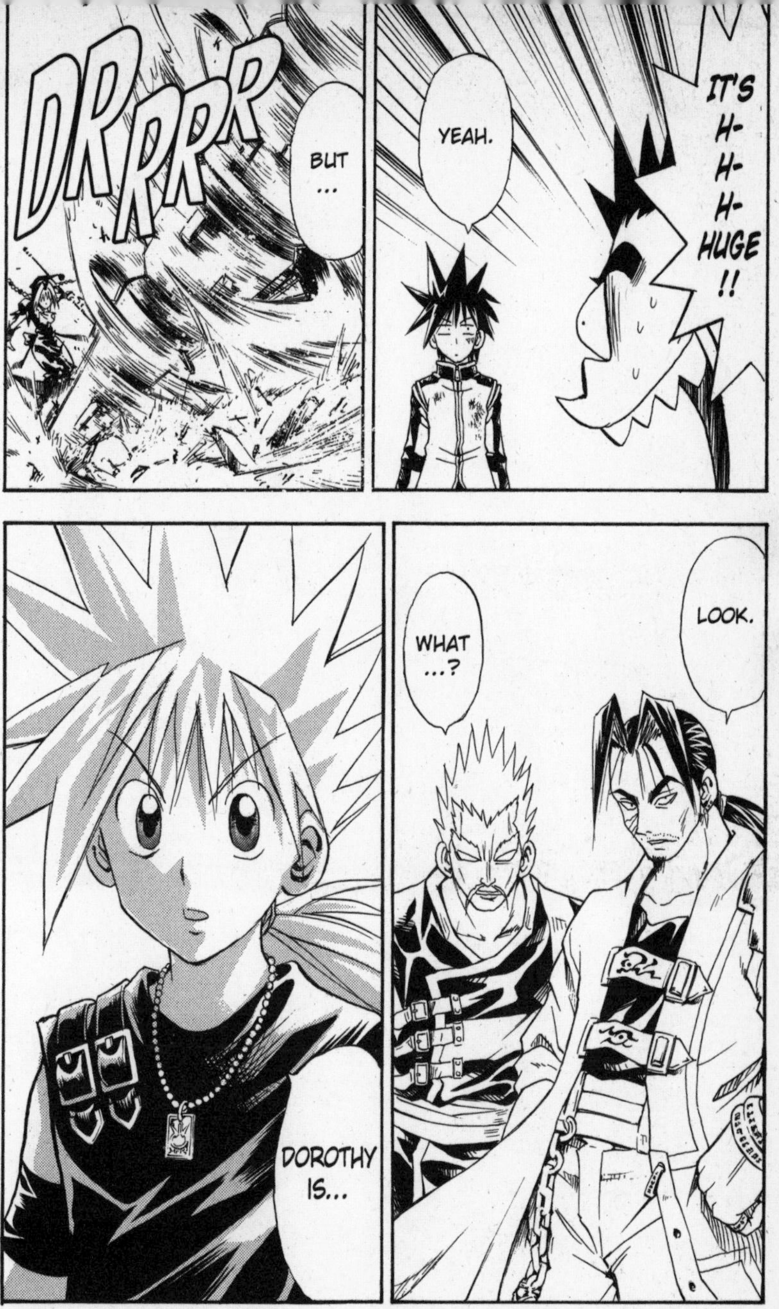
IT'S H-H-H-HUGE!!
YEAH.
BUT ...
DRRRRR
LOOK.
WHAT ...?
DOROTHY IS...

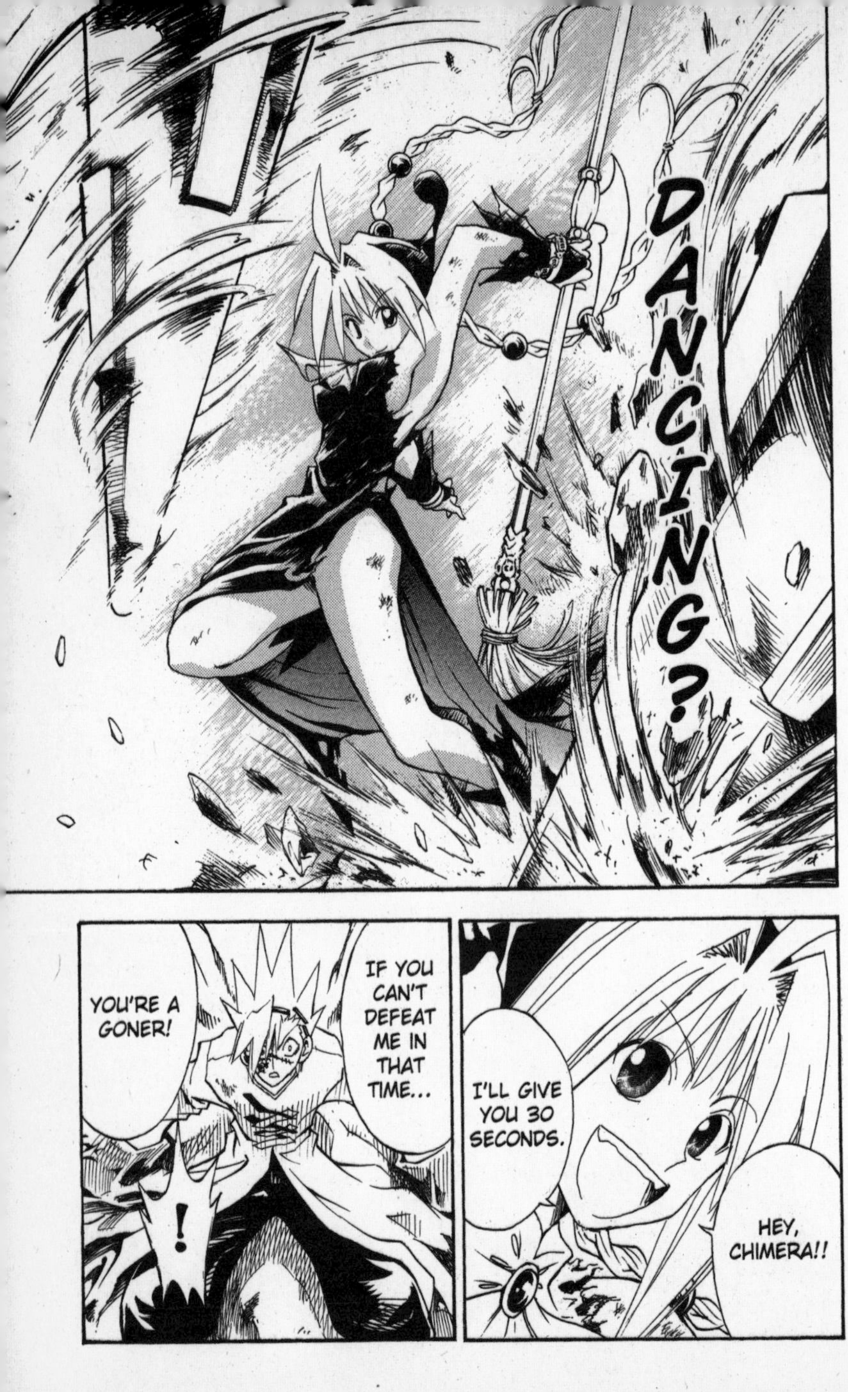
DANCING?
HEY, CHIMERA!!
I'LL GIVE YOU 30 SECONDS.
IF YOU CAN'T DEFEAT ME IN THAT TIME...
YOU'RE A GONER!
!

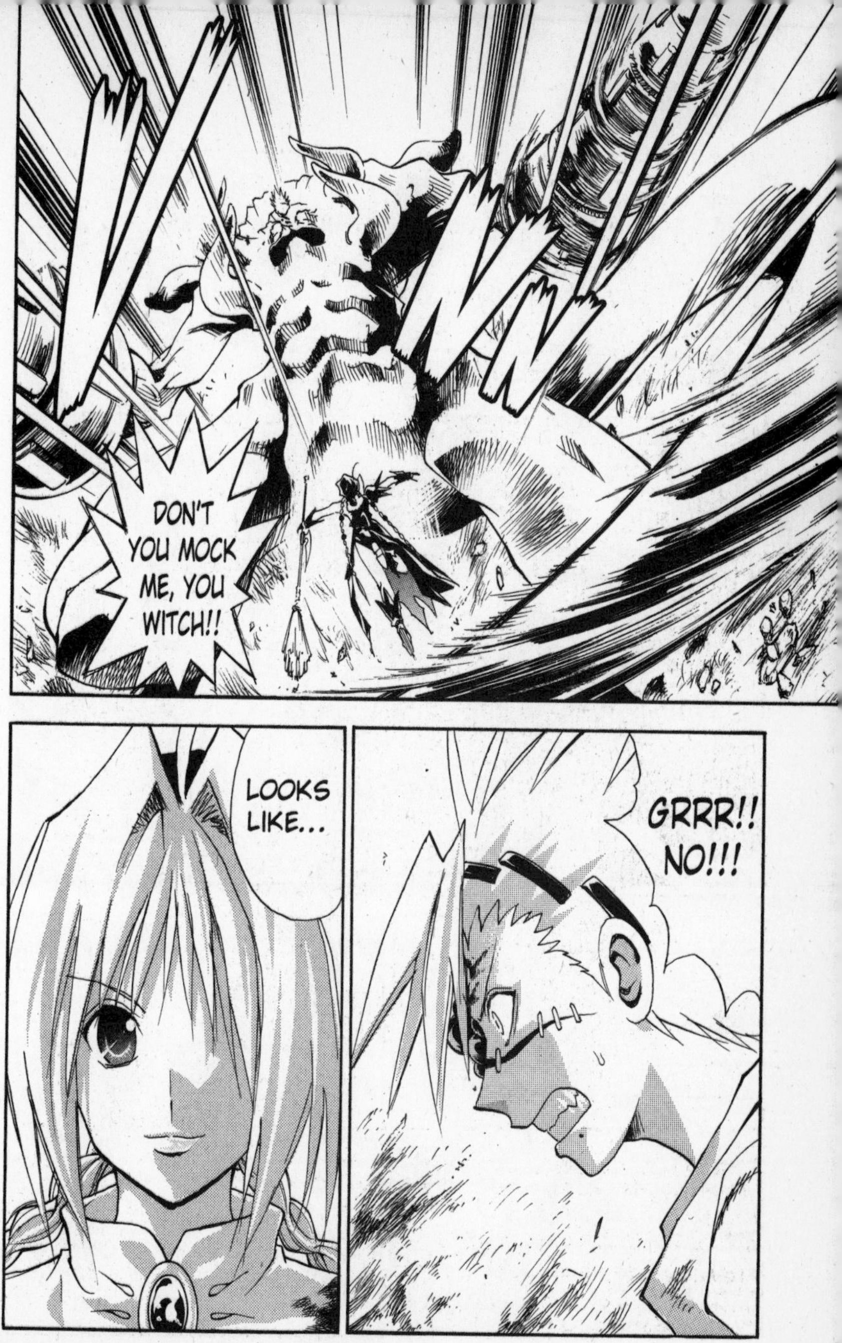
DON'T YOU MOCK ME, YOU WITCH!!
GRRR!! NO!!!
LOOKS LIKE...

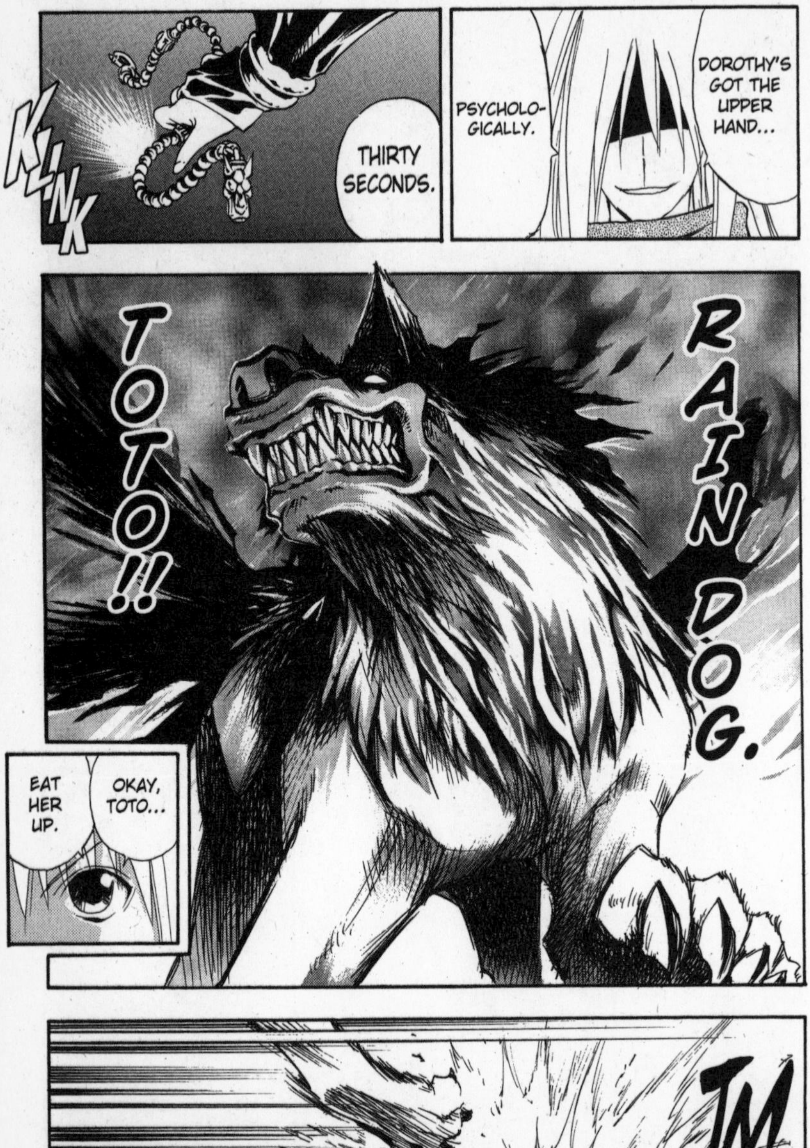
DOROTHY'S GOT THE UPPER HAND...
PSYCHOLO-GICALLY.
THIRTY SECONDS.
KLINK
RAIN DOG.
TOTO!!
OKAY, TOTO...
EAT HER UP.
TM

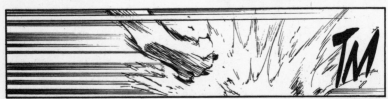

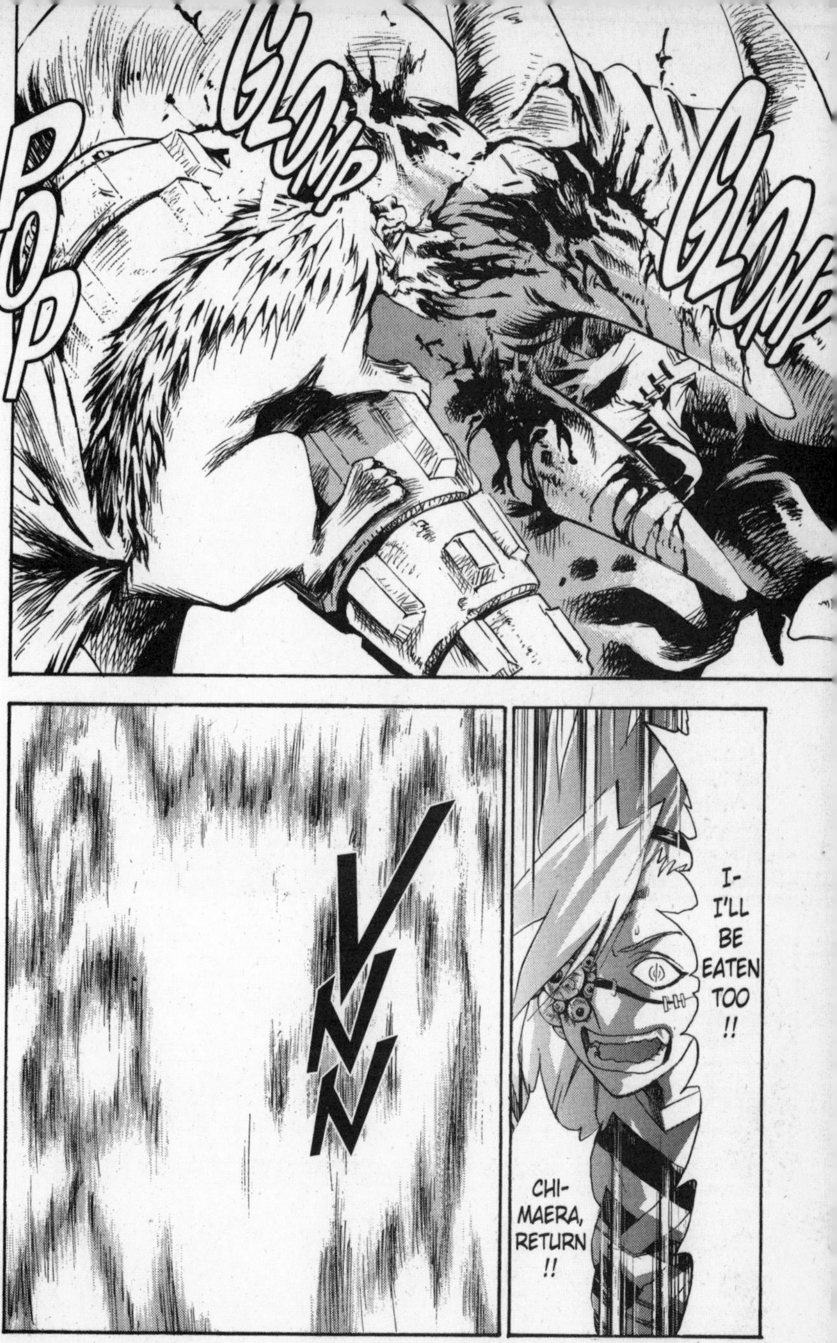
GLOMP
GLOMP
POP
I- I'LL BE EATEN TOO !!
CHI-MAERA, RETURN !!

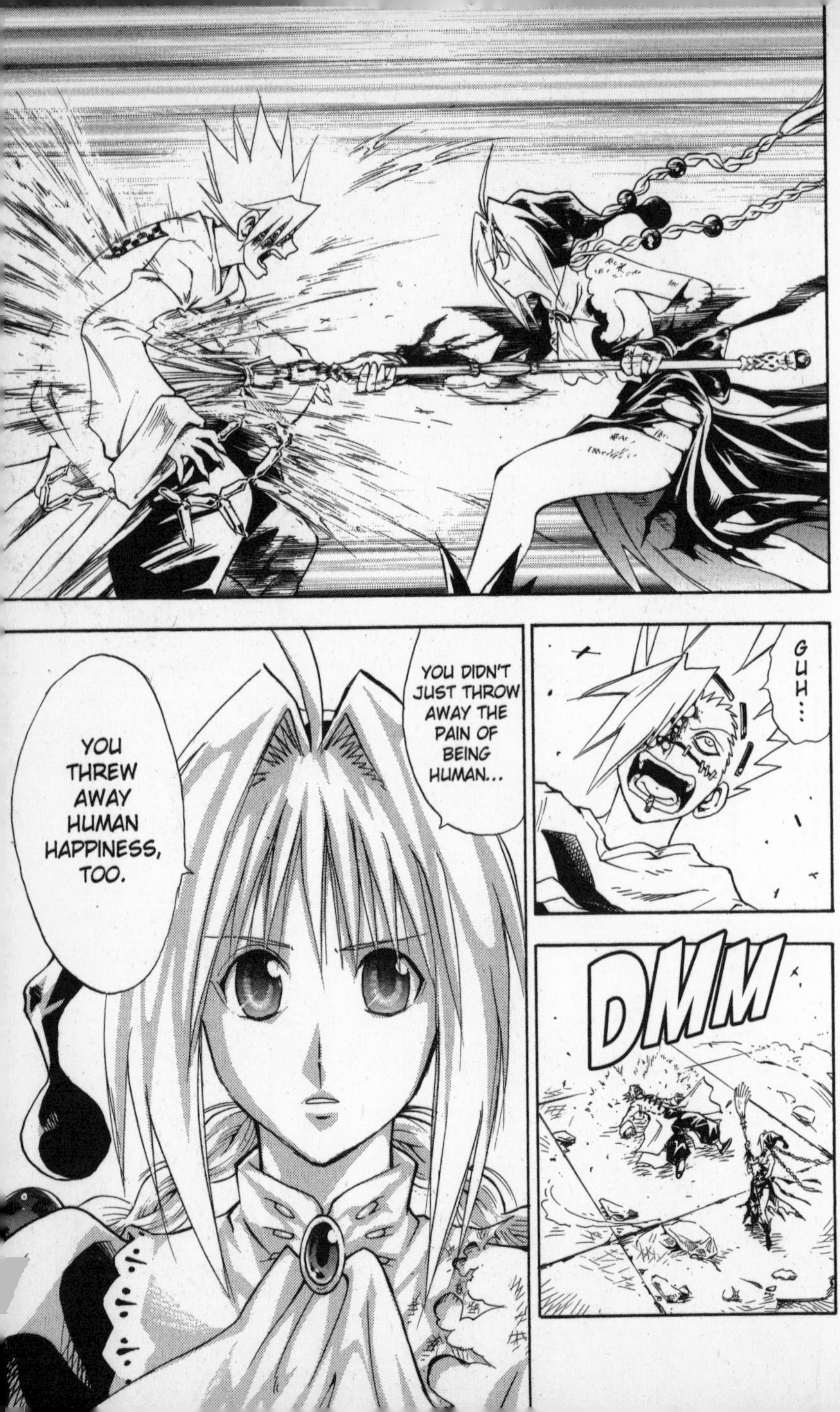
GUH...
DMM
YOU DIDN'T JUST THROW AWAY THE PAIN OF BEING HUMAN...
YOU THREW AWAY HUMAN HAPPINESS, TOO.

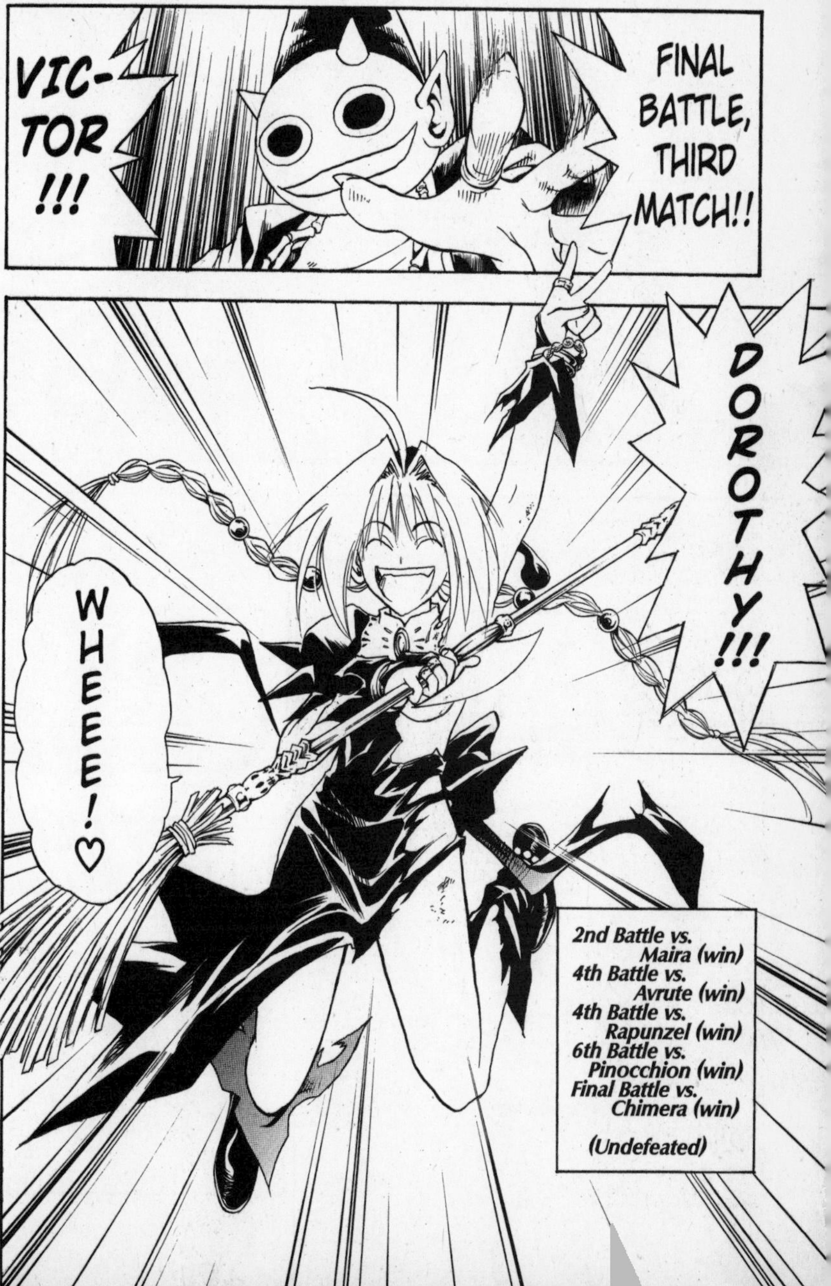
FINAL BATTLE, THIRD MATCH!!
VIC-TOR!!!
DOROTHY!!!
WHEEE!♡
2nd Battle vs. Maira (win)
4th Battle vs. Avrute (win)
4th Battle vs. Rapunzel (win)
6th Battle vs. Pinocchion (win)
Final Battle vs. Chimera (win)
(Undefeated)

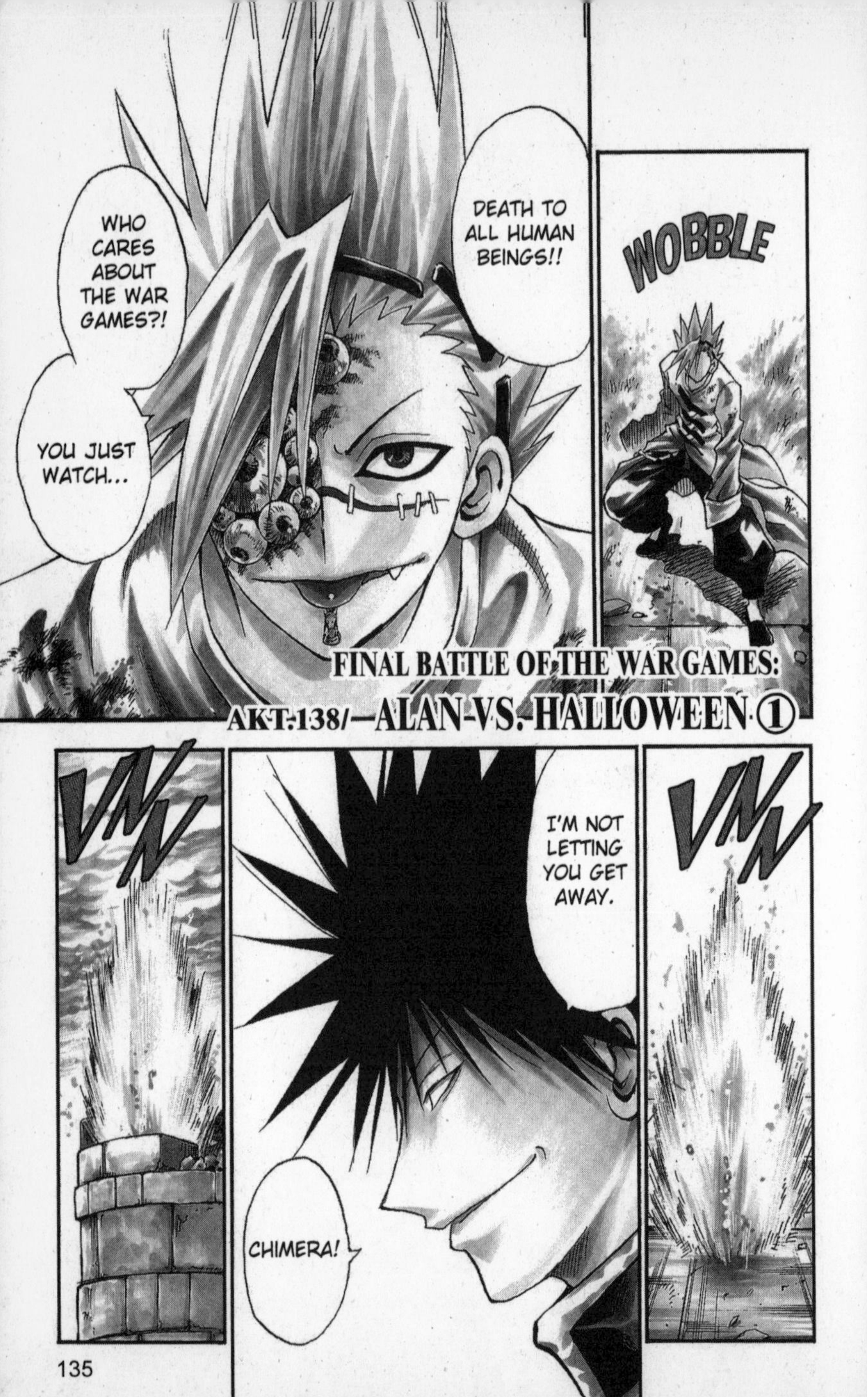
WOBBLE
DEATH TO ALL HUMAN BEINGS!!
WHO CARES ABOUT THE WAR GAMES?!
YOU JUST WATCH...
FINAL BATTLE OF THE WAR GAMES:
AKT.138/—ALAN VS. HALLOWEEN ①
VNN
I'M NOT LETTING YOU GET AWAY.
CHIMERA!
VNN

AKT.138/ FINAL BATTLE OF THE WAR GAMES: ALAN VS. HALLOWEEN ①

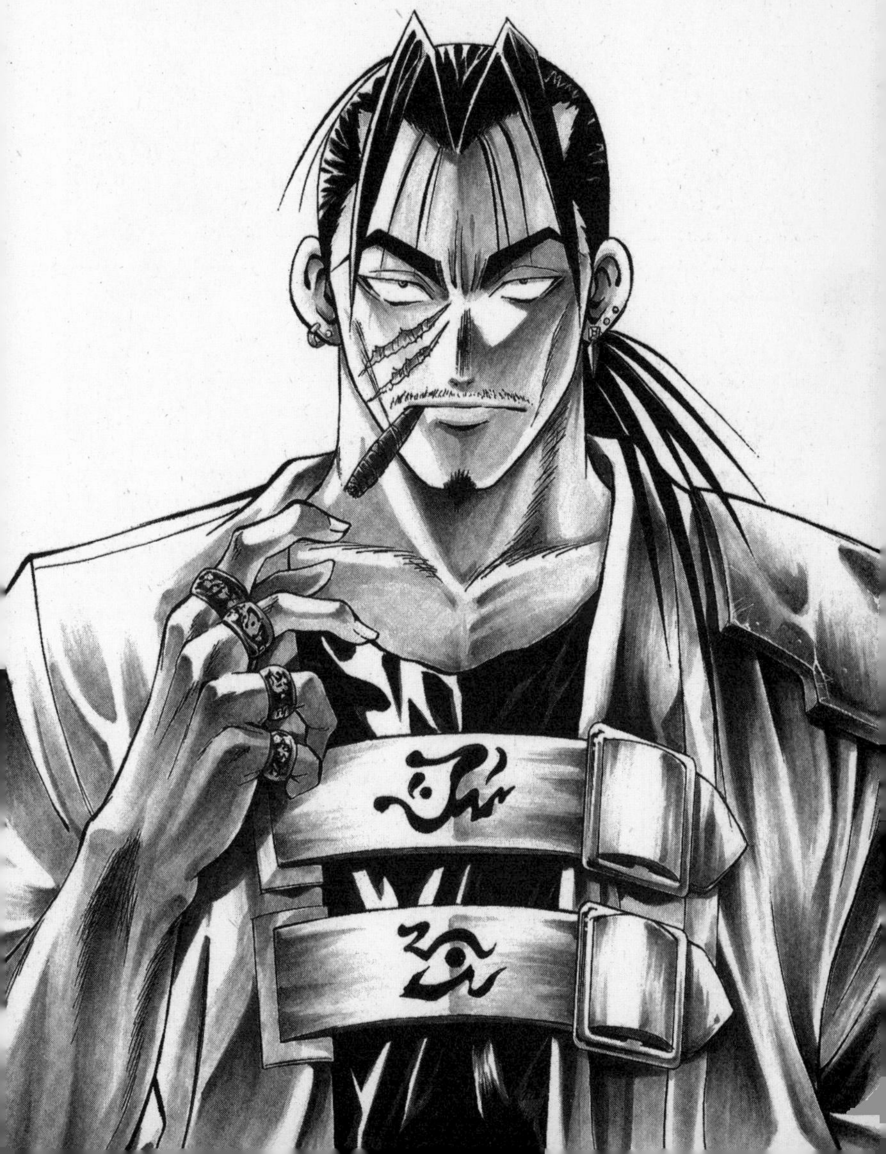

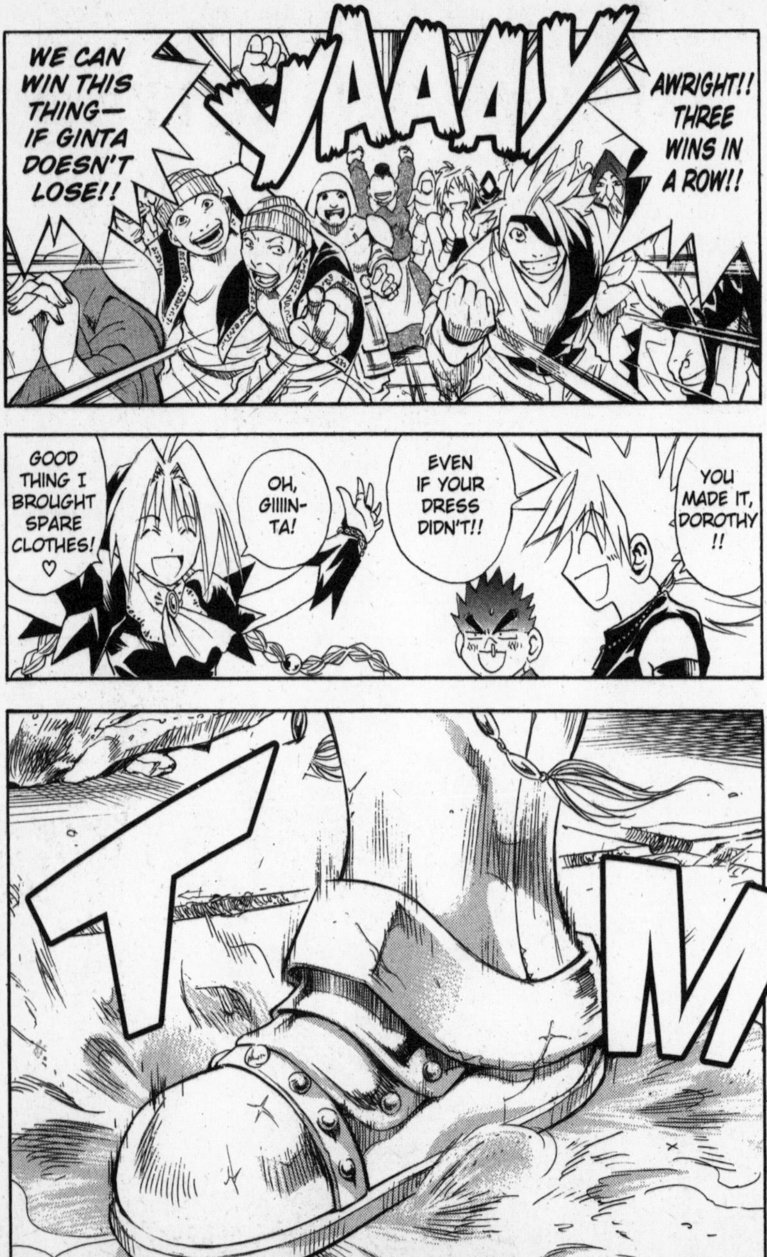
AWRIGHT!! THREE WINS IN A ROW!!
YAAAY
WE CAN WIN THIS THING— IF GINTA DOESN'T LOSE!!
YOU MADE IT, DOROTHY!!
EVEN IF YOUR DRESS DIDN'T!!
OH, GIIIN-TA!
GOOD THING I BROUGHT SPARE CLOTHES! ♡
T M

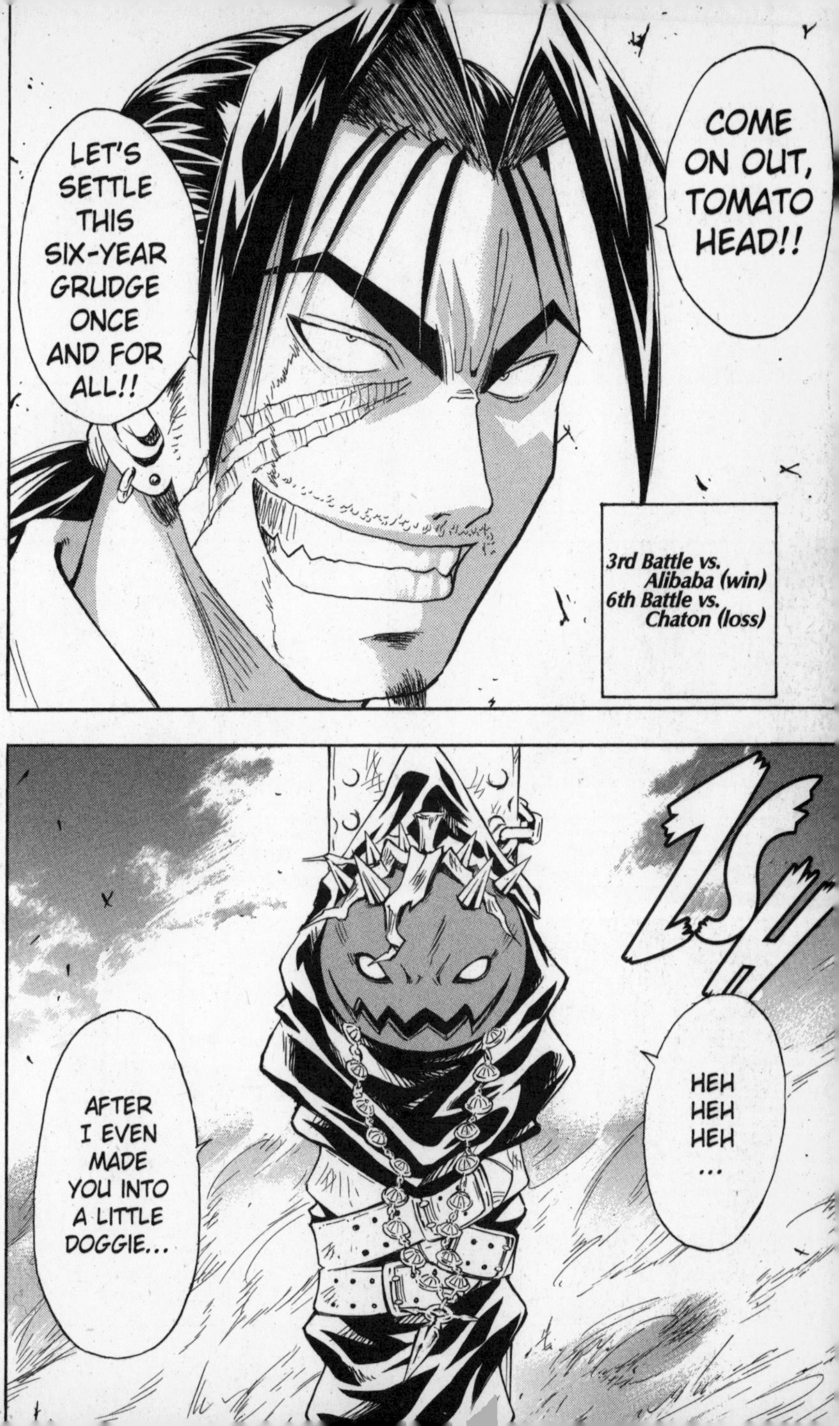
COME ON OUT, TOMATO HEAD!!
LET'S SETTLE THIS SIX-YEAR GRUDGE ONCE AND FOR ALL!!
3rd Battle vs. Alibaba (win)
6th Battle vs. Chaton (loss)
TSH
HEH HEH HEH ...
AFTER I EVEN MADE YOU INTO A LITTLE DOGGIE...

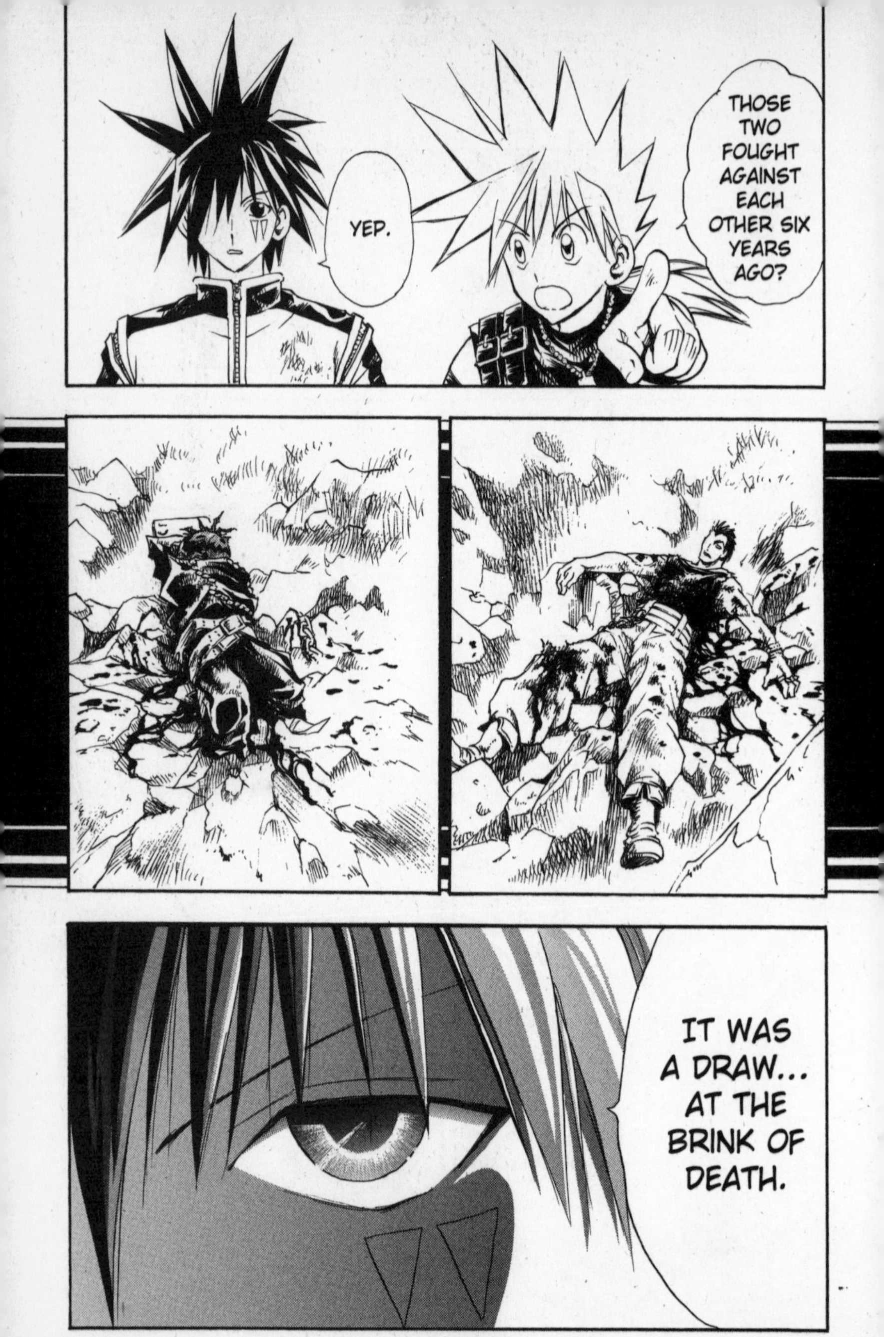
THOSE TWO FOUGHT AGAINST EACH OTHER SIX YEARS AGO?
YEP.
IT WAS A DRAW... AT THE BRINK OF DEATH.

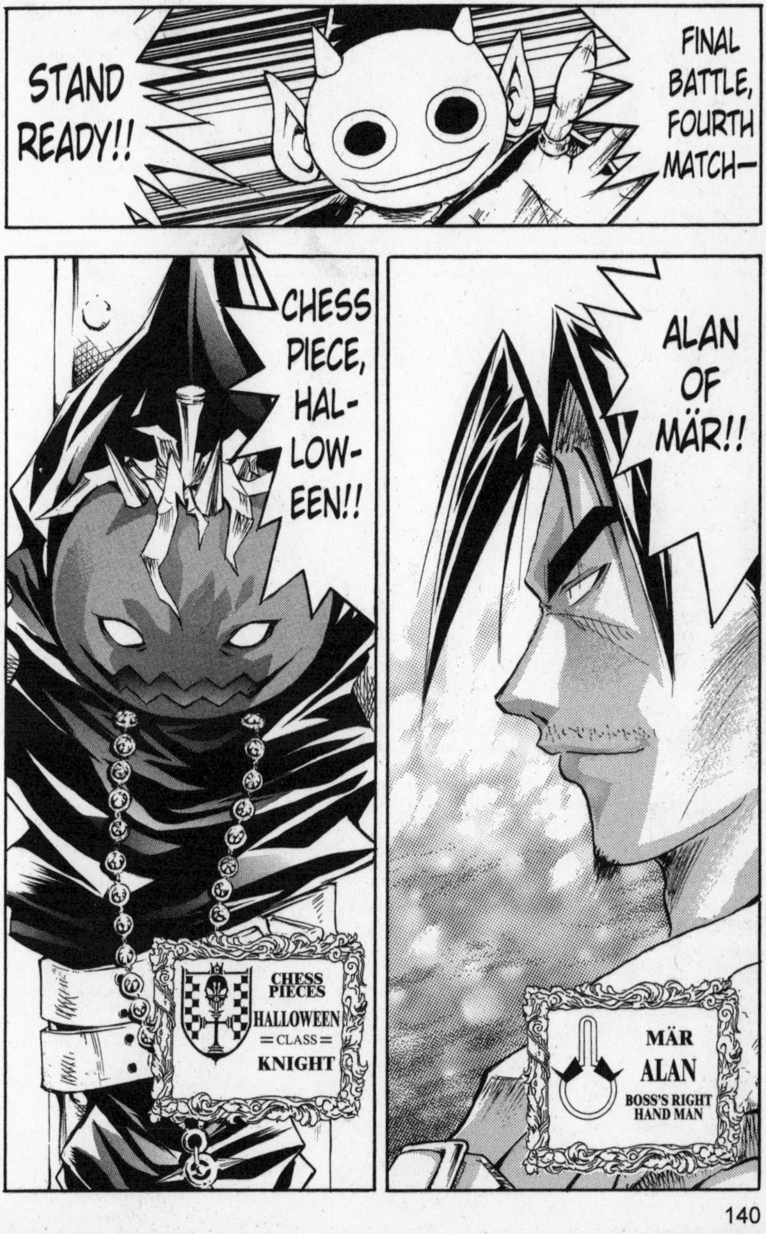
FINAL BATTLE, FOURTH MATCH—
STAND READY!!
ALAN OF MÄR!!
MÄR
ALAN
BOSS'S RIGHT HAND MAN
CHESS PIECE, HAL-LOW-EEN!!
CHESS PIECES
HALLOWEEN
CLASS
KNIGHT

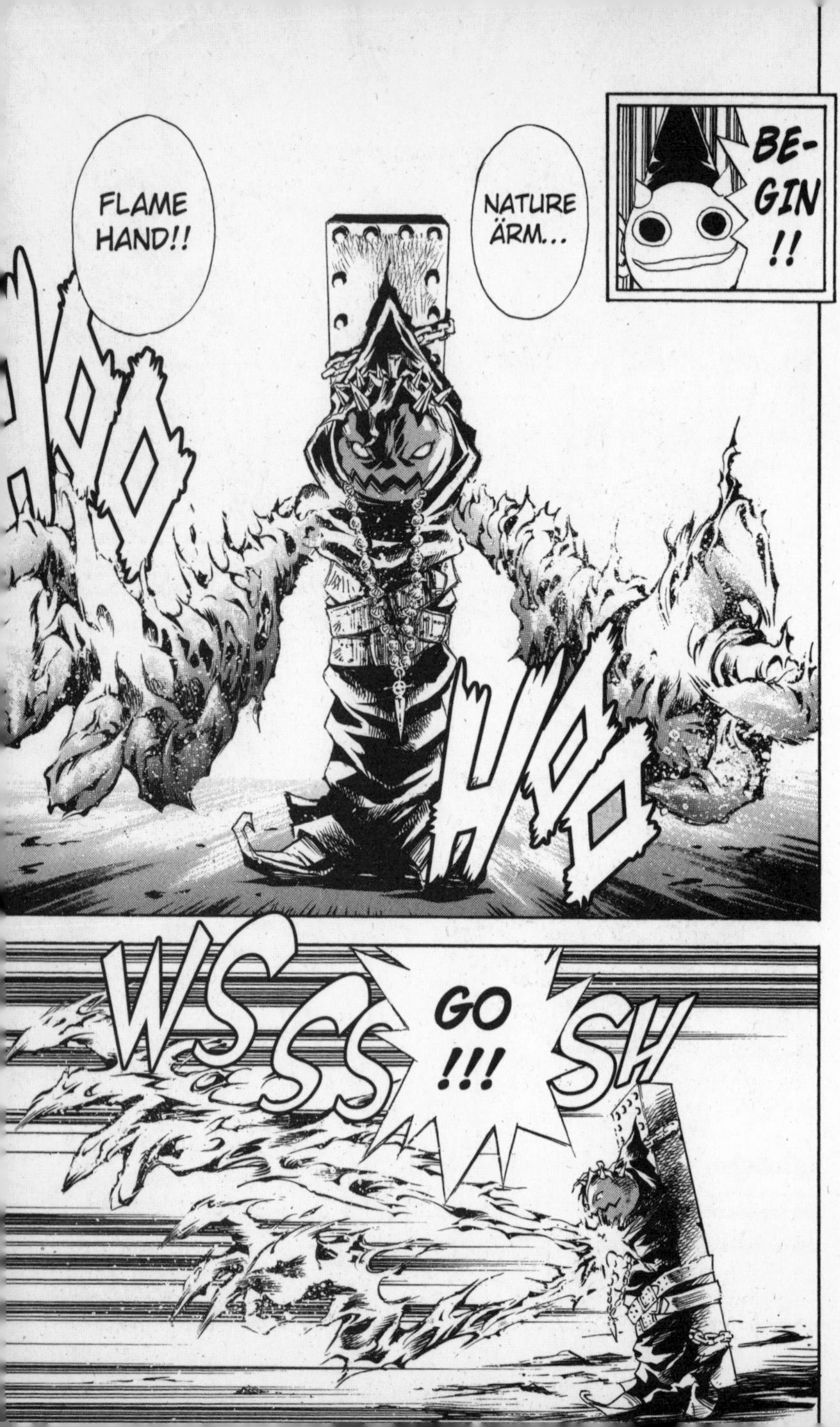
BE-GIN!!
NATURE ÄRM...
FLAME HAND!!
WSSSSH
GO!!!

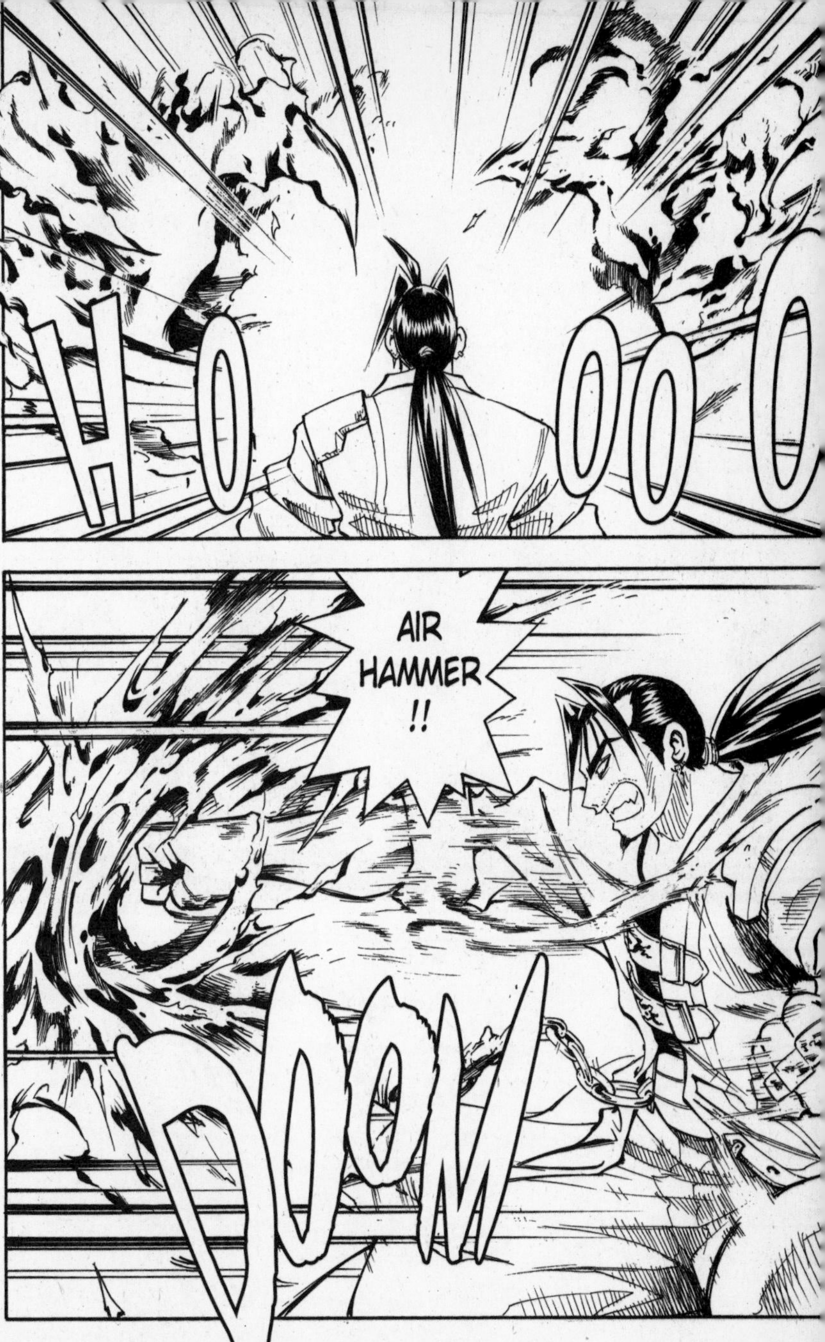
HOOOO
AIR HAMMER !!
DOOM

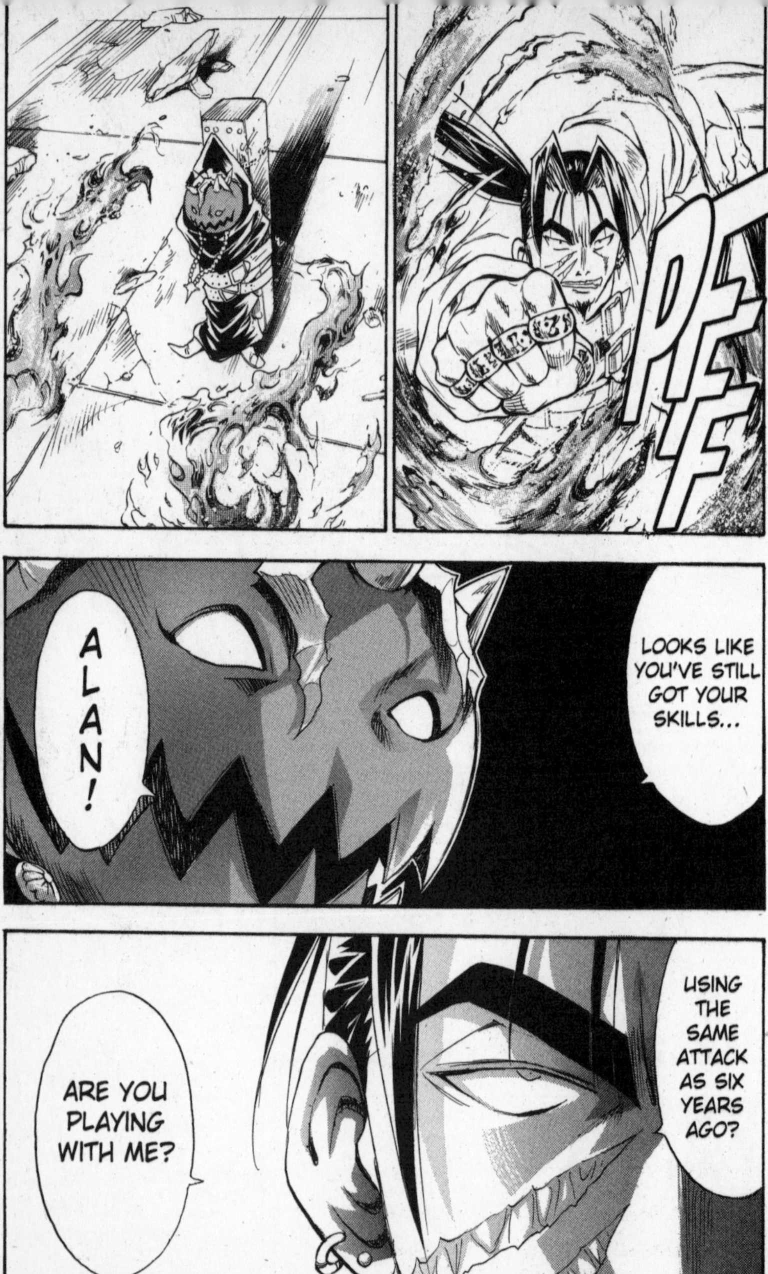
PFFF
LOOKS LIKE YOU'VE STILL GOT YOUR SKILLS...
ALAN!
USING THE SAME ATTACK AS SIX YEARS AGO?
ARE YOU PLAYING WITH ME?

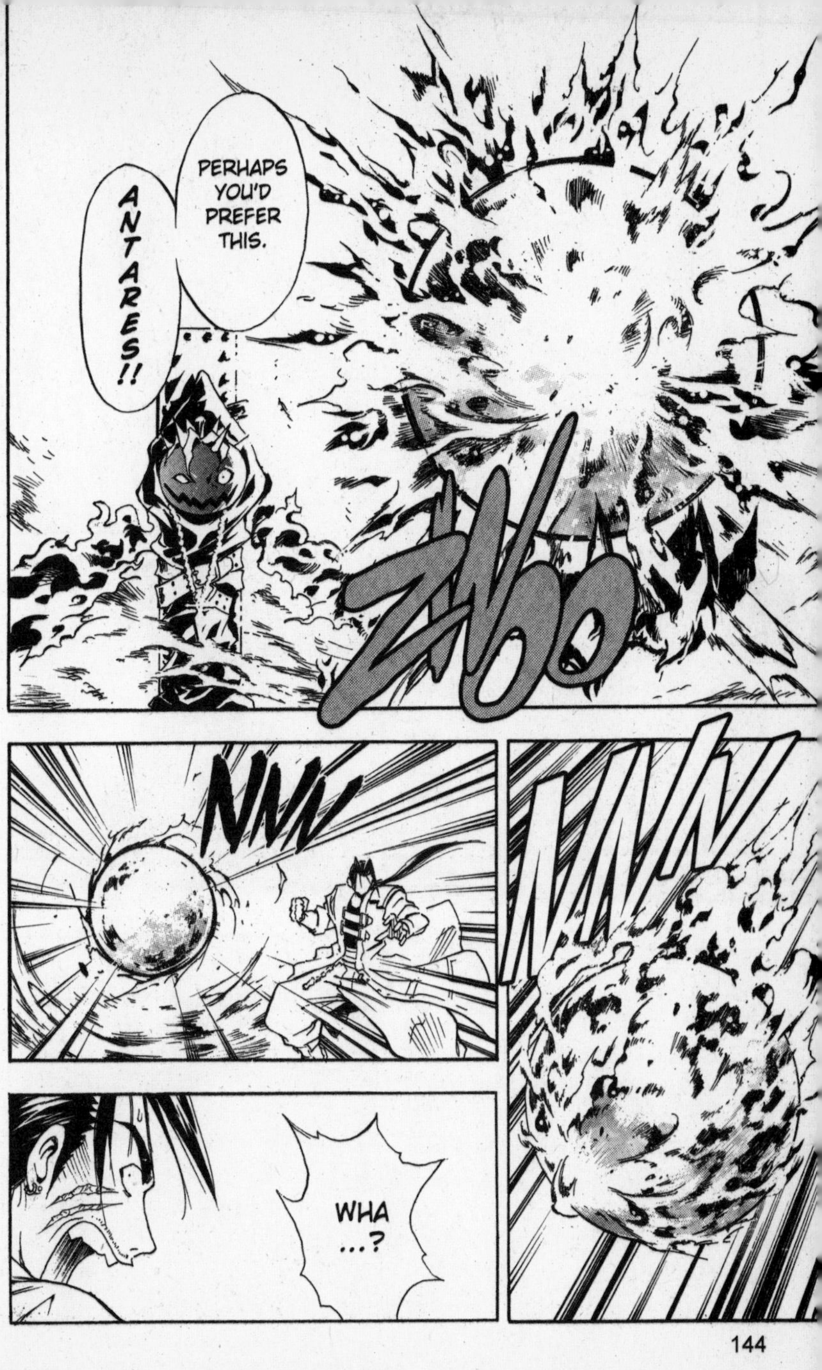
PERHAPS YOU'D PREFER THIS.
ANTARES!!
WHA ...?

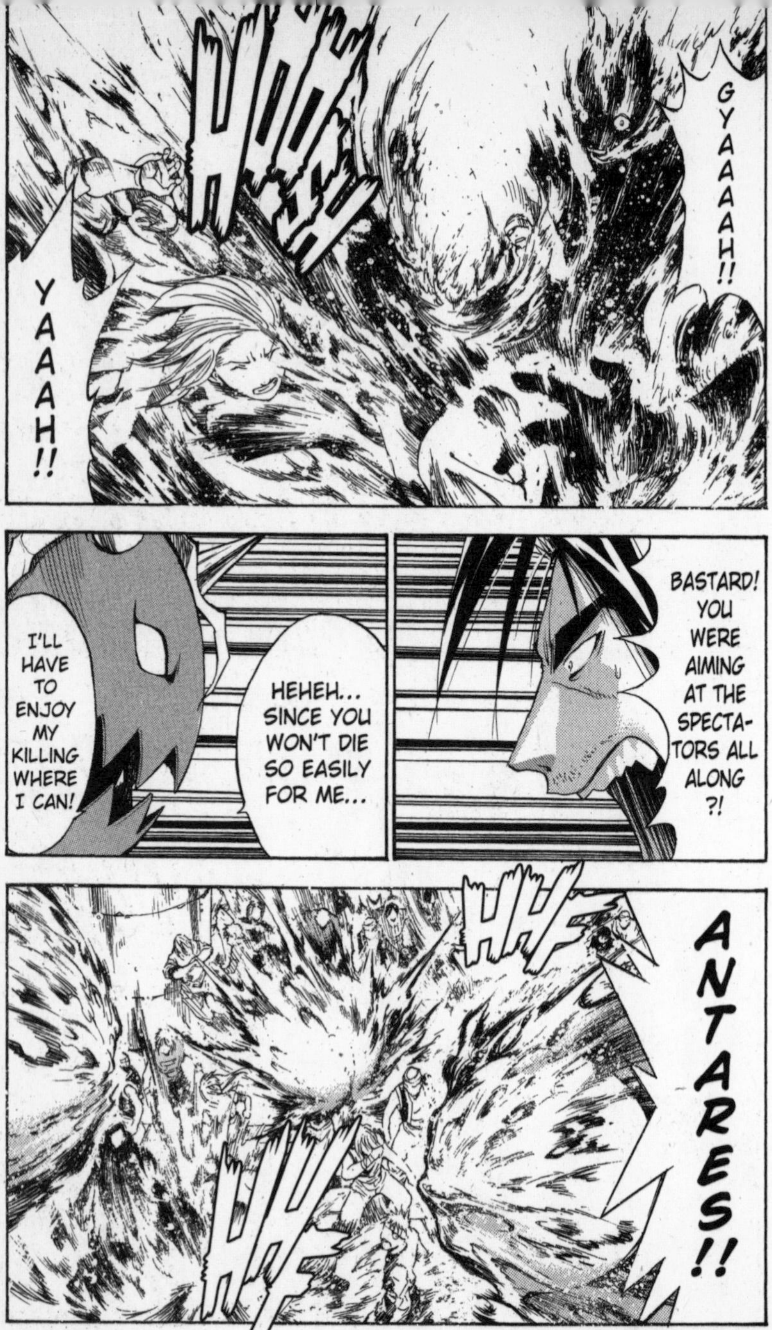
GYAAAAAAH!!
YAAAAH!!
BASTARD! YOU WERE AIMING AT THE SPECTATORS ALL ALONG?!
HEHEH... SINCE YOU WON'T DIE SO EASILY FOR ME...
I'LL HAVE TO ENJOY MY KILLING WHERE I CAN!
ANTARES!!

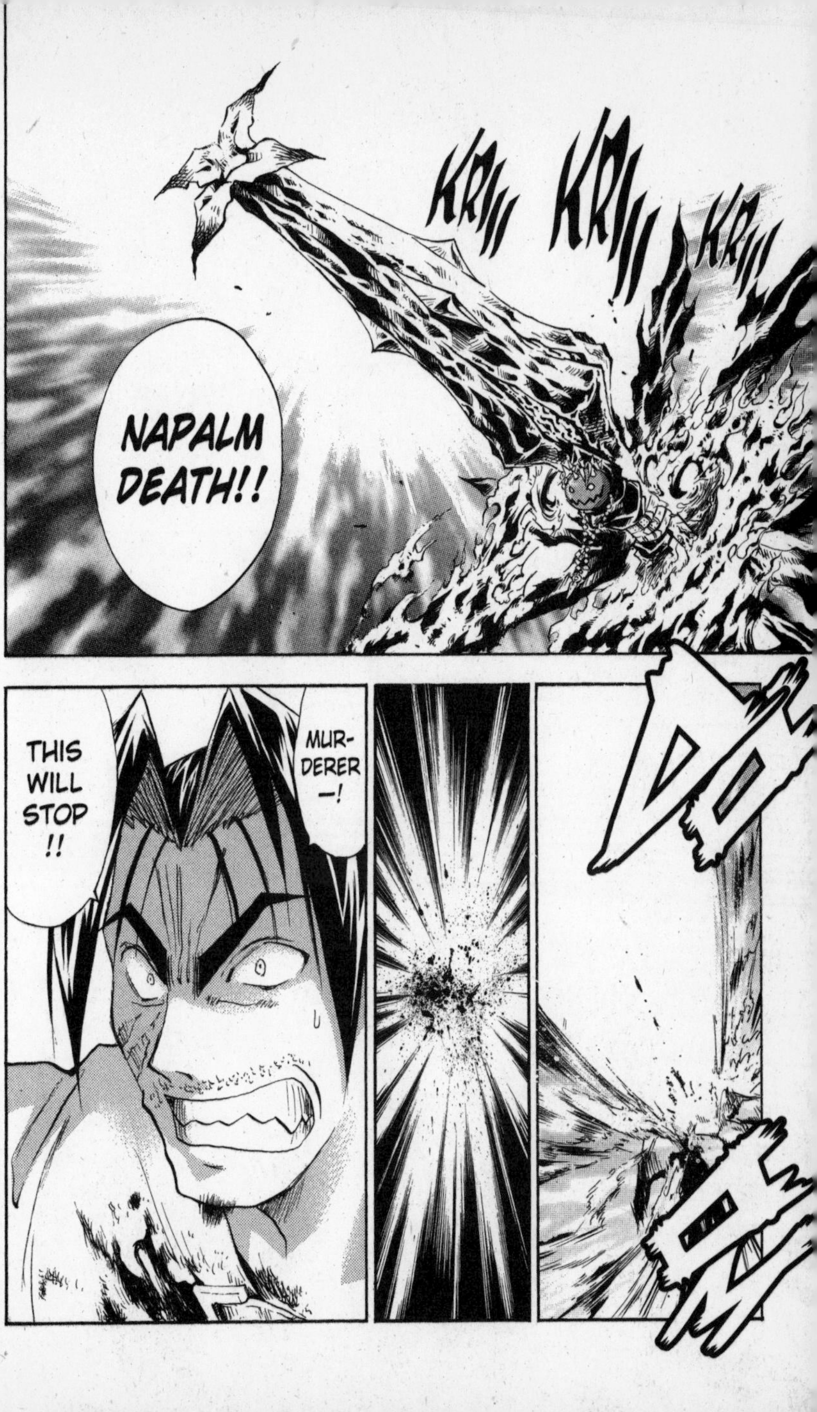
KRIII KRIII KRIII
NAPALM DEATH!!
MUR-DERER—!
THIS WILL STOP!!

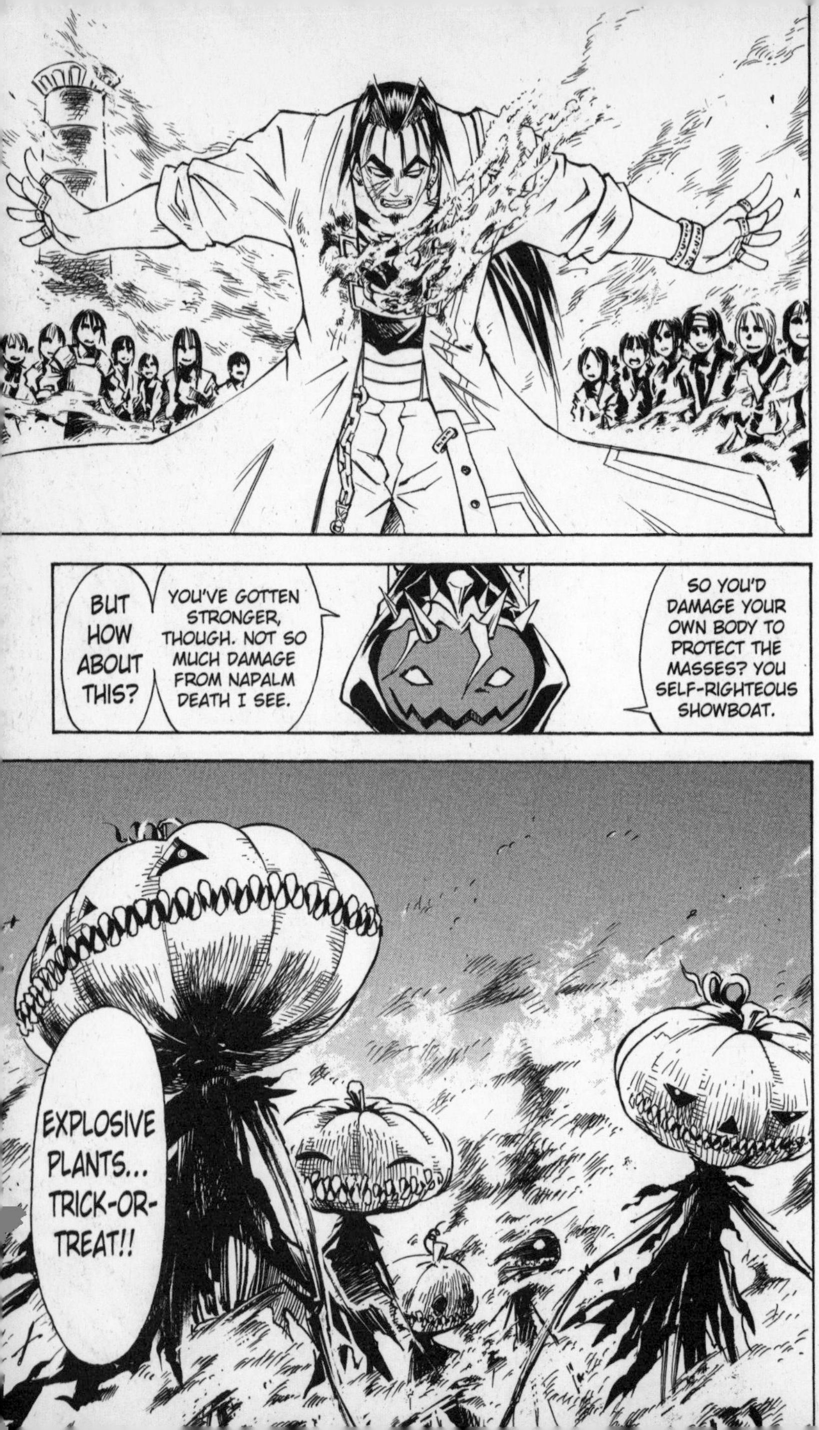
SO YOU'D DAMAGE YOUR OWN BODY TO PROTECT THE MASSES? YOU SELF-RIGHTEOUS SHOWBOAT.
YOU'VE GOTTEN STRONGER, THOUGH. NOT SO MUCH DAMAGE FROM NAPALM DEATH I SEE.
BUT HOW ABOUT THIS?
EXPLOSIVE PLANTS... TRICK-OR-TREAT!!

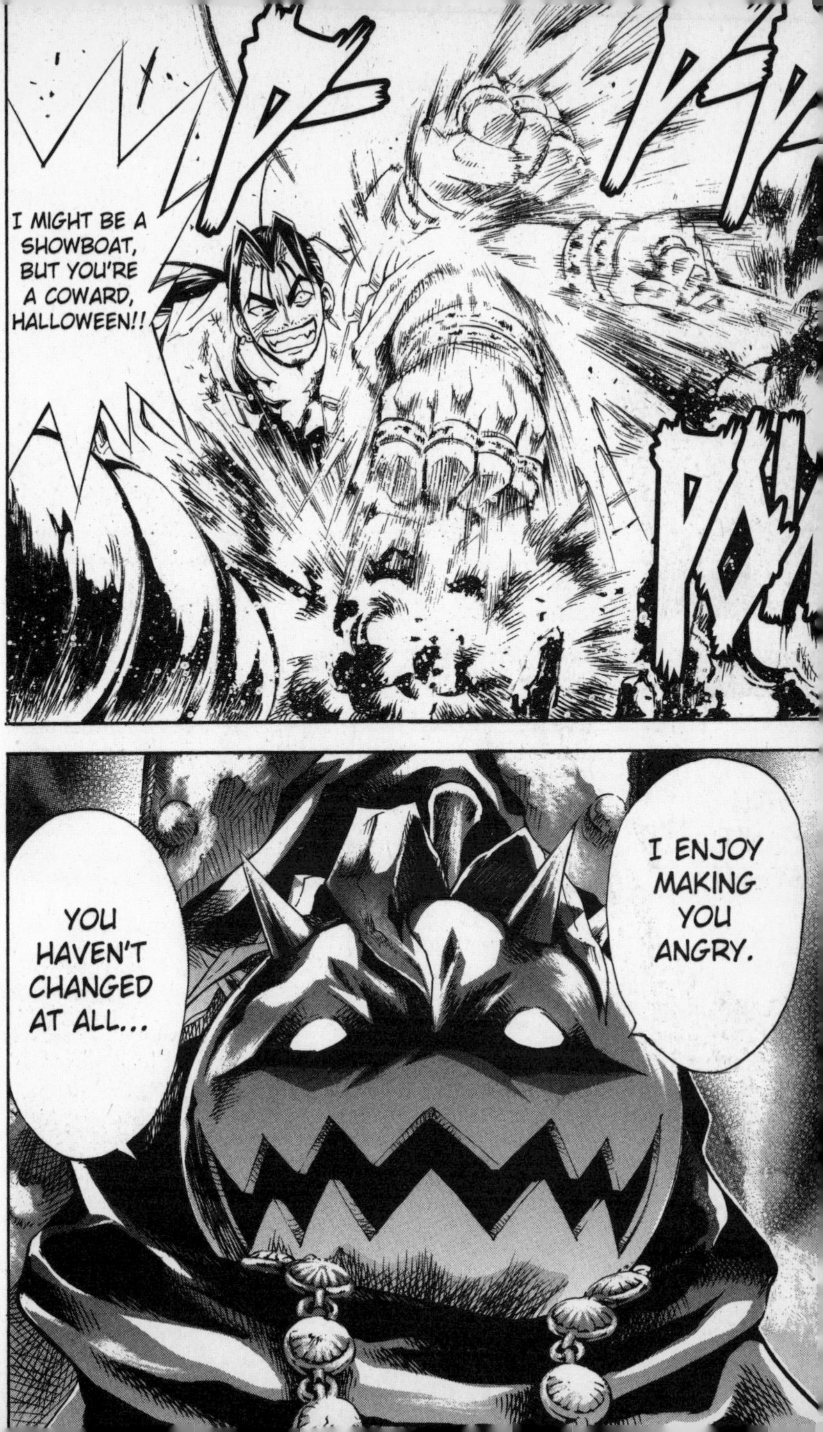
I MIGHT BE A SHOWBOAT, BUT YOU'RE A COWARD, HALLOWEEN!!
I ENJOY MAKING YOU ANGRY.
YOU HAVEN'T CHANGED AT ALL...

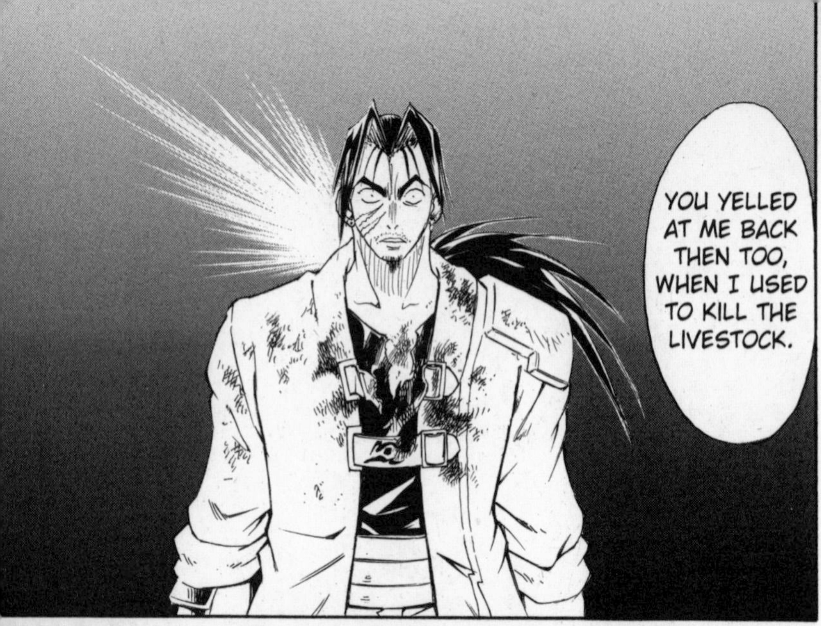
YOU YELLED AT ME BACK THEN TOO, WHEN I USED TO KILL THE LIVESTOCK.

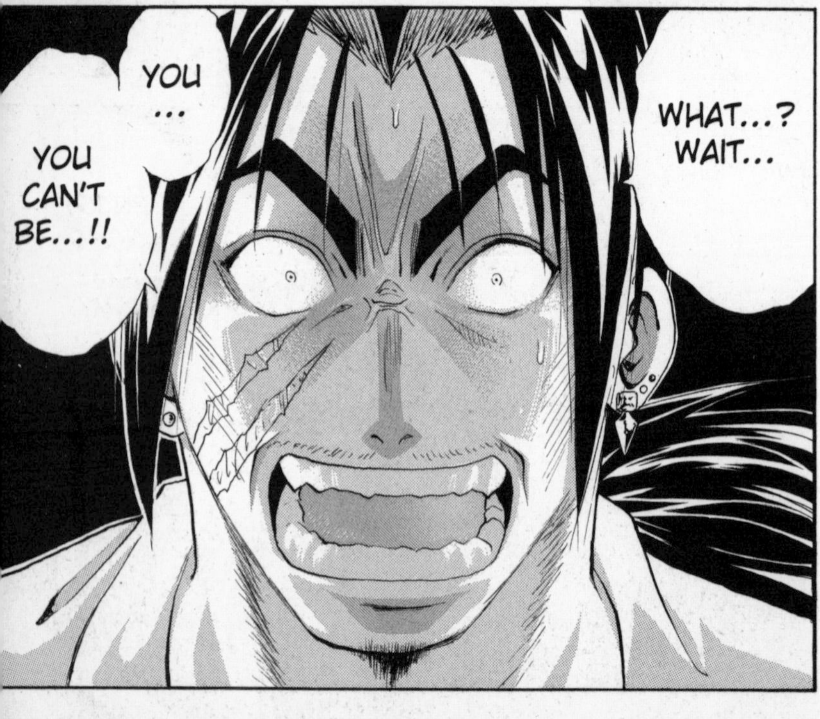
WHAT...? WAIT...
YOU ...
YOU CAN'T BE...!!

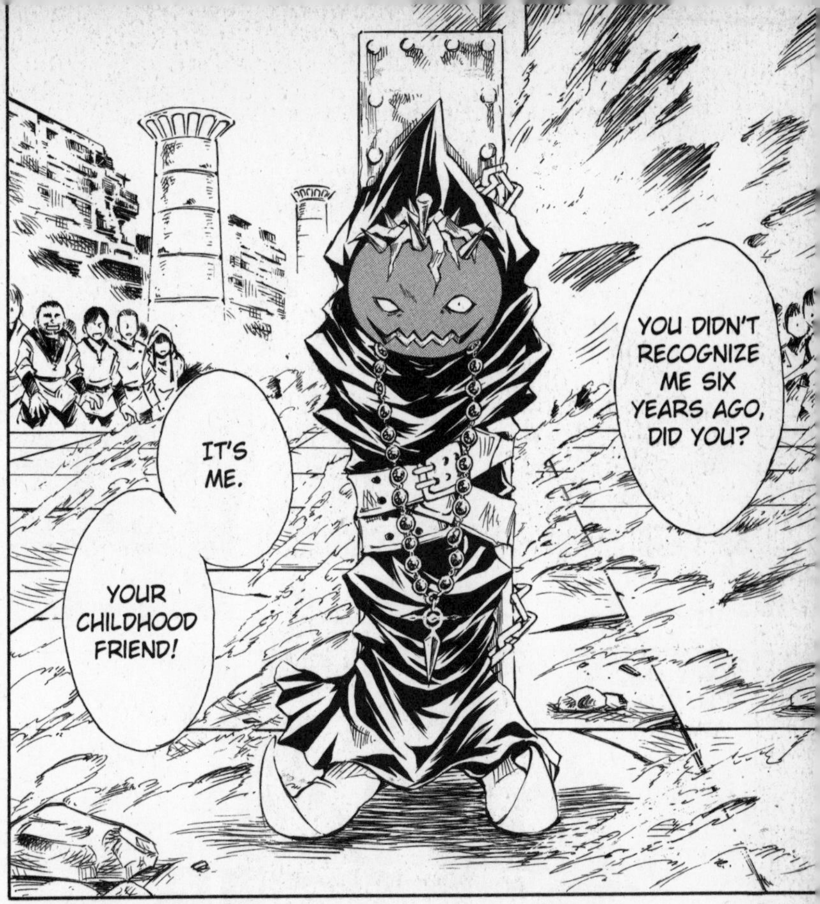
YOU DIDN'T RECOGNIZE ME SIX YEARS AGO, DID YOU?
IT'S ME.
YOUR CHILDHOOD FRIEND!

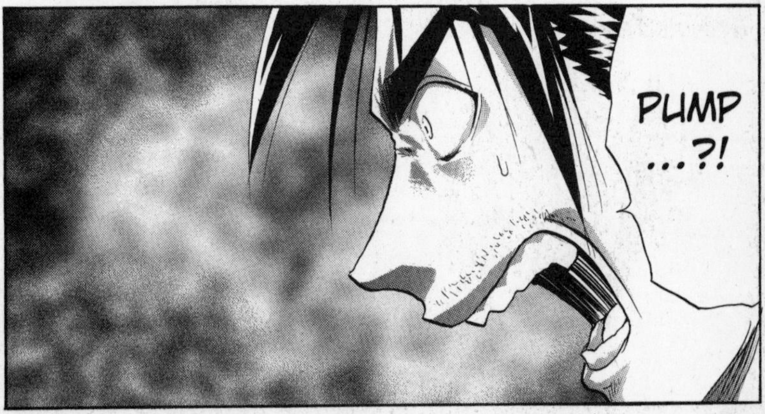
PUMP ...?!

FINAL BATTLE OF THE WAR GAMES:
ALAN VS. HALLOWEEN ②

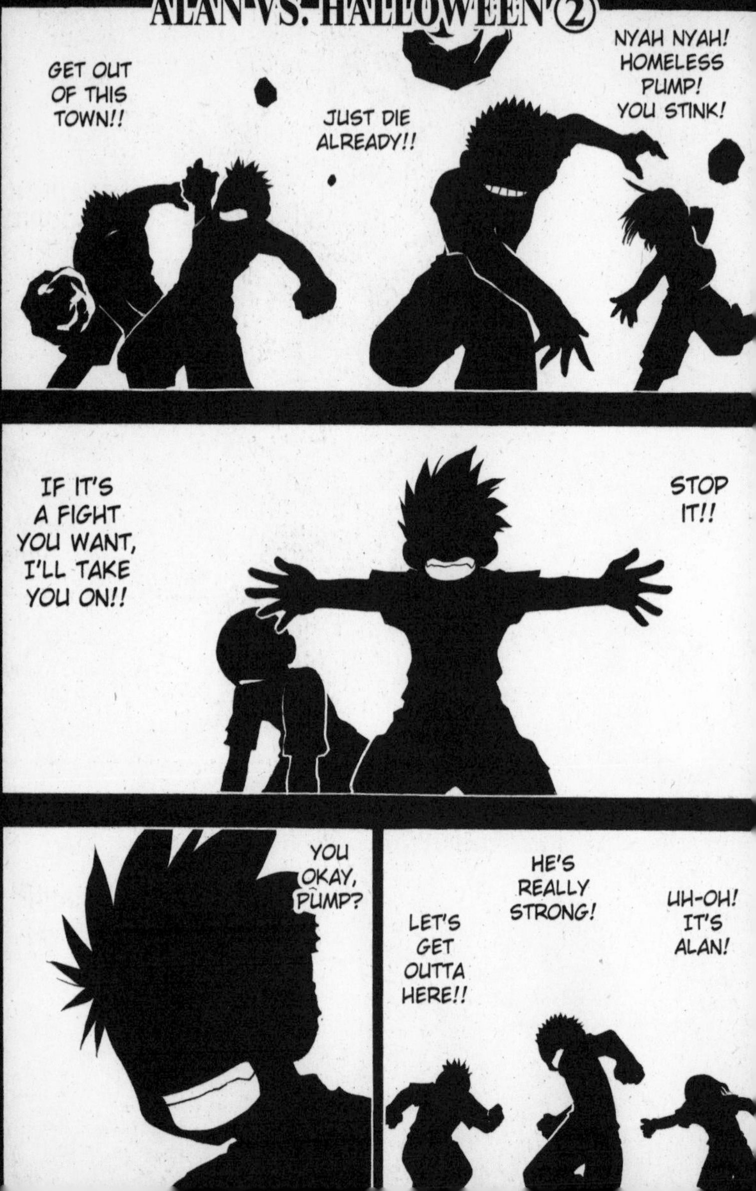
NYAH NYAH! HOMELESS PUMP! YOU STINK!
JUST DIE ALREADY!!
GET OUT OF THIS TOWN!!
STOP IT!!
IF IT'S A FIGHT YOU WANT, I'LL TAKE YOU ON!!
UH-OH! IT'S ALAN!
HE'S REALLY STRONG!
LET'S GET OUTTA HERE!!
YOU OKAY, PUMP?

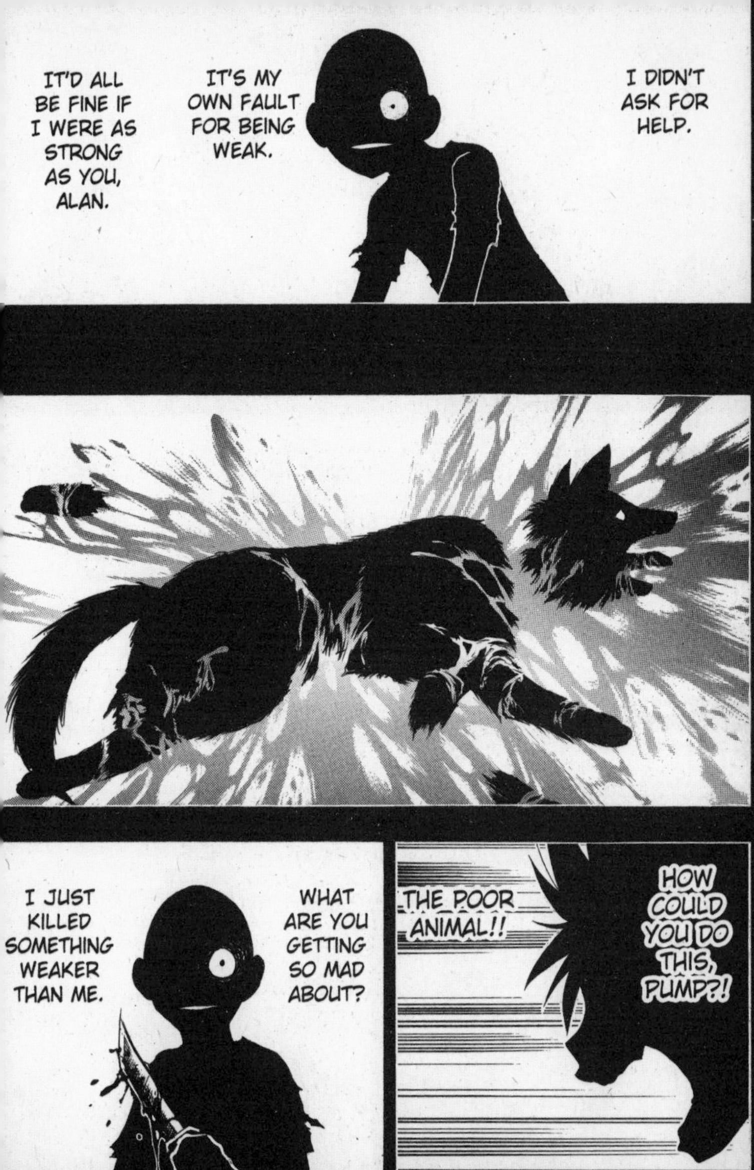
I DIDN'T ASK FOR HELP.
IT'S MY OWN FAULT FOR BEING WEAK.
IT'D ALL BE FINE IF I WERE AS STRONG AS YOU, ALAN.
HOW COULD YOU DO THIS, PUMP?!
THE POOR ANIMAL!!
WHAT ARE YOU GETTING SO MAD ABOUT?
I JUST KILLED SOMETHING WEAKER THAN ME.

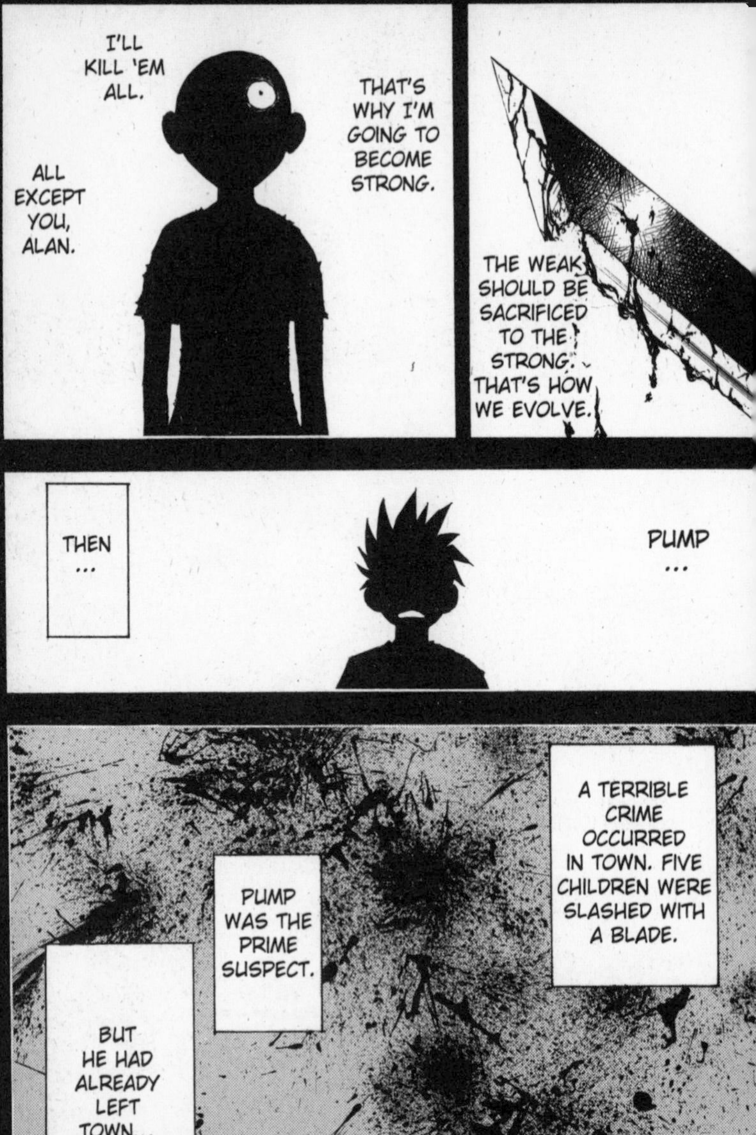
THE WEAK SHOULD BE SACRIFICED TO THE STRONG. THAT'S HOW WE EVOLVE.
THAT'S WHY I'M GOING TO BECOME STRONG.
I'LL KILL 'EM ALL.
ALL EXCEPT YOU, ALAN.
PUMP ...
THEN ...
A TERRIBLE CRIME OCCURRED IN TOWN. FIVE CHILDREN WERE SLASHED WITH A BLADE.
PUMP WAS THE PRIME SUSPECT.
BUT HE HAD ALREADY LEFT TOWN...

AKT.139/ FINAL BATTLE OF THE WAR GAMES: ALAN VS. HALLOWEEN ②

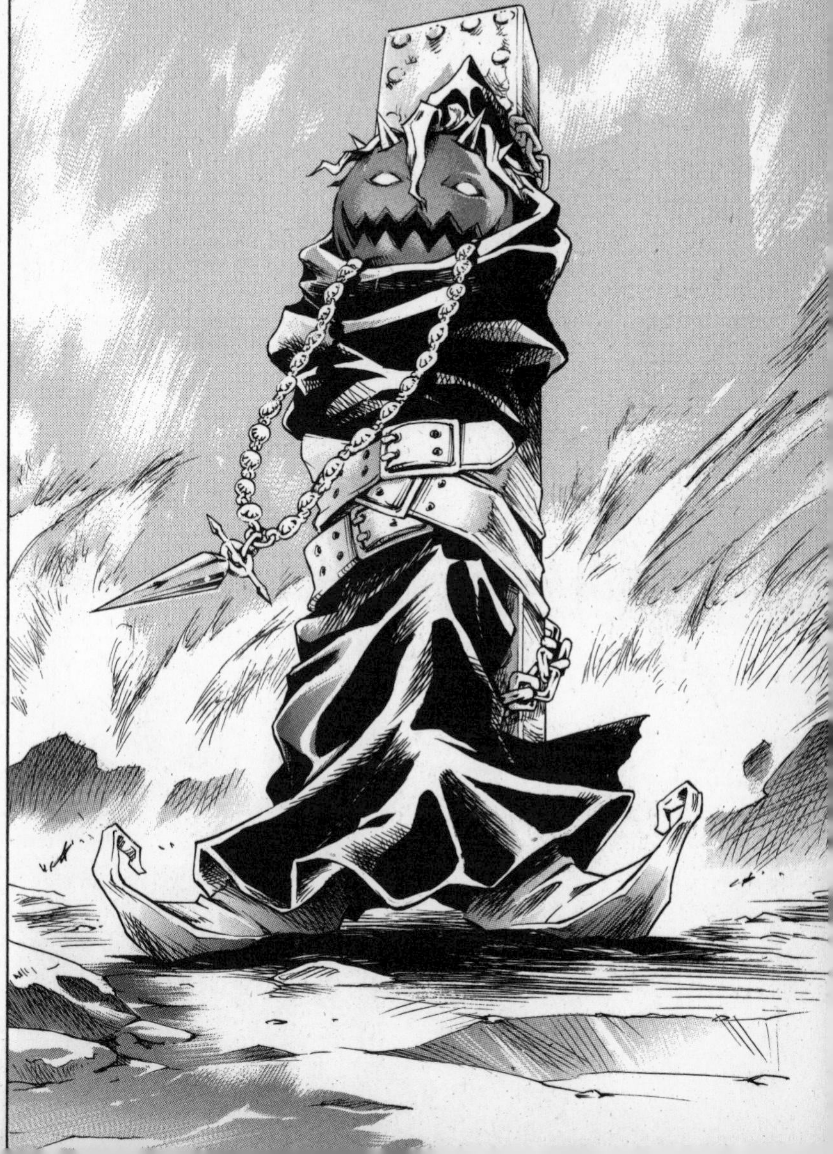

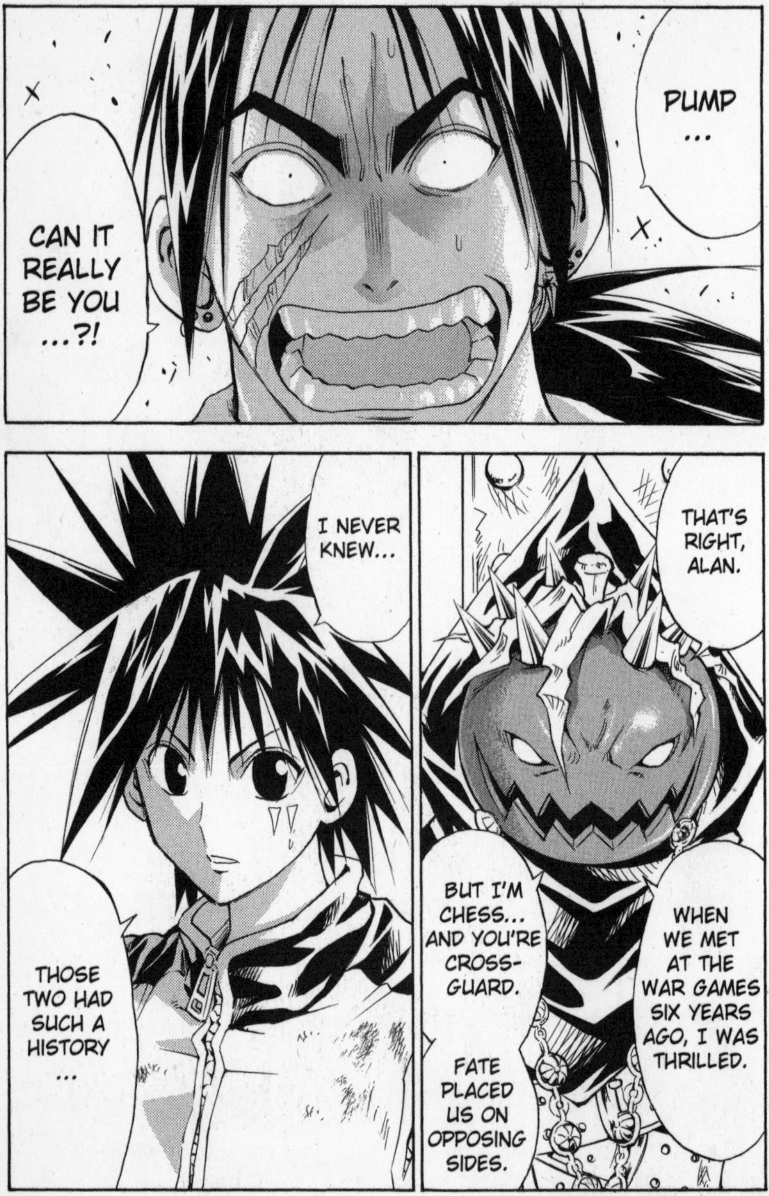
PUMP...
CAN IT REALLY BE YOU...?!
THAT'S RIGHT, ALAN.
WHEN WE MET AT THE WAR GAMES SIX YEARS AGO, I WAS THRILLED.
BUT I'M CHESS... AND YOU'RE CROSS-GUARD.
FATE PLACED US ON OPPOSING SIDES.
I NEVER KNEW...
THOSE TWO HAD SUCH A HISTORY...

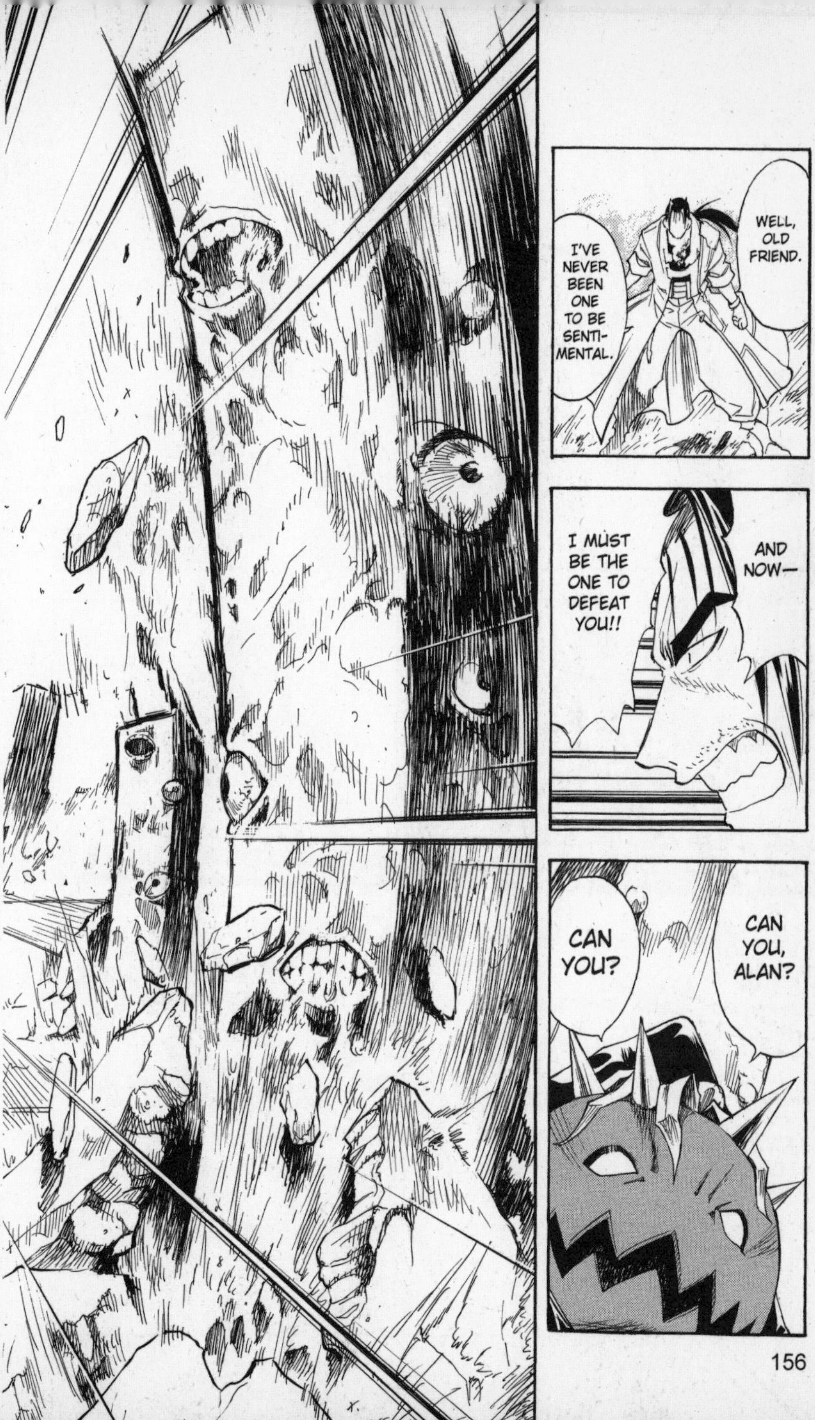
WELL, OLD FRIEND.
I'VE NEVER BEEN ONE TO BE SENTI-MENTAL.
AND NOW—
I MUST BE THE ONE TO DEFEAT YOU!!
CAN YOU, ALAN?
CAN YOU?

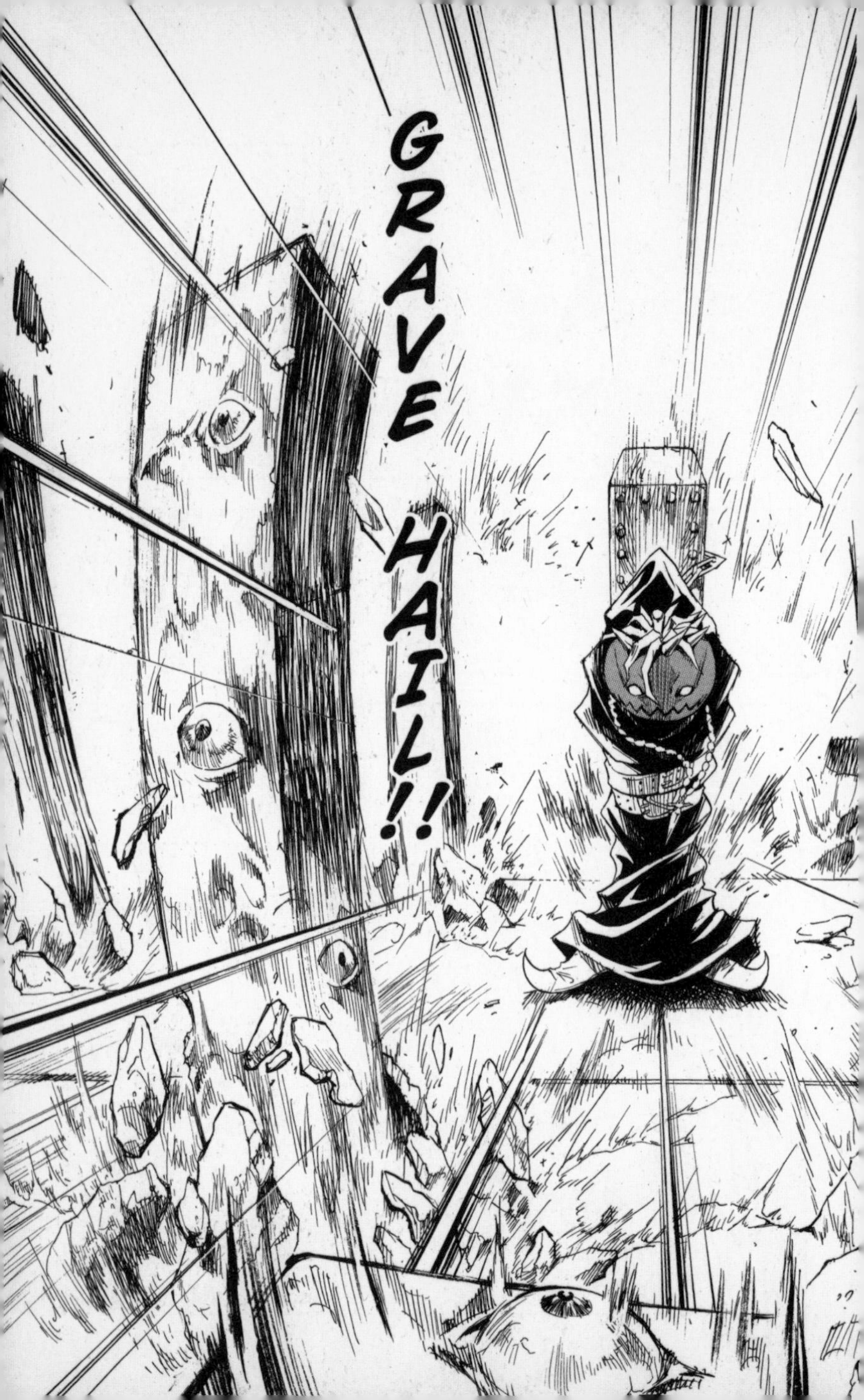
GRAVE HAIL!!

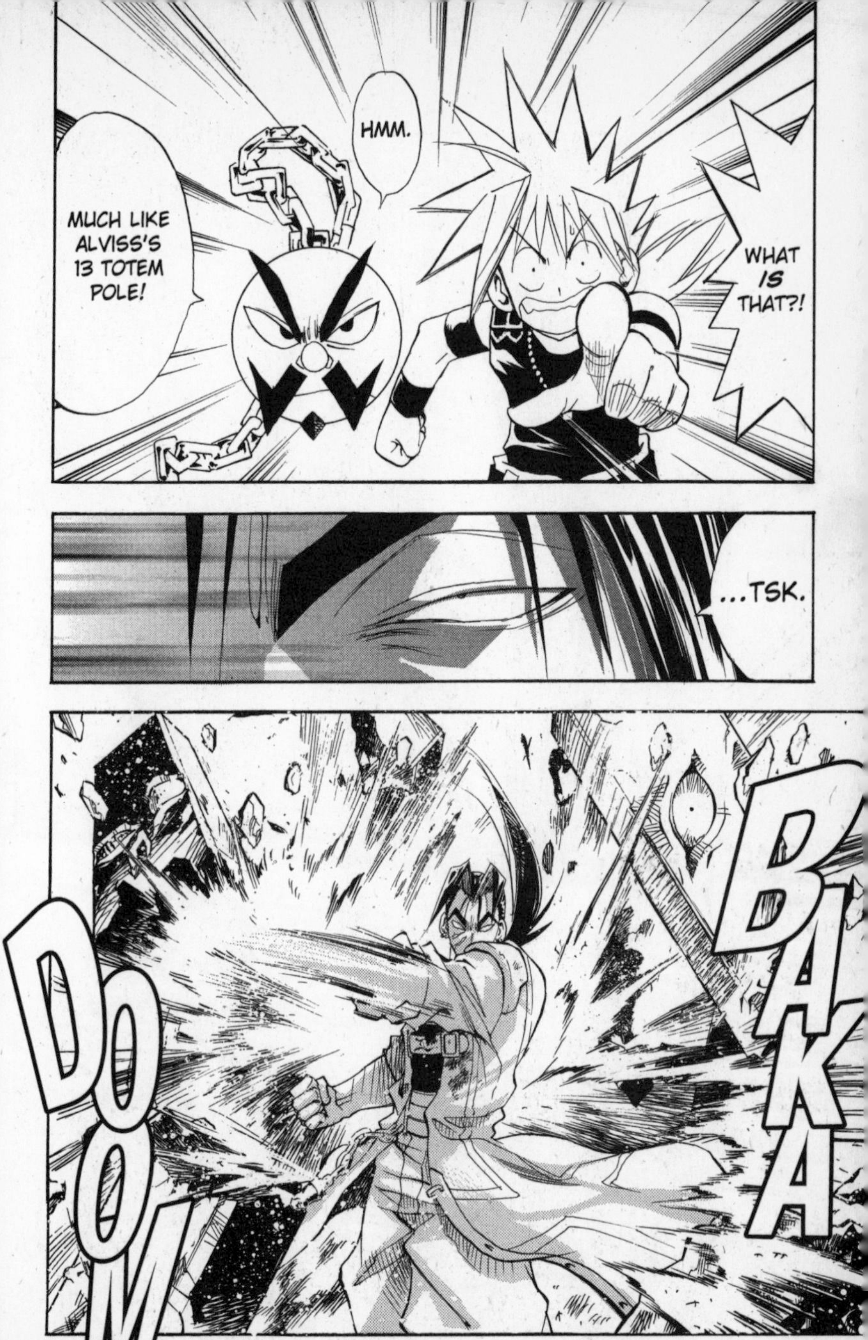
WHAT IS THAT?!
HMM.
MUCH LIKE ALVISS'S 13 TOTEM POLE!
...TSK.
BAKA
DOOM

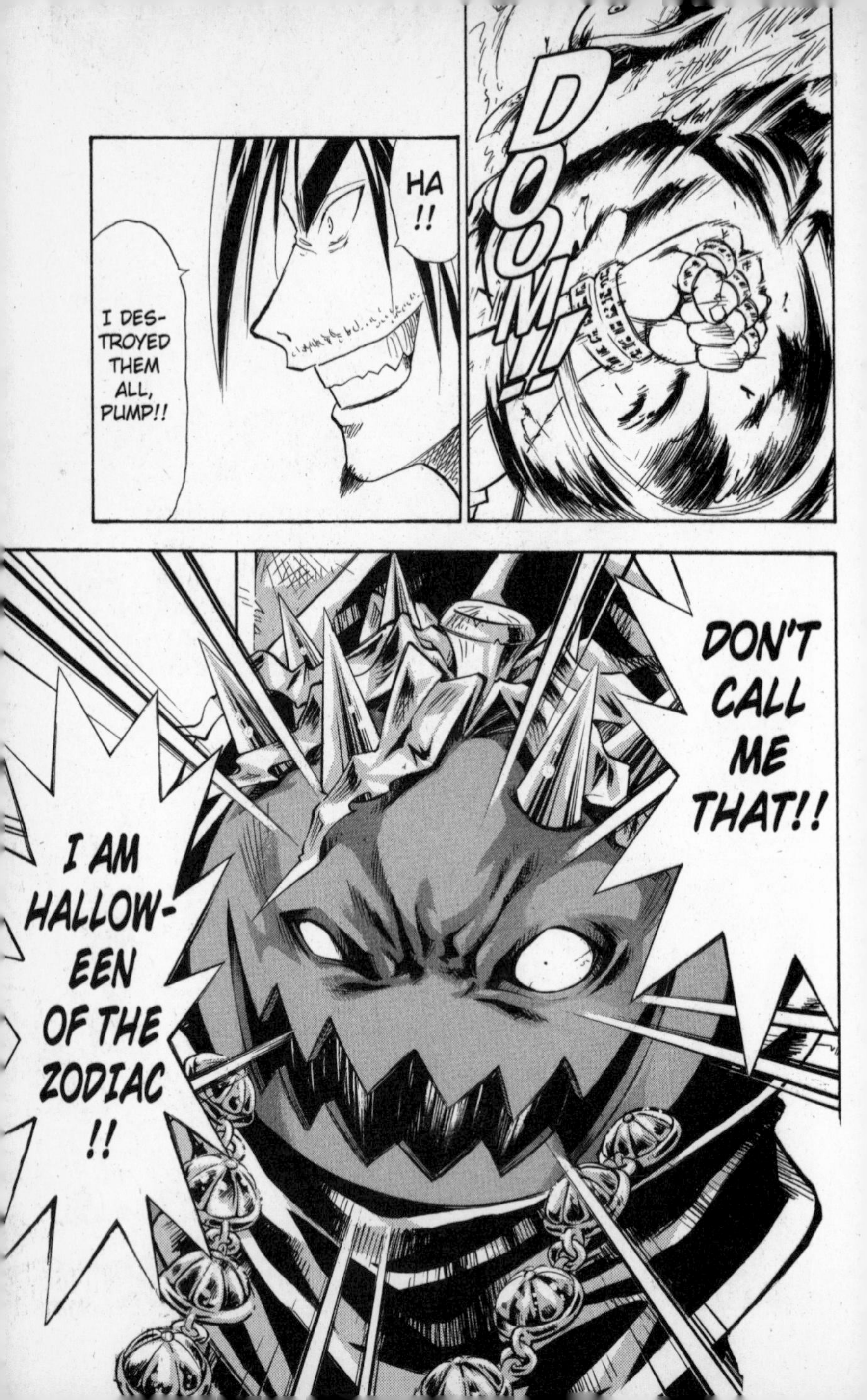
DOOM!!
HA !!
I DES-TROYED THEM ALL, PUMP!!
DON'T CALL ME THAT!!
I AM HALLOW-EEN OF THE ZODIAC !!

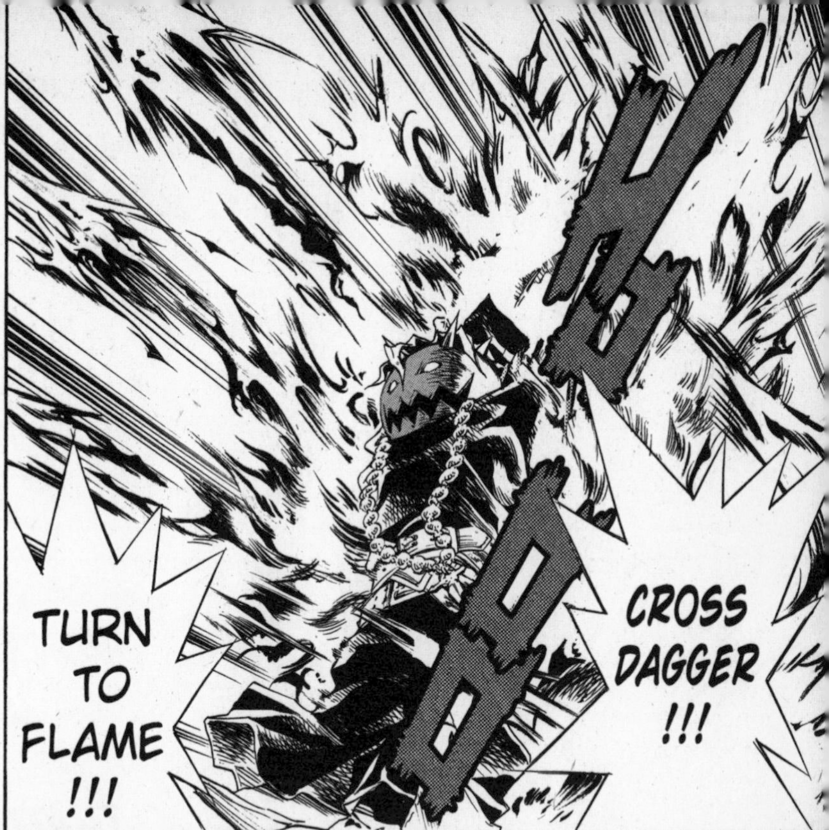
CROSS DAGGER !!!
TURN TO FLAME !!!
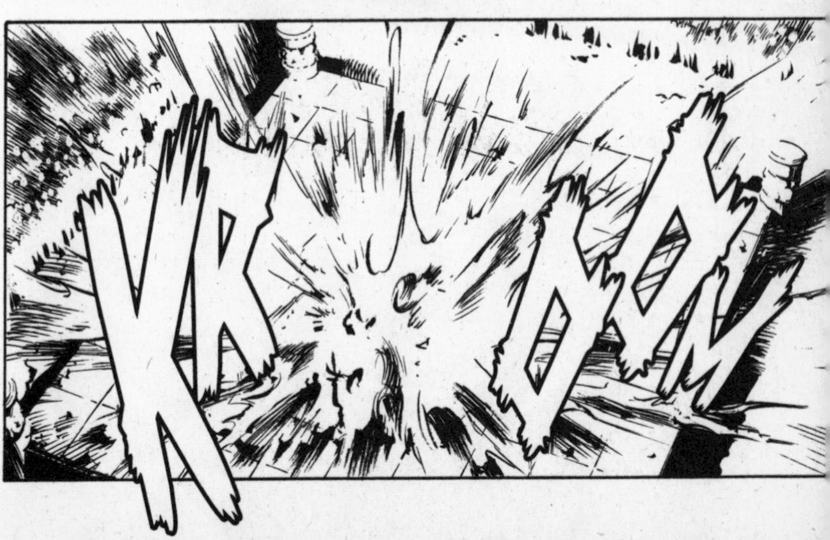

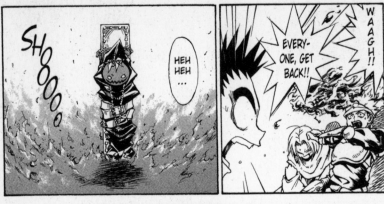

SHOOOOOO

HEH HEH ...

EVERY- ONE, GET BACK!!

WAAGH!!

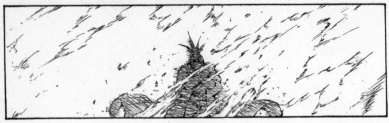

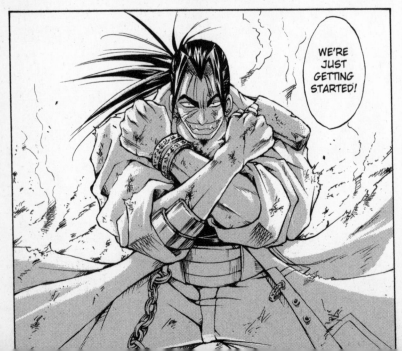

WE'RE JUST GETTING STARTED!

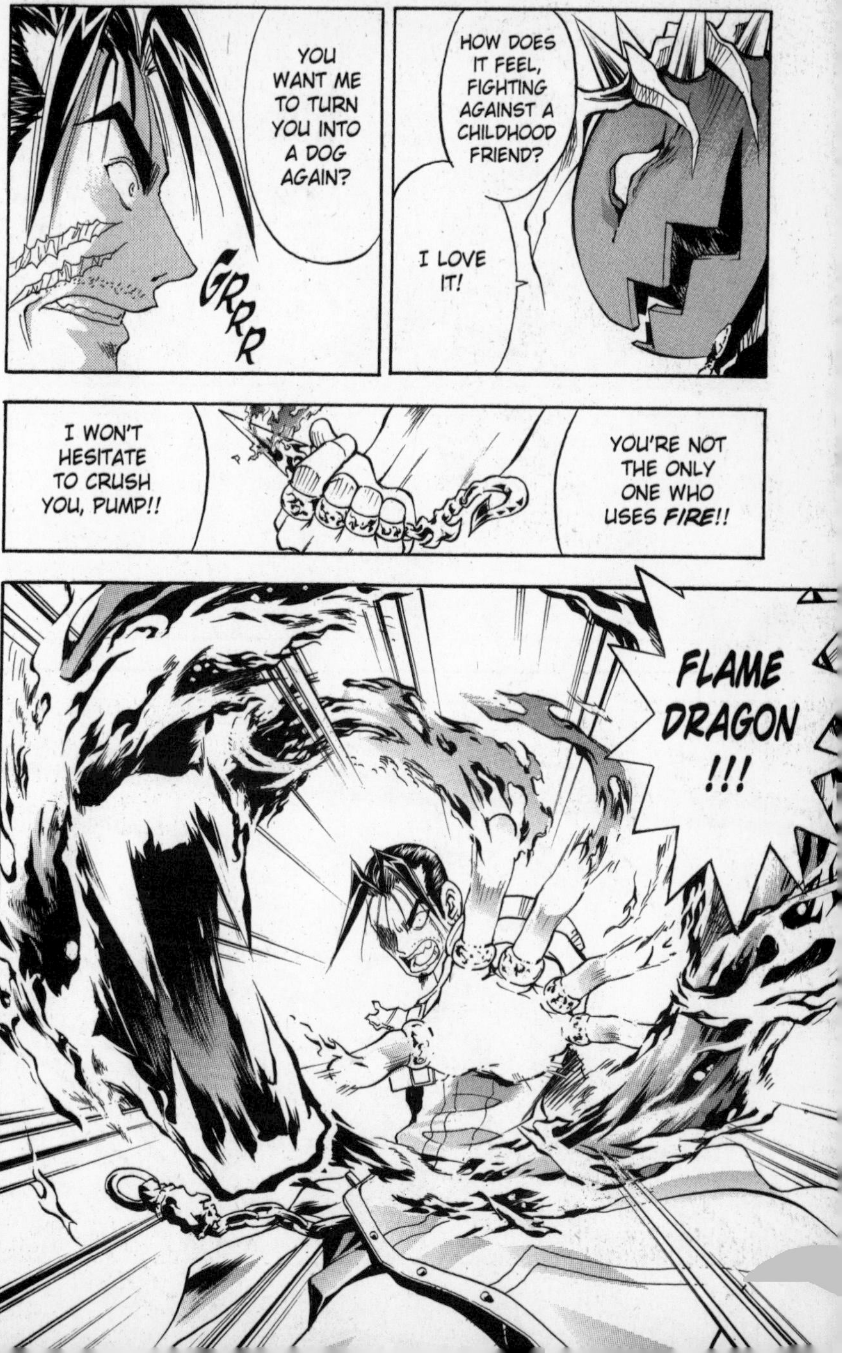
HOW DOES IT FEEL, FIGHTING AGAINST A CHILDHOOD FRIEND?
I LOVE IT!
YOU WANT ME TO TURN YOU INTO A DOG AGAIN?
GRRR
YOU'RE NOT THE ONLY ONE WHO USES *FIRE*!!
I WON'T HESITATE TO CRUSH YOU, PUMP!!
FLAME DRAGON !!!

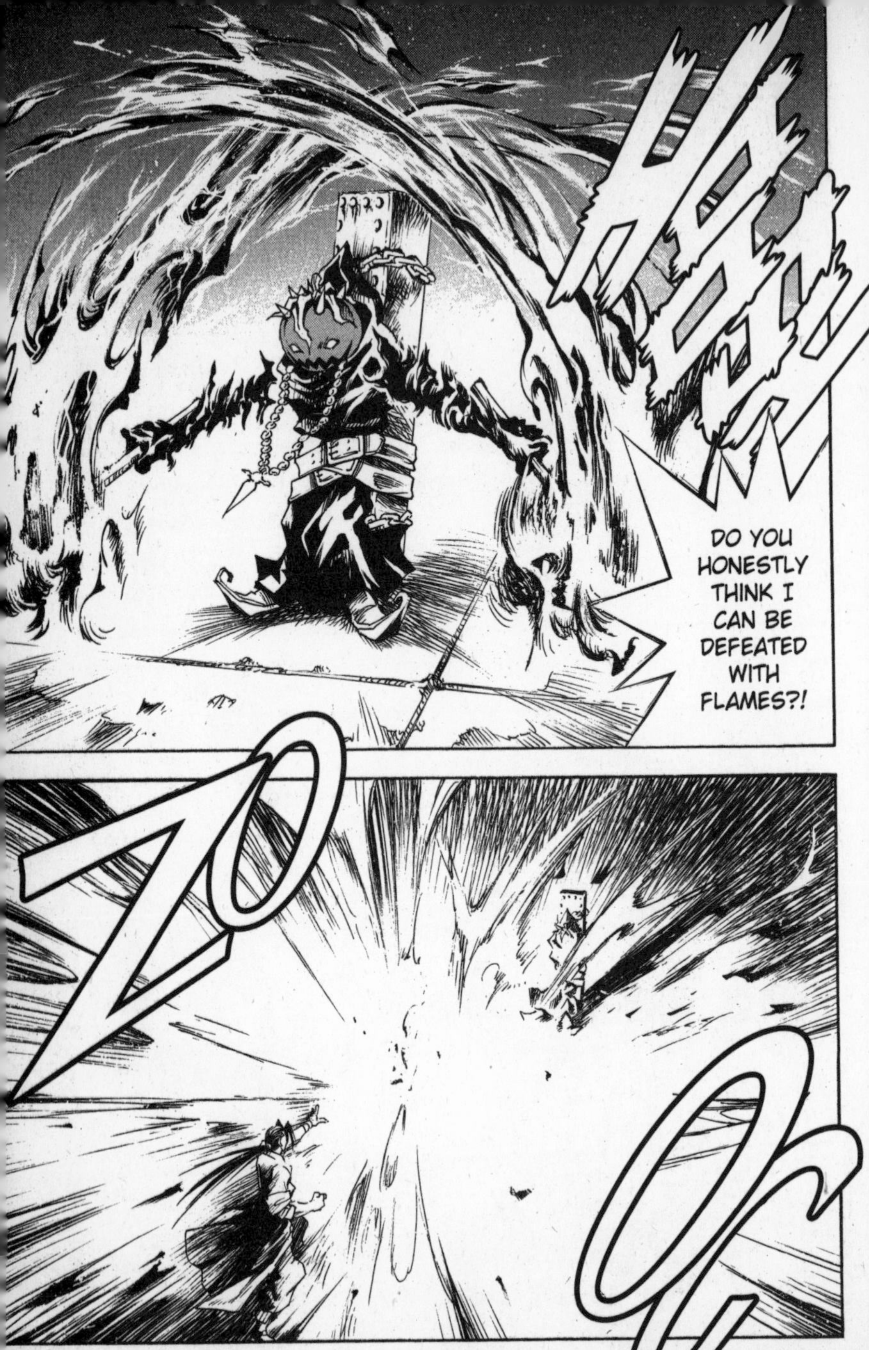
DO YOU HONESTLY THINK I CAN BE DEFEATED WITH FLAMES?!

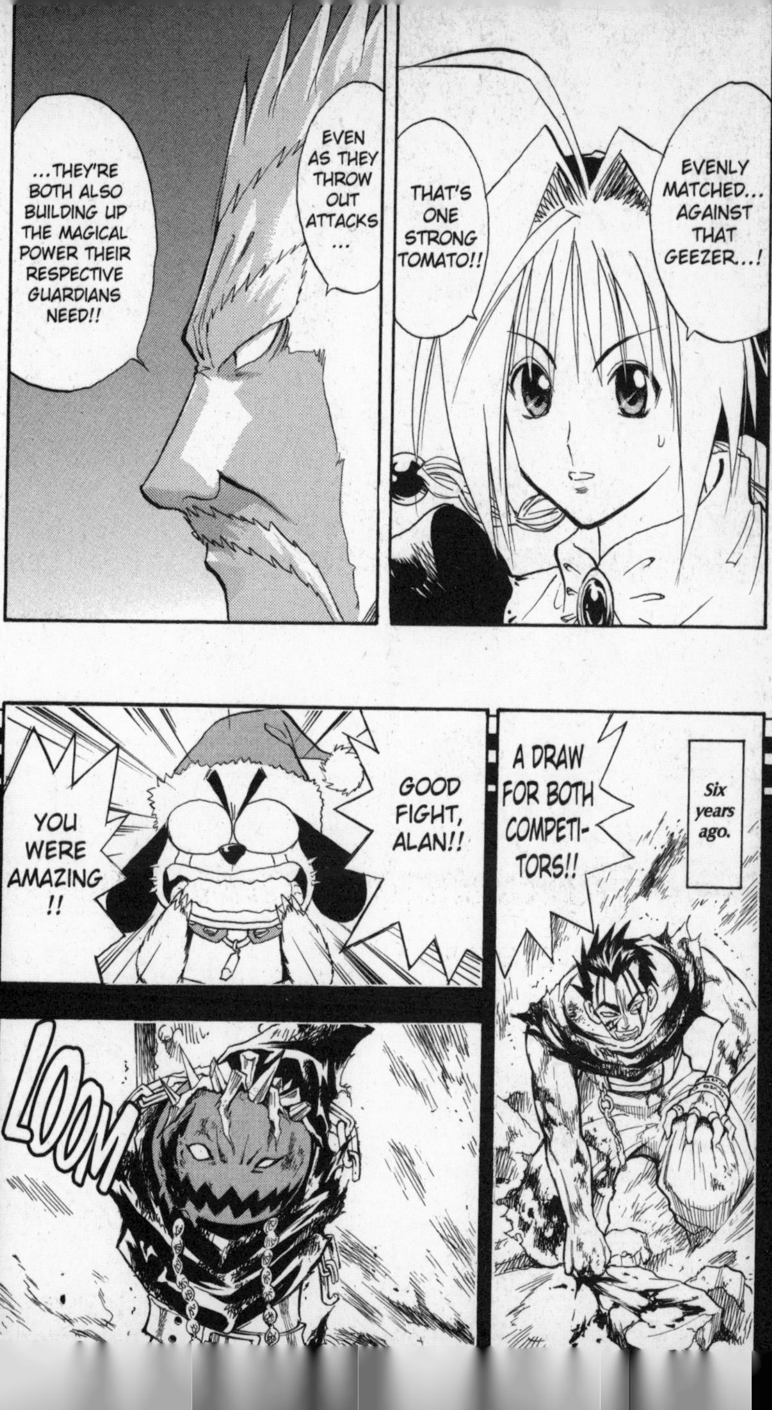
EVENLY MATCHED... AGAINST THAT GEEZER...!
THAT'S ONE STRONG TOMATO!!
EVEN AS THEY THROW OUT ATTACKS ...
...THEY'RE BOTH ALSO BUILDING UP THE MAGICAL POWER THEIR RESPECTIVE GUARDIANS NEED!!
Six years ago.
A DRAW FOR BOTH COMPETITORS!!
GOOD FIGHT, ALAN!!
YOU WERE AMAZING!!
LOOM

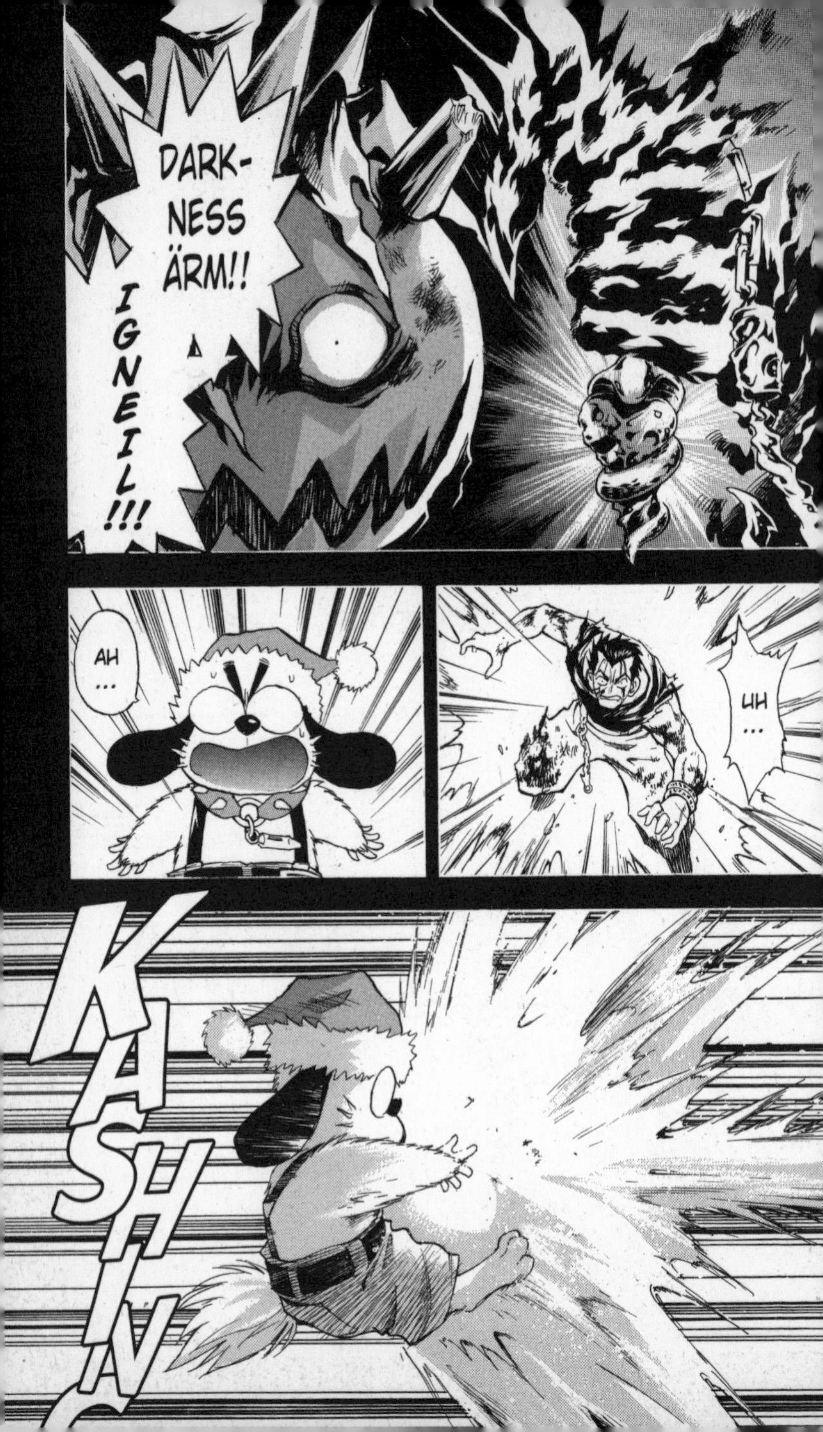
DARK-NESS ÄRM!!
IGNEEIL!!!
UH ...
AH ...
KASHIN

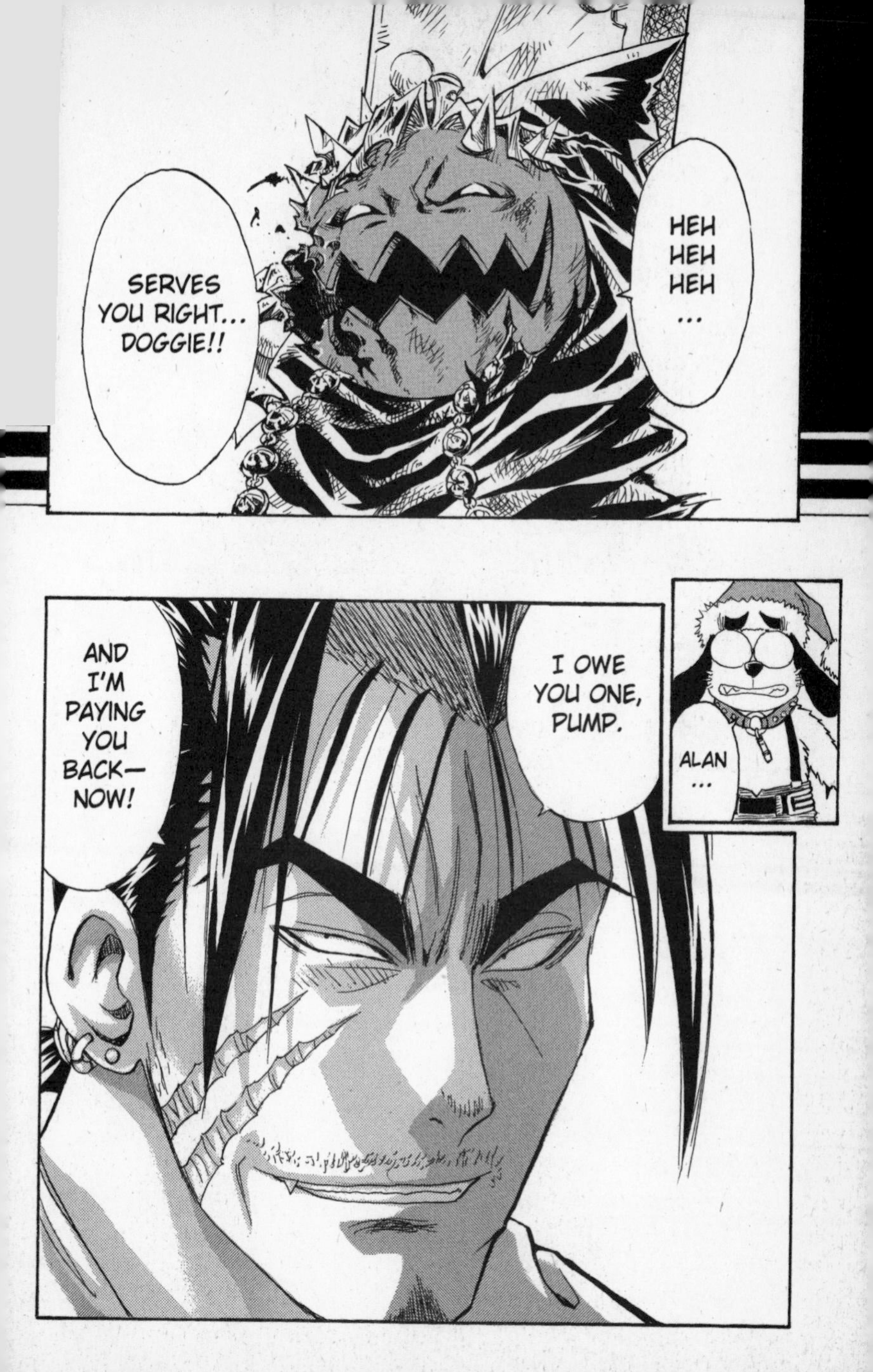
HEH HEH HEH ...
SERVES YOU RIGHT... DOGGIE!!
ALAN ...
I OWE YOU ONE, PUMP.
AND I'M PAYING YOU BACK— NOW!

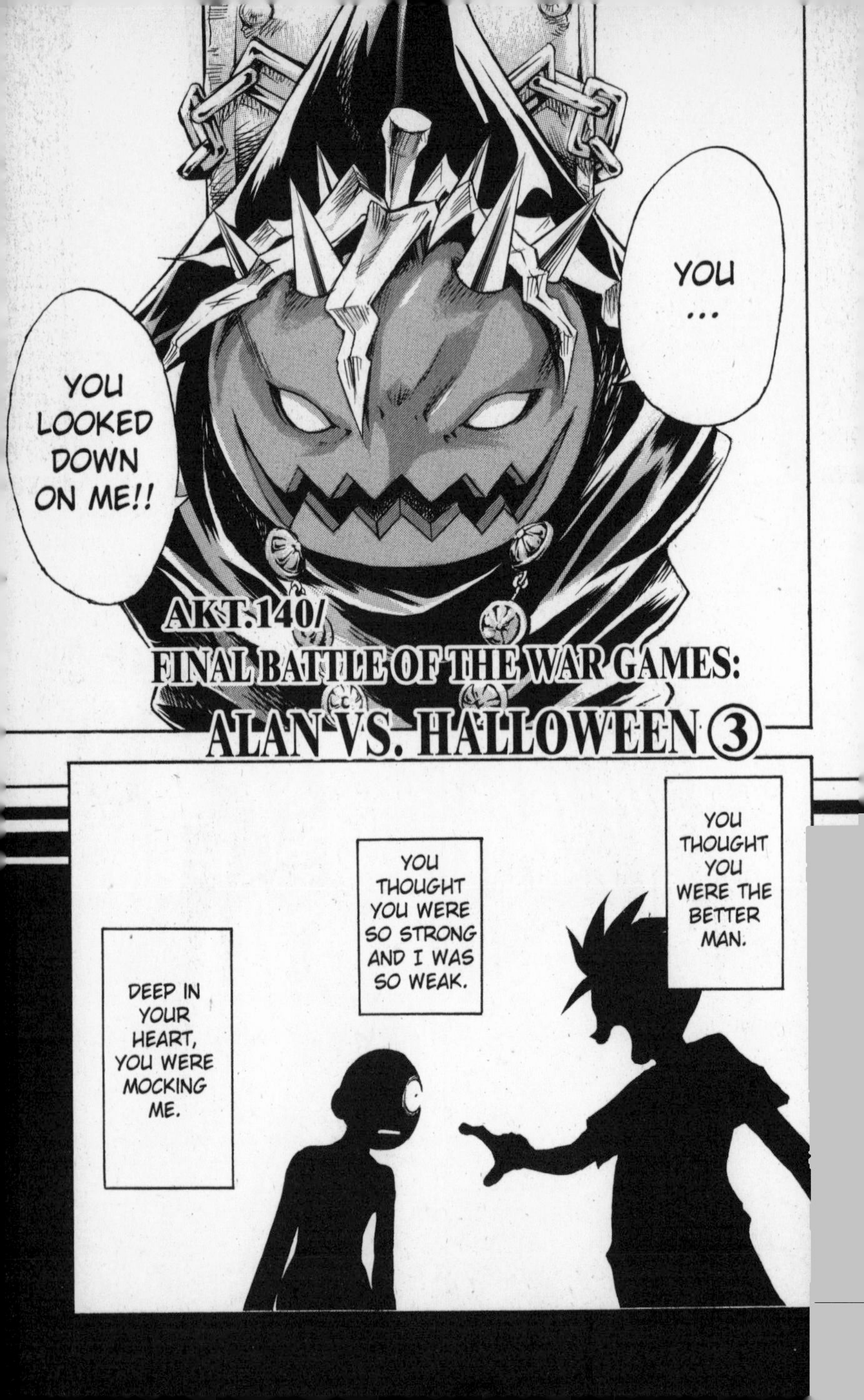
YOU ...
YOU LOOKED DOWN ON ME!!
AKT.140/ FINAL BATTLE OF THE WAR GAMES: ALAN VS. HALLOWEEN ③
YOU THOUGHT YOU WERE THE BETTER MAN.
YOU THOUGHT YOU WERE SO STRONG AND I WAS SO WEAK.
DEEP IN YOUR HEART, YOU WERE MOCKING ME.

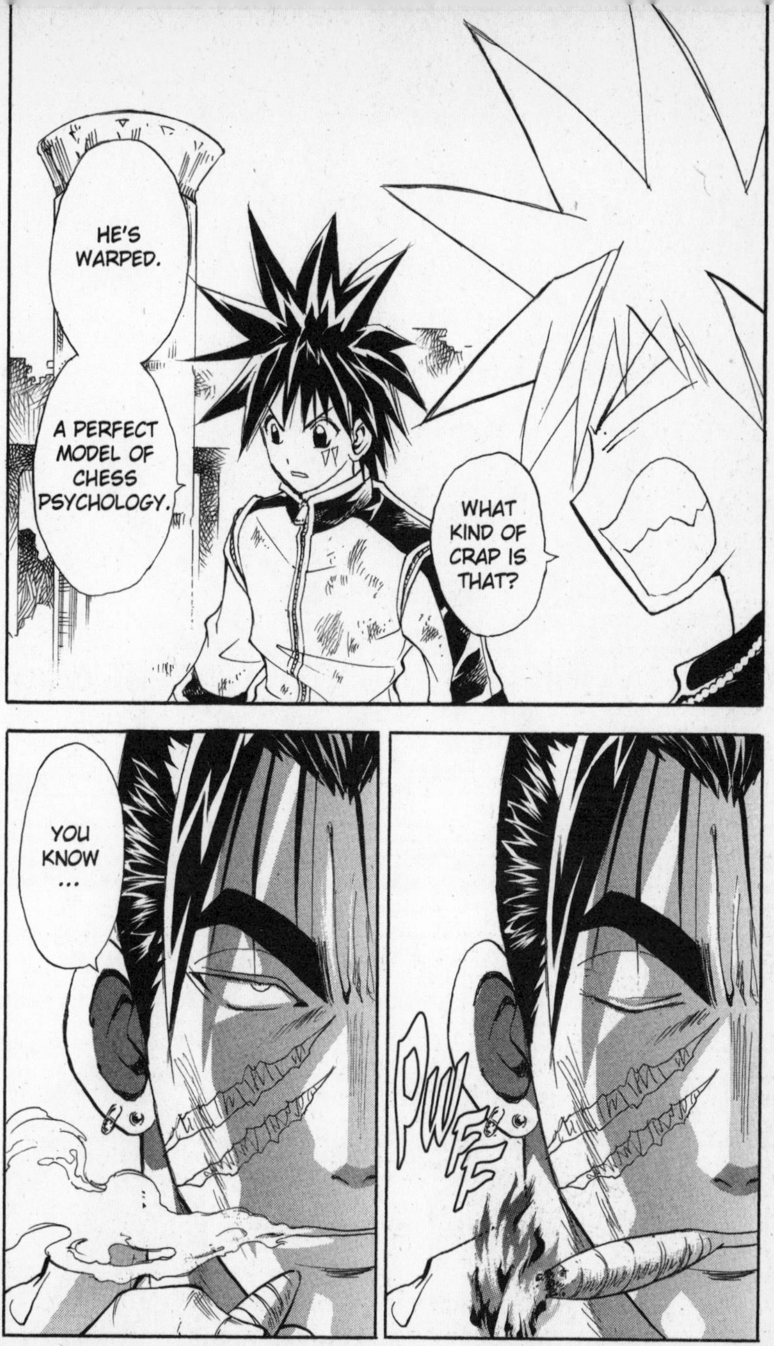
WHAT KIND OF CRAP IS THAT?
HE'S WARPED.
A PERFECT MODEL OF CHESS PSYCHOLOGY.
PWFF
YOU KNOW ...

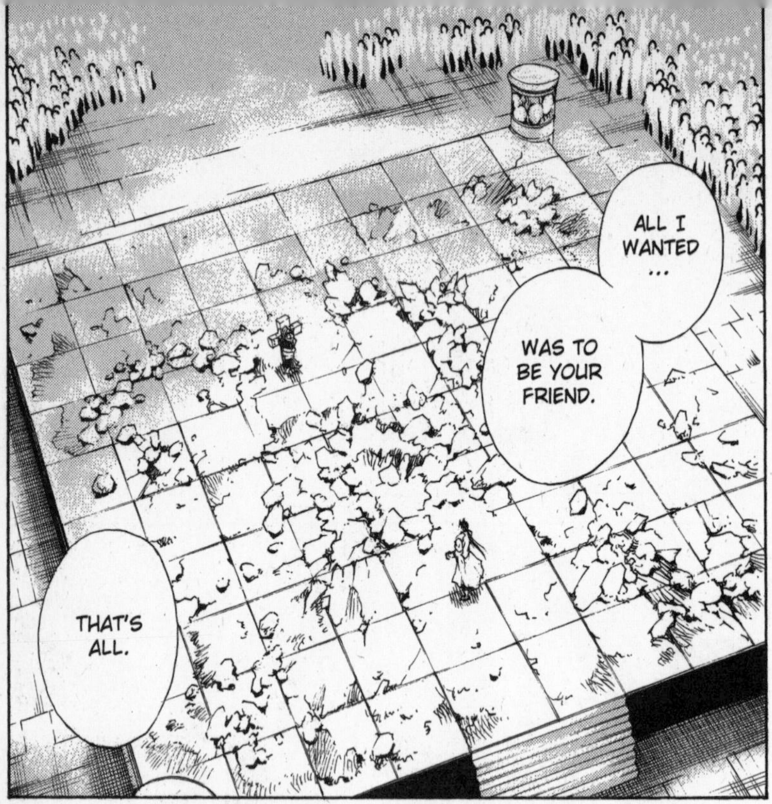
ALL I WANTED ...
WAS TO BE YOUR FRIEND.
THAT'S ALL.

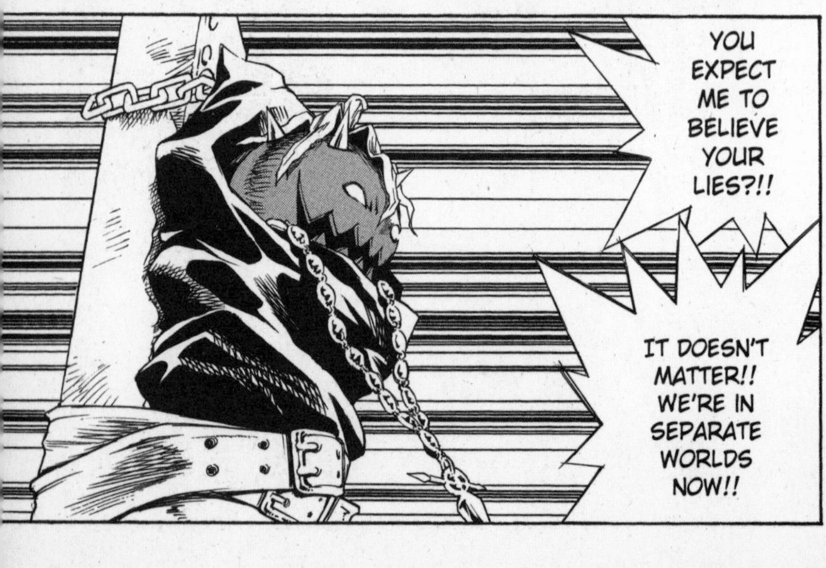
YOU EXPECT ME TO BELIEVE YOUR LIES?!!
IT DOESN'T MATTER!! WE'RE IN SEPARATE WORLDS NOW!!

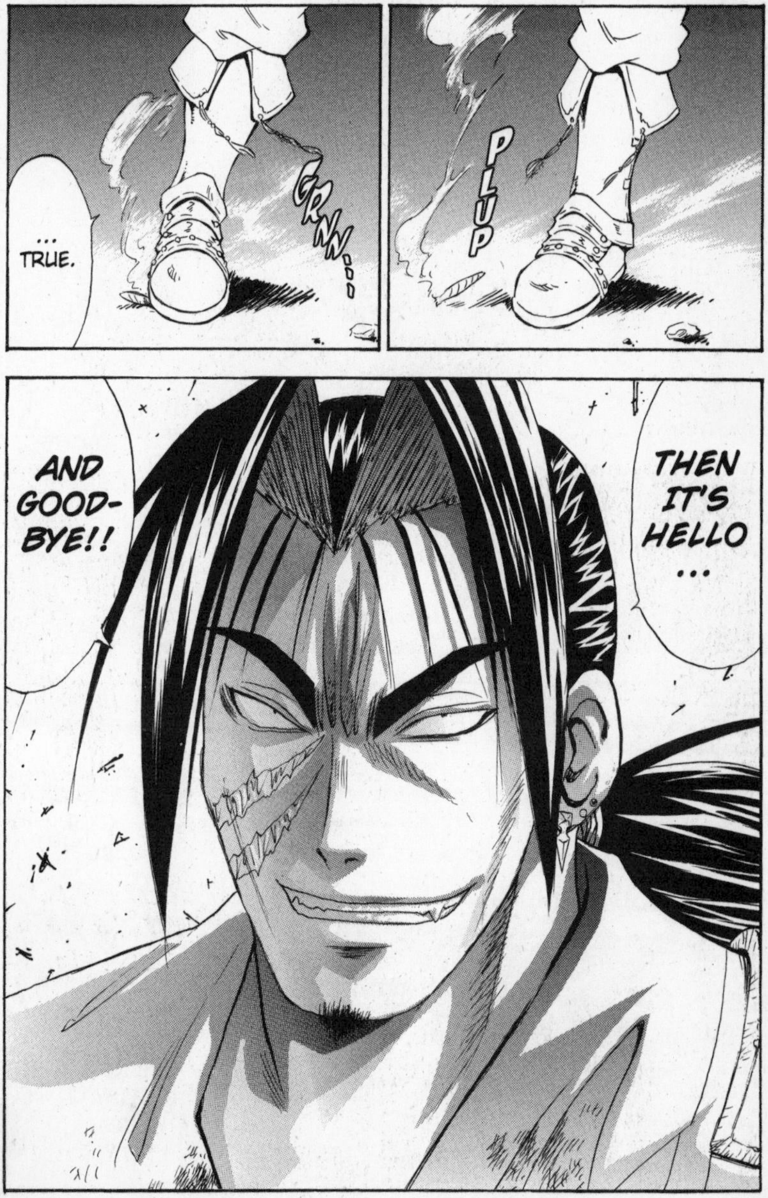
PLUP
GRNN...
... TRUE.
THEN IT'S HELLO ...
AND GOOD-BYE!!

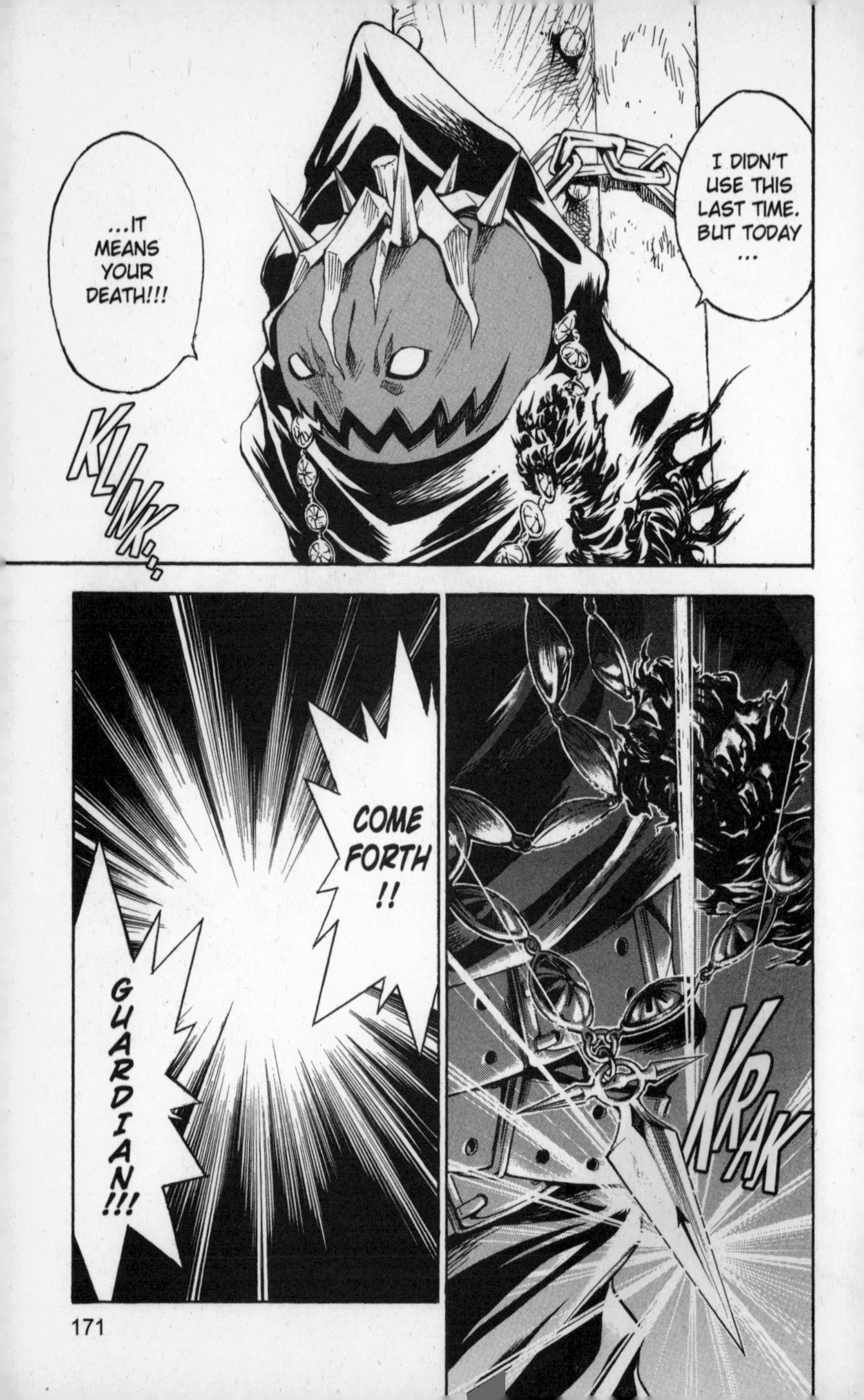
I DIDN'T USE THIS LAST TIME. BUT TODAY ...
...IT MEANS YOUR DEATH!!!
KLINK...
KRAK
COME FORTH !!
GUARDIAN!!!

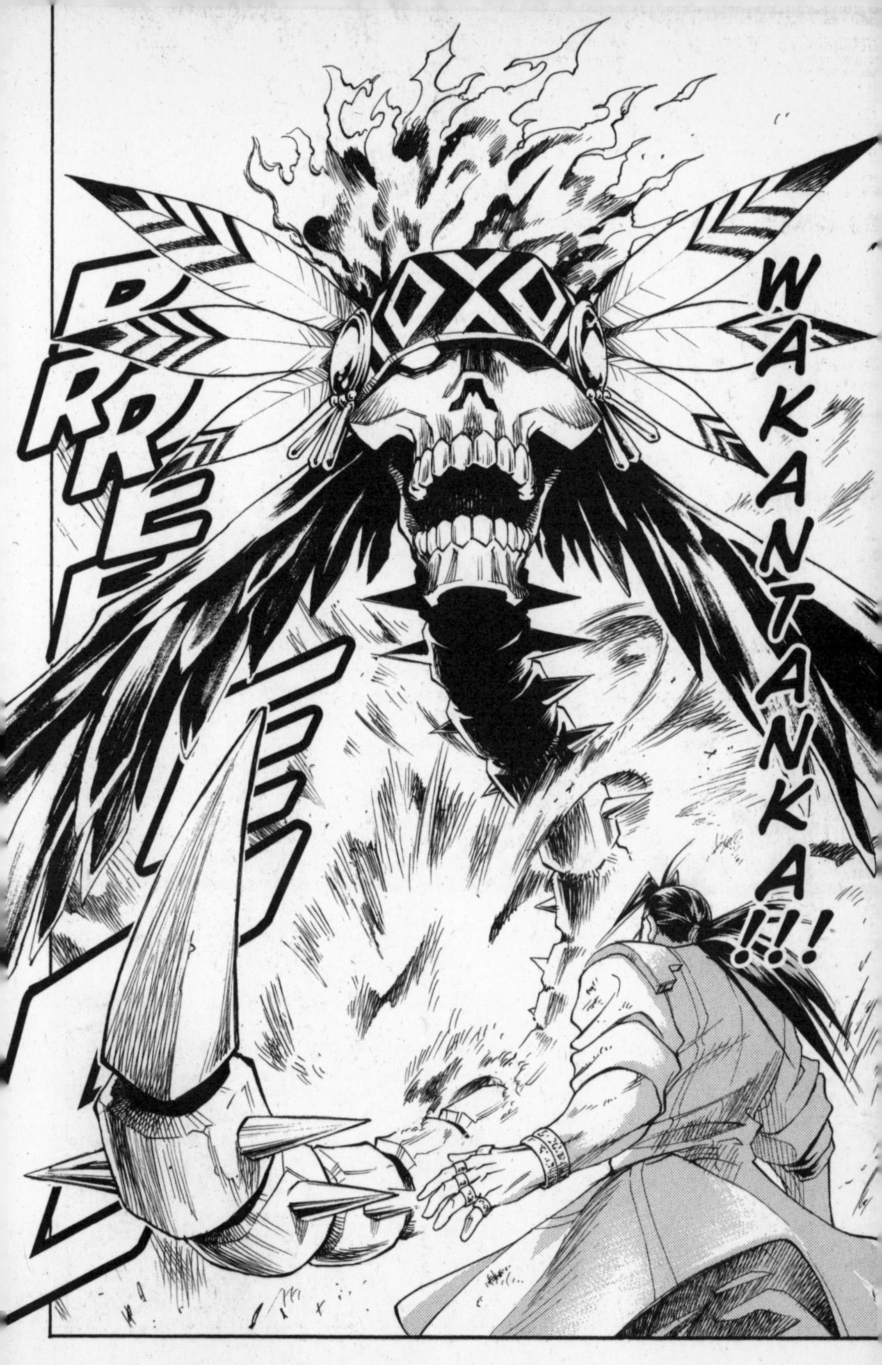
WAKANTANKA!!!

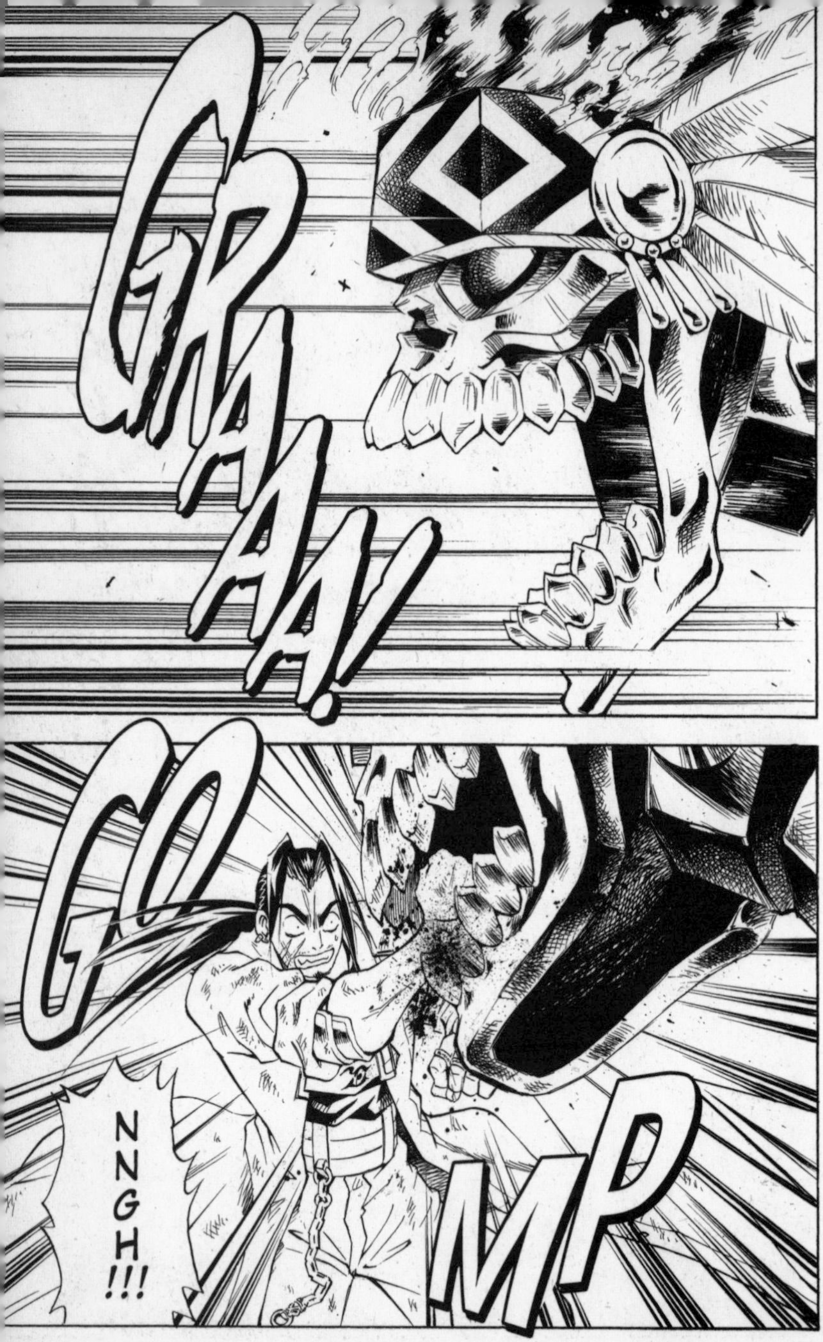
GRAAAA!
GOMP
NNGH!!!

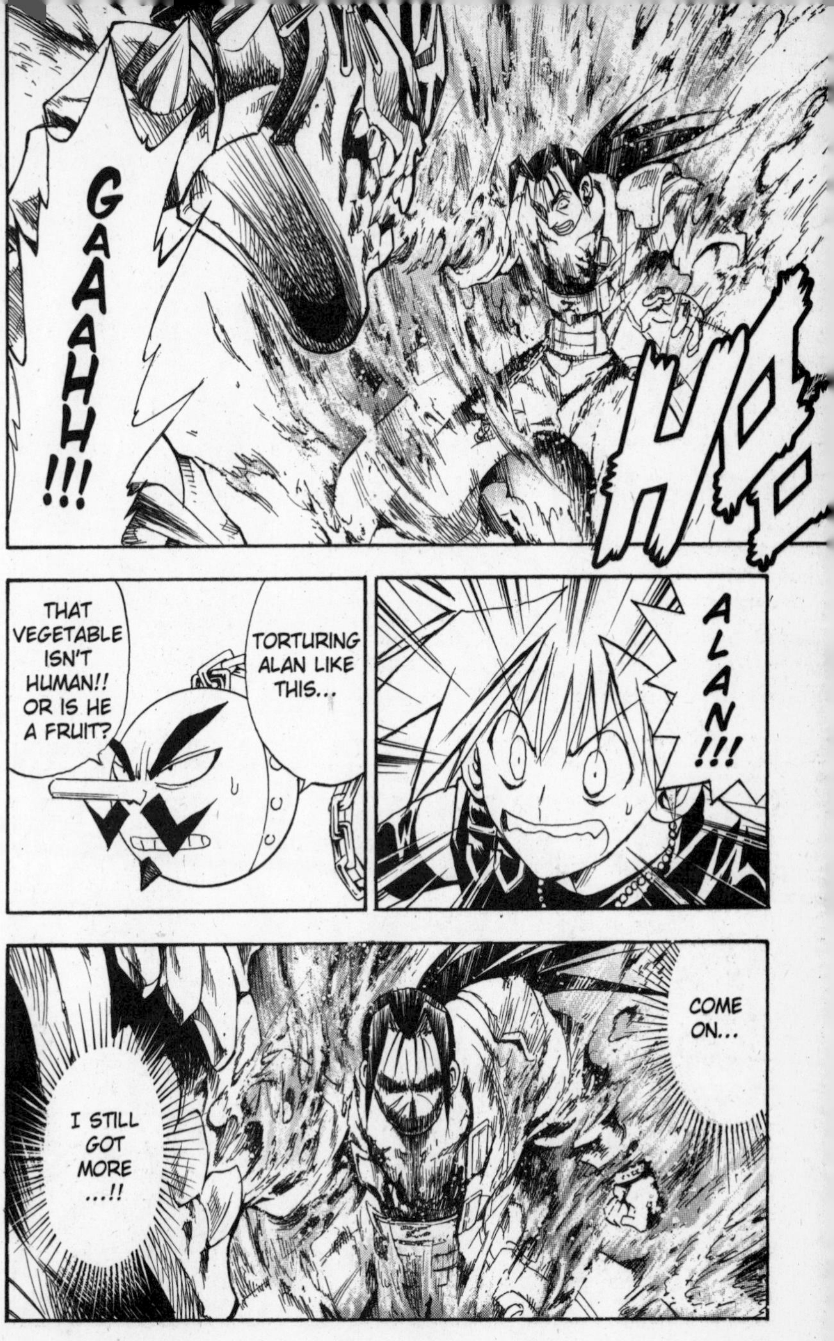
HA
GAAAHH!!!
ALAN!!!
TORTURING ALAN LIKE THIS...
THAT VEGETABLE ISN'T HUMAN!! OR IS HE A FRUIT?
COME ON...
I STILL GOT MORE ...!!

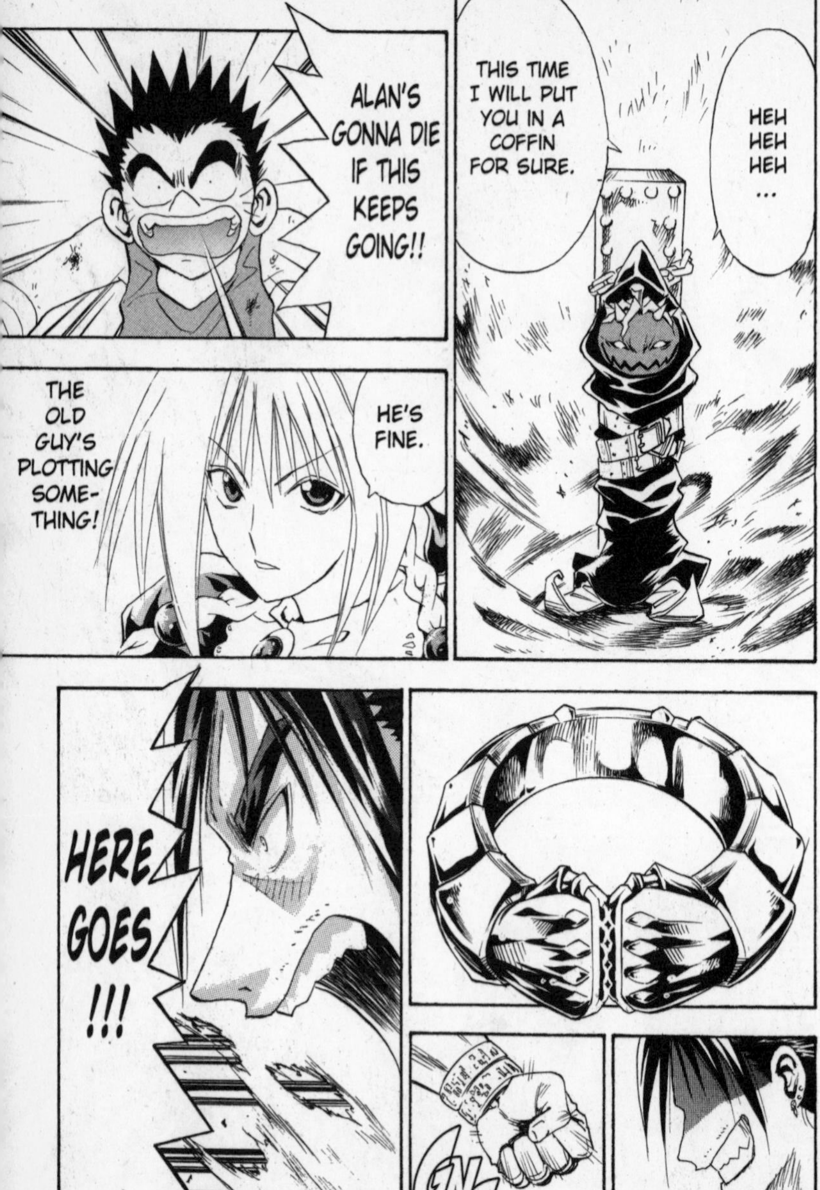
HEH HEH HEH ...
THIS TIME I WILL PUT YOU IN A COFFIN FOR SURE.
ALAN'S GONNA DIE IF THIS KEEPS GOING!!
HE'S FINE.
THE OLD GUY'S PLOTTING SOME-THING!
GNG
HERE GOES !!!

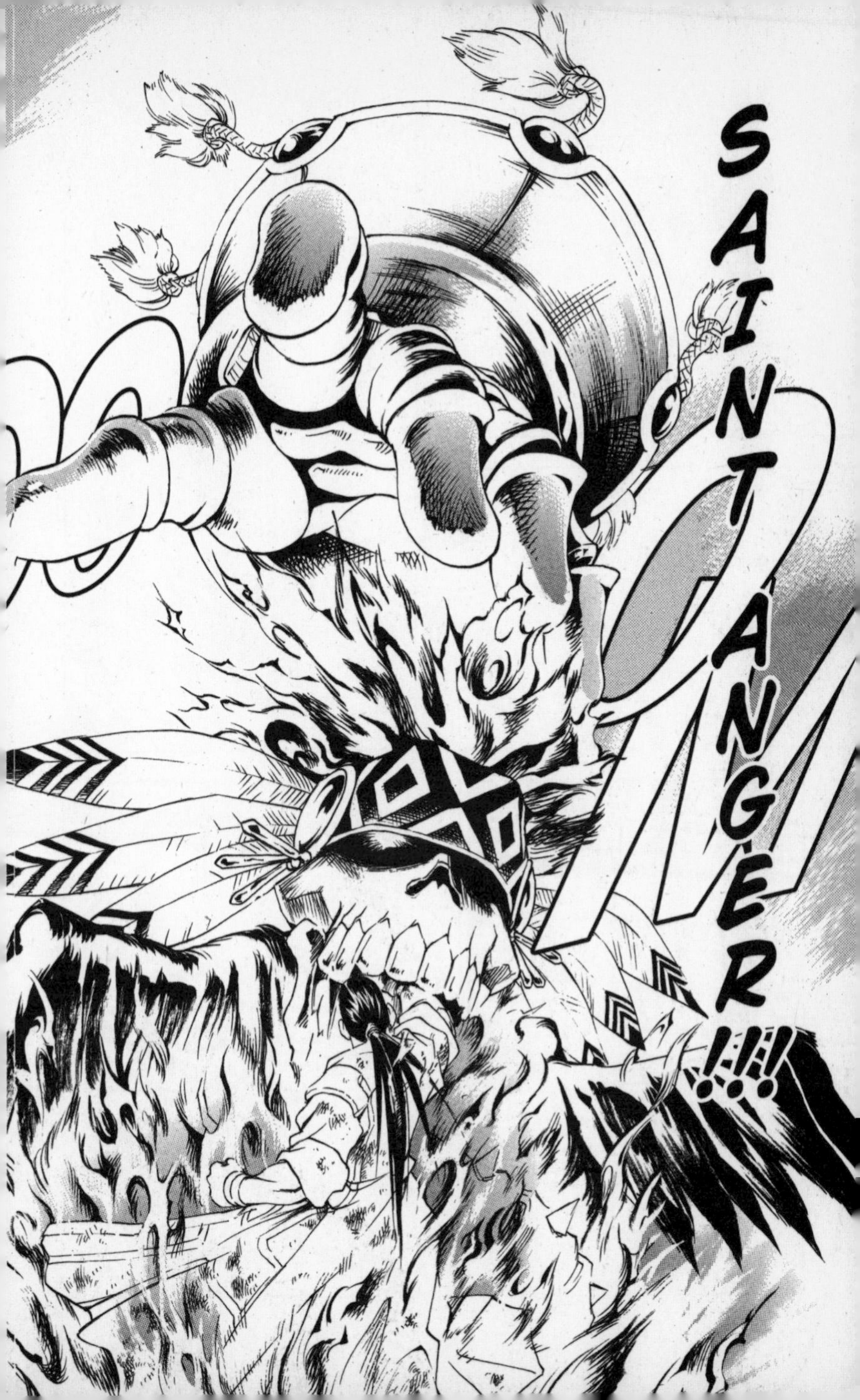
SAINT ANGER!!!!

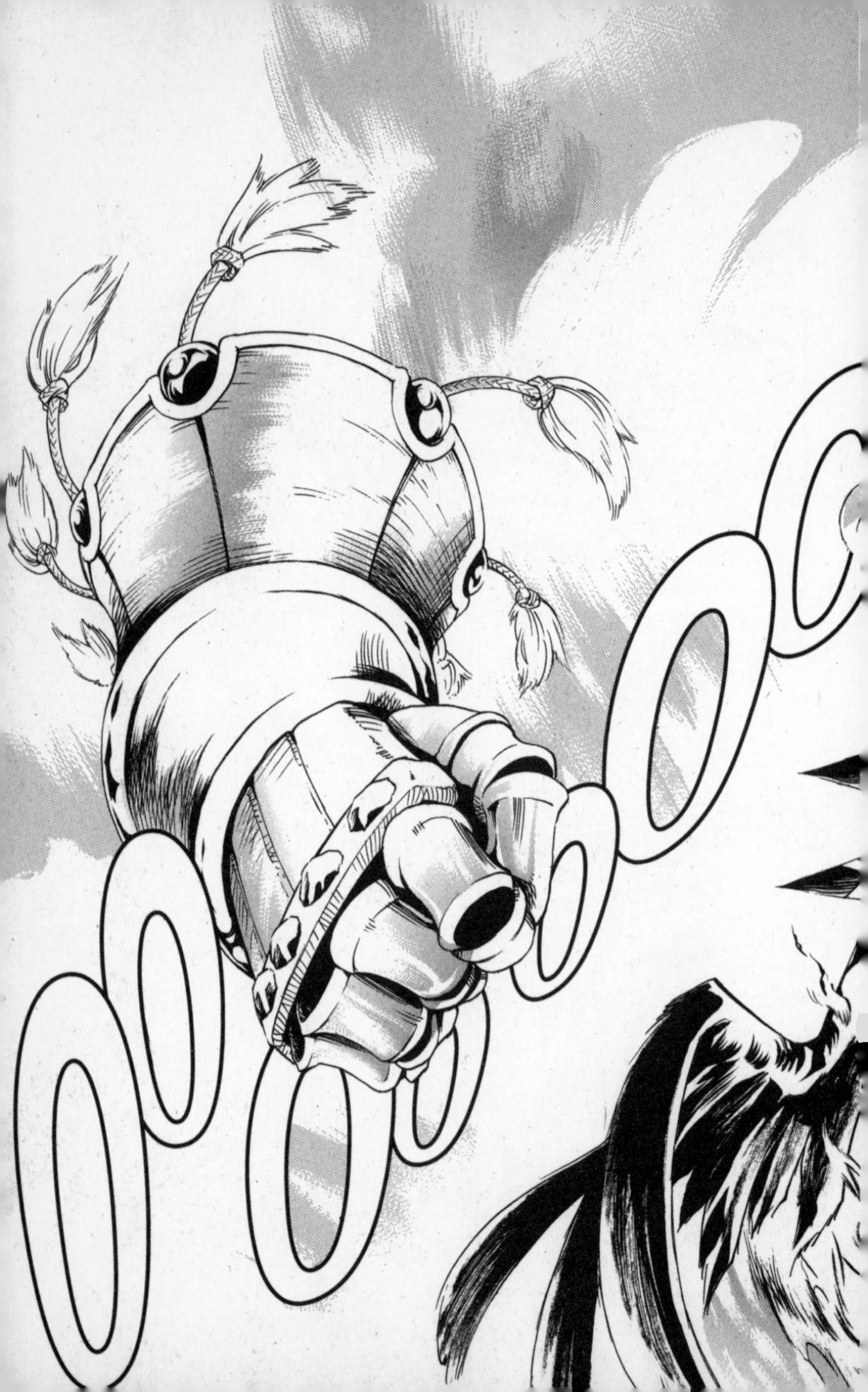

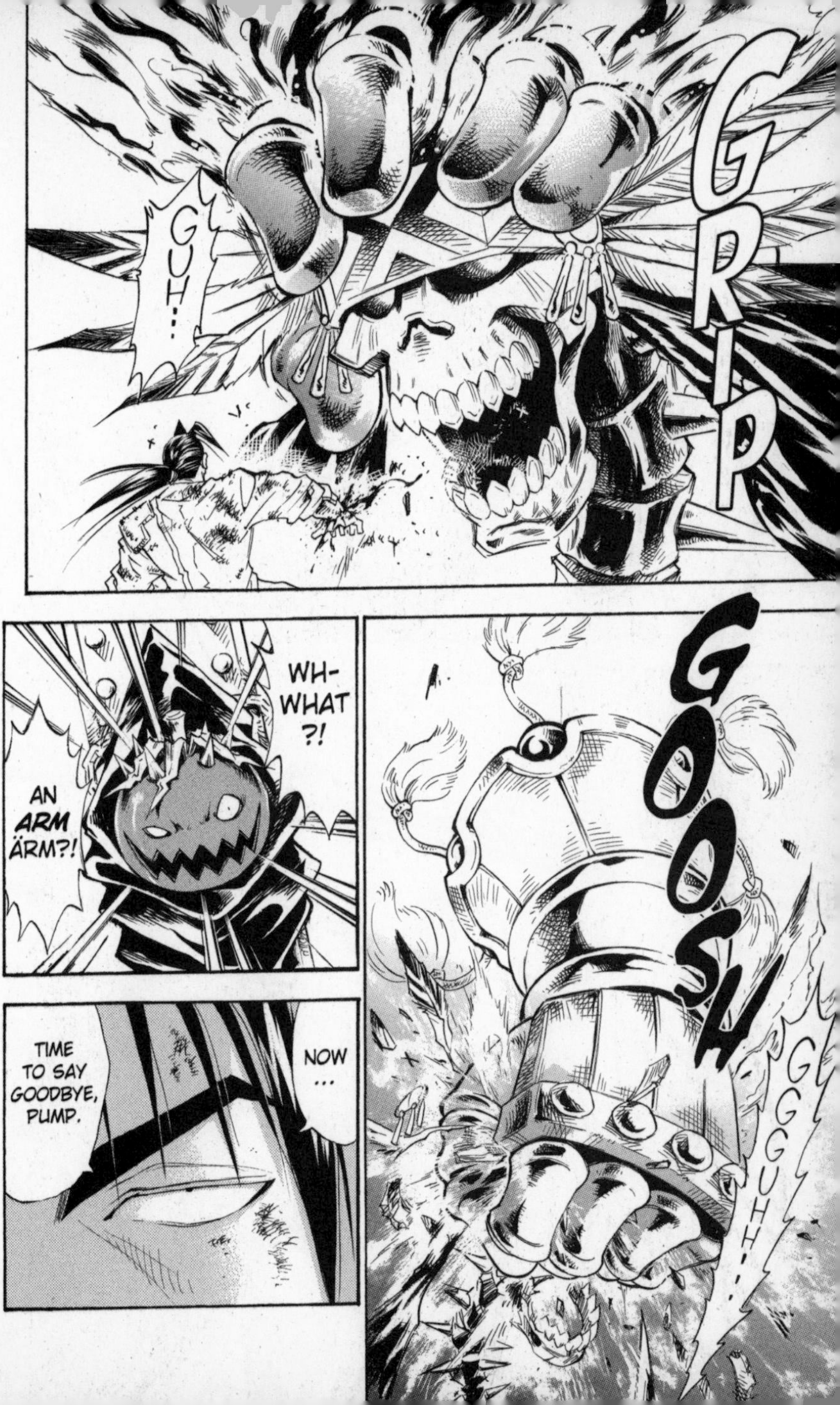
GRIP
GUH...
GOOOSH
GGGGUHH...
WH-WHAT?!
AN ARM ÄRM?!
NOW...
TIME TO SAY GOODBYE, PUMP.

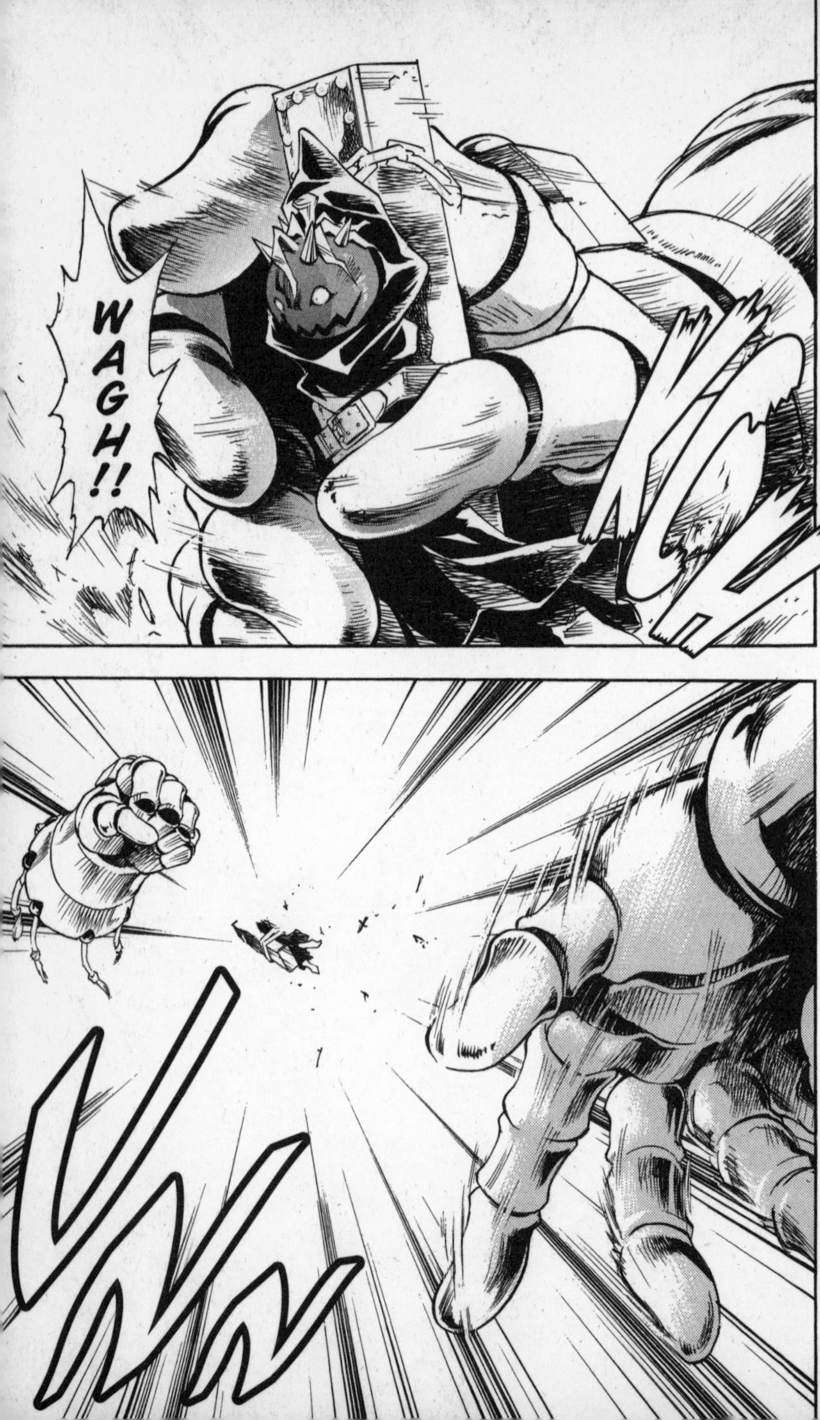
WAGH!!

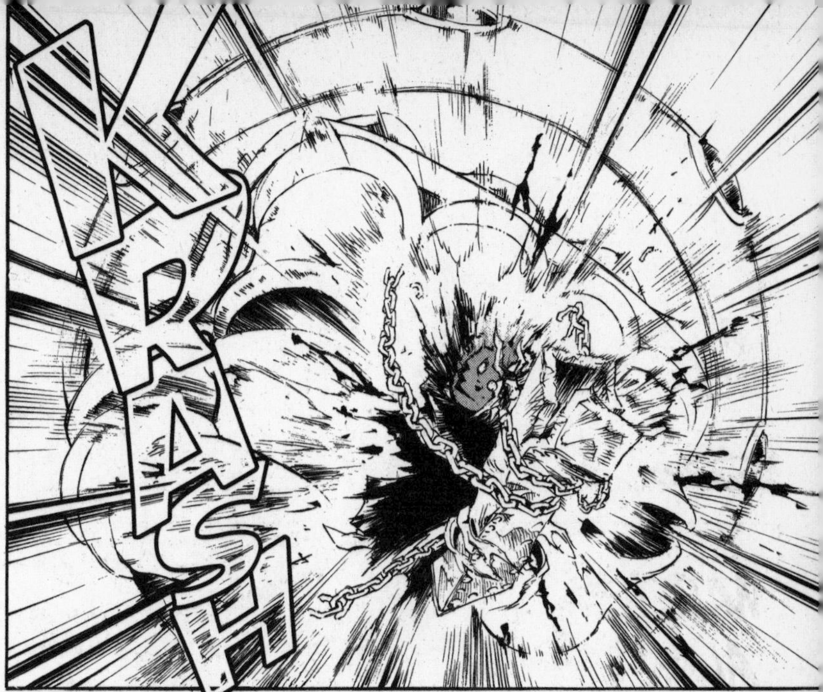
KRASH

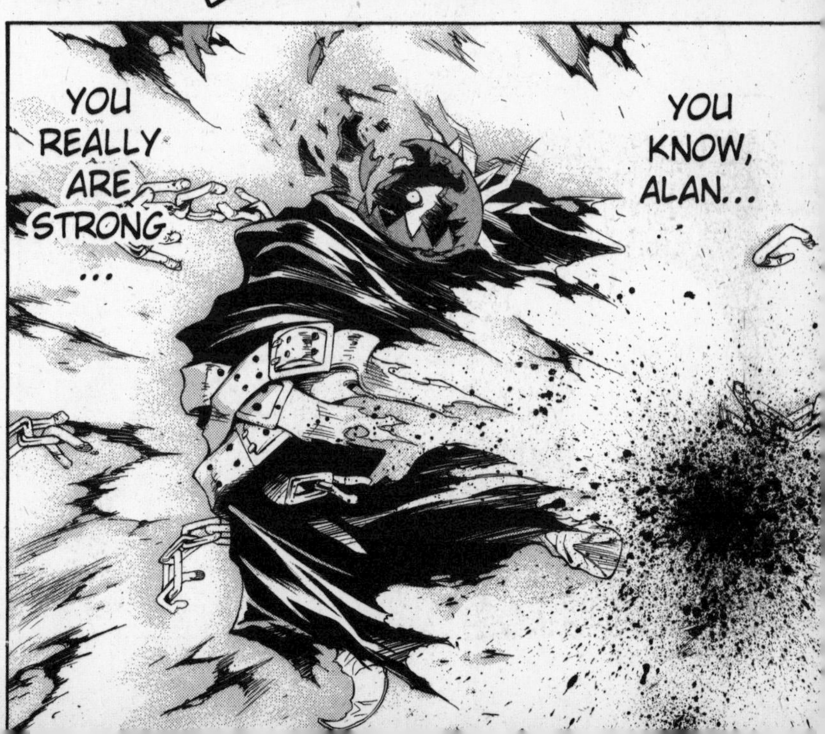
YOU KNOW, ALAN...
YOU REALLY ARE STRONG...

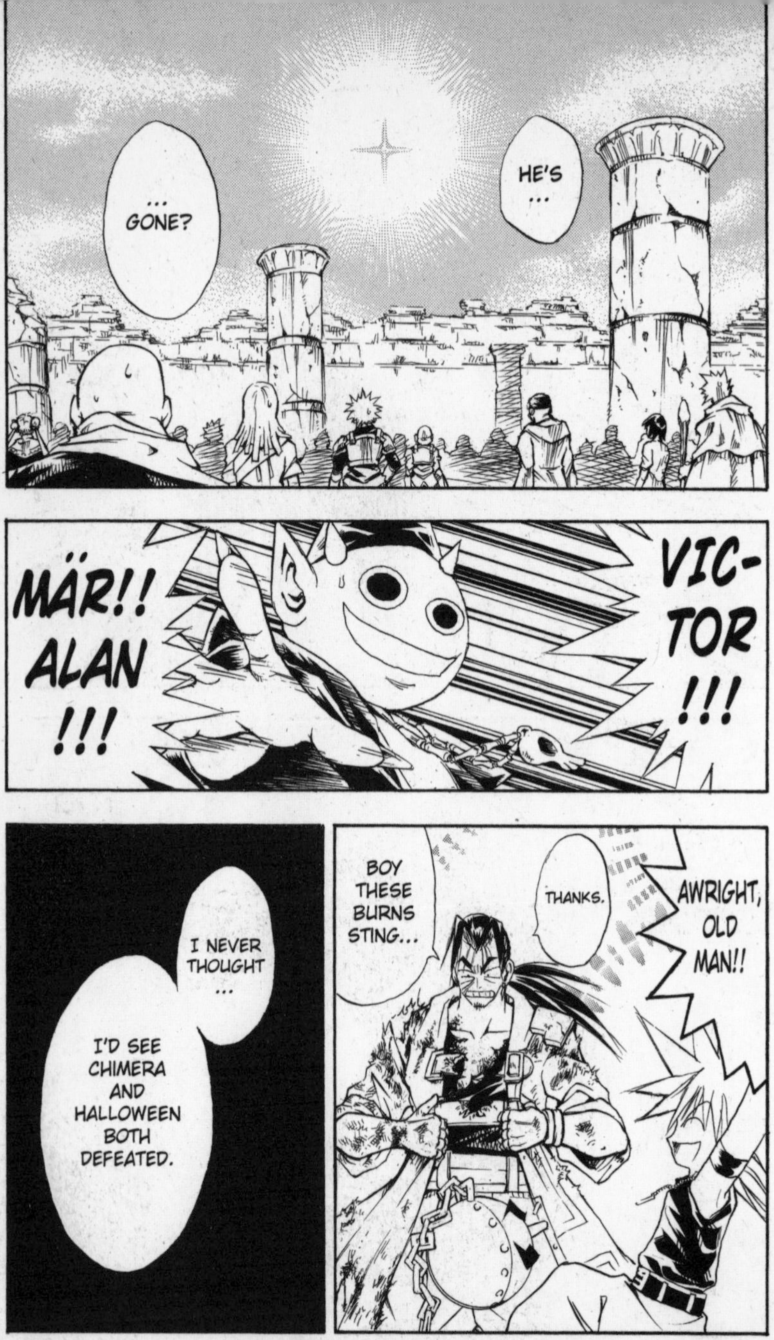
HE'S ...
... GONE?
VIC-TOR!!!
MÄR!! ALAN!!!
AWRIGHT, OLD MAN!!
THANKS.
BOY THESE BURNS STING...
I NEVER THOUGHT ...
I'D SEE CHIMERA AND HALLOWEEN BOTH DEFEATED.

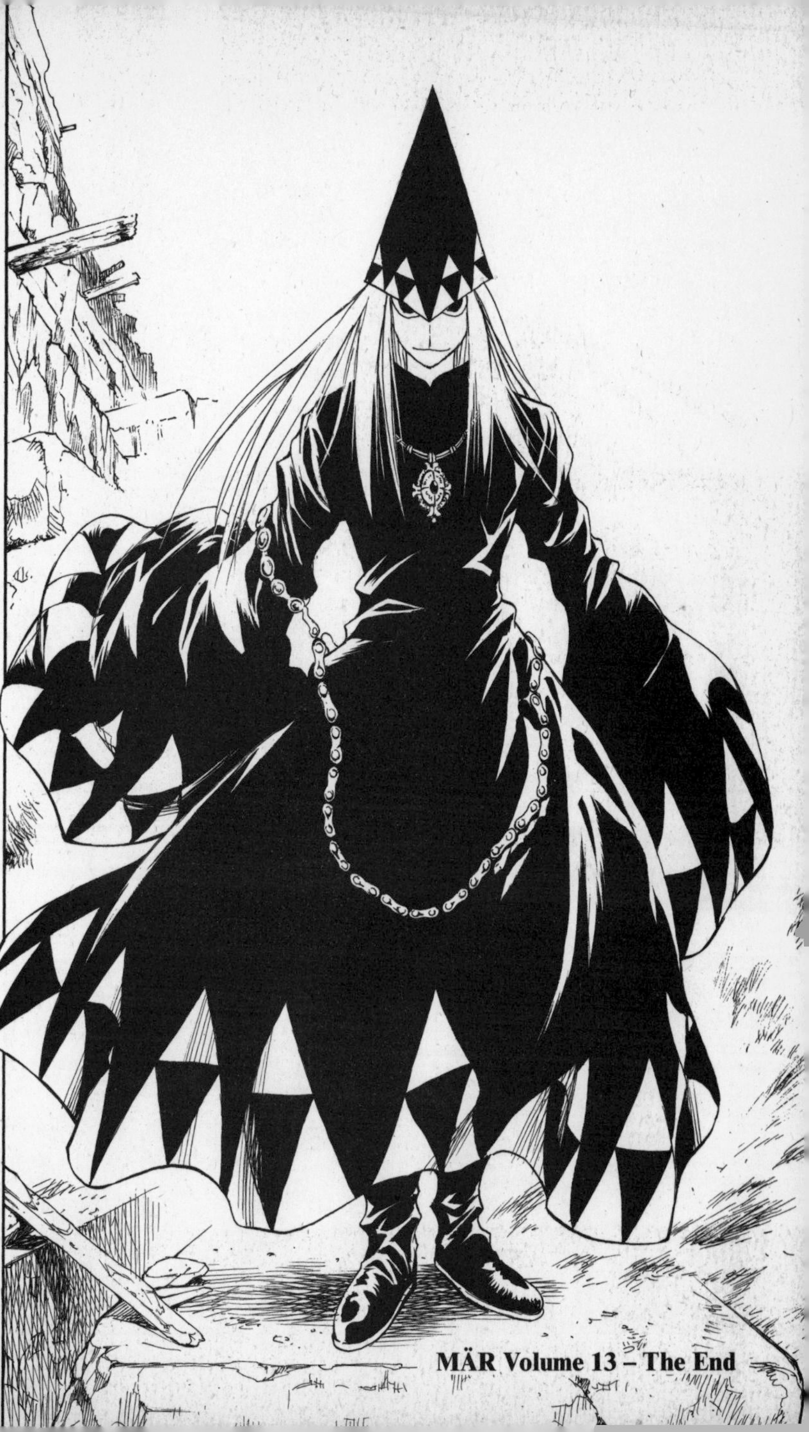

MÄR Volume 13 – The End

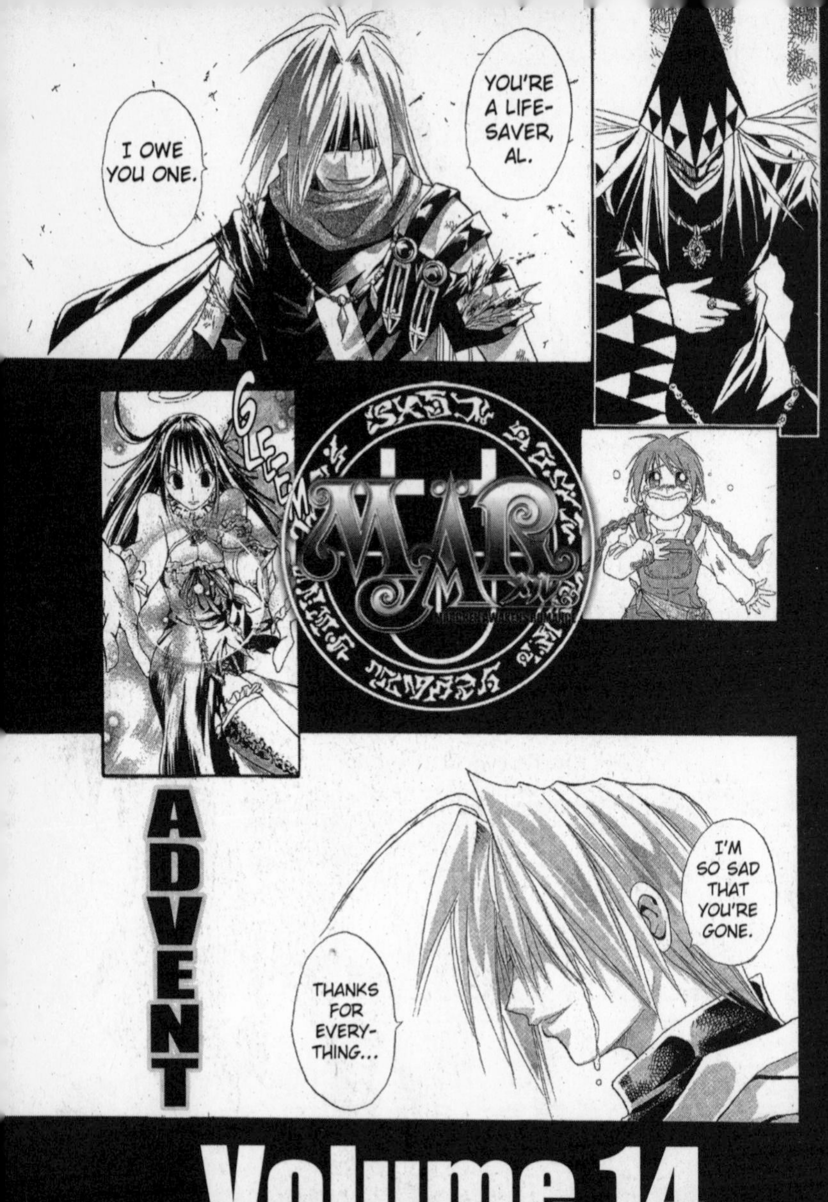
YOU'RE A LIFE-SAVER, AL.
I OWE YOU ONE.
MÄR
I'M SO SAD THAT YOU'RE GONE.
THANKS FOR EVERY-THING...
ADVENT

Volume 14

DUE TO THE STRESS OF THE NEVER-ENDING BATTLES, I WAS HALLUCINATING...SERIOUSLY.

THIS NEVER HAPPENED!

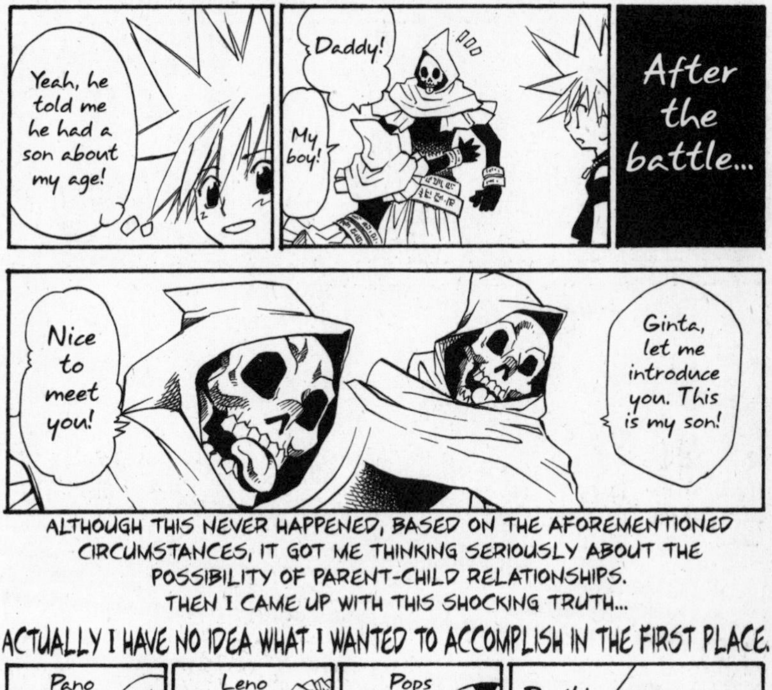
After the battle...
Daddy!
My boy!
Yeah, he told me he had a son about my age!
Ginta, let me introduce you. This is my son!
Nice to meet you!

ALTHOUGH THIS NEVER HAPPENED, BASED ON THE AFOREMENTIONED CIRCUMSTANCES, IT GOT ME THINKING SERIOUSLY ABOUT THE POSSIBILITY OF PARENT-CHILD RELATIONSHIPS. THEN I CAME UP WITH THIS SHOCKING TRUTH...

ACTUALLY I HAVE NO IDEA WHAT I WANTED TO ACCOMPLISH IN THE FIRST PLACE.

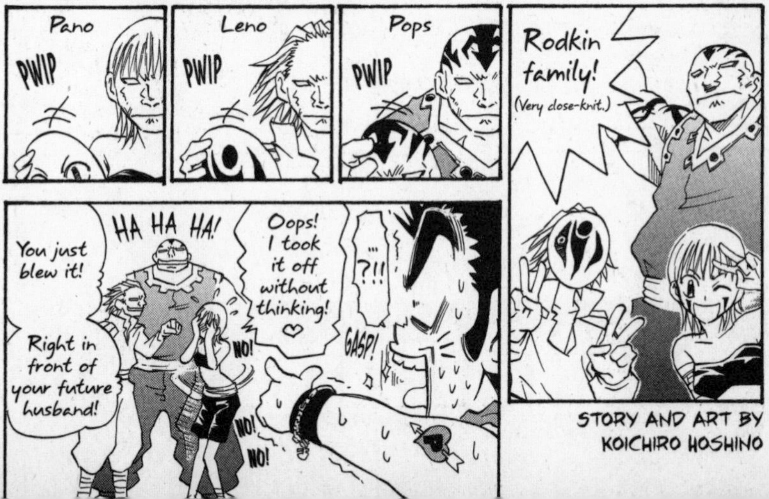
Rodkin family!
(Very close-knit.)
Pops
PWIP
Leno
PWIP
Pano
PWIP
...?!!
GASP!
Oops! I took it off without thinking!
HA HA HA!
You just blew it!
Right in front of your future husband!
NO!
NO!
NO!

STORY AND ART BY
KOICHIRO HOSHINO

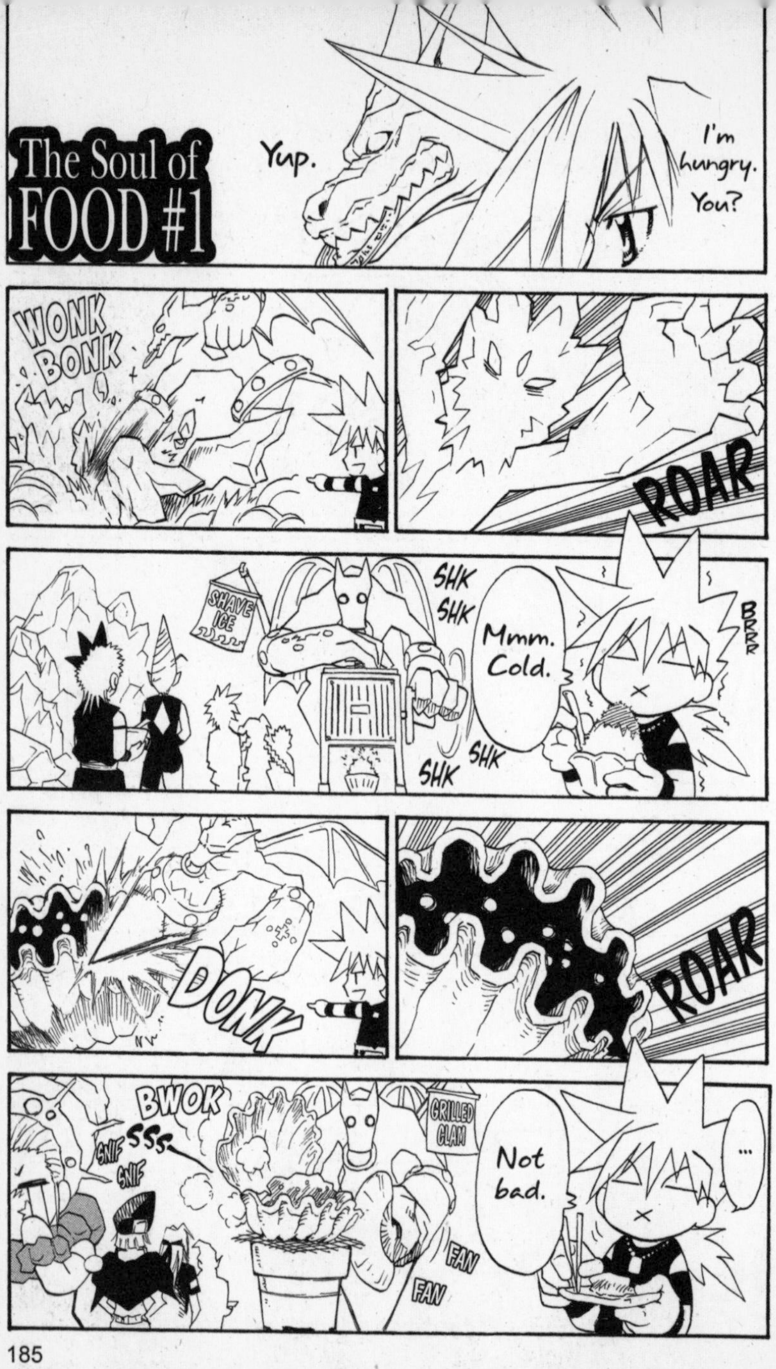
I'm hungry. You?
Yup.
The Soul of FOOD #1
ROAR
WONK BONK
BRRR
Mmm. Cold.
SHK SHK
SHAVE ICE
SHK SHK
ROAR
DONK
...
Not bad.
GRILLED CLAM
BWOK
FAN FAN
SSS
SNIF SNIF

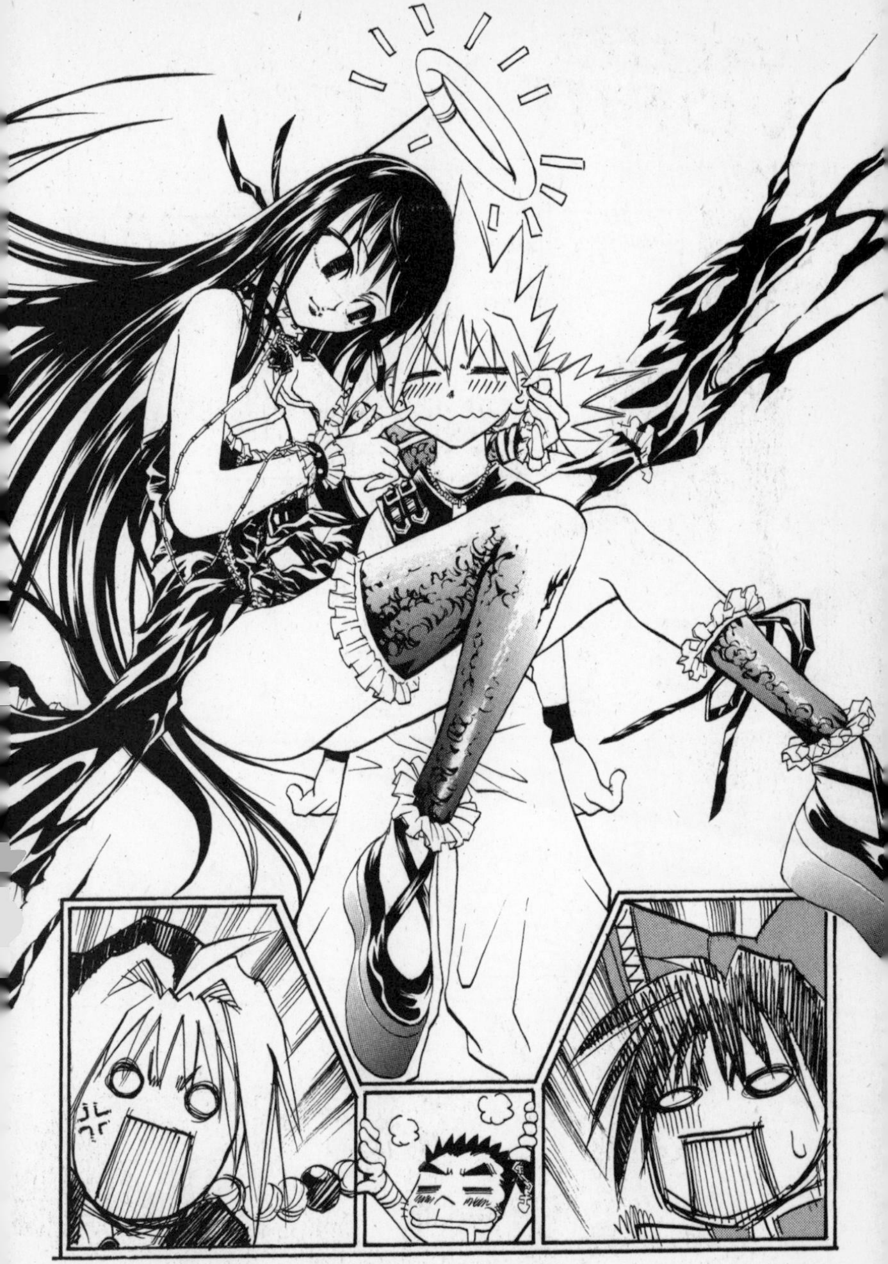

ACID VOMIT

Mini mini theater
Narrative by G.B.

Act 1

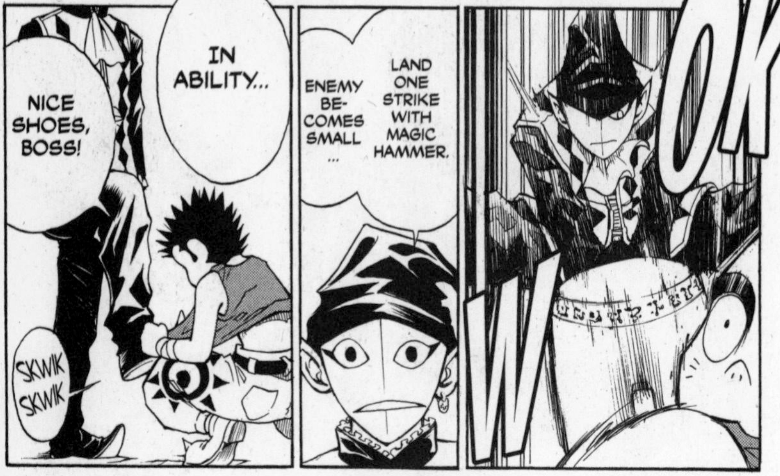
WOK
ENEMY BE-COMES SMALL ... LAND ONE STRIKE WITH MAGIC HAMMER.
IN ABILITY...
NICE SHOES, BOSS!
SKWIK SKWIK

Mini mini theater

Second Act.

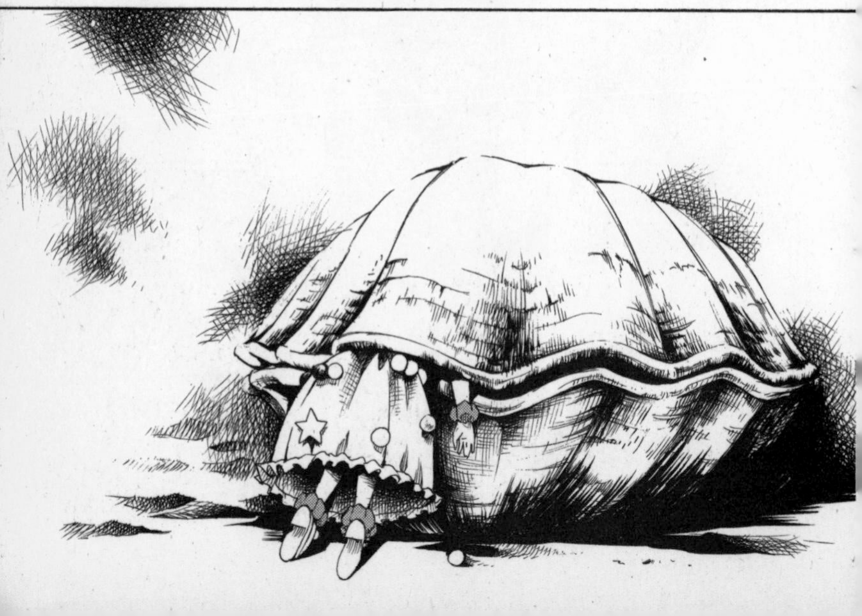

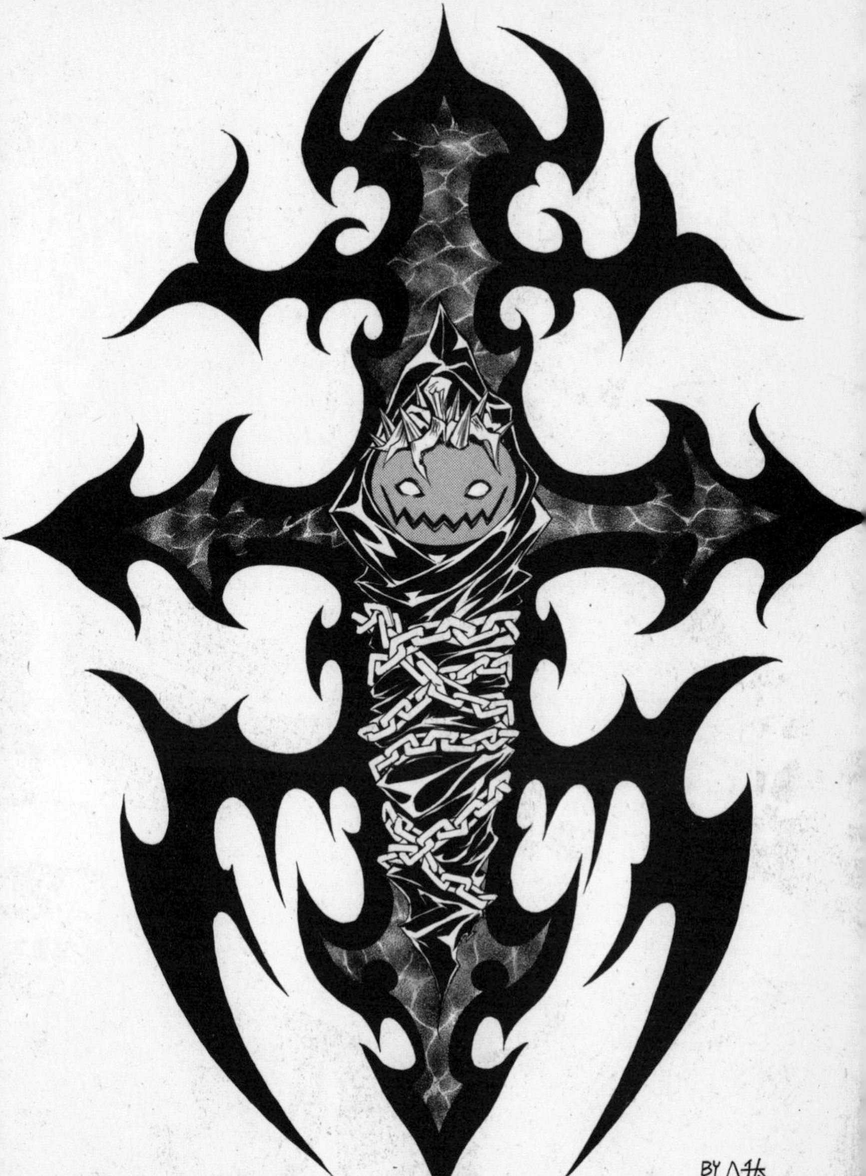

BY ヘチ太
By Hechita

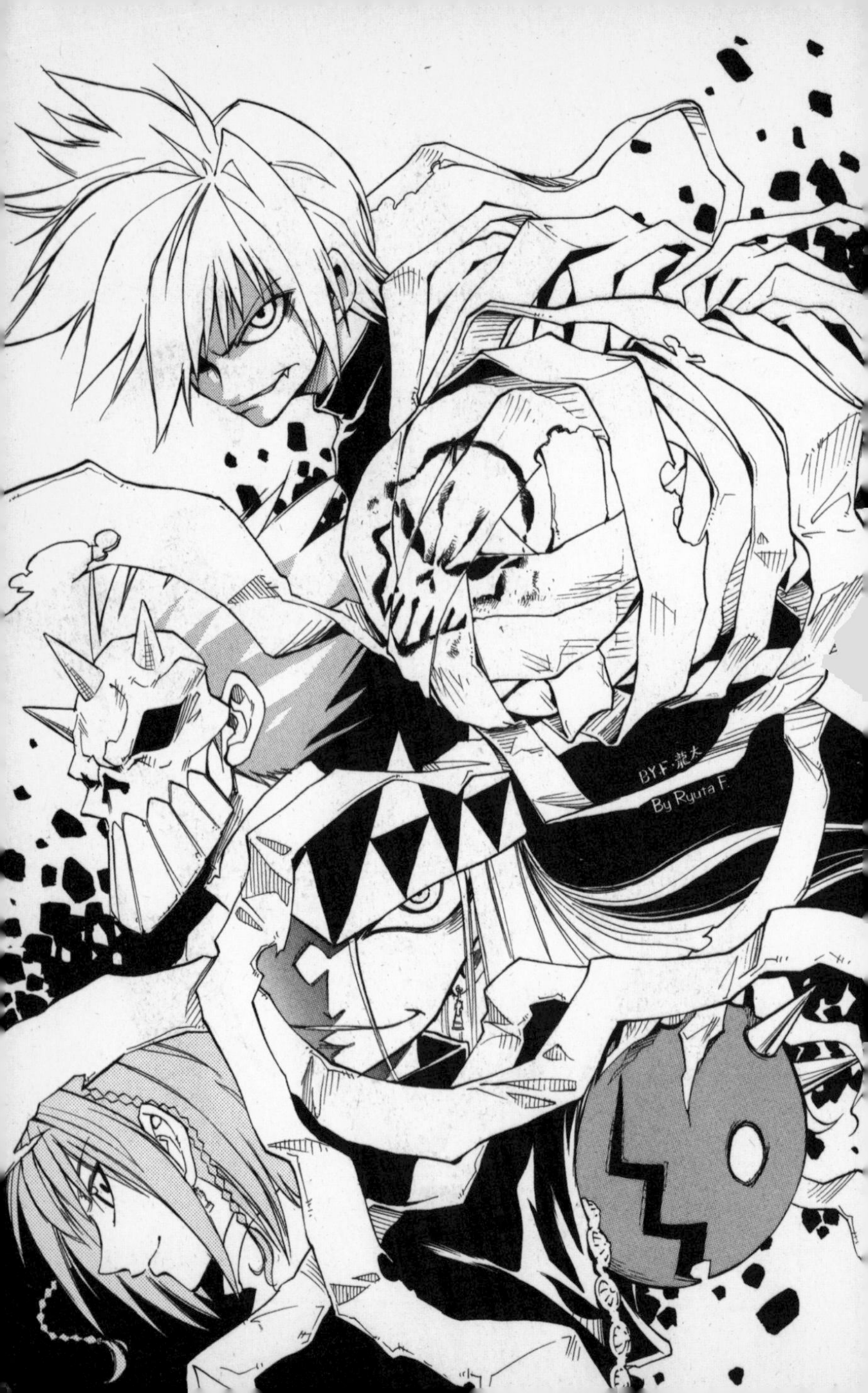
BY.F·龍太
By Ryuta F.

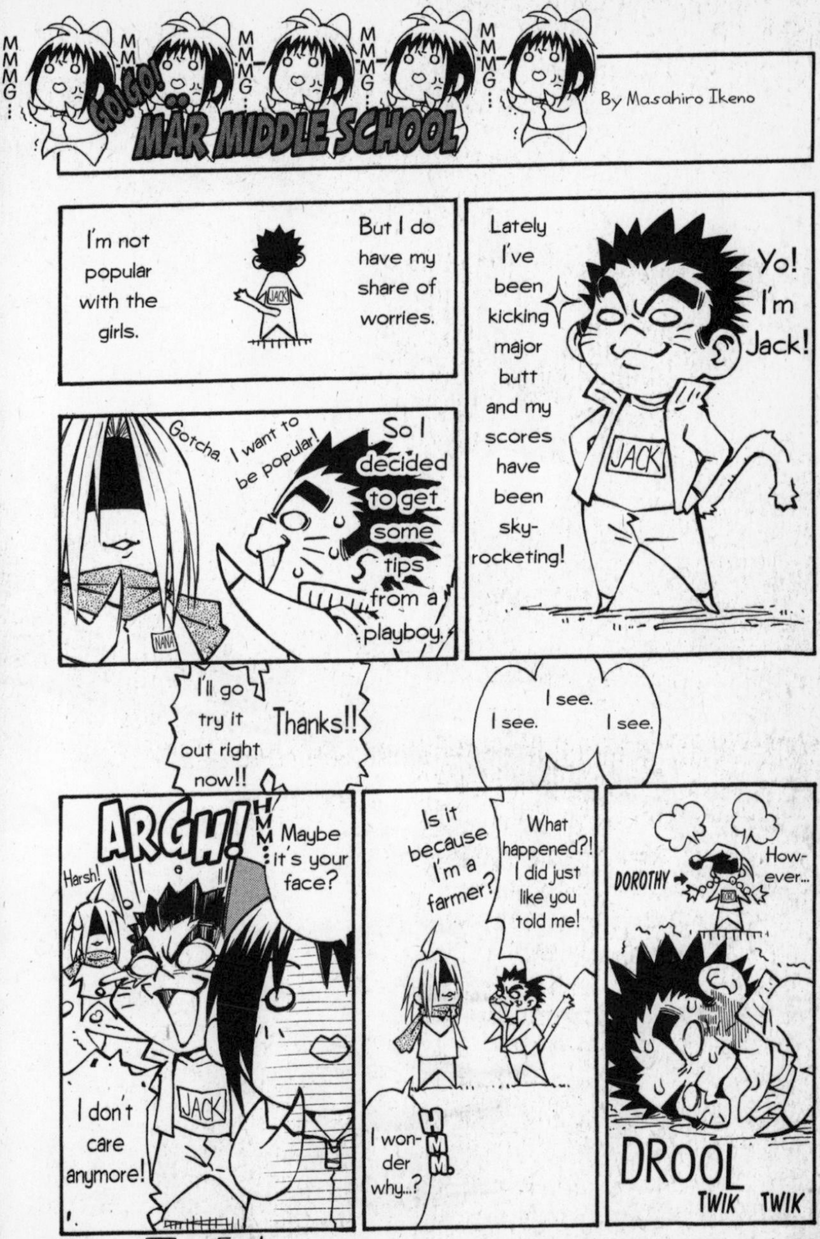
MMMG...
GO! GO! MÄR MIDDLE SCHOOL
By Masahiro Ikeno
Yo! I'm Jack!
Lately I've been kicking major butt and my scores have been sky-rocketing!
But I do have my share of worries.
I'm not popular with the girls.
JACK
So I decided to get some tips from a playboy.
Gotcha. I want to be popular!
NANA
I see. I see. I see.
Thanks!!
I'll go try it out right now!!
How-ever...
DOROTHY
DROOL
TWIK TWIK
What happened?! I did just like you told me!
Is it because I'm a farmer?
HMM...
I won-der why...?
HMM...
Maybe it's your face?
ARGH!
Harsh!
I don't care anymore!
JACK

The End

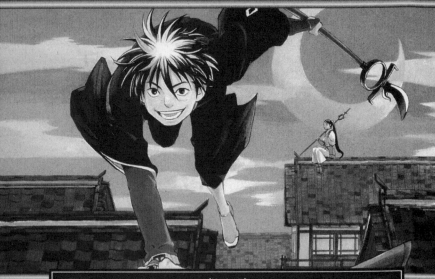
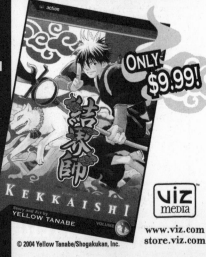

LOVE MANGA

LET US KNOW WHAT YOU THINK!

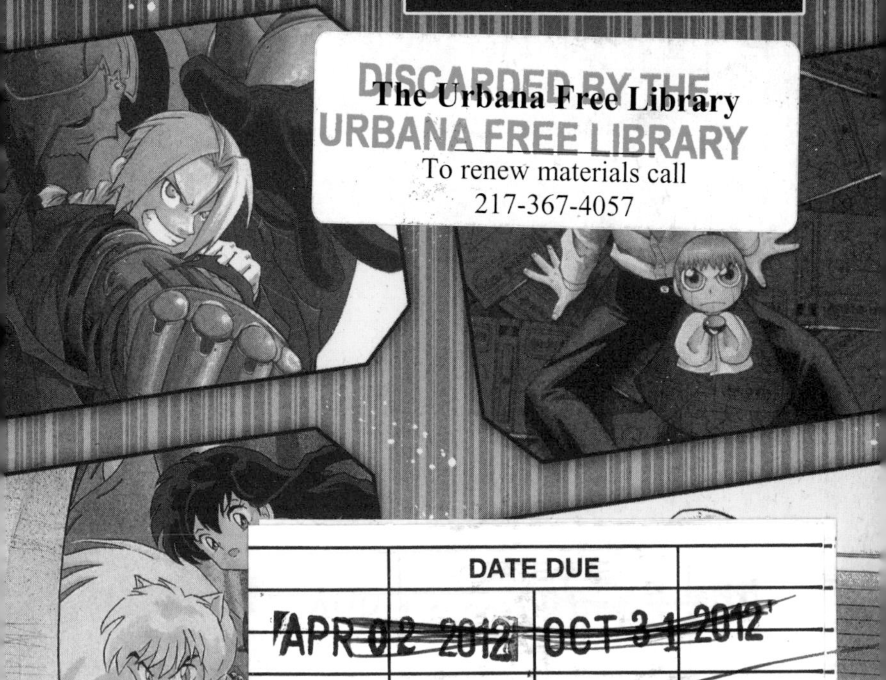

HELP US M
YOU LOVE